Calling It Quits

ALSO BY DEIRDRE BAIR

Jung: A Biography

Anaïs Nin: A Biography

Simone de Beauvoir: A Biography

Samuel Beckett: A Biography

CALLING IT QUITS

*Late-Life Divorce
and Starting Over*

DEIRDRE BAIR

Calling It Quits is a work of nonfiction, but the names of the individuals portrayed (other than those whose stories have already appeared in print) have been changed, along with a number of potentially identifying details. Some of the portraits are composites.

Print ISBN: 9780786754885
ebook ISBN: 9780786754892

Distributed by
Argo Navis Author Services
www.argonavisdigital.com

For
Judith G. Bartolotta

CONTENTS

INTRODUCTION

NOT EVERY writer finds inspiration for a new book in a dentist's office on a sweltering summer day. I was a nervous wreck waiting for what I knew would be the bad news that I needed an implant, and so I thought I'd divert myself by reading magazines. There wasn't much on the table and most of it—about hot rods, golf, raising babies—was old and tattered, but at the bottom of the pile I spied what I thought was the best of a bad lot, the magazine for oldsters sponsored by AARP (American Association of Retired Persons).

The cover was like all its others, featuring a photo of a woman who didn't look old enough to be on it (Cybill Shepherd this time), but it was the blurb for one of the articles that caught my attention: "The New Divorce: Why More Women Than Ever Are Calling It Quits (and Why Men Don't See It Coming)."[1] This was certainly intriguing, because my own divorce happened after forty-three years of marriage, and in the years since I had been told countless stories (whether I wanted to hear them or not) by men and women who had been married a very long time but who had, for whatever the reason, decided to live the next stage of their lives as a single.

Some gave the usual reasons: "He traded me in for a trophy wife younger than our daughter" or "We had nothing in common anymore" or "I couldn't take his [fill in the blank—gambling, drinking, womanizing]." But I also heard a lot of stories from men and women who I thought lived comfortable, contented lives in financially secure marriages and who said that they didn't care what the future might hold, that they divorced because they could not go on living the same old life in the same old rut with the same old boring person. I heard a lot of remarks that all came down to one word: freedom. Women—especially those women who had jobs outside the home—were tired of taking care of husband, house, and children. Men who divorced told me they, too, were tired of the same old daily grind of working to support wives who did not "appreciate" them and children who did not "respect" them. Another remark I heard often from both was "It's my time and if I don't take it now, I never will."

So I was naturally intrigued when I saw that the magazine's story was about a survey that AARP had commissioned of 1,147 people aged forty to seventy-nine, all of whom divorced between their forties and sixties. The reporter called it "groundbreaking" because it put the lie to the usual assumptions, that men leave and women seldom find love and/or companionship ever again. The study found that women initiated the divorce more often than men, and if they wanted new love or companionship, they were usually able, eventually, to find it.

The article corresponded in large part to the stories I had been hearing from friends, associates in publishing and academe, and acquaintances everywhere from Paris to Zurich to Sydney, where the research for my biographies took me. People rushed to tell me their stories while I kept mostly silent, probably because I am a curious anomaly: a biographer who writes the intimate details of other people's lives and tells few of her own. To cover my reticence, I joked, asking if there was something in the drinking water that was making late divorce the worldwide phenomenon it seemed to be.

Some of the stories I heard fell into the same patterns as those in the AARP survey, but most had original and interesting twists. I knew several couples in their eighties who divorced after sixty years of marriage. I knew women who celebrated their fifty-year golden anniversaries by announcing that they would be divorcing within the coming year. One woman had been married for fifty-three years, had never worked outside her home, had no clear idea of how she would survive financially, and had just undergone an organ transplant. She told me, "I don't know how many years I have left,

I just know I don't want to live them with him!" Her ex-husband said he "didn't know what hit him" when she walked out because he always thought "everything was just fine. We never fought, we never raised our voices." And I knew high-level businessmen approaching retirement who told me they were "frightened" into divorcing because, even though their wives fulfilled every lifestyle-supporting role they needed, from giving exquisite dinner parties to entertaining clients to raising the children alone so they could concentrate on work, there was no intimacy between them in their show-case "McMansion" homes. One of these men said he "could not stand the loneliness any longer," especially now that he and his wife would be together "24/7."

I thought about these stories in the dentist's office. Yes, I did need an implant, and we did set up the necessary appointments, but the dentist was puzzled that I seemed more interested in telling him I needed to filch his AARP magazine and beat a hasty exit than in his description of the dire procedures that awaited me. All I could think of was how fast could I get out of his chair and onto the phone with my agent in New York. I had barely be-gun to explore with her the possibility of turning the intriguing stories I had been hearing into a book when she burst in excitedly to tell me about the "late divorces" that were almost an epidemic among the "chattering classes," as the publishing and writing communities are called. We talked about the writer whose wife of thirty-seven years grew tired of washing his socks—yes, washing his socks, not typing his pages—and left him to fend for him-self in a Brooklyn loft while she went to Cape Cod "to find herself" and write her own book, "a self-help for other women who call it quits." There was the very rich "lady poet" (she styled herself that way) whose husband of twenty-nine years (and a figure of respect in his own right but in a different line of work) got tired of holding her two tiny dogs at readings in obscure storefront locations, especially after they became old and incontinent. He left her to go and live in a studio apartment in a poorer part of Manhattan, where he watched television sports and drank beer from the bottle in soli-tary splendor at the end of his busy workday.

That evening, the agent who represents me in Europe phoned and in the course of conversation I told her about this book about late-life divorce

I intended to write. She called the phenomenon "the European epidemic" and surprised me by saying that it was rampant in France and Germany. Germany, perhaps, I replied, but France? Didn't husbands and wives just go their separate ways, as all the movies and books portrayed French marriage, and didn't they stay married just to keep the money in the family? No longer, the agent said. European divorce statistics are fast catching up to those in the rest of the world. Even China was jumping on the bandwagon.

In the spring and summer of 2005 I had a chance to see for myself how common late-life divorce was becoming when I went to Australia and New Zealand to lecture, participate in writers' festivals, and be a writer-in-residence at a Sydney university People everywhere asked what my new book would be, and when I told them, so many came forward to tell me their stories that I realized it was truly a worldwide phenomenon.

But how, I wondered, would I tell these many different stories? As I am neither a sociologist nor a cultural anthropologist, I knew from the beginning that the book would not be a statistical survey or a scientific treatise. What I thought the book needed to be, and what I wanted it to be, and what it has become, is a collection of stories told to me by husbands and wives who chose to end long marriages, as well as the stories of adult children of late-life divorce, who told me how their parents' breakups affected them. My main objective was to let real people talk so that others might find in their stories something helpful—utility (guidance on how to divorce if they believed they had no other option), information (about the financial reality they would have to face after divorce, for example), or comfort (ways to live a satisfying life as a single after many years of being part of a couple).

I set out to collect as many stories as people wanted to tell me and to let them fall naturally into whatever categories or patterns they assumed. The AARP survey had 1,147 respondents, and initially I was hoping to amass about one tenth that number, or approximately 150 case histories. I began to interview in October 2004, and to my amazement, by the time I finished writing in early 2006, I had interviewed 126 men, 184 women, and 84 adult children. I continued to interview people until the writing was finished, for I learned something new with every interview and I wanted to incorporate everything I thought would be useful, helpful, and informative for those already divorced or for those contemplating it.

I found my subjects by word of mouth, as people learned that I was writing this book and one person told another, who had a friend, who told another friend, and so on. When I tried to describe my research methods, my sociologist friends told me I was using the well-respected technique of "snowball sampling," in which information accretes to a point where it can be interpreted to give legitimate findings. Almost two thirds of my interviewees found *me* and volunteered to talk. In general, women were more open and eager, whereas men were not only hesitant about being interviewed, they were also more guarded and circumspect about what they wanted to tell me. Whenever possible, I tried to interview both parties to the divorce, but frequently—with about a third of the ex-couples—one or the other was so angry and bitter that he or she would threaten me with the dire things that would happen if I dared to contact the ex-spouse. I honored the request and did not initiate contact, but if the ex got in touch with me, then I conducted an interview. All the while I was interviewing, I kept remembering what a man in Switzerland told me when his wife ended their thirty-seven-year marriage: "There are five truths in my divorce: mine, my wife's, and our three children's." That was why I thought it was so important to get all sides of the story whenever I could, and why I also interviewed the adult children of divorced parents. It was interesting to me to explore just how the parental divorce affected the adult children's relationships and their attitudes toward marriage.

My respondents include straight, gay, and lesbian couples. They came from many social classes, from (to use some simplistic terms here) "high society," business elites (CEOs), and high-level politicians, to the stable managerial and working classes, to those I call the working poor, who hold service jobs or irregular employment. I also talked to divorce lawyers, mediators, and judges who specialize in what is euphemistically known as "family law." To my regret, my study population is mostly white: I had too few Hispanic and African and Asian American respondents to relate their stories as being representative of a larger group.

Most of my interviews were conducted by telephone because my respondents lived throughout the world and the time and money needed for travel precluded face-to-face conversations. Initially I was disappointed that I would not have in-person interviews with everyone, but overall, when I compared personal interviews with those on the telephone, I found that the phone provided exactly the right degree of separation and the perfect buffer between people who were often hurt, angry, or confused and the stranger at the other end to whom they were confiding such intimate details of their lives.

I asked all the respondents the usual questions about how long the marriage had lasted and what role each partner played within it. Then I let them tell me how and why they came to believe divorce was their only option. I also asked about life after divorce and whether or not it had turned out to be what they hoped for. In general, my findings supported the AARP survey in that the greater percentage of divorces among the longmarried are initiated by women. Most of them stressed the positive and told me they were "pleased," "satisfied," or "downright happy" with their lives. The men, many of whom called themselves "the dumped," "the duped," or "the abandoned," are for the most part learning "to adjust," "to accommodate," "to get along."

One man who coped better than most is the eighty-three-year-old whose wife of fifty-three years tossed him out. Calling her the "dumper" and himself the "dumpee," he decided that, having had a woman look after him all his life, he needed to find a new one. He remembered how the cruises he had taken as a married man were filled with single women, all seemingly on the lookout for a new man. It took three cruises, all of which "exhausted" him (he said euphemistically), until he found "a good-looking sixty-year-old who doesn't mind doing my laundry." His ex-wife says she is happy for him, as she fills her days with part-time volunteer work, plays bridge with friends, and dances in the evening with men her age whom she meets in church groups and at senior centers. What she likes best about her single life is that she has male companionship when she wants it but at the end of the evening she goes home to her own bed and they depart for theirs. "I'll never pick up a man's socks again," she vows.

Divorce is different for the rich and famous. Here I found the largest categories of men who initiated divorce and women who are sad and sometimes angry because their husbands have left them for "trophy wives." A Jungian analyst told me she describes these men as afflicted with "CEO-itis." All their lives they have been taken care of by wives, secretaries, and various assistants who fulfill their every need and desire. They are imbued with a sense of entitlement, that they can have and should be given everything they want and as soon as they want it. An English man described himself as a "serial marryer," who likes his wives in their twenties and wants to dump them as soon as they reach thirty because "they get broody and want babies." That, he said, would interrupt their concentration on him. Another told me to think of a man like himself (chief financial officer of an international corporation) in a way that his several wives had never accepted, as a "prize stud bull." It was his "obligation to service as many cows" as he could.

Throughout the book, I have used two different forms to tell the stories. One is the composite, in which I create a fictional person to stand for the cluster of persons whose stories are so similar that one can almost stand for them all. The second is the case study, where one couples experience either provides a blueprint for what causes a marriage to end or else is so unusual that it needs to be told separately. Because I promised everyone who talked to me confidentiality, I have disguised their identities by changing their names and sometimes their professions and places of residence. All the information contained in this book is the truth as they told it to me, but I have created fictional personae to protect their privacy.

I don't know how many answers I've provided to the question of why there is so much late divorce throughout the world, but I have certainly raised a lot of questions. There are the obvious reasons, such as the fact that people are living longer and healthier lives and many have more disposable income. It is only natural that they change and even more natural that they don't always change at the same time as their spouse: he may be ready for retirement and she may be deeply involved with a career or hobby; she may want to move to a retirement community and he might not want to leave the old neighborhood. One or the other becomes bored or disenchanted with the old, wrinkled person sitting across the dinner table and might want someone new and exciting.

Margaret Mead thought every woman needs three husbands: one for youthful sex, one for security as she raises her children, and one for the joyful companionship of old age. Perhaps this is what people want today and why so much divorce is happening. The feminist revolution that started in the 1970s got women out of the kitchen and into the workforce, where they learned to be self-sufficient and discovered that they liked it. There are still many women today who are financially dependent on the man they married a long time ago, but it is surprising how many of them are willing to risk the uncertainty of life on their own just to get away from the "control" (another big word often cited in divorces) their husbands exerted.

I use the phrase "social earthquake" to describe what is happening today. It was coined by the revered American feminist Elizabeth Cady Stanton to describe a sensational adultery scandal of her time that led to a late-nineteenth-century divorce, and it remains resonant here in the twenty-first. Our contemporaries have tried to name the phenomenon; British writer Margaret Drabble deems life after divorce "the Third Age." Drabbles heroine thinks, in the novel *The Seven Sisters*, "Our dependents have died or matured. For good or ill, we are free."

A woman in New Zealand put it more bluntly when she told a newspaper interviewer that she looked at her husband one day after her children had left home and thought, "I don't want to be here, I don't need you, and I really don't like you."

Could that be the simplest and most direct answer to all the questions about late-life divorce? We need to find out, and I hope this book will be a good way to get the dialogue going.

CHAPTER ONE

THE THIRD AGE

People change and forget to tell each other.
—LILLIAN HELLMAN

This then was marriage! The old things didn't matter any more. . . . All
that mattered was that he should love her and she should love him.
—D. H. LAWRENCE, *The Rainbow*

JAN, A MIDDLE-AGED WOMAN whose parents were in their eighties, told me that with great trepidation she had just brought them to live in her house. Growing up in Margaret and Harry's house had been like living on a battleground, as they argued, shouted, and threw things on an almost daily basis. Their marriage lasted forty-two years, until both were in their sixties and Margaret decided to end it. Now she and Harry were in their eighties and had not seen or spoken to each other for the twenty-plus years since the decree was granted. Jan, who had never taken sides and always saw her parents separately, now faced a serious problem. Both her parents had Alzheimer's and needed supervision, and as their only child, she had no option but to take them into her home until she could arrange for permanent care elsewhere.

"Here's the amazing thing," she told me. "They have become best friends because they can't remember they were ever married to each other." Margaret and Harry spend their days in Jan's living room, happily comparing tales of their miserable marriages to "perfect shits" and telling Jan how nice she was to introduce them, and how they wish they had met when they were young so they could have married each other. They are sure that theirs would have been a blissful marriage that lasted forever. Jan sighed, rolled her eyeballs, and said, "Go figger!"

Margaret and Harry's story is certainly one of the more unusual ones I heard in my interviews of 126 men, 184 women, and 84 adult children of late-life divorce. I learned that divorce happens for many reasons, takes many different forms, and has many, often surprising, outcomes. My investigations parallel the groundbreaking study commissioned by AARP in 2004, of 581 men and 566 women, to investigate what the directors called "a common experience among midlifers and older people."[1] In many respects, the reasons for divorce given by people I interviewed correspond to the formal findings of the AARP study, but in other, key instances, they are strikingly different. Also, the AARP study was limited to residents of the United States, whereas my respondents included citizens of Mexico, Canada, Ireland, England, France, Germany, Switzerland, Italy, Australia, and New Zealand. Granted, my international participants were random, self-selecting, and few in number, so I cannot claim statistical accuracy for what I report. However, I do believe their stories are representative of their cultures and their social classes and that they provide insights into the universal ramifications of divorce.

In attempting to identify some of the causes of divorce, the AARP study pointed to life-changing events that create upheavals in midlife. Husbands and wives may be facing the death of a parent or the last child leaving home—or, in a growing number of cases, children moving back in, sometimes after their own divorces and often with children of their own. These couples may have reached the age and stage of life where they begin to worry about growing old, or if they are already older, they may think about how the years are flying by and their mortality is catching up with them. Not surprisingly, if they look at their mate and see someone with whom they have not communicated for years, they may ponder what their lives have been and what they still might become. Into these volatile situations, events both major and minor trigger life-changing decisions, and more and more frequently, older couples in long marriages see divorce as the answer.

"I JUST WANT OUT!"

Take, for example, the story of Caroline and Ted, who had been married for fifty-three placid years when Caroline's kidneys failed and she needed a transplant. After a harrowing near-death experience, the first thing she said to Ted when she recovered was "I don't know how many years I have left, but I do know I don't want to spend them with you." Both were in their mid-eighties when the divorce became final two years ago. Caroline said she "almost didn't know where the words came from" but that from the moment she said them, she was (and still is) convinced that divorce was the right thing for her; Ted, who had just settled into a new relationship, was still puzzled about why his old one had to end but thought "everything will work out okay." After a pause, he added, "I guess."

"Surprise" was a word several people who initiated the divorce used—often to describe themselves when they talked to me, wondering where the words "I want a divorce" came from when they first said them. Rachel was among those who "almost didn't know where the words came from" when she told Murray after twenty-nine years of marriage that enough was enough and she wanted out of the marriage. It was the night before the Passover seder and she was in the kitchen surrounded by all the foodstuffs required to prepare a meal for the dozen or so members of her extended family She was "up to [her] elbows in chopped liver" while he was sprawled on their bed upstairs watching television. When Rachel yelled up to ask him to come to the kitchen and hand her a spatula just out of reach, he shouted back that she should keep her voice down so he could hear the program. Suddenly, the differences in how they approached the holiday celebration "became a metaphor for the entire marriage." Rachel was tired of being "the family social director," the one who brought family and friends together and convinced them all that hers was the perfect marriage and she was the perfect wife, mother, and hostess. Suddenly she knew she "just wanted out."

Franklin, a gay man who ended his twenty-two-year partnership with Terry, also described himself as both the "social director and the enabler."

Their breakup also happened because "one day there was just one thing too many. There was no huge dramatic incident; nothing out of the ordinary, only more of the same. But one day 'more of the same' became the trigger on the gun I was holding and I pulled it."

Patricia was in a similar situation. After so many problems became an avalanche, she sought psychotherapy for the first time in her life at the age of sixty-three. She was tired of juggling her demanding profession as the senior administrator for a midsized law firm with running her complex household. She organized all the functions for her firm and also had to participate in much of Donald's; as a midlevel executive in a manufacturing company, he was charged with entertaining difficult clients and wooing them into signing contracts.

Both Patricia and Donald came from large families who always expected to come to their house for social occasions and major holidays. She was tired of being the sounding board for everyone in the two families, but she was especially tired of listening to her two adult children tell her about the roller-coaster ups and downs of their marriages. Patricia was of the generation that left their parents' house for good from the moment they married. She was in her early twenties when she became a self-sufficient adult who never told her parents her troubles or asked for help or advice. Patricia joked about "the child from one to forty" because her own children were in their thirties and still depended on "Mommy" to solve most of their problems. She was tired of a generation that refused to grow up and be independent, but most of all, she was tired of a husband who became increasingly passive-aggressive as he stubbornly and silently refused to recognize her emotional needs. As she put it, "Never a hug now and then, never a compliment that I cooked a good dinner or put on a good party for his business. Heaven forfend that he'd tell me I looked good!"

Therapy helped Patricia to see that it was not her responsibility—as her therapist told her—"to make the world safe for democracy." She knew she could not continue to be all things for all the people who expected her "to do, to be, to give, to smooth the way," but she did not expect the fury directed toward her by everyone who took it for granted that she would always be there for whatever they needed her to give them. When she announced that she was divorcing in order to make time for her own needs as she entered the last third of her life, the overwhelming response from her relatives and children was resentment that she was being "so selfish."

David felt that he bore many of the same burdens as Patricia, and he, too, ended his marriage of thirty-two years in his mid-sixties. He was a retired air force officer whose wife, Marlene, had never worked outside the home because they moved so often during his years in the service. She kept the house and raised their three children while he was away on various deployments, and that, she said, "was job enough" for her. Even though David's postings made him absent from home so much of the time, Marlene had always depended on him to balance her budget, tell her which bills to pay and when to pay them, remind her to have the car serviced, keep her focused on the children's activity schedules, and even remind her to participate in the activities of the officers' wives club wherever they were stationed. He never minded doing all these things because it was his way "to stay connected" to family life. After he retired from the air force, David took a job with a defense contractor that required him to travel for several weeks each month, and so the pattern of family life established during his service years more or less continued—until one day, when an "ordinary little thing" happened that made him ask Marlene for a divorce.

Marlene insisted that David's secretary put through her "urgent" phone call during a crucial meeting—an arrow light was flashing on her car's dashboard and she had forgotten what David told her it indicated on the two previous times it happened. Rather than read the manual, she phoned him to take care of it. That night David told Marlene that he was "too tired of propping her and the kids up time after time after time." He had no idea "what was out there" for himself, but he wanted to find out.

For many of the men and women I interviewed, not just in the United States but throughout the world, the path to divorce seems to have been paved with a steady accumulation of insults or abuses (mental or physical) throughout the marriage until they reached a single, defining moment when they knew they "just wanted out." The event itself was often quite ordinary, but the spontaneous recognition that they wanted a divorce often came as a surprise even to themselves, let alone to their mates and others in their families. Afterward, many wondered aloud what it was about that particular incident, so harmless in itself, that triggered the stunning realization that they needed to end their marriages.

A New Zealand psychologist put it bluntly when she told an interviewer why she thought so many older women in her country were divorcing: "You're left looking at your partner thinking, 'I don't want to be here, I don't need you, and I don't really like you.' "[2] With the people I interviewed, I found that various forms of this attitude cut across all spectrums of society, no matter what the ethnic culture, social class, income, or education. And it was true no matter where they lived.

Anne was an Australian in her seventies when she knew she "just wanted out." A war bride transplanted first from England to Canada and then to a remote town in the Australian outback, she had a vivid recollection of the day she decided to divorce: "I got up that morning and cooked breakfast for Des and my two grown sons who still lived with us and worked our farm. Then I did the washing up and several loads of laundry and hung it out to dry. I fed the chooks [chickens] and was weeding the garden in the broiling sun when Des came to the back door and said, 'Where's my lunch? It's time for my lunch.' And that was it. I thought to myself 'What about me? What nourishment do I get?' I knew it was then or never."

Anne had never worked outside the home, but she represented a surprisingly large number of women in the same situation who were so desperate to leave their marriages that they were willing to risk whatever financial consequences came their way.

Martha holds dual citizenship in the United States and Switzerland. She was a senior at Wellesley when she married Hans, a Swiss, who was at Harvard Business School. On the outside, their forty-nine-year marriage looked like something from a romance novel, replete with financial security, easy travel around the world, and three adult children, over-achievers with first-class educations and successful marriages and careers. Martha's moment of wanting out came when Hans, as he had done all their married life, changed the carefully made plans for travel and entertaining that, because of his complicated schedule, had taken her months to arrange. On the one hand, this was nothing new for Martha because changing plans at a moment's notice was "how we always lived." Her role in the marriage was to make, then be ready to abandon, a succession of plans and schedules. On the other hand, this time became the one time too many, the defining moment when Martha knew "it was time for me." She initiated divorce proceedings in a country that does not look kindly on women who do so. Everyone in their social setting was aghast, but, as she recalled dryly, "no one was really surprised, for even though I have lived here for half a century, I am still thought of as 'the American.' Everyone here is convinced we do these things all the time."

Nevertheless, Martha's decision, stunning as it was in the rigid, tightly structured, and socially conservative society in which she lived, started something: her sister-in-law Regula, married to Hans's brother, Rolf, came from a family embedded in the Swiss upper classes for centuries. When she decided that she wanted out of her marriage of forty-one years, their entire social community was thrown into turmoil. If she and Martha were not actual pariahs, they were certainly to be avoided as if contagious. But worst of all, according to the husbands, was the disrespect their wives were showing toward them. Hans was puzzled when his card-playing and golfing cronies tried to avoid him, "as if what happened to me might rub off on them." Sheepishly they told him that their wives were warning: "You'd better be careful—you could be next!" They were not willing to bear the shame, so better to avoid Hans and Rolf, who soon found themselves cold-shouldered by their former buddies.

PLANNING CAREFULLY FOR DIVORCE

For every man or woman who spontaneously "wanted out," I encountered many others who had given long and careful thought to the decision, sometimes waiting for years before they actually looked into the possibility, let alone took action. A number of these spouses came to the sad realization that economic realities meant they would have to stay married. Some of these drifted on, together yet alone, living separate lives in the same house. They had separate bedrooms, prepared and ate their meals separately, and did not speak to each other unless third parties were present. Others continued to live in the same house, going their separate ways while sometimes bringing new partners or lovers into what had been the family home. They, and others who actually established separate households, used the same term to describe their status: "divorced while still married." For whatever reason (but the main one was financial), they led entirely separate lives but never got around to making their status legal. Those who did divorce generally echoed what Janet, who now lives in Oregon, told me: "I knew I had to prepare for it very carefully, because otherwise I'd be a sixty-year-old woman living in poverty."

Janet met Trey in the late 1950s, when both were twenty-two-year-old students at Boston University. He had accelerated his studies to graduate in three years and was in his first year of business school. Janet was a senior and they married as soon as she graduated. During Trey's last two years, she supported them by teaching in the Boston public schools. "He got his MBA and I got my "Ph.T. (putting hubby through)." Trey breezed through his studies happily, while Janet, who had been assigned to one of the most violence-ridden of the inner-city schools, suffered terrible emotional distress. She managed to hide her depression and hold herself together until Trey graduated and they moved to California. Once there, her black mood "lifted with the sunshine," and for the next thirty-eight years, she thought she had "died and gone to heaven." They lived on a large plot of land with their three children and the many horses, dogs, and cats they considered part of the family. As Trey's entrepreneurial-investment business grew and prospered, Janet knew his holdings were many, varied, and mostly hidden. He was so secretive that even though he kept an office complex with a good-sized staff in town, he did his most important work at home, in several rooms that were off-limits to everyone in the family, including Janet.

Five years before the marriage officially ended she knew they were headed for divorce court, and she knew Trey would not want to reveal his assets and net worth to "strangers," as he would deem their lawyers. During their long marriage, Janet worked only occasionally, as a substitute teacher, and so she had no income of her own. When Trey was away on business trips, she systematically culled the files to find out what her share of the marital assets would be. Her lawyer praised her diligence, for Trey's original financial disclosure was only a fraction of what Janet discovered to be his total worth, half of which was hers according to California law.

Mary was a housewife in Queens, New York, for the forty-seven years of her marriage to Phil, a retired construction worker. She also tried to prepare for divorce, but her situation was nothing like Janet's. She knew what Phil's salary was, a generous portion of which he gave her to run the household. He never told her what he did with the rest, except to say that it was safe and she would never have to worry. Mary had never sought a job outside the home, but as soon as their three children started school, the nuns in charge of their local Catholic elementary school noticed how good she was with numbers at parent-teacher fund-raisers and asked her to work part-time in the school office. During the school year Mary worked four half-days a week so that she could rush home in the afternoons to do her housework and cook the evening meal. She saved most of the money she earned, first in her banks Christmas club, then in a simple savings account, for she had no knowledge of how to invest elsewhere and was too afraid of losing her money to find out. It never occurred to her to ask Phil what he was doing with the rest of the family money because she thought of it as "his." During her years keeping the books for the school, Mary learned enough about office procedures and simple bookkeeping that even though she was sixty when she left Phil, she was hired to work full-time in the office of a large family-owned grocery store where she had always shopped. She has been self-supporting ever since. Mary did not have a lawyer when Phil, in frustration, filed to divorce her, so she never asked him for a portion of "his" money, nor did he ever offer to share it with her.

David paid the same careful attention to financial planning when he made up his mind to leave Marlene, but he fully intended to share everything equally He had made safe and prudent investments during his air force years, and she would be entitled to half of those, plus half his pension and current salary. She wanted to stay in their current home, but he persuaded her that it was unwise, as she could not care for it herself and would not be able to afford its upkeep. David helped Marlene buy a town house and saw that she was settled before he moved on to his own new life. Still, despite all his generosity, the divorce caused so much unhappiness among their three children that they described how they felt with the same word used by so many adult children of divorce that I interviewed: "devastated."

These snippets are from the lives of people who choose to enter "the Third Age"[3] and to create a new way of living. Their stories of life before and life after divorce are fascinating, and I will tell them in more detail in the chapters to come.

CHAPTER TWO

INFIDELITY

I've had five husbands. Four were mine; one was someone else's.
—MARGO HOWARD, "I Was Between Husbands,
He Was Between Cupcakes"

DIVORCE WAS RARE in centuries past, mostly because unhappy marriages usually ended in early funerals. Men, mainly, didn't live long enough to drive their spouses to desperation, or to be driven to desperate measures themselves. In fact, the rate at which marriages ended in 1860 (based on the number of those who became widows and widowers in that year) is practically the same as the rate of marriages that ended in divorce throughout the 1960s. The only difference is that marital dissolution in the nineteenth century most often took place at the graveside while twentieth-century terminations usually happened in a courtroom, for reasons that are many.

Until divorce laws were radically restructured throughout the mid-to-late twentieth century, infidelity was the primary—and often the only—grounds to end a marriage. The movies had a field day with scenes of staged adulteries, usually slapstick and highly comedic, where one spouse or the other cavorted in a slinky peignoir or suave dressing gown in a seedy hotel. Detectives burst in, always with photographer in tow, flashbulbs popped, and the screen usually dissolved into a spinning whirl of newspaper headlines as the story became front-page news for avid tabloid readers. There were usually two photos on these mythical front pages, one of the mock lovers in the hotel bedroom and the other of the aggrieved party (usually the wife clad in a collar of fox furs) snuffling into a lace handkerchief as she boarded a train for Reno and the six-week residency required to make the divorce final. Ah, the glamour days of Hollywood's Silver Screen, when everything took on a rosy glow as soon as the train huffed and puffed its way out of the station.

In recent films, however, as in real life, there has been a decidedly different perspective. From Ingmar Bergman's *Scenes from a Marriage*, to Noah Baumbach's *The Squid and the Whale*, infidelity is depicted as a far more painful approximation of what happens in real life. In the AARP survey, infidelity is the third-most-often cited reason for divorce (after verbal, physical, and emotional abuse and different values and lifestyles). In my interviews, more women than men cited infidelity as the cause of divorce, with more men than women committing it.

The kinds of male adultery differed, and according to both husbands and wives, the most common form was when a husband took a mistress. Usually, she was a colleague in the workplace who was content to maintain a discreet silence in what was often a kind of parallel marriage. Lillian Ross, a staff writer for *The New Yorker*, became one of the more famous long-term mistresses when she wrote a memoir revealing her liaison with the magazine's famous editor William Shawn.[1] Ross and Shawn had a child together, and she lived in an apartment fairly close to the one Shawn shared with his wife and their children. Their story was similar to quite a few from my interviews, but the outcome was different. Shawn and his wife stayed married, as did the architect Louis Kahn and his wife, despite his fathering two other children by different women with whom he had long liaisons.[2] But when most of the wives I spoke to learned of their husband's other relationship(s), they ended the legal marriage in one of two ways: either the wife asked for a divorce without first asking the husband to renounce the mistress and stay in the marriage, or, if she did ask him to choose, she divorced when he chose the mistress.

In most cases the wives learned of the affair through some sort of slipup, but there are others in which the husband tells the wife straight out, saying he is tired of the duplicity and equally tired of a sterile marriage. Jessica and Jake were in the first category; Richard and Priscilla in the second.

Jess (as everyone called her) and Jake had known each other since the third grade, were "going steady" by junior high, and were "unofficially engaged" all through their college years while he was at West Point and she attended a nearby girls' college. They married at graduation, in the West Point chapel and under crossed swords. Jake left the service at the earliest opportunity and became first a business-machine salesman and then, as the personal-computer age began, an entrepreneur. As his business grew and prospered and he amassed enormous wealth, he joked of being a "minor-league Ross Perot." Jess, an outspoken and dynamic woman, was his perfect partner who gave him four brilliant sons and kept whatever homes and apartments Jake decided to buy gorgeously decorated and running smoothly. They were the envy of everyone who knew them, the perfect couple with the ideal marriage that all others aspired to but despaired of ever attaining.

They had been married for almost forty years and were flying to Aspen for a ski vacation when Jess inadvertently pressed a button on Jake's cell phone that connected her to a steamy voice mail from a woman who said she was "busy giving herself an orgasm" while remembering the one he had just given her that morning. In front of their two married sons and their wives, and the other two sons with their girlfriends, plus assorted couples who were their close friends, Jess confronted Jake, who admitted that the woman was his mistress and had been for the past five years. Later, in private, he told her that there had been "others, on the side," but "they didn't mean anything." As for the mistress, he said he could not and would not give her up; Jess would have to accept that she was a part of his life—at least for the indefinite future.

As of this writing two years later, they are separated but not divorced. Jake wants to stay married while Jess insists that she will never take him back. Their family life is in total disarray: the eldest son says his wife left him because he is "a chip off the old block," which he claims is totally unfounded; the other married son refuses to see Jake or let him visit the only grandson; the older of the two unmarried sons had a "breakdown" and had to leave his university for a year (he has since returned); and the youngest moved across the country and won't speak to either parent, although he continues to live on the money they put into his bank account each month.

Jake told me he knows his sons will "come around," once they realize that his behavior is "normal" for men who have the financial wherewithal to support extramarital liaisons. He said he has had "girlfriends" through out his marriage but the woman he calls his "mistress" is one of "only three" to whom he has granted such status. He said that Jess should be more understanding because "after all, forty years is a long time to be married." He said he "tells her this, but she won't listen."

Richard had only one mistress, of long duration, and he chose to tell his wife, Priscilla, about her, and to end the marriage. A physician in a group practice, Richard was approaching sixty-four at the time, and he'd had a relationship with his office manager, Evelyn, then fifty-two, for more than fifteen years. When the affair began, Evelyn was divorced, the mother of two young sons, and sharing custody with her ex-husband. She and Richard were discreet and only got together at her home during the alternate weeks when the boys lived with their father. If there was a medical conference in another city, Evelyn usually attended, traveling alone whenever Richard took Priscilla. Interestingly, they all lived in the same suburb of a midsized New England city and in fairly close proximity. Richard and Priscilla lived in the "posh" part, while Evelyn lived in the more modest section. Priscilla worked as a director of volunteer docents at the community museum, and she and Richard had two children, a son and daughter in their thirties who were both married and had children of their own. I interviewed them all (and will tell the children's stories later), and all three insisted they knew nothing of Richard's double life until he told them about it.

Richard told Priscilla about his relationship with Evelyn over their evening cocktails, which Priscilla described as "the way we WASPs conduct our lives." When I talked to her, she insisted that she'd had no idea of the affair and that it came as a total shock. Nevertheless, after their ritual two double scotches, they went into the dining room and sat down to eat the dinner their housekeeper had prepared. Priscilla excused herself halfway through and went to their bedroom. Richard finished eating and cleared the table before going upstairs to see if she was all right. She told him she had phoned their children—Barry, who lived in the western part of their state, and Amanda, who lived in the same town. Telling them there was "a family emergency," she asked them to come home the following evening in time for the cocktail hour and to stay for dinner, and to come alone, without their spouses.

Barry and Amanda used the same word to describe how they felt, drink in hand, when Richard told them he was leaving Priscilla and that he hoped they would remain friendly with both parents: "devastated." No one could eat dinner that night, and Barry drank so much that he had to spend the night at Amanda's, where they were up until the wee hours wondering how the affair could have gone on "under [their] noses" for so many years.

Richard moved out of the house the following weekend and told Priscilla he wanted only a few mementos that had been in his family. He said he would leave it to her to sell the house, which she had to do because there was not enough money for her to keep up such a large and expensive property. He said she could keep the profit plus anything she took in by selling the household furnishings. Unfortunately, Richard's announcement left Priscilla in no condition to deal with anything concerning the destruction of the life she loved and thought she would lead forever, especially as it came just before the Thanksgiving holiday Barry and Amanda loved Thanksgiving and agreed that it meant more to them than all other holidays put together. They had always celebrated it at their parents' house, but that year it was a gloomy occasion as Amanda cooked a meal they only picked at. When Richard dropped in during the afternoon, Priscilla went to her bedroom, and Barry and Amanda and their spouses had nothing to say to him. Christmas was even worse, as Barry insisted that he would not drag his children to an unhappy house and told Priscilla she had to spend it at his home. She came and did nothing but cry, deeply upsetting his three little children.

For the next six months, Barry went back and forth from his house to his mother's every weekend and sometimes during the week as well. He convinced her that she had to look for an apartment, and he helped her find a large one close to where she worked. He also helped her to organize a lifetime of possessions, and to decide which to keep and which to sell or give away. As the things left the house and it became increasingly empty and desolate, he and Amanda talked Priscilla into moving into her new apartment and only visiting the house to work on preparing to vacate it.

When I spoke to Richard he said he is happy with his new life, and Priscilla told me she is coming to terms with hers. She finds it difficult to live in the same city as Richard, where she hears news of how happy he and his mistress are, but she was born and raised there and cannot imagine living elsewhere. She has a circle of friends, most of them connected with an amateur theatrical society where she has worked on stage sets and costumes for many years. They, too, are either divorced or widowed, so she always has company for a movie or a concert. Even so, she admits that she is depressed and other people must initiate the engagements or else she will "just stay at home, eat cheese and crackers for dinner, and watch stupid TV until bedtime."

She finds it hard to believe that the man she lived with for so many years could have been "so duplicitious." But then, she added, "I guess he really loved her, and not me."

SERIALLY UNFAITHFUL

Another variant of male infidelity happens when one partner (usually the husband) engages in a series of extramarital relationships, often throughout most of the marriage. When these men are asked about why they are unfaithful to their marriage vows, their answers range from excuses—most told me, "I just wasn't good husband material"—to various expressions of entitlement, such as Sean's, who asked me a question and then provided his own answer with an analogy that I heard from a half dozen other men, all of whom offered it in a tone of voice that combined pride with prowess.

"You know how bulls behave with a herd of cows, don't you? They have an obligation to fertilize them. Just think of me as a bull, doing his job." When I asked why he used such an analogy, he said it was "the only truthful way to describe what I do."

Sean was a professor at a midwestern university, a handsome and popular lecturer who fit the academic stereotype of the pipe-smoking, graying-at-the-temples, tweed-jacketed, slightly sardonic man of the world who had seen it all and done most of it. Colleagues and students of both sexes vied for his attention, but women vied to have sex with him—at least to hear him tell it. Ramona, his wife of twenty-seven years, told the story of their divorce in a slightly different manner: Sean could not accept the fact that he had not made it to the top of his field, which would have meant a chaired professorship at an Ivy League university, and so in order to convince himself that he was first-rate, he seduced women as compensation.

Sean and Ramona had two adopted children, a twenty-year-old daughter in nursing school and a seventeen-year-old son with learning disabilities who lived in a residential facility where he was learning a trade. Ramona was a permanent adjunct who received a modest salary teaching at a small Catholic college in the next town. She said she had long ago accepted Sean's philandering for a reason I heard repeatedly when I asked why some couples stayed married so long after the marriage had obviously failed: "for the sake of the children." Ramona described both of her children as "fragile," and she had no intention of divorcing Sean and breaking up their home until she thought her children could cope with it. Ramona knew for years that she would eventually divorce Sean, but until she was sure her children would not be emotionally devastated, she intended "to get along by going along." She was, therefore, understandably shocked when Sean told her he wanted a divorce. He thought the time had come for him to be free to pursue his "avocation of being available to women" without the need for the discretion with which he had always conducted his affairs.

"The one thing I always made sure of," he told me, "was never to put Ramona in a position where she would be embarrassed. That was probably the only way I was a good husband. I always protected her."

After her initial reaction of shock and "outrage, that he did it first, before I could," Ramona's practical nature very quickly snapped into operation. She had been careful with her salary and had always taken advantage of her college's retirement plan, so she knew that she would have almost but not quite enough money to maintain herself and the children. She would need a substantial portion of the marital assets, and she intended to consult a divorce lawyer to make sure she received whatever she was entitled to from Sean's pension, investments, and Social Security when the time came.

Just when all this was settled to her satisfaction, she received another shock: Sean had been diagnosed with multiple sclerosis in an advanced stage and would soon need extensive care. Ramona offered to put the divorce on hold and to take him back. He refused, telling her it was an intellectual opportunity he could not refuse, to observe his illness unaided. He planned to live alone in the town house he rented near the campus. He would take a sabbatical to learn what he could do to slow the progression of his illness, and he would also do some of the things he had never had the time to do before, particularly to write poetry. He did not tell her his secret reason, that even though "Ramona does not have a vindictive bone in her body," he feared becoming dependent on her after all the emotional pain he had caused her.

Sean and Ramona went ahead with the divorce and became one of the few couples I spoke to who cited infidelity as their reason but who managed to remain (as both put it) "civil, if not downright friendly." And yes, Sean continued to attract a succession of women, including a middle-aged widow who wanted him to marry her so she could care for him until the end. He refused, saying he was enjoying life too much to settle down. Ramona lives alone and even though she has had the occasional drink or dinner with a colleague, she chooses not to pursue another relationship. For the first time since her marriage to Sean, she has "control" over her life, and she likes it.

WOMEN WHO "CHEAT"

Men may say they are just not husband material, or that they feel entitled to have multiple affairs, but when women are unfaithful, it is usually for an entirely different reason. Men seldom told me they committed infidelity because they "fell in love with someone else," but it was the reason most women offered. And because of that, these women did not believe they had committed adultery in all the ugliness and pain of its reality. Women who described themselves as "strongly religious" did not feel they had "committed a sin," and women who said they believe they possess a "strong moral and ethical code of conduct" did not feel "stigma" or "shame." Time after time women told me their infidelity was "different" and could not and should not be compared with the ways in which men betray their wives. Only two women told me they had begun an affair "to get even" with their husbands, and both regretted doing so, saying if the situation were reversed, they might have been able to forgive their husbands, but their husbands could not forgive them and the affairs hastened their divorces.

Most of the women who committed infidelity were married to men they believed had always been faithful to them. The majority told me there had not been any overt problem between them and their husbands. In this respect, they were falling into another major category of the reasons for divorce—the lack of communication between spouses, synonymous with "falling out of love." What made most of them receptive to an affair was that there hadn't been an emotional connection between them and their husbands, often for many years. One woman who divorced after twenty-nine years said, "We were living together without love, sex, or affection." Another said, "All I ever wanted was to be spoken to as if I am cared for, and to feel that I am valued." Her lover made her feel this way, which her husband of twenty-eight years had never been able to do.

This was Fiona, and when she told her husband, Trevor, that that was the reason she was divorcing him, he was perplexed.

Trevor told Fiona, "I did everything I was supposed to do. I went to work and supported this family and made things nice for you. What more do you want?" After several months of couples' therapy, when Trevor was unable or unwilling to say more than this or to accept any responsibility for his role in the disintegration of the marriage, the counselor told him and Fiona, "You people don't belong together." Shortly afterward, Fiona filed for divorce.[3]

I would ask every woman I interviewed when and why she thought she and her husband began to experience emotional distance between them. Many of them, when they reflected back, were surprised to discover that the reason they divorced went all the way back to the reason they married in the first place. One couple, who were each fifty-five when they divorced, told me the same thing in their separate interviews about why they married: "We were both thirty and tired of being single." Another couple, whose marriage of thirty years had recently ended, told me, "We grabbed hold as if we were the answer to each other's prayers. Unfortunately, we weren't." A man who divorced after thirty-nine years said, "My idea of a good marriage is that the husband, the breadwinner, has to come first. She was too needy, so I just tuned her out to shut her up." This man thought the most important part of the marriage ceremony was the admonition that wives should "obey" their husbands. His wife said, "He was an old-fashioned Irishman, just like his miserable father and grandfather. I was supposed to know he appreciated a clean house and good meals and be grateful for sex once a week on Saturday night, and he was under no obligation to tell me anything nice."

Marianne was unusual in that she committed infidelity but denied having had long-term problems in her marriage to Michael, which she described as "neither good nor bad, it was just there, and we were okay with it." She was surprised by the emotions that led her to infidelity but was not ashamed of them, even though she was cocky, feisty, combative, and perhaps a little defensive when we first talked.

"I suppose you are going to call me a stereotype and lump me in with all the other cheating wives," she said early in our initial conversation. She had e-mailed me from her new home in Oklahoma after one of her friends in the Dallas area told her I was interviewing people she knew, among them Marianne's ex-husband. Marianne had lived in Dallas during her marriage, and she wanted to be sure that I had her side of the story as well. I asked why she thought I would call her a stereotype, and she told me her story.

Both she and Michael were fifty-four when they divorced; they had been married for thirty-two years, since the summer after they graduated from the University of Iowa. Michael was a certified public accountant for a large corporation, and they had moved four or five times during their marriage, mainly throughout the Southwest. Most of the time they lived in Dallas, where their three adult children (whom I also interviewed) were settled. Kelly was thirty, married with three children; Jason was twenty-eight and newly engaged; Kim was twenty-four and single, living with a female room-mate. Marianne thought Kim was gay and would be relieved if she were to declare her relationship but feared she "will never be strong enough to come out of the closet."

The entire family was always active in a conservative Christian church in their community because "everyone else went there." They kept their cultural attitudes and political leanings to themselves, calling themselves "quietly liberal" and "Texans for the other [Democratic] party." They were all athletic and liked hiking and camping in southern Utah and Colorado and hunting fossils in Wyoming and Montana.

Marianne trained as an elementary-school teacher but did not work until Kim started school. Very quickly she discovered that she did not like teaching, and after a succession of part-time jobs in other fields, she decided to become a real estate agent. She liked the work and did it well, but until Kim was in high school, Marianne put her family first and worked only enough to keep her place in the agency and bring "spending money" to the family coffers.

Michael comes into the telling of Marianne's story at this point. I had interviewed him before I spoke to her, and he told me he was "embarrassed and ashamed" to admit that she left him for another man. I asked if he might have felt different if she had given another reason for leaving. He told me no matter what the reason, the very fact that she divorced him made him think of himself as a "failure." I asked him to tell me how he felt when Marianne told him she wanted a divorce, and without hesitating, he said, "surprised," before adding, "I guess I thought everything was okay. There were never any problems between us."

When I interviewed Marianne, she described the first twenty or so years of their marriage in much the same way. There had been "no real problems," but what she called her "I don't know—discontent maybe" began around the time Kim entered college. When her first two children were both away at college, Marianne began to sell real estate at a faster clip because educating them was expensive. She did so well that she became a top seller for her firm and earned frequent rewards, some of which included holidays and vacations such as the one she and Michael took on a Caribbean island. Her strongest memory is that they "slept on the beach all day and didn't talk to each other across the dinner table at night." With their last child now enrolled in college and no longer living at home, Marianne noticed that she and Michael were only together at bedtime, "and even then we just said good night and turned our backs to each other without a hug or a kiss." After that, even when spouses were invited, Marianne went alone to sales conferences and other professional meetings held at posh resorts.

"Here's where I become the stereotype," she said and then laughed as she told me how she met Bill in Orlando, at a coaching conference just out-side Disney World. Bill, also fifty-four, recently divorced after thirty years, worked for a real estate agency in Tulsa. His marriage to his high school sweetheart, Doreen, "just fizzled out," when they became "another couple who married too young." Bill had been faithful throughout his marriage, and they had never quarreled. The separation was "amicable enough," so much so that Bill could not remember if he or Doreen had been the one to ask for the divorce. He had none of the feelings about the dissolution of his marriage that Michael had. Bill had little contact with Doreen afterward, but they were polite to each other for the sake of their two unmarried adult sons, William and James.

Bill was immediately attracted to Marianne, who sat next to him in the coaching workshop and so became his partner for the exercises they played. Both thought it was a "fun session," and afterward they sat together at lunch and shared horror stories of selling houses to difficult clients. Marianne said Bill made her laugh; Bill, a shy man who had been dating several "really nice women" since his divorce, was delighted that such an attractive woman found him amusing. He said he could not believe how "corny" he felt about Marianne as soon as he met her, like "falling in love for the first time in my life." Marianne said Bill revived "all those feelings you have when you date but put away when you marry." Still, both were shy, timid, and of the genera-tion that believed "nice people like us, people our age, don't just fall into bed like in the movies or on TV." They hid behind a euphemism for sex, saying they didn't believe it was possible for people their age to experience "ro-mantic love." For them, infidelity was tantamount to sin, and sex belonged only in legal marriage, so they did not become lovers until several months later, when (as Marianne described it) "passion just took over." From the day they met, they had barraged each other with daily e-mails and run up huge overages on their cell phones until another conference was announced, this one "terrible, not worth the time or trouble to go to." However, it presented Marianne with an excuse to be away from Michael, so she and Bill attended anyway and their affair began. Afterward, the distance between Dallas and Tulsa was just too great and Marianne could neither lie nor invent enough excuses to cover the times she wanted to be with Bill.

At this point in her career, she was earning as much as Michael (and in some years more) and knew she could support herself. Michael was stunned when she walked into the den one evening and asked him to turn off the television and listen to what she had to say. Determined to be with Bill, she offered to walk away from everything she and Michael owned if he would give her an uncontested divorce (she didn't know that in her state, grounds were not necessary).

Michael said he walked around in a daze for a week or so. He had asked Marianne not to tell their children, thinking she might "come to her senses" and he could persuade her to stay married. Kelly, their oldest child, the one to whom he was closest, learned about her parents' separation when she phoned to ask why Michael wasn't dropping in to visit the grandchildren as he often did. As she listened to his evasions, Kelly sensed something was wrong, so she showed up unannounced at Michael's office to take him to lunch, when she asked him point-blank what was wrong. She thought he would tell her "he had cancer or something"; she "never imagined" he would tell her he and Marianne were getting divorced. Kelly said he blurted out that he was "humiliated" and "so depressed it felt like walking underwater, with ten-ton weights on his head holding him down." She was furious with her mother but did not confront her. Instead, she acted to help her father and did something that Michael said "saved my sanity."

Kelly was trained as a social worker but had not worked since her children were born. She knew about a divorce recovery program that had a chapter in Dallas,[4] and not only did she insist that Michael go to a meeting, she went with him to make sure he stayed until the entire program was over and then signed himself up for future sessions. In the divorce recovery workshop, he met a lot of people just like himself, who had never thought they would end up alone after so many years of marriage. His loneliness was "crushing," and he depended on his children and his twice-weekly recovery sessions in equal part. It took almost a year before he was able to get over the shock of Marianne leaving him.

Meanwhile, Marianne was engaging an attorney to begin the divorce proceedings and going about the business of packing only the things she wanted to take to her new home, which for the immediate future was Bills apartment in Tulsa. She arranged to be transferred to her firms office there, and within weeks she was busily selling real estate and enjoying her new life, both professional and romantic. For her, the infidelity appears to have led to a happy second marriage, which was not the case for some of the other women I interviewed.

UNFORTUNATE INFIDELITIES

Donna and Frances fell into the unfortunate group whose infidelity did not have the results they desired. The initial experience of each woman was similar to Marianne's, but in both cases, the men turned out to be disappointing. Donna's fellow told her he was divorcing his wife, so she left her home to be with him. "But of course he wasn't, and of course he didn't, and eventually I got tired of not being divorced and not being married either." By the time disillusion set in and she knew she should end the affair, her husband told her he had learned to like living alone and didn't want to resume a loveless marriage. She said she was "disgusted" with herself for "making such a dumb mistake" but soon adjusted to being "a middle-aged woman on her own with a low-level sales job and not much future." However, she has decided to "look on the bright side, and look forward to whatever comes."

Frances continued to have feelings for her lover and to hope he would change despite his addictive behavior, but eventually she had to face the fact that it was never going to happen. "Now I know why he told me I had to put the apartment lease in my name and pay for it myself," she said, when she learned about his enormous gambling and credit-card debt. She asked him to leave and he did, but she decided not to try to return to her marriage. She planned to let the divorce become final, learn how to live alone and take care of herself in the hope that she would find "the satisfying, sustaining relationship" she now realized she had never had with her husband.

"UNWAVERING MONOGAMY" WITH MULTIPLE AFFAIRS

One of the most interesting tales of a woman's infidelity I encountered was that of an Australian couple I never met: Mary Moody, fifty, the Australian gardening writer and TV presenter, and her film-producer husband of thirty-plus years, David Hannay, fifty-four.[5] After a marriage of "unwavering monogamy," Mary convinced David to buy a house in a French village where she could live without him and where, during the summer of 2002, she took one lover, who was soon followed by another. David learned about the first affair, and Mary ended it. "Well, sort of," said the reporter who wrote about the couple's further adventures. Mary wrote a book about the first affair, *Au Revoir*, in which she hinted about her lover but confessed to sleeping with nobody but her cats, and it still became a runaway bestseller in Australia among "women of a certain age." By the time she wrote her second book in 2003, *Last Tango in Toulouse*, the word was out and these enthralled women were flocking in droves to the lunches arranged to promote Mary and sell her books.

Only one man was seated among the six or seven hundred women who eagerly bought tickets for the luncheons, and that was David, who always said, "I'm willing to forgive Mary Moody anything." When the ladies asked him to sign Mary's book, he did so graciously even as they told him how their own husbands would never have tolerated such behavior. What they didn't know and what David didn't tell them was that the marriage was on precarious grounds because Mary had had not one, but two affairs, and a third book was under way that exposed every detail of her liaisons. Entitled *The Long Hot Summer*, it was published in 2005 in Australia with the same success as her first two.

Mary said her problem was that she fell in love with her lovers, even though the first one was married and had no intention of divorcing and the second was much younger than she and not nearly as involved in the relationship as she was. David described himself as "livid, shattered, stunned," by her infidelities, but he did not direct his anger at his wife. Instead, he attacked (verbally) her lovers, her publisher, and even his own best friend. David insists that he is not the amazingly civilized husband Mary's fans think he is. "Actually I'm a barbarian. I'd very happily kill the lover, or two. That's why I went to the talks. . . . There is a suggestion of tolerance, which I really haven't felt at all."

Mary does worry about her children's reaction (one from David's earlier marriage and three from theirs), but she thinks they probably haven't read any of the books. Why, then, did she write them? Because she was "keen to cash in." The problem, however, was that writing the books meant that David learned about the affairs, but, Mary said, once he knew about them, "there was no point in not including it in the story."

They still own the house in France, but neither has been there recently and there are no plans for either to return any time soon. Mary says their marriage crisis has not been resolved and she has no idea if they will still be together in the future. Since the third book was published, "it's been two steps forward, one step back, one step forward, two back." She has decided she needs to try to write something different and told David that she wants to live in a village in Nepal for three to six months.

Why, he asked her—has she met "some Sherpa?"

CHAPTER THREE

ABUSE TAKES MANY FORMS

The crisis of middle life confronts us with a need to change our lives, but it does not invite us toward any pattern of changes; and thus it is a source of personal dilemma. It's as if we had to invent the rest of our lives, and we don't believe we know how to do that. . . . Survival is what happens afterward in the life we are inventing.

—ELIZABETH JANEWAY, *Cross Sections:*
From a Decade of Change

ABUSE TAKES MANY FORMS, from random and haphazard physical violence to the constantly relentless humiliation of verbal insult, to the cruelty of emotional abandonment by a spouse who "just wasn't there, in any way, shape, or form." Perhaps it is not surprising that the majority of people who cite abuse as the reason they divorce are women, for until recent times men in long-term marriages have wielded the power to ordain the role each partner played in the relationship. Their authority was largely financial because men were the primary wage earners and controllers of the family's finances, and most women did not work at all, let alone have careers. The husband's work dictated where the wife and children lived, what their standard of living would be, and by extension, where they would fit in the world outside their household door.

Many wives, especially those who were married to corporate or military men, could not have had careers even if they wanted them because of the frequent moves their husbands' work entailed. When these women relate their stories, they often describe how they had to remain in unhappy, abusive marriages because they were frightened not only by their inability to support themselves but also by the lack of support or even the hostility they feared to find in a community of strangers. The wife of an army enlisted man whose chest was festooned with ribbons and decorations asked who, on their isolated army post, would believe he was responsible for her broken ribs and bruised torso, when he was prepared to tell them she fell down the cellar steps while carrying an overloaded laundry basket. "He never woulda done that if we were back home with our folks," she insisted. "His daddy would not let him disrespect a woman that way."

Corporate wives living in foreign countries where they did not know the languages told me how they bore the brunt of their husbands' frustration with having to do business in cultures that did not follow the patterns and practices of the Western world. One woman whose husband's career was spent mostly in the Mideast told me how she survived the early years of her marriage: "When he came home ready for bear and headed directly for the bottle, I just took the kids into their bedroom and read to them quietly, hoping he'd drink himself stupid and fall asleep. Otherwise I'd know I was in for it." Throughout those twenty-some years, she "put up with it" by excusing him for behaving as he never would have done in the United States. When the children grew up and left home, she "stood up to him one time only" and spent several weeks in a Jordanian hospital after he beat her senseless for her "disobedience." When she was released, she sought help from a charity she would not name and was given enough money to return to the southern city where his firm had its corporate headquarters. She went there because her only "friends," a word she used "loosely" after a lifetime of "pulling up stakes and moving on," agreed to take her in until she could get settled elsewhere.

In the AARP study, 34 percent of the respondents cited abuse as the main reason for their divorce, but no breakdown was given for the three main categories into which it was divided: physical, verbal, and emotional. Women outnumbered men (86 percent to 60 percent) in claiming that abuse led them to divorce, with both insisting that they were not the abusers but the abused; both men and women put the blame on their spouses. My interviews paralleled the AARP study, in that more women claimed "abuse" (the actual word they used) as their primary reason, but very few told me they were victims of *physical* abuse. When they did admit to physical abuse, they did so offhandedly, claiming it was "infrequent," "sporadic," "not really painful," or "just hurtful inside." Physical abuse cuts across class lines, and among my respondents, those who cited it ranged from the highest social strata to the working classes.

My respondents described physical abuse in a variety of degrees. One woman, who classified herself as an "upper-middle-class corporate wife," said, "It wasn't like the Saturday-night drunk coming home and beating the hell out of everybody. Once early in the marriage I provoked him to the point where he shook me hard and slapped me lightly. Ten years later he threw a glass of booze at me but missed, and a couple of years after that, we were standing at the bottom of the staircase arguing, and he pushed me down so hard I hurt my tailbone." Another woman, who said she was "in the middle of the middle class" and was married to a construction worker, admitted to "two black eyes in twenty-four years, but that was enough," and she divorced him. Several women who admitted to physical violence declined to go into detail. Among them were wives of a senior officer in the navy, an artist-teacher, a CEO of a major international corporation, and a New York City police officer.

Almost every woman I interviewed who cited some degree of abuse as a primary reason for divorcing used the same expression: they "gave up" on their marriages. I found it interesting that so many used the same wording to describe how, after years of trying to "make things work," they "gave up." When I asked if they regretted being the one who initiated the divorce, many said they had regrets about things that happened during the marriage but not about getting the divorce. They described different kinds of regret, but primary among them was "failure." The senior naval officers wife elaborated: "Divorce is failure, no matter what the reason for it and the outcome of it." The CEO's wife said her primary feeling was "more like resentment than regret," that after all the years she had "walked the walk" in order to keep her wealthy and pampered existence, she was still going to "end up alone" and "on the short end of the financial stick." A seventy-four-year-old woman who ended a fifty-one-year marriage asked rhetorically, "Why did I spend so many years trying and trying to make him show me the least little bit of tenderness? Why did I wait to leave him until it was too late for me to make a new life with someone else?"

Another woman, whose divorce came after thirty-nine years, regretted not the end of her marriage but rather that she had obeyed her husband's command never to have children. He had persuaded her that their life together was perfect and children, with their many needs, would spoil it. She admits to one abortion that she never told him about, even though she knew that for more than half their marriage he was unfaithful to her and she yearned all through it for children to fill her "emotional void." When he left her for a divorced woman with three teenagers to whom he became a "soccer dad," she regretted letting him "brainwash" her, saying in retrospect, "What he did was the worst kind of emotional abuse." She was one of the many abused women who believed divorce was her only option, but she, too, expressed the primary regret of them all: that she would be alone in her old age. "It wasn't supposed to be this way," she said.

When men spoke to me about the "battles" they had in their marriages, of how "things got thrown" or "broken" or "destroyed," I would always ask if perhaps they had been the abused as well as the abuser. Every single one of them vehemently denied being the abuser, and when they described how crockery or other objects flew back and forth between them, the battle was always "mutual." However, there are stories, such as the anonymous accounts on various radio and television programs in which men describe how their wives are physically violent toward them. When asked why they did not report their wives to the authorities, they said something like, "Who would believe me? She'd say I was beating her, and then I'd get arrested." When asked why they didn't divorce these battering wives, the men who had children said they stayed in the marriage for two reasons: they feared that if they left, the wife would turn her fury onto the children, or else she would find a way to convince the judge in a divorce action that she should have custody of the children and would do all she could to deny the husband access to them.

I may not have interviewed any abused men, but the growing interest in the topic and the burgeoning number of programs and articles dedicated to this phenomenon must be an indication that it happens in larger numbers than were previously known. And that it is as crushing, humiliating, and demoralizing for men as it is for women.

ABUSE AS A "GENERATIONAL THING"

Sandy, a woman who divorced her physician husband, Sherwin, after thirty-seven years of marriage, described the ways in which she subjugated her needs and her children's to his, and how she allowed him to control the family by controlling its finances. She concluded that "a younger woman today would never allow herself to be as compromised as I allowed myself to be." She is convinced that younger women have opportunities that she did not have to take more control of their marriages early enough to stop abuse in any of its forms before it reaches the point of no return. What she calls "the younger generation" has grown up assuming that women will work, will have their own money, and will have a say in how family life is conducted. If they cannot take this control or they choose not to have it, Sandy believes "they will divorce, but quite simply, they will do it earlier."

Sandy offered her own example as an illustration of how and why women of her generation (those who married in the late 1950s and early 1960s) remained for so long in abusive marriages. She was the only child of a widowed alcoholic mother, and her upbringing had been "just above the poverty line." She attended college on a tuition scholarship but worked to pay for room, board, and all her other expenses. She and Sherwin both graduated from Boston University, but she gave up a fellowship in comparative literature at Cornell to stay in Boston and put him through medical school. After he graduated they remained in the Boston area and Sherwin became a partner in a medical consortium, specializing in reconstructive facial surgery. He was highly successful and he and Sandy were able to live in one of the best houses in one of the area's richest residential enclaves.

Sandy gave birth to three daughters in quick succession, and her "work," as she put it, was to keep them "fedded and bedded and out of his way." Everything in the household revolved around Sherwin, but it was a comfortable life that gave Sandy all she thought she would ever want or need;

to her, the life Sherwin's career gave her was "a dream." To live the dream, she was willing to endure his unrelenting criticism, which soon became his only form of communication with her and the three girls. Nothing Sandy did was good enough, from the elegant parties he expected her to give, to the designer clothes he expected her to wear, to the good grades the girls brought home from school, to the breakfast grapefruit that was never sweet enough. Sherwin, according to Sandy, "thought life was out to get him and everything was all my fault."

However much he criticized, Sherwin was faithful and had no bad habits such as gambling or drinking, so Sandy learned not to react, not to respond, and above all, never to argue. When the last daughter entered school, she parlayed her volunteer work of writing and editing newsletters for several medical organizations into paying work as a freelance feature writer for the local weekly newspaper. Soon, she had local recognition and people were praising her writing wherever they went socially. When they returned home after these occasions, Sherwin would find a reason "to throw a tantrum about something in the house." Her local writings led to commissions for articles in a large metropolitan daily newspaper and eventually to a small book commissioned by a local historical group and published privately. On a trip to New York with Sherman while he attended a medical conference, Sandy visited her college roommate, who introduced her to a literary agent living in the same apartment building. "One thing led to another," is how she describes landing the contract for her first book, a collection of articles based on her newspaper interviews with teenagers about how they envisioned their future.

Was Sherwin proud of her? I asked. Sandy paused for a long time and then said quietly, "No." If anything, "his daily ridicule became far more scathing."

"You must have had a very strong sense of your self-worth to put up with it," I said.

"Yes," she responded, "and that in the end is what saved me."

Sandy published the book about teenagers and received a contract to write another. Both were well received by the few reviewers who took notice, but neither was a runaway bestseller, which Sherwin did not let her forget. He treated her "with a mixture of indifference and hatred." He accused her of wasting her time writing what nobody wanted to read. He berated her for neglecting him personally and not taking care of his needs ("he said it was my fault when the maid put too much starch in his collars"). He complained about the condition of the house even though they always had a full-time cook and a resident couple to care for the house and garden. He even extended his criticisms to the three girls, who to this day say they hardly saw their father when they were growing up because they spent most of their time staying out of his way.

Whenever Sandy had a deadline, Sherwin would demand her attention in all sorts of ways she could not refuse. "Interestingly," she told me, "this is when he became highly sexual, something he otherwise was not." When sex did not deter Sandy from her writing, he became so depressed that she begged him to go into therapy. He refused and "got into a sadistic routine: I love you. I don't love you. You are tainting my good life. You're a nobody and you came from nothing. You can't do anything right. I can't make it without you." Sandy ignored his "manic highs and depressed lows." She persevered, managing to meet Sherwin's needs, deflect his criticisms, nurture her daughters, and meet her deadlines. Her capability made him furious.

In retaliation, he took up athletics and became a triathlon competitor, in the process filling their house with his newfound friends who competed in the same meets. He demanded that Sandy feed them, find beds for them when events were held locally, and even accompany them to provide the different kinds of support their activities required, from guarding equipment to preparing elaborate carb-loading meals. Sandy did these things, even though Sherwin had no qualms about berating her for anything that did not meet his approval or listing her other alleged failures in front of anyone who happened to be around.

Did she ever think of leaving him? No, she said, "not then, and probably I never would have. At least that's how I felt then." I asked her to explain, and she blushed in embarrassment: "I liked all the things being married to him gave me, so I was willing to put up with him." Also, and equally important to her, Sandy believed that "women of my generation did not divorce. We made our beds when we married and we learned to lie in them." In saying this, she represented the majority of the women I interviewed who were around fifty-five or older. I asked if they held this belief because they felt divorce left them with a stigma, or if perhaps they were religious enough to consider it forbidden. Most women thought these were secondary considerations to the primary one: once a woman was married, "it was like the vows said, till death (and *only* death) do us part."

Sandy said she intended to stay married even after she began to suspect that Sherwin was having an affair with a triathlete who was often their houseguest. Sherwin scoffed and told her that when he decided to have an affair, she would be the first to know She believed him because throughout their marriage, "sex was never that important to him." How about to her? "When I became a married woman, romance took a backseat." Didn't she miss ordinary touching or cuddling? "Even in the courtship I never had too much of that. After the marriage he was always on duty at the hospital in the early days, and later on, he was too tired when he came home."

Several years after Sandy first asked him about the other woman, Sherwin told her the friendship had become "occasionally" sexual and he expected her to "deal with it." He did not want a divorce and would fight her if she filed for one, threatening that he would see to it that she got next to nothing financially. It frightened Sandy because, like so many women of her generation, she had no clear idea of their financial worth. Sherwin and his partners had a business manager who took care of their investments and paid their household bills, and so she stayed married out of fear of the unknown. Soon after, she was relieved when Sherwin told her the affair was over because the triathlete bored him. It was not until after her divorce that Sandy learned the other woman (in her early forties and of a different generation) ended the affair because she refused to put up with Sherwin's sarcastic criticism. "See," Sandy pointed out to me, "that's what I mean about younger women taking control far earlier!"

What made Sandy finally file for divorce was the discovery that Sherwin's partners had grown weary of his constant criticism, which was driving patients away. Also, they feared for their own reputations when several patients threatened to bring lawsuits against Sherwin, so they asked him to leave the practice. He was enraged. For the first time, he turned the full force of the venom he had unleashed mostly upon Sandy upon his daughters as well.

Fortunately, the older two were away at college but the youngest was still at home. Sandy was determined to protect her and enrolled her in a nearby boarding school where she could visit her on weekends so she wouldn't have to come home to face her rampaging father.

When Sandy told Sherwin she wanted a divorce, he set every obstacle in her way. Hoping to frighten her into staying, he told her he was broke, that their lavish lifestyle left him with no resources, especially now that he had to start all over again to rebuild his medical career. By this time, his behavior was so erratic and abusive that Sandy, fearing his words would turn to blows, asked him to leave the house. He refused to go, so she moved into a guest bedroom. He dismissed the servants, and what meals she ate at home, she bolted down, standing up in the kitchen, fearful that he would come home before she finished. Mostly, she found reasons to be away except when sleeping. One day when she came home, she found a sign on the front lawn. Sherwin had put the house on the market, saying they had to sell it, as they had no income. Even though she had no clear idea of their total financial worth, Sandy knew that half of it would not be enough for her to maintain the house on her own, so she accepted what he had done and concentrated all her energies on dismantling the showcase she had spent years furnishing and decorating. At that point, Sherwin, saying he could not stand the chaos, moved out and left her to deal with everything, including selling it.

Sandy had "adequate legal counsel but not the best" for her divorce. Sherwin "did his number about how he was down, his partners were kicking him out, et cetera. Like a good girl, I didn't go to a ball-busting big-city lawyer but to one in the burbs where I lived. To make this sorry story short: he got off easily and I didn't."

She is convinced that "had I been younger, with a real career and some kind of parental or family support network, I could have taken him for my fair share, but by that time all I wanted was to be rid of him." Her "eyes were opened," she said. "He made a fool out of me as a woman. He made me give up grad school and give up work to decorate his house and build his reputation. He used me and exploited me to the nth degree—and then I lost everything anyway."

Sandy took a "shorter alimony" just to get the divorce over with quickly.

She was entitled to half of Sherwin's investment and retirement accounts, but they had suffered in various market reverses, and as she suspected, almost everything else was tied up in the house and its contents. She cried "every day for months on end" as the house did not sell and dealers came to haggle over the prices of the Early American and English antiques, the paintings, the museum-quality silver. In the end, she got "a third to a fourth" of what she had paid for everything but had to accept it because she could not take them to a tiny apartment and, more important, she needed the money. She still had two children whose tuition had to be paid, and Sherwin was abdicating responsibility because they were over eighteen. He so resented Sandy for divorcing him that he used his refusal to support the children as one of the ways to try to insert himself into her life: "If he could raise an obstacle, no matter how serious or how trivial, he did it." He would also phone at all hours and leave messages demanding to know what had become of an object he had never shown any interest in before, ordering her to find and return it to him at once. The worst came after the house was sold, when he invoked a clause in the divorce agreement. Even though all responsibility for the support of the house fell to her until it was sold, he threatened to sue if she did not hand over one third of the modest profit it brought. She had no option but to give him the money, which put her even closer to the poverty line.

The house finally sold after a year on the market. To be able to pay the mortgage and utilities, Sandy sold its contents, her designer wardrobe, and her Mercedes. After she paid the lawyers, credit-cards companies, and other assorted debts that Sherwin assigned to her, she faced the grim reality that she had barely enough money left to get herself into a one-bedroom apartment in a triple-decker house in a working-class suburb of Boston. Recalling that grim time, she said, "I ate peanut butter and cereal to survive until I found a full-time job." She could not afford a professional mover, so she hired "two guys from the new neighborhood with a big truck." When she got to her new home, she discovered that some of the larger pieces of furniture would not fit through the doorway and up the stairs to the second floor. Frazzled, exhausted, and filthy from the move, she left them in the backyard, covered with a thick tarpaulin. The hot water in her apartment had not been turned on, so she ate a bowl of cold cereal and flopped into bed unwashed.

It rained that night and all the next day and night, a classic nor'easter, and everything under the tarp was ruined. The low point of her life came the morning after the skies cleared, when Sherwin drove up in their other Mercedes (which he kept), showered, shaved, "looking like a Brooks Brothers ad," to ask her to sign several papers pertaining to the house sale that had mistakenly been sent to him.

Sandy said she wanted to get into bed and pull the covers over her head, but her "strong sense of self-worth" saved her. She learned that "possessions, even the ones you hold most dear, are all replaceable. But we are creatures of habit and we want our things. This is a terrible stumbling block for women."

After Sherwin left, she spent the morning arranging for what the rain had ruined to be picked up and hauled away, and for the "two guys with the truck" to take the rest to a charity that collected household goods for battered women's shelters. She set up her desk in a corner of the bedroom and sat down to collect her thoughts and make notes about the several writing projects whose deadlines were fast approaching. Knowing she could not support herself on freelance assignments, she studied the help-wanted ads. Three weeks later, she had several interviews, and within a month, she accepted a job at the public relations office of a small women's college. She took this job because the salary was decent and after a probationary period, she would receive medical benefits and could contribute to a pension plan. For the first time in her life, she was in charge of her own money, and dealing with it wisely became the most important event in her recovery from the trauma of divorce. Financial security brought "self-sufficiency, and self-sufficiency brought self-worth and self-value."

I wanted to know what sorts of things or people she thought were important enough to bring into her new life from her previous one. Had she kept the friends who had been part of her life when she was part of a couple? "Sadly, no," she told me. The medical community has many marriages—among the male doctors that is—so the women who were still married to them and who I thought were my friends all dropped away. Doctors' wives are very frightened of any doctor's wife who has been divorced. They fear it might happen to them."

Having gone from college to marriage, Sandy had never lived alone before. "I'm not a person who sits around and cries, so I had to learn to amuse myself." She had "to figure out what to do on long, lost weekends to keep from getting depressed," so she got up the courage to go to movies alone (something she had never done), to take a book to a good restaurant and insist upon a decent table so she could enjoy eating a meal alone. She joined a writing group but didn't find it as pleasant as she hoped. "I was with a lot of women who had been single for too long and men who had been married for two minutes to lots of women."

Sandy fit the AARP statistic of women who ask for the divorce (66 percent) and who want a relationship after divorce and enter into one within two to five years (79 percent), and who then remarry (32 percent). She is one of the 76 percent who think they made the correct decision to divorce, and one of the 67 percent who believe their new relationship is stable and secure. Like 31 percent of the AARP respondents, Sandy wanted no contact at all with Sherwin, but six months after their divorce was final, he begged her to come back to him, vowing to atone for every wrong he had ever committed. This, too, fits a pattern, but AARP gave no statistic for it. In my interviews, slightly less than a third of the abusive partners asked to resume the marriage. None of my respondents accepted. Sherwin sent her several letters of apology as he pled his case, and they made Sandy "very happy," but she still declined. She is among the AARP's 35 percent of those who are not friendly with their former spouses and who have contact only when necessary.

By the time Sherwin made his overtures, Sandy had joined a group of divorced people who were graduates of pretigious colleges and were interested in meeting new people. She met some of these men for lunch or a drink after work but was careful not to become involved in anything serious. This behavior was typical of most of the women I interviewed. Many of them wanted male companionship but hesitated for fairly long periods before allowing it to evolve into more than casual meetings in public places. One year after her divorce, Sandy met a divorced man totally unlike the "high-strung, overachieving" Sherwin, whom she described as "the kind of man who doesn't put much value on human relationships, who can't sustain intimacy, especially friendship. Now I know it's a sure sign that marriage to these men will eventually fail."

The new man in Sandy's life was "calm, measured, logical, warm, quiet, and with a sense of humor, attractive but not gorgeous." They were engaged shortly after they met, but like 26 percent of the AARP respondents, they lived together for almost two years before deciding it was "safe to marry." Sandy knew even before she divorced that she wanted to be remarried, and she advises any woman who divorces to "visualize what you want in life and then go after it until you get it." Four years after her own divorce, with a stable and supportive relationship, she said she becomes more convinced each day that she has found it.

"IT WAS ALL HIS/HER FAULT, NOT MINE!"

When verbal or emotional abuse is cited as the main reason for divorce, men and women alike tend to blame their spouse for the breakdown of the marriage. Still, more men than women, perhaps in an attempt to seem chivalrous, say they are willing to accept the greater part of the blame than their mates, even as they equivocate to show that it really was not their fault. In my interviews with men, about half said their wives had been "cold," "withdrawn for years," "disapproving and sarcastic," "passive-aggressive," "stubborn," "disapproving of everything I did," or "constantly putting me down." When I asked if they considered this to be verbal or emotional abuse, they all agreed that the reasons for their divorces fell solidly into one or both categories; when I asked them to give me actual examples of what they meant by the phrases above, they were either unwilling or unable to be more specific. They retreated into metaphor, euphemism, or outright evasion, like some of the men whose stories I tell below.

However, no matter who blamed whom for verbal or emotional abuse, whenever I asked who actually began the divorce proceedings, slightly more than 60 percent of the men I interviewed said their wives filed, not them. Almost 100 percent of the men I interviewed told me they were "surprised," "puzzled," or "bewildered" when their wives told them the marriage was over and initiated the divorce, because they thought "everything was all right." Many of them offered a variation of this comment, too: "We didn't talk all that much, but we never fought about anything."

Writers Penny Kaganoff and Susan Spano asked other writers, both men and women, to contribute the stories of their divorces for companion volumes in the late 1990s.[1] Reviewing the submissions, Kaganoff and Spano found that women were far more comfortable revealing all the details of what went wrong, no matter how painful, embarrassing, or downright sordid; whereas men "were uncomfortable with the sort of emotionally intense self-examination common in the women's volume."[2] From my own interviews, I made the same observation, particularly with men who insisted their wives should share responsibility for verbal and emotional abuse even though the wives initiated the divorces.

Among the men who spoke in metaphor and generality, one in Switzerland told me the end of his marriage was "like a symphony ending, or a fountain that has no more water coming from the well." Gottfried and Elisabeth had been married for forty-one years and had three grown sons. He was eager to talk to me about what happened to him, hoping it would help him to understand it, for he could not "risk" going to a therapist in the tightly knit community where they lived. He also said he had a specific reason for wanting to tell me his story because he knew I would interview Elisabeth, and when she asked for a divorce, he realized there would be "five truths here, for every one of us [this included their three children] experienced the separation in a different way with different pain and sorrow, but also as a freedom to form a new gestalt within the family."

Throughout the interview, Gottfried spoke in a language of such artifice that, while he may have wanted to arrive at "his truth," he still had to maintain distance from it in order to assimilate and digest the pain it caused him. He stated his only direct admission firmly, even angrily: that he expected his wife, his children, and his home to be "adjuncts, satellites" to him and his professional life. "That is what marriage is supposed to be in this country," he insisted. Gottfried was an admistrator in the legal division of a large Swiss corporation, the equivalent of a well-paid midlevel civil servant in the United States. At the end of his workday, he expected to return to a home organized so efficiently that his evening would unfold smoothly; his wife would serve an excellent meal, and his children would fill the dinner hour with polite conversation, after which they would go off to their own pursuits. He would read or listen to music before retiring early, to his own bedroom, to which Elisabeth had banished him some years before because of his thunderous snoring. When Gottfried attended weekly lodge meetings or monthly hiking or fishing trips with male friends, he expected Elisabeth to get up before dawn to lay out his gear, make his breakfast, prepare coffee, and pack fresh lunches for him that included enough extra to share with his companions.

Elisabeth's "truth" was far more direct and emotional. "You see these clothes," she said, pointing to her well-tailored designer clothing and expensive jewelry. "I wear them when I go to the supermarket because I have them and I have nowhere else to wear them." She used her elegant wardrobe and all the trappings of her beautifully appointed apartment as an example of the sterility of her marriage: "I have *things*, and that's all," she insisted. When I asked how she filled her days now that her children were off on their own and she no longer needed to be at home to prepare their lunch, she said that was exactly her reason for wanting a divorce—that she was "not needed anymore." All her life she had patterned her activity on the needs of others, and now it was her turn. She was "terrified" at the thought of being alone, unsure what, if any, "personal needs" she herself had, but she had to "make the leap to freedom" to find out, for if she waited any longer, it would be too late.

Hidden beneath her need to find out about her own need was a tremendous surge of anger toward Gottfried for leaving her no alternative but divorce: "There were so many ways he could have included me in his life but he chose to be selfish and think only of himself." She claimed that over the years, she had told him to "let me in" repeatedly, but he had no idea what she was talking about. Gottfried saw it differently: "I went to work every day to provide a good home for my wife and children, and they always came first. Was I not entitled to some pleasures of my own when my workday was done?" This, too, was a common refrain in my interviews.

In Australia, Edmund said he "had been conscious for some weeks" that his forty-nine-year marriage to Margaret "was under strain," and that he had been trying hard "to think of some not-unacceptable way to initiate discussion as to how to improve it." After breakfast one morning, he tried to start a conversation, beginning with the remark that "everything I have ever done for us and our family has been done with the best of intentions," at which point she interrupted and launched a verbal barrage of (in his words) "every dreadful thing I was supposed to have done in the past forty-nine years." Margaret told him this conversation was his "third strike. And three strikes and you're out, and now this marriage is over." Edmund felt "dreadful; there was such a sense of unreality about it." He asked Margaret to explain what his "three strikes" were, and she went back to the beginning of their marriage to accuse him of infidelities when, as a construction engineer building roads in western Australia, he was often away from home. He told her again, as he had told her all those years ago, that she was imagining things and that he had never been unfaithful. His second strike was midway through the marriage when he invested some money that was earmarked for their retirement into high-risk stocks and lost it. His third was "staying out of her way, not unleashing her terrible temper, tiptoeing around the house after I retired." Margaret's version was that Edmund may or may not have been unfaithful, he "was always a dunce about money," and he was "cold and unfeeling and would not change." Edmund said he was not a gambler and the bad stock investment was only one of two such instances in their marriage. What she resented was that he took these risks without first consulting her. "She wanted to be in on everything, but I stopped trying to include her because she always criticized. No matter what I did, it was always wrong."

Both agreed that the marriage lasted as long as it did because of Edmund's business trips and the long days he spent at work. Once he retired, Margaret complained that "I cannot call my house, my only refuge throughout these forty-nine years, mine any longer." She could not stand to live her final years "under the same roof with a stranger." Their divorce is still being contested because Margaret told Edmund to give her the house and to move out at once. He said they needed to agree about "a fifty-fifty distribution of the assets, with the house being the largest." Margaret never worked outside the home and was furious that he would not give her the entire house plus

50 percent of their assets. She threatened that anything less would leave her "no option but suicide." Edmund countered that "to give her what she wants is to leave myself with nothing." Margaret said, "no quarter would be given," and Edmund fears that when the lawyers finally "finish dithering, she, being the forceful one, will get what she wants and I will be in difficult straits."

James, in Upstate New York, takes "some of the blame" for ending his marriage of thirty-three years but insists that divorce "has to be seen as a joint decision." Eight years before the official end of the marriage, his wife, Karen, started to spend six months of each year in Southern California. James ran a small family business, and Karen was an artist who concentrated on painting patterns and designs on clothing, mostly sweatshirts, hats, and jackets. She told him she could not make a decent living in Upstate New York because the weather did not permit year-round crafts festivals and sales. When she began to paint purses, she experimented with selling them at winter crafts festivals and outdoor markets throughout the Southwest, and she told James she did very well. Karen had a family inheritance, which was paid to her through a trust, and she kept this money separate from what James gave her to run the household. She insisted that she was making a good living selling her crafts, so he did not learn until they were divorcing that the crafts never paid well and were only her excuse for living away from him. All the years they lived apart, Karen was supporting herself not on her earnings but on money she withdrew from their joint accounts, and when that was not enough, she supplemented it with small amounts from her inheritance.

In the third year of her annual six-month absences, James was so lonely that he began "to date innocently." He took women out to dinner or a movie but did not have sexual relationships. Karen insists to this day that she had no other relationships while she was away from James, but he insists without elaborating that "evidence suggests otherwise." In the fourth year, when she returned from her annual absence, she told him she wanted a divorce but that they would have to live together in the family house until things were settled because there would not be enough money otherwise to pay for her next six-month sojourn in Arizona. Thus, they spent the last four years of their marriage living separately in the same house six months out of every year, fighting over their "bitterly contested" divorce.

All this time, James said he never understood what he had done to inspire such rancor in Karen. She, he said, "merely shrieked" when he asked her to explain. She said, "All he had to do was think about every single day of the last thirty-three years" and he would know what he had done. He described her as "volatile and difficult" and himself as "easier and more resilient." She described him as "dull as dishwater" and herself as "high-strung, artistic, temperamental." She accused James of "not being able to let go, to get over things," adding that "he still brings up all the things I allegedly did wrong when I was a bride as if they happened only yesterday." Karen handled disagreements far differently: "I just blow up when something bothers me. I let it all out. And then it's over and I forget about it and go on. James can't do that; he has to go over and over things and rehash them again and again. After a while, I just couldn't stand it anymore. I had to get away."

Even so, they continued to do things together during the last eight years of the disintegrating marriage. They entertained their friends at Friday-night bridge parties when it was their turn, and they had family celebrations with their two adult children (both married) and three grandchildren. They even took vacations together, although the marriage became "each day more contentious." Gradually, according to James, "there was less marriage and more and more just living in the same house without love, affection, or a sex life." Still, when all the fighting was done and the divorce decree was final, when the assets were allocated "fairly" according to Karen and "unfairly" according to James, he was consumed by "anger," all of it connected with the financial settlement, which he could not stop thinking about.

Under New York law, marital assets would normally be divided fifty-fifty, but Karen insisted on keeping her inheritance and James agreed to let her have it. Only then did Karen confess that she had amassed a lot of debts connected to her allegedly "successful" crafts business, which she demanded that James pay or she would demand a greater settlement. If he did not agree, she was willing to put him through a protracted court case in which the legal costs for each would have been higher than all her debts. He gave in and agreed to her demands, which significantly diminished his half of the marital assets. It took them the last four years of the marriage to reach this agreement, and throughout those years both agreed that "the need for divorce was clearly there and very great."

Nevertheless, even after all that time James's "anger" did not go away, but was coupled with "a lasting puzzle: What did I do wrong?" He retraced their entire marriage, going back to their first meeting at a party in New York's Greenwich Village. He was thirty and Karen was twenty-nine and "trying to be an artist." He persuaded her to give up that pursuit to marry him and move to the small upstate town where he had just taken over his father's business. His version of why she accepted his proposal was that "her talent was modest and she probably would not have made it and I gave her an easy out." She insisted that she "could have made it, but my hormones were kicking in and I was tired of working and wanted kids."

Like the Swiss Gottfried, James believed that he had done everything possible to create a good life for his family. Karen agreed that he had always met their family's physical needs but that otherwise "there was always something missing." Also, like so many other couples, Karen and James admitted that when they met, everyone they knew was married and starting families, so they "grabbed on to each other." With hindsight they admitted that "maybe we should have taken a closer look before hooking up permanently."

I interviewed them separately seven years after the divorce and I asked what they each hoped to gain in their new lives. Karen said she gained the "freedom" to live where she wanted (first in Arizona, then briefly in New Mexico, and finally in Utah) and to work at her crafts. She has learned to market her purses on the Internet and is now making "enough of a living" that she doesn't need to supplement it with her other assets. She remarried a year ago in 2005 but will not talk about how much support she receives from her new husband.

James stayed on in the family home for the first few years after the divorce, saying he "relished the tranquility but didn't like the loneliness." Because he had never lived alone, he went to the supermarket weekly to buy "seven Hungry Man dinners, a box of cereal, and a bottle of milk." His bi-weekly cleaning woman took pity and made him casseroles, meat loaves, and spaghetti sauces. For a social life, he tried to keep the card-playing friends from the marriage but was uncomfortable, feeling that Karen had turned them against him, so he joined a gym to get in shape. There, he met Sally, a widow whose husband belonged to his fraternal lodge and whom he had seen on various social occasions. Their marriages had been "like night and day," for Sally's was blissful and ended only with her husband's death by a sudden heart attack. James said hearing her talk about how close they had been made him realize how emotionally distant he had been in his own marriage, but he still wonders if changing his behavior would have been enough to make it last.

After a period of "being together while living in separate houses," James and Sally recognized how much they had in common and moved in together. Both agree that it makes better financial sense to remain single even though they consider themselves "married in every way but legally."

DEALING WITH ANGER

James was like so many of the men I interviewed who described how they assuaged the "anger" that enveloped them during their divorces. Most managed to resolve the issues that created it on their own, others addressed it through therapy, and still others by establishing a new relationship that diminished or dissolved it. However, I spoke to quite a few who remained consumed by anger years after their divorces were final. One man told me he had to "hold on to it because its all I have left of her." Another said he had no intention of "giving [anger] up because its the only thing that makes me feel alive." The majority of the men who held on to anger as if to a lifeline were like Robert, who told me he needed an "edge" to get by in life: "Basically I have always been a very angry person, and the way I am now is not so unusual. My children always say I deal with my anger very well for an angry person, but I am still angry about what my wife did."

Robert, of all the angry men I interviewed, was the most impolite. I didn't know this when I agreed to interview him after he told a mutual friend that he wanted to tell me his story. I phoned him in Sarasota, Florida, where he had moved from Winnipeg, one year after his divorce was final. Trying to soften his truly insulting remarks about both me and his wife and to get him to change his snide, superior, and disparaging tone of voice, I made a joke about snowbirds. It did not sit well with him and he did not respond.

Instead, he shouted into the phone: "You better not talk to my wife! You better not contact her or my kids." I told him I regretted that my phone call was upsetting him, and perhaps it would be best if we spoke at another time or perhaps not at all. It was all right with me if he chose not to participate. He ignored my remarks and launched into his version of why his wife left him: "I thought we had a good marriage. Oh, sure, there are negative things in every forty-four year marriage, bad stuff you just shuck off. Then all of a sudden, whammo! She announces she doesn't want to be my wife anymore and she's moving out and she'll get a restraining order if I come near her."

Why would she want a restraining order? I asked. Is it because he had been physically violent?

By this time he was shrieking in anger: "No! No! Never! Never!" Perhaps, then, now that she was divorced, she wanted to restrain him from speaking to her the way he had throughout their marriage? Was it perhaps the same tone of voice that he was using to speak to me?

"What's wrong with my tone of voice?" he shouted, but I didn't respond. I asked instead if he wanted to tell me what reasons his wife claimed she had for leaving him. Without hesitating, he said it was "because I had to retire early." Robert worked for a company that designed and manufactured machine parts for other companies. He was the consultant who drummed up business and was very proficient at what he did. He traveled fairly often and sometimes was away from home part of every week. When he was sixty-two, Robert was one of a large group of employees who were asked to take early retirement, but he wanted a larger pension and managed to keep working for another year, until he was sixty-three. One month "to the day" after his retirement, his wife walked out.

He stayed in Winnipeg for a year, living in the house, phoning her daily at first, then weekly, to demand that she "come home." I imagine he must have screamed at her as he was screaming these words long-distance at me. Robert refused to hire an attorney, but his wife, Roberta (always called Bobbi to distinguish her from him), a retired high school math teacher, hired her own and proceeded calmly and logically to get the divorce. It went fairly quickly once Robert accepted that Bobbi was not coming back, and when it was final, he moved to Florida. Two of his three children are in Canada and one lives in England, but he has no contact with them, dismissing them as "worthless; they side with their mother."

In Sarasota, he bragged to me about the many women he "goes out with." He claimed they all "come on" to him but he won't let them "get their hooks in." He insisted on telling me of one woman who pursued him for two and a half years, but "she finally got the picture that she's a dog, and now she lets me alone."

I have to admit that I stopped taking notes at this point, as Robert raved on and on, boasting of his prowess with women when not talking about how important his anger was to him and how he would never let go of it. When I finally succeeded in bringing the conversation to an end, the last words Robert said to me were about Bobbi: "She'll be back. She'll come back someday, you wait and see."

Bobbi told the mutual friend from whom Robert learned about my book that she would not consent to be interviewed about her marriage, but she did want our friend to tell me that her life afterward was "everything" she never had while married. She remains in Winnipeg, takes great joy in her children and grandchildren, has a large network of friends from her teaching career, and is active in her synagogue. She "loves doing things without always looking over my shoulder," but she declined to say what, if anything, she was looking for, or more likely, looking out for.

"WHO ELSE WILL DO IT?"

Millie Hayes, a sixty-seven-year-old woman in Louisiana, divorced her husband, Karl Decker Hayes, in 1998 after forty-two years of marriage because he had been so cruel and controlling that he "picked out her car and her clothes, and checked the walls for smudges after she cleaned house."[3] She "despised" everything he had done to her, but four years after she divorced him she volunteered to care for him when he developed Alzheimer's disease. "There is nobody else," Millie Hayes said. "You can't throw a human being away."

She is typical of a newly emerging pattern in American life, in which sick or dying spouses are being cared for by those who could not bear to live with them but will not allow them to ail or die all alone and uncared for. Millie Hayes believes that even when anger is the prevailing emotion toward the divorced spouse, "you have to come to terms with yourself and get rid of the bitterness . . . not for their sake, but for your own."

Caring for a divorced spouse might well become commonplace as time goes on. The last time the government collected census report statistics was 2003, and in that year there were 2.7 million divorced Americans who were older than sixty-five and who had not remarried. Although most of these re-unions happen because the ex-spouses have reached the point where there are no recriminations and nothing left to fight over, practical reasons enter into it as well: some dying people have actually asked their divorced part-ners to remarry them for estate-planning purposes, in the belief that this is how they can preserve the value of their assets.

Catherine and Arthur were one such couple. They had been divorced for fifteen years after a thirty-three-year marriage in which there were few as-sets to divide. Catherine had never worked, so when all her resources were exhausted, she had no recourse but to move in with her married daugh-ter, Lorrie, who converted the third floor of her large house into a sepa-rate apartment. Meanwhile, Arthur was busy investing his few assets into a mutual fund that ballooned throughout the 1990s, giving him a lot more money to invest. He amassed a sizeable fortune, which, of course, was all his because it came after the divorce, but he felt guilty about Catherine's poverty and wanted to find a way to make this "proud and bitter" woman accept some of it.

At just about this time, he was diagnosed with a fast-moving Parkinson's disease. Knowing that he would need care, he telephoned Catherine to tell her he wanted to make "a business proposition" and asked her to set up a meeting with Lorrie present to "keep things on an even keel—translation: so Catherine wouldn't throw something at me." Arthurs investments had made him a millionaire several times over, and he had wisely set up a se-ries of trusts, but he was still worried about their eventual distribution. His business proposition was that he and Catherine should remarry, but that it should be in name only because (according to Arthur) "neither one of us could stand the ground the other walks on" and he feared that Catherine would give the money away just to spite him. He wanted Lorrie to convert the basement of her house into an apartment for him, one in which a caregiver could also live when the time came that he would need one. Catherine's only responsibility would be to inherit his money and see that it was passed on after his death, according to his legal directives. Catherine agreed and they were remarried in 2002. As of this writing, she still lives on the top floor of Lorrie's house and Arthur is in the basement with Judd, who looks after him.

Meanwhile, a judge in Massachusetts recalled presiding over the divorce of an elderly couple in their seventies who had been married for fifty years. He urged them to consider the consequences of being alone at their age and to reconsider the divorce. Who would take care of them if one or the other became seriously ill? The wife had an immediate answer: "If he gets sick, I'll take care of him. I just can't live with him anymore."

The judge granted the divorce.

CHAPTER FOUR

THE "LAST CHANCE" DIVORCE

A woman on a highjacked airplane told herself, "If I get out of this alive, I'm going to divorce my husband. I have to have something that makes my life worthwhile before I die."

—JUDITH WALLERSTEIN and SANDRA BLAKESLEE,
The Good Marriage: How and Why Love Lasts

THE AIRPLANE PASSENGER'S MARRIAGE HAD not been one of "overt conflict," and until the hijacking it "had functioned reasonably well." This seemed to be true of the many women I interviewed who did not make the decision to divorce until or just after a traumatic event. Several told me they had been in auto accidents—either serious or relatively minor ones—and when they left the crash scene found themselves thinking not of car repair or replacement but, rather, of their "wake-up call" to divorce. A woman in Texas said her "moment of truth" happened at a Friday night high school football game when her quarter-back son was carried off the field on a stretcher. "Let him live, God," she bargained, "and I'll divorce that bastard and give me and my kids the life we deserve." Several other women used a similiar gesture to describe how their "moment of truth" hit: making a fist of one hand and slamming it into the palm of the other, "bam!" was the word one used, saying, "It was like I heard thunder and then lightning struck, and I was left breathless. I knew it was time to go."

Women who knew they had to walk out and end their marriages

often surprised themselves by their decision, but even more often they left behind husbands who were "bewildered, bereft, and baffled." Three men from New York who met in a restaurant in the summer of 2004 to talk about how they had reacted to such news were typical.[1] Prompted by the AARP survey, a reporter from *The New York Times* invited the three, in their late fifties or early sixties and friends of long standing, to talk about their divorces.

Hal Klopper, married twice (the first time for twenty-five years and the second for three), had been alone for two years. Now that he was single again, what he missed most was the "companionship." He thought women said the reason they divorced was so they would not have "to answer to anybody anymore," and he could accept this as a reason. But now that he was unencumbered, he was "lonely" because he had enjoyed having "to answer to somebody." He was puzzled by his latest divorce because he "really didn't know what went wrong or what happened."

His friend Frank Freitag asked if Hal's wife (he did not specify which, but most likely he meant the second) ever explained her version of what went wrong. Hal said, "Not really . . . Maybe I didn't ask the question because I didn't want to know the answer. Maybe things were going through her head that I didn't realize." Frank and the third friend, Marshall Farr, said they both had "a glimmer of warning" that they and their wives were "drifting apart," but they managed to convince themselves it was a "passing phase." Marshall said he could always find something to blame his wife's behavior on, and Frank added, "I thought if I gave her some time, she'd come around."

Hal had gone back into "the dating game," but even though he did want "companionship," he didn't think he wanted to marry for a third time. Frank, who was separated for four months at the time the article appeared, was reluctant to begin dating. His wife was a "gregarious woman," and he had relied upon her to smooth his way with other people. Now that he was divorced and had to go into social situations alone, he was "not sure who I am without my wife." He was "more resigned than angry" that she left him, and he wondered if resuming the dating game would be worth the effort. After initial hesitation, he concluded that "something in me says yes."

Marshall's marriage had been built around a comfortable lifestyle that he relished, with two incomes, a Brooklyn brownstone, a house in the country, and two nearly adult children. When his wife divorced him, he had to reassess his situation: "What do I want? Who am I?" He did not think it necessary to think about such things until then because "in a marriage you can stop thinking about that. Its a given. So you can do other things." Now that he is on his own, he points to his deepening rapport with his two friends as an "unexpected, enriching thing," and he "also pours out his feelings in a journal."

THE NINE

The three men in Brooklyn reminded me of nine men I interviewed who had similar experiences when their wives of long standing initiated divorces without offering (according to the husbands they left behind) any compelling reason for wanting out. Four of the men knew one another but had not met until after they were single and had joined a divorce recovery group, and they still considered themselves acquaintances rather than friends. The histories and marital experiences of these men struck me as so similar that when I began to write about them, they fell into an informal grouping that I took to calling "the Nine."

The four men who knew one another lived in the greater Philadelphia area, comprising southeastern Pennsylvania, southern New Jersey, and northern Delaware. Three of the men were from Westchester County, New York, and two were from Fairfield County, Connecticut. All considered themselves "middle-class" and had some form of higher education: five were college graduates, two had "some" higher education (a year or two of college), and two had certificates for vocational or technical training. Six worked for large companies in departments of accounting and human resources. One worked in a family home-repair business started by a father and an older brother, and the last was a shop manager for an automobile dealer. They all had children (twenty-five among them), and their marriages lasted from twenty-eight to thirty-five years. Some of their wives had worked throughout most of their marriage—among them were a teacher, a registered nurse, and a licensed practical nurse. Two of the wives had joined the workforce after their children started school and had worked steadily since then, one as a receptionist in a veterinarian's office and the other as a secretary in a high school principal's office. Four had worked sporadically or occasionally, three as salespersons in stores during the holidays, and the fourth in the office of the family business when she was needed.

All the Nine owned their own homes in modest but comfortable suburbs, and all their children were high school graduates, with most graduating from college or university and four with graduate or professional degrees. Every one of the Nine owned at least two cars while they were married. Four were active in various Protestant churches, two were Catholics who attended mass sporadically, and three described themselves as Reform Jews who observed the high holidays. These families did not have a lot of discretionary money after the monthly bills were paid; vacations were not a given, even though most managed some sort of getaway every other year or so, usually to the Jersey shore or Cape Cod. Once the children were on their own, holidays and excursions for the parents became an overnight stay in a New York hotel with dinner and a Broadway show, usually to celebrate an anniversary or a milestone birthday.

Some of the Nine had hobbies that consumed a lot of their time. They all claimed to enjoy gardening, landscaping, and working on their houses themselves, even though they admitted their primary reason for doing it was to save money. Some resented that it took so much of their spare time, while others shrugged and said it had to be done and doing it themselves was the only option. One of the Nine led a Boy Scout troop, another coached Little League baseball. One never missed Friday-night football games at his high school (where he had been a star halfback), and in baseball season he watched every Yankee game on television and recorded many to watch again during the winter months when he needed a "baseball fix" (his wife did not enjoy sports, and so he watched them alone). Two were active in the Rotary Club and enjoyed attending lunches, social programs in the evenings, and weekend planning sessions for future events. Several liked to spend time alone in basement or garage workshops on "nothing special, just whatever needed doing." Two admitted that after a grueling workday, all they wanted to do was "stretch out in front of the TV with a beer."

I asked all nine what they thought were their major contributions to their marriages. All began by telling me how proud they were to fulfill their responsibilities as breadwinners and how they went to work every day to ensure that "the wife and kids never went without." Although they all worked at jobs that fell roughly into the nine-to-five category, only two said they regularly attended programs at their children's schools, and only those involved in sports and the Boy Scouts talked of spending time with their sons. None used the expression "quality time," and when I did most seemed puzzled by what it was supposed to represent. Those who had daughters seemed surprised when I asked about how they interacted with them, saying "girls" were "mostly with their mothers." Most added that their daughters "knew" their fathers loved them so they did not "have to say it." All nine expressed pride in their children and believed they had raised "fine adults." Some admitted that their children had been "in trouble" as teenagers, with three "smoking the occasional joint," one arrested a single time for drunk driving, and another for "serious Halloween mischief." One had a child with health issues, juvenile diabetes, and another had two daughters with scoliosis who had endured surgery, back braces, and physical therapy. In short, all nine seemed to have escaped the severe conflict that can sometimes arise from problems with children.

I asked how they related to their wives, and all thought they were "pretty good" about remembering birthdays and anniversaries. About half the men became sheepish or embarrassed when I asked if their wives appreciated what they did on these occasions. Several said they "did not always hit on the right gift." One mentioned a "surprise party that backfired" but gave no details, and the rest seemed puzzled that I would ask. One said he always gave his wife "an envelope" (money) and "she seemed okay with it." Two others said their wives knew they were "not good with that stuff," which, they explained, meant showing their emotions. All said they always "helped out around the house," but when I asked for specifics, the examples they gave were putting up Christmas decorations or raking leaves. They took out the garbage and took care of the maintenance on both cars on a regular basis.

Well, then, if they had so many activities that kept them from participating in the lives of their families and if their contribution to the work of the household was periodic rather than routine, what did they and their wives do together? What did they do "for fun"? Nearly all had not moved far from the communities (or from the family homes) in which they had grown up, and about half had fairly large extended families nearby. Their idea of fun was getting together with their brothers' and sisters' families and their parents (where they were still living). They spoke of community obligations that filled time, from weddings to funerals, church suppers, and fund-raisers. When their children were in high school, "there was always something going on there."

Did they and their wives ever do anything together that was just the two of them? "Sometimes but not too often" was the answer. Many said their wives had "her girlfriends, her card club, her gym class," and a host of other activities. Or "She has her daughters, her grandchildren," or "She's always over at her mothers, or her sisters, or with her girlfriends."

Did they and their wives fight, argue, dispute anything, no matter how trivial or how serious? Did they argue about money or how to raise the children? They either said "never" or "hardly ever," and if they did disagree about something, "it was never anything serious." When I asked these questions, I usually got the following response: "For the life of me, I didn't know anything was wrong. I thought everything was all right." This, too, fits a common pattern: women frequently said "lack of communication" was the reason they divorced, while their husbands seldom, if ever, did.[2]

WOMEN WHO LEAVE

The ex-wives of the three friends in the *Times* story declined to tell the reporter their reasons for divorcing, so to find a woman's perspective, she interviewed an editor at the AARP magazine, Karen Reyes. Then fifty-seven, Karen had divorced in her mid-forties after a twenty-five-year marriage. She said she'd stayed in a loveless relationship for almost ten years before she divorced because she was "a good Catholic girl who took her vows seriously." When her husband (who has since died) confessed to infidelity, she was relieved to have a reason to leave him.

I was struck by her description of how her husband reacted when she told him she was divorcing because it paralleled the seven wives of the Nine who consented to be interviewed (two declined). Karen said her husband cried and offered to do anything to save the marriage, while she remained adamant that it had to end. Only two of the seven wives told me how unnerving it was to see their otherwise "cold and distant" husbands (or the "lying and cheating" husband as one woman put it), "turn to blubber and cry and beg and promise to do anything if only I'd stay." The others all said their minds were made up and no amount of begging or pleading could convince them to stay married. None of the Nine men admitted having expressed such strong emotional reactions, and all insisted they had never been unfaithful (as one of their wives insisted her husband had been). Still, all nine volunteered, albeit in fairly formal rather than emotionally loaded language, that they had "asked" their wives to remain in the marriage. The closest they would come to an admission that they had been distraught was to say that they asked for "another chance."

At this fragile moment in collapsing marriages, a preponderance of divorcing couples turn to therapy in the hope of saving them. In my interviews, an interesting statistic emerged: about 80 percent of the 184 women had been in therapy for a sustained period, sometimes for years, before they finally initiated divorce. At the crisis point in their last years together, almost half asked their husbands to join them, either separately or in couples' therapy. The experiences of the women I interviewed coincided with what several family therapists told me. In the words of one: "It is not too often that couples come to me because both parties want to save the marriage. By the time I see them, one partner wants to work on it but usually the other is already out the door."

A Jungian analyst told me that he made an informal study of the phenomenon of late-life divorce once he realized that the largest part of his practice was counseling women "either contemplating late-life divorce, in the middle of one, or just coming out of one." Most were ending marriages of from twenty to forty years, and he thought it would be useful if he tried to elucidate some of the issues that they had in common. He couched his insights in Jungian terms, but they also fit neatly into categories from the AARP survey and my own informal findings as well.

Jung believed that the first half of life, roughly the years between birth and thirty-five to forty-five, are those when the individual concentrates on forging a place in society. The person gives the major amount of time and attention to a variety of spheres: education, career, and human relationships, including dynamics within the birth family to choosing a partner *for life* (for that is the choice most think they are making at the time). For many of these people, things changed in midlife as careers soared or stalled, children grew up and left home, partners developed other interests and led separate lives. Once the pace of daily life either speeds up or slows down and things happen that are beyond their control, a couple is forced to take a new, intense look at themselves as well as each other, and suddenly, many things that they may have ignored, glossed over, or covered up assume enormous proportion in their lives. They simply ask themselves "How did I get here? Who am I now, and when did I become this person?"

The Jungian analyst found that couples rarely grow in the same direction at the same pace, and that they almost never arrive in tandem at things they want to change. A husband may be ready to retire, while a wife wants to keep working for another dozen or so years; he may want to leave their Rust-Belt community for life in the Sun Belt, and she wants to stay put. Or one rises in social status through job promotion or an educational degree, while the other remains solidly where he or she was when the marriage began. The analyst concluded that there are "periods of extreme tension" in every marriage, but some of the best turn out to be "those that have weathered all these tensions" and somehow or other manage to remain intact.

I talked to this analyst at length about women who initiate divorce after long marriage, and he presented me with some case studies he had prepared for a professional meeting. He saw them, in general, as women for whom "the first half of life went all right [because] their adaptation as traditional wives and mothers worked. But in midlife that cycle broke down and they sought analytic therapy to reorient themselves to the circumstances in which they find themselves today."

I was curious to know how the husbands reacted to these changes and what was happening to them at the same time. The analyst found that they were about evenly divided: half wanted their wives to "quit the shrink stuff" and go back to being the way they had always been, while the other half wanted the women to stay in analysis as long as they felt they needed it, but to stay married once the analysis was completed. He also said that the wives told him that their husbands had decided against therapy for themselves, preferring to "tough it out and go it alone."

In observing how his women patients navigated the process that encouraged them "to choose their individual way," he tried to present them with some of the "pros and cons" of divorce. He asked them to consider how the taking of a "more individual, more independent way" did not necessarily mean that divorce was the only answer, and advised them to explore whether it was possible to maintain their newfound independent identities within traditional marriage. Very few of his women patients thought "the new self could return to and be sustained by the old way," and they almost always chose divorce. Many said "divorce became a necessity because they could no longer tolerate the old pattern."

WHAT, THEN, DO WOMEN WANT?

So, then, what made 66 percent of women in the AARP survey and about 75 percent of the women in my interviews initiate divorce? And why were all the husbands they left behind, particularly the Nine, as "bereft, baffled, and bewildered" as the three friends in the *New York Times* article?

Karen Reyes, the magazine editor mentioned earlier, typified the response I heard over and over again from the women I interviewed. When I asked them why they believed divorce was the necessary next step in their lives, their answers boiled down to one word: "freedom." For Karen Reyes, it was "having my house the way I want it, doing what I want, and spending my money the way I want." Catherine Kohler Riessman did a study of how women and men talk about their divorces and found that although both use the word "freedom" as something they gained, it meant different things to each of them.[3] To women, it meant "independence and autonomy" and not having to be "responsive to a disgruntled spouse." To men, it meant freedom from the obligations imposed by familial responsibilities. Even though they felt "less confined" and "less claustrophobic," many men said freedom or "independence" were not "gifts" given to them by divorce. One described himself as having "always felt independent and I guess its just more so now."

Among the wives of the Nine, some gave reasons that were variations on "freedom." One said: "This was my time and I knew if I didn't take it now,

I never would." Others spoke of years of "increasing frustration," and how they got tired of "always accommodating." Some said: "The kids were gone, which made it painfully obvious how little we had in common." Theirs were "perfectly good" husbands, who were "decent provider[s]," but who were also completely unaware of their wives' needs and the emotional distance that had grown between them. These were the women who let their husbands know that the birthday presents or anniversary dinners were not what they wanted, and who asked their husbands repeatedly to join them in celebrating the occasions in ways more to their liking. They were the wives who "sometimes begged" their husbands to take a greater part in their children's lives or, especially, "to do something just with me." Several talked about the lack of "touching," never mind the paucity of sex.

One woman called herself "the married nun" as she described how, for several years before her divorce, she would stand close behind her husband while he stood at the kitchen sink fixing his evening drink after work. They had slept in separate bedrooms and had not had sex for almost four years; "desperate for warmth and affection," she would hug his waist and press her breasts into his back, "just to feel close to him." Every time she did this, she could feel him "recoil, whether consciously or not," but she still continued to hug him in the hope of sparking a response. Only after she told him she was definitely ending the marriage and he was in tears begging to know what he did wrong did she get the nerve to use the "kitchen-sink example" to ask why he did not return her affection. He told her he could no longer stand to look at her naked body, let alone to touch her, and that she should "get over that romantic crap." He said they had "three kids together" and she should "settle down and act [her] age." She was fifty-six years old and an aerobics buff who was often told how young she looked. She told me, "that was when I knew I was doing the right thing to leave. I knew I deserved more from life than that."

Lack of physical affection was a strong reason given by very many women for ending their marriages. One said her husband hid behind the excuse of his snoring to move into another bedroom, even though she volunteered to wear earplugs and put up with it. They had not had sexual relations for three years before their divorce. Common, too, was the more general assertion that they had "fallen out of love" with their husbands. Many spoke of managing to make the marriage last as long as it did because "we went our separate ways so early and were polite to each other and made peace along the way." Others put it more succinctly: "We accommodated."

Often a catalyst happened to make them realize how distant they had become to each other. Several spoke of living "like two strangers in the same house." The woman whose husband recoiled from her told how they began to eat meals separately shortly after he moved into another bedroom. Because her best hours for working were in the late afternoon and early evening, she began to stay late at the office, whereas he was at home shortly after five and wanted dinner soon afterward. He learned to prepare simple "one-pot meals" and took pleasure in cooking for himself while he listened to music and sipped his one drink. "You do everything else without me, so you might as well do your own laundry," she told him one day, and to her surprise he did. She was upset when he did not complain but seemed to enjoy "living alone in the same house with me." The only times they did anything together were when the children came to visit or there was a function or event they had to attend as a couple. Then, like Debbie Reynolds and Dick Van Dyke in the movie *Divorce American Style*, who had violent fights in the privacy of their apartment, they learned how to "put on a happy face" when they opened the door to their guests. No one could believe it when "such a happy, contented couple" announced their separation.

LIVING ALONE TOGETHER

Living separate lives in separate places creates friction that can lead to divorce. I talked to quite a few two-career couples in the baby boom generation who complained that commuting made it impossible to sustain a marriage. To my surprise, far fewer than I expected said they divorced because they had affairs and were found out, or met someone else with whom they wanted to start a new life. The greater number told me they "just drifted apart, and all of a sudden it wasn't any fun to make that long weekend schlep to be with somebody I didn't know anymore."

In the military, husbands who have been away from home on frequent deployments often find that when they are stationed in places where they can live daily life with their families, they and their wives have serious problems adjusting to living with each other. With military service requiring separations that can last a year or longer, wives need to become the authority figure if they are to keep their households functioning on an even keel. They pay the bills, balance the budget, deal with the children, take care of the house, car, and animals. They have to be strong and independent, as their family's well-being depends on it. When husbands come home, they often try to reestablish their primacy and "take command" in ways that are often disastrous. Not only is there spousal abuse but there may also be physical violence to children who do not obey a fathers orders with military precision. Most of these troubled marriages limp along for years because the husbands are often posted elsewhere for long periods. Only when they transfer from sea duty to shore duty or from a combat zone to an army base does the trouble really start. Several military wives gave the same reason for their divorces given by the wife of a staff sergeant who divorced her husband of twenty-two years: "He is in the army, and me and my children and my house and my dog are not."

In civilian life, retirement often leads to divorce, but it is even more the case in the military. One couple who spent half or more of every year living apart while the husband rose through the ranks commanding navy ships discovered that when he retired and it came time to live together permanently, each looked at the other and saw a stranger. This woman said her moment of truth "was probably silly," but she knew she would have to divorce him when he moved most of her cosmetics out of the bathroom cabinet to make room for his toiletries, "That little thing stood for so many others that were a whole lot bigger."

WHEN A PARENT DIES

The death of a parent can often trigger a divorce, and often the one asking for it is unable to give a specific reason for wanting it at that particular moment. In my interviews, I found that, although men often cited the death of a parent as the reason they asked for a divorce, it was more often named by women as the galvanizing factor. One wife told me that when her mother died, she felt "free to become the person I always wanted to be." I asked her to explain.

"We were of the Jewish immigrant experience; my parents got out of Germany before the war, and they expected my brother to do well and he did—he's a judge. My sisters and I were expected to marry well, and they did—to a doctor and a lawyer. I was the disappointment because Ira is only an accountant, but I would have been the family failure if I divorced him before Mama died."

Observing the reality of their parents' lives can also spark an intense self-realization that can lead to divorce. Some years go, Andrea, a woman I knew, told me she was resigned to staying married to Mort even though they had no common interests. She worried how long she could "stick it out" every time she thought of her parents and of how both grew into "embittered drudges." Even though there was no overt hostility between Andrea and Mort, she feared they were becoming so distant that "one day soon he'll resent the hell out of me and I won't like him very much either." Her prediction came true, for as I was writing this book, she volunteered to tell me that her thirty-three-year marriage "withered away, died on the vine," and that she had filed for divorce.

Even more frequent, now that people are living to a very old age, is the tension induced in a marriage when a parent becomes ill or disabled and either has to be taken into the adult child's home or institutionalized. Caring for elderly and infirm parents is often the proverbial "straw" that breaks the camel's back; it "certainly broke my back," one woman told me. Many said they could barely cope when the parent was their own, but the situation became insupportable when they were asked to assume most of the responsibility for the care of a husband's parent or, in some cases, both his parents.

CHILDREN AS MARRIAGE BREAKERS

Children induce stress into already troubled marriages to such a degree that they often tip them over the brink and into divorce. Caroline, part of whose story I told in chapter 1, said she had many reasons for leaving Ted after fifty-three years of marriage, but the way he treated the youngest of their four sons was the main reason she divorced him. Terry had a drug problem that Ted tried to resolve by paying for several lengthy stays in expensive detoxification clinics. After each one, Terry was back on drugs as soon as he could buy them. Ted said he would no longer "throw good money after bad," so Terry supported his habit by using his skills as a computer programmer to commit identity theft. He was arrested but not sent to jail because Ted made financial restitution to the few persons Terry bilked and because Terry promised to enter one more clinic and swore he would come out clean and stay that way. Caroline claims that Terry kept his promise but Ted insists he did not. Still, he allowed Caroline to persuade him to give Terry half a million dollars to buy a town house in Arizona, where he promised to set up a "clean" computer-programming business. Within six months, Terry lost the house to pay for drug debts and restitution for another spate of identity theft. At that point, Ted said, he "really washed [his] hands" of Terry, and Caroline retaliated by divorcing him.

She and Ted were wealthy, but they had earned every penny of their significant assets, both working long hard hours in scrap-metal businesses that Ted began the day he was discharged from the army in 1945. When Ted retired, the two middle sons took over the daily running of the business and the eldest son, Chad (a lawyer), took care of the family's legal affairs. These three sons made sure all the marital assets were split equally and without acrimony, but they were unable to convince Caroline to protect her money so that Terry could not dissipate it. Indeed, her first purchase was a house big enough for her and Terry and, by this time, for his lover, as he had declared himself gay and was living with another man. Caroline swears that Terry is "clean and committed [to his lover]," while Ted is convinced "its just another one of Terry's scams. He's Caroline's baby and she'll always take his side." The three older sons worry that her money will be gone far sooner than she thinks but she refuses to follow their advice on how to protect it.

Two of the more unusual interviews in which a child's behavior was the reason both parents gave for divorcing were those I had with Jane and Tom. They went to different high schools in adjoining small towns in southern Illinois and met at a Friday-night dance when Tom was discharged from the army in 1952. They married several months later, when Tom went to work as an electrician for the local utility company, a job he retired from thirty years later. Of their three children, the older son and daughter were married and lived in the same town and only "young Janey" (as the family called their youngest daughter, named for her mother) went to college and moved away. When I met her, she was a thirty-five-year-old professor of education at a college in a larger midwestern city and was married and the mother of two small girls. She was also the mother of an older daughter, now seventeen and in college, whom she had raised for many years on her own as a single mother.

Despite the disapproval of everyone in their conservative community, especially in their fundamentalist church, Tom bowed to Janey's wish to keep her child. Jane, her mother, believed herself "disgraced" and was so against it that she moved out of her own house on the day Janey brought the baby home from the hospital. In the years following, Jane's only contact with her daughter was what she deemed absolutely necessary, and she had none at all with her eldest granddaughter. It was Tom who rallied to Janey's defense, taking her in at a time when small-town morality did not approve of out-of-wedlock babies. He helped to care for the child during Janey's last year in high school, and he supported them both when she won a scholarship to a state university. He remains a doting grandfather, and he and Ellen, his companion, often visit Janey and her husband.

Jane and Tom lived separately for almost seven years after she moved out of their house. Both swear that during that time, neither ever asked the other to return to the marriage; Janey's pregnancy was simply the catalyst that made them realize how "different" they were, and how they "didn't think alike about anything." Unlike many women of her social class and family background—she had never worked and had no independent financial resources—Jane was fortunate that she had someplace to go to when she left Tom. She was an only child who moved into her widowed mothers house and lived there until her mother died, when she sold it and moved into an apartment. She was quite content with this life, as her two older children lived nearby and were attentive to her needs.

At the end of their fourth year apart, Tom "connected" with Ellen, a neighbor whose husband had just died after a protracted illness. He asked Jane to divorce him and she agreed. Even though the divorce was "straightforward and simple," it took almost two years to finalize while Tom sold the family house. He moved in with Ellen and both he and Jane agreed to the equitable division of their modest assets, so there was no acrimony. They have no contact with each other and see their children separately, especially on holidays or birthdays, but to this day Tom cannot understand "how a mother could turn her back on her own child." He shakes his head and adds, "You can live with somebody for most of your life and still never understand what goes on in their head."

WHEN MONEY CAUSES PROBLEMS

Issues about money and the fear that they will not be able to support themselves often keep women in marriages they would prefer to end, but there are also financial reasons that convince them they must shed their spouses as an act of self-preservation. Many women who deal with husbands drowning in seas of gambling debt or substance abuse have straightforward reasons for divorce. Still, in many of my interviews, "financial irresponsibility" was a factor that loomed larger than I expected and cut across class lines.

Betty, who lived in a pretty town in northern Michigan, spent the twenty-seven years of her marriage working in a job she despised because "it was a steady salary with benefits and health insurance," neither of which her husband, George, provided. She discovered his staggering credit-card debts about eight years into the marriage when she was routinely putting away his laundry. Her hand bumped something hard in his sock drawer, and inside one was a bulging stack of credit cards bound by a rubber band. She confronted George, and when he told her that most of them were "maxed out," she immediately separated her finances from his. She thought he would "go ballistic," but instead he told her that it was "probably the logical thing to do" because she was "the more sensible one." Betty found out what George owed and thought she was paying off the debt and that he was not creating more, until bill collectors began to call at the house routinely, and once the sheriff even came to arrest him. Betty paid George's bond, bailed him out, and made arrangements with the new creditors to add them to the list of others she was gradually paying off.

She stayed married to George for "much longer than was wise" because of a "combination of things: I married him for better or for worse, and besides, he was always on the verge of a 'really big thing' that never came to pass, even though some of them really sounded good." But George had no "stick-to-it-iveness" and was always looking for an easy way out. To him, "credit was found money." To Betty, his disregard for money became "a question of ethics and morality" as well as a source of constant anxiety over what debt he might incur next. Eventually the worry made her ill and she divorced him. Because George had no assets, Betty was required by law to share hers. She had to sell the house for which her premarital savings made the down payment and her wages paid the monthly mortgage. By law, she had to give George one third of the profit of the sale.

Because all the credit cards she didn't know he had were in her name as well, she struggled for years after the divorce until she eventually paid them off. These were debts that "he didn't think were real and therefore he didn't have to pay them. They were only little plastic cards."

Sue, whose marriage to Nick, an entrepreneur, lasted thirty-three years, had just the opposite experience. She cheerfully signed all the papers Nick set in front of her, confident that her "Hollywood lifestyle" in an affluent New Jersey community was secure forever. She didn't realize how perilous their financial underpinnings were until Nick was indicted on tax and secu-rity fraud and everything they owned was seized and put into receivership. Two years later, Sue still marvels at the speed of events that dropped her, penniless, into her sister's spare bedroom in a run-down section of Newark, from which she scrambled to find an office job after so many years out of the workforce. She was one of the luckier women who had never held a paying job, as her family had "contacts," and a friend of her sister's created a posi-tion for Sue in his legal firm.

In most ordinary lives, businesses fail, jobs are lost, investments dissipate in market crashes, and suddenly there is nothing to cushion the blow of a disintegrating way of life. People in their late fifties and early sixties who spent all their working lives with one company and who thought their re-tirement was secure now find themselves standing in long lines for some form of government compensation. If they are lucky enough to find new jobs, they are often far beneath what they had before.

All too often, women must scramble to pay the bills and feed their families. In western Pennsylvania, where steel mills and coal mines shut down years ago, housewives take their kitchen appliances or their few trinkets to thrift stores, hoping to get a few needed dollars. In affluent Fairfield County, Connecticut, women leave their McMansions wearing dark glasses and their heads covered in babushkas for the drive to Bridgeport or Stamford, where they park their SUVs a block away from the charitable food-distribution center that gives them free bricks of cheese and bags of canned goods. They rattle around in empty houses as they sell off furnishings and decorations piecemeal, and in the worst-case scenarios, they lose the grand houses in default of mortgage payments. The husbands retreat in shame or despair; the wives become shrill and shrewish as they struggle grimly to "save face."

All too frequently divorce follows, as both partners seize upon separation as the only way to get out of the mess. In what used to be coal country, where blue-collar workers in a manufacturing economy once made a good living, there is now a mostly service-based economy with salaries a fraction of what the lost jobs paid. A lawyer who works in the "reddest part of the blue state" of Pennsylvania says her practice consists of "the nonsexy part of divorce, the bread-and-butter reality of people who don't have much money." There is no job security to speak of, and many families carry enormous credit-card debt. If they do consult divorce lawyers, they generally "have things sorted out" before they ever enter the office; "they just want to get it over with quickly but, more important, cheaply."

This attorney finds that many older women have to stay in miserable marriages because the economic consequences of divorce—bad though they may be in married life—are so great that they have no recourse. In these situations the only women who insist upon divorce are those whose circumstances are so desperate that they don't care about money or what will happen to them. They tell the divorce attorney, "I'll deal with whatever I have to deal with; I just have to get out of that marriage."

WHO IS IN CONTROL?

I spoke to a great many lawyers (I'll tell their stories later in chapter 8) who cited the differences in how husbands and wives handle finances as the primary reason for their divorces. They found that control of money was often combined with another important reason given for divorce: matters of "control" in general. A large percentage of the lawyers who listed "issues of control" as the most frequent reason women consult them about divorce say this is particularly true in instances where their "clueless husbands" thought "everything was just fine" and their wives had no "good reason" to leave them.

Some were in situations like Anna's, with husbands who demand to know where they are at every moment of their day. Anna tolerated Martin's constant checking up on her for twenty-four years until she grew tired of his twenty or thirty daily telephone calls and his screeching hysteria if she was in the basement or the backyard and didn't hear the phone ring. She offered, in what she thought was jest, to keep a journal in which she would record everything she did in any given day, for him to read every night—if only he would stop phoning. He thought it was a fine idea, and for several days she kept up the travesty until one evening he told her that "On toilet. Taking crap" was no excuse for not answering the phone and ordered her to take it into the bathroom with her. She spent the next several days making appointments with lawyers, looking for the one she thought would be the least expensive. Because she had never worked and Martin always doled out money to her, she pawned her late mother's engagement ring to pay for a legal retainer. After hearing her story, one lawyer she interviewed told her to retrieve the ring and he would take her case without a retainer. So she hired him, paying him after the divorce, when she found a job.

Many women go into divorce court admitting that they spent years having to ask their husbands for every penny and that they never had control of money of their own unless they managed to hide away part of what they were given. These are women who almost always insist that their husbands were generous and gave them all they asked for if not more, but the point was that it was not given freely and they had to ask for it. Eventually, many refused to go on living this way, and as their husbands would not change, the women often divorced.

VERBAL ABUSE

Many women added "verbal abuse" to "control issues" as their reason for divorcing husbands who told them they needed to be controlled because they were too stupid, ugly, or incompetent to manage anything on their own. Many women are strong enough to tune out this humiliating message, trying to create daily routines that will help them cope, but others fall prey to depression and depression-related sicknesses. The Pennsylvania divorce attorney said she is convinced that when she tells the many poor women who consult her that they cannot survive financially unless they stay married, they begin "to doctor," a euphemism for seeking medical attention for a host of vague and unidentifiable ailments. "Doctoring" becomes a way of insulating themselves from their untenable lives; they can't be asked to clean and cook or provide sex if they are ill, which is a way of opting out of marriage without being divorced.

Mary, who lived in Queens, New York, chose another way to opt out of her fifty-two-year marriage to Phil: passive resistance. She was newly divorced when I met her through her adult daughter, Angie, who was furious with Mary for "ruining the family." Over and over, Angie said there was "no good reason" for what Mary did, that Phil "never mistreated, never dishonored" her. Angie said, "What my mother did is a disgrace to the Church [Catholic], our neighborhood, and our family. Divorce is something other people do, not us."

I was particularly eager to have this family's story because at the time I interviewed them, most of the people I talked to were from the upper and middle classes and I wanted to learn how and why working-class couples divorced. It was not easy to convince Mary to be interviewed. She would not talk on the phone but wanted to see me "in person," to "size [me] up," so I met her during her lunch hour at a coffee shop near the large discount grocery store on Queens Boulevard where she worked in the accounting office. We talked for an hour, and when she had to return to work before we were far from finished, I asked if I could see her again in the house where she now lived with two other women. She said she would have to check first with them.

In the initial conversation, this is what Mary told me. She was the middle daughter of three, all of whom were high school graduates. They were second-generation Italian Americans, children of immigrant parents. After she graduated, Mary worked for a year as a clerk and a part-time bookkeeper in a neighborhood drugstore. She met Phil there in 1950 when she was nineteen and he was almost twenty-two. He did not graduate from high school but left for a good-paying job as a construction laborer, eventually to become a master carpenter.

Mary said she could not really call their courtship a romance: "He would come into the store, maybe buy something, maybe talk to me. There were Friday-night dances at the church, and I went with my sisters and girlfriends. He started coming even though he didn't like to dance. He'd hang around and wait for me and eventually everyone took it for granted he'd walk me home. Then he started coming to the house and everyone took it for granted we were a couple."

Mary's older sister was already engaged, and she married while Phil's courtship progressed. People teased Mary that she would be next, so "Phil sort of said something like 'I guess we better do it, too.' " That was his proposal, and they married in May 1952. Phil was proud that, unlike so many other young couples in their neighborhood, they did not have to move in with his family or into the basement apartment of her widowed mother's house. He made enough money for them to set up housekeeping in a modest apartment near both families in their tightly knit ethnic community. Phil insisted that Mary quit her job so others would see that he could support his wife, and she did. Within months she was pregnant, and the following March, 1953, Phil junior was born. Angie followed at the end of 1954 and Tom in 1956. By this time, they had bought half of a two-family house in the neighborhood where they had always lived. Phil's long-term plan was to buy the other half, but it never happened because the family who lived there never moved out. As happens in such neighborhoods, when they died, one of their children moved in.

Mary didn't work throughout these years except to do "little things." When the church needed office help, she did it on a volunteer basis. The man for whom she had worked before her marriage asked her from time to time to "deal with the paperwork," and she discovered that she was good with figures. He paid her a modest sum, which she usually saved for Christmas presents, which was "okay with Phil." When the children started school, she worked at parent-teacher fund-raisers or church benefits, usually as the treasurer. Here, too, she was "doing real work but not getting paid for it." Phil wanted it this way because "it was important for him to be the man of the family." He gave her "house money," from which she was to buy the food and take care of anything else connected with running the house. When the monthly bills came in (mortgage, utilities, phone), she showed them to him before she wrote the checks to pay them, checks that he signed, not her. She never really knew how much money Phil brought home, what with overtime, bonuses, and "off-the-books work," because he put the money into bank accounts to which she had no access. If she wanted anything for herself or the house, she either had to ask Phil for the money or else secrete small amounts from her household allowance until she had enough. Even so, she always asked Phil before she bought anything. She said he gave her everything she asked for "because he knew I was good with money and wouldn't spend it foolishly."

Their life continued in this fashion until Tom was entering the seventh grade. The nuns at the parochial school told Mary and Phil that he was too intelligent for the local junior high and should go to a special Catholic boys' school in Manhattan. The tuition was more than Phil wanted to pay, but Mary persuaded him that she could work in the local parochial school office for a modest salary that would cover the cost. Phil reluctantly agreed, and so Mary began to leave the house regularly to go to work. She went to school with the children but was back at home before they were, and in the summers she only went to the school two mornings each week.

At home, she continued to be responsible for everything. She did the cooking, cleaning, laundry, and shopping. A hot meal was always on the table by 6 P.M., and she always cleaned up afterward. She "really didn't think about it. That's what women were supposed to do. He worked hard all day to bring in our money, so I couldn't expect him to come home and work." Mary said "women's lib passed [her] by." She couldn't understand why women wanted men to vacuum rugs or change diapers. She was satisfied with her role and liked her life.

Mary's younger sister became what is known in Italian families as "the sacrifice." She never married but went to work every day to a civil-service "city job" and lived at home to care for their mother. The married elder sister lived within walking distance of their mothers house, as did Mary, and both visited her frequently. Mary liked the couple who lived in the other half of the house, and she had friends from her church. "There was always a kitchen where I was welcome, where there was always coffee and cake on the table— just like in my house." Everybody she cared about was "a local call away if I couldn't get there in person."

When their own children finally married and left home, they didn't move far. Phil junior became a policeman in a nearby town on Long Island; Angie worked for the city of New York and lived in Brooklyn; Tom worked as a computer programmer for a Long Island firm, married a girl from the neighborhood, and lived four blocks away from his parents' home.

Years passed and Phil went to work, came home to his dinner, his TV, and his basement workshop. He kept their house in immaculate repair, and in the summers he and Mary planted a large garden, the only activity they shared. They didn't take vacations or do anything socially that did not involve the church or their families. She went to Tupperware parties and baby or wedding showers, but he never went out with other men and did not have any he considered close friends. He did not play cards and didn't attend sports events unless it was something at his children's schools, and even then his attendance was spotty. He was not at ease in social situations and preferred to be at home.

Mary brought her salary check home to Phil, who deposited it and continued to dole out money. If she needed a winter coat and asked for a hundred dollars, "he would always give me a hundred and fifty. He was generous." Theirs was a cash economy and they never used credit cards, accepting a MasterCard from their bank "for emergencies only." They never argued over money. Mary said Phil was "the man of the house and he was in charge."

The crisis happened when Phil decided to retire on his company pension, savings, and Social Security. Mary worried about what he would do all day long to fill his time, especially because she had just applied for the office job she was holding when I spoke to her. She wanted the job primarily because she was bored at the parochial school and had been for years but did not know how to go about finding other work. A friend from the church who worked at the store told her of the opening and insisted that Mary apply. She thought the job was heaven-sent, as she could run home at lunchtime to take care of Phil after he retired. He, however, was angry that she intended to disobey him to go to work full-time; when he retired, her said her full-time job would be to take care of him. For the first time in her life, Mary rebelled.

She told Phil the new job paid a considerably higher salary and he should "let" her work, at least for a little while to see if she could fit it into her household responsibilities. Her ploy was to keep telling Phil that the money was "so good" he could not afford to turn it down, so Phil, who had always been a cautious saver, was enticed by it and eventually agreed. Mary went to work thinking everything was settled to her satisfaction, but what Phil didn't tell her was that he planned to use her salary to bolster what he needed for the down payment on a condo in a Florida retirement community.

One night, an uncharacteristically cheerful Phil came to the dinner table with a cluster of brochures about Florida retirement living. Mary was "flabbergasted." He told her he had been thinking about moving there for years, but this was the first she had ever heard of it. He told her he had been talking to "some guys at the church" who thought their house was worth "quite a bit." If they sold it, they could "live off the fat of the land" in Florida for the rest of their lives. He told her to read the brochures and "maybe pick a place." In the winter, he wanted to take a week or two to go down and "look things over." Mary could not believe her ears. She remembered "sitting there, with blood pounding in my head. I couldn't eat. I couldn't swallow. I just sat there." Their roles at the dinner table that night were exactly the opposite of their usual ones: Phil, who never conversed during meals, laughed and talked about the good life they would have; Mary, who always tried to make pleasant conversation, sat in silence because she was afraid if she tried to talk, she would choke. Phil said he would ask "one of the guys from the church" who sold real estate to "set a price" on their house. Mary told him "not so fast," because she needed to think about it. Phil said what was there to think about, it was the start of "easy street." Mary wanted to buy time to think, so she persuaded him not to call anyone into the house until she could "clean it good." He gave her a week.

She went to their room after dinner and climbed into bed, lying for hours "like almost in a coma, in a fog." She knew the house was in both their names, so he could not sell without her permission, or—could he? She had no idea. She knew they had a will, a basic one in which their assets were to go to the surviving partner if one died. But if a wife chose not to do what her husband wanted, what happened then? At this point, "divorce never entered my mind. All I could think of was that I did not want to move out of my house." I asked her why She said she had not been able to think "logically" about everything that happened to upset her traditional life until many months later, but at that time, all she could think was that she did not want to move away "from everything I knew." Later, when she could describe her feelings "logically," she said, "it was because my kids are at the end of a local phone call. So are my sisters and my friends. I can go sit in their houses at their kitchen tables. We can talk. I couldn't do this in Florida. I wouldn't know anybody. What would I do there all day long? Sit at my own kitchen table, all by myself." She tried to explain this to Phil, who "pooh-poohed" her. He said she always made friends easily, so she could join a new church, play bingo, learn hobbies. Mary said, "I don't play bingo up here and I don't like hobbies. It's my family I need."

Several months passed until one night when Mary was in the kitchen preparing dinner. Phil told her to turn off the stove and come into the living room. He had festooned the coffee table with brochures of a particular condominium community and told her he was tired of waiting for her to "come around." She needed to "get serious," as he had to act fast to secure the unit he wanted. He said some of the men he worked with had moved there and they and their wives liked it. They would become "instant friends" for Mary. Mary remembered feeling the same way she had when he first told her of his plans, but this time she did not go to her bedroom in a fog. She told him she was not moving to Florida and she wanted him to reconsider. If caring for the house had become too much for him with the arthritis he claimed to have ("conveniently, when it suited him"), she was willing to sell it and move into a one-floor house or apartment. But she would not leave Queens unless it was for something in Brooklyn or Long Island near their children. This was not an argument, she told him; it was instead "something we never have, an exchange of information." Phil raised his voice, something he almost never did, blaming her "stubbornness" on "those women libbers" she worked with; he told her he was the head of the family and she would have to go along with him.

At this point in my first interview with Mary, her lunch hour ended and she returned to work, promising to ask her "roommates" if she could see me again in the house they shared. She could not have picked a more dramatic moment in her story to leave, and I could not wait for the next appointment.

Mary's daughter, Angie, said she, Tom, and Phil junior all thought it was a good idea for their parents to retire to Florida and were surprised that Mary was so reluctant. The children thought it a good way "to live out the golden years." Mary was visibly upset when her sisters and friends agreed with them. Angie blamed everything that subsequently happened between her parents on the women Mary worked with, for only at work did she get different advice. She had begun to talk to them over sandwiches, as they all ate lunch together (she fixed a plate for Phil's lunch in the morning, telling him there was not enough time for her to come home to cook and then get back to the office on time). The younger women were mostly married and in their thirties, and the older, more traditional ones (all married but one, who was divorced) affectionately lumped them together as "the bra burners." The older ones thought Mary should enjoy retirement without working, and most of them thought "a cushy life in Florida sounds pretty good," but the younger ones all agreed that Mary should stand up for what she wanted.

They suggested that she ask Phil to rent at first, to see if he really wanted to be in Florida. They told her to agree to a vacation, so Mary and Phil went to a small town in southwest Florida for two weeks in a housekeeping motel near several of the condos in which he was interested. They went to some activities in each condo community, had early-bird dinners with some of the residents, and even attended a dance at a community center. Phil was content to sit and watch, so Mary did not accept the several invitations to dance offered by friendly men. When they returned to Queens, Mary told Phil it had been fun, and she would like to take such a vacation every winter, but she was not moving permanently It was after this, Angie said, that Mary came to believe that everyone had "turned against" her.

All three children took Phils side, but none said they told Mary (as she insisted to me they had) that she was "crazy, nuts," not to go along with him. Her sisters did warn her that she was "risking everything" if she disobeyed him, and her friends from the church told her that no matter what she wanted, it was her "duty" to do what her husband wanted. Phil told her she was "shaming" him and stopped talking to her.

I heard the rest of the story from Mary herself, when she invited me to the house she shared with two other women, where she had moved several months after Phil stopped talking to her. She was driven to leave because they were eating the meals she cooked in total silence, and if they were in the house at the same time, Phil was never in the same room with her. He moved into the boys' bedroom to sleep and spoke to her only on matters pertaining to household bills or repairs. Mary began to lose weight. At work she continued to be her usual efficient self but said little. One day at lunch one of the younger women asked what was wrong and Mary burst into tears. When she told them, they agreed that Mary needed to get out of her house for a while to get a new perspective.

One of the women had a cousin, a widow named Louise, whom Mary knew slightly. In order to keep her house, Louise had taken in one boarder, Alma, who also worked in the store but in another office. Louise needed one more boarder, so they suggested that Mary ask if she could live in the house as a stopgap measure until she sorted out what she wanted to do, away from all the pressures caused by her family. Mary said she could not possibly leave her home and thought the matter was ended. The next day, Alma told her Louise would be happy to have a little extra money for the holidays if Mary wanted to stay just for a week or two. But Mary still did nothing about it.

Things came to a head when Mary returned from work a week later to find that Phil had been showing the house to real estate agents. She begged him not to do this, for it made her "feel dirty" to think that strangers were coming into her home and prying into her closets and cupboards. She began to cry, and he retreated to the basement without answering; still crying, she followed him. He told her to "get out," meaning out of the basement, but she thought he meant the house itself. She packed the only suitcase she owned, the small one she had bought for the Florida trip, and went to Louise's. The next day at work, her colleagues praised her and told her to stay there until Phil "saw reason," or at least until he listened to her side of the story. She refused their advice and went directly home after work. She asked Phil if they could talk, and he said not until she "came to her senses." Until then, she could stay where she was. She packed a few more of her things in two large shopping bags and returned to Louise's.

The next day, she received a phone call from her parish priest asking her to go home after work, where he would be waiting with Phil. She had always thought this priest to be rigid and old-fashioned, and so she was surprised when he turned out to be open-minded and fair, as he gently asked them both to try to compromise. Phil said he did not expect his own priest to turn against him and stomped down to the basement. Mary tried to make polite conversation, for the priest was a guest in her home, but he quietly brought the meeting to a quick, dignified end. Once he heard the priest leave, Phil came upstairs, so angry that for the first time in their long marriage, he frightened Mary. She left hastily, went to Louise's, and called Angie, asking her to get her brothers and go to Phil.

Late that night, Tom came to Louise's house, pounding on the door to wake the three sleeping roommates. By this time, Mary had become a disturbing element in the household, more than Louise had "bargained for." She told Mary that if things continued this way, Mary would have to find someplace else to live. Tom said that he was speaking on behalf of his siblings, and Mary had to "come home and knuckle under." Mary said she was "too scared" even to consider it. After a sleepless night, she asked Louise if she could stay on a "temporarily permanent basis," and Louise agreed, but only if there were no more incidents. Mary phoned Phil and told him she would not be coming home. She said she would no longer give him her paycheck but would set up a separate account for herself. He swore and said she would not get a penny of his money unless she came home. She thought she could live on her salary if she was careful, but at no time did she consider divorce. She truly thought Phil would "wise up" and she would eventually go home and resume the life she had always known. She envisioned going with him to Florida for part of every year, but she also saw herself as working for the indefinite future and taking care of her own needs.

Several months passed, and Mary discovered that she liked living in Louises house. She liked the way the three women gathered in the kitchen to share a glass of wine as they prepared the evening meal. She liked it when workmates invited her to birthday parties or baby showers. One day Mary went into Manhattan to see the daughter of one of her coworkers appear in an off-Broadway play, after which they ate at a theater-district restaurant. Mary thought it one of the more magical days of her life. On her own one Saturday, she went to Manhattan to spend the entire day at the Museum of Modern Art. She felt as if "a whole new world was opening up." When she went back to her old neighborhood, such as to her church's sodality meetings, half the women ignored her or told her she'd better be careful because "lots of women would like to put the moves on Phil," while the other half told her surreptitiously how much they admired her "courage" and how "great" she was looking. From Phil himself, she heard nothing for the better part of a year.

When he finally contacted her, it was to say that he was going to Florida for a month and she needed to make up her mind about what she would do. If she did not go with him, he planned to "see a lawyer" as soon as he returned. She asked if he planned to divorce her and remembered later how she was "really so calm about it, no panic at all." He said he did not plan to divorce, he just wanted to find out what his rights were, "about the house and all." Mary told this to her "new family," Louise and Alma and the people she worked with, and they all urged her to see a lawyer herself. She said she had no money, as she was barely able support herself, and they said she had been a fool not to take any support from Phil. Even worse, she had abandoned her marital home and they were sure this would count against her. They told her to go to a local legal services office that helped battered women. She was not battered, she answered truthfully, but she went anyway.

There a lawyer advised her of her rights in the situation. Residence in New York entitled her to half the marital assets. Also, they had been living separately for more than a year, and so under that state's archaic family-law system, they could qualify for a divorce. She telephoned Phil and told him, but all he said was that he would think about it while he was in Florida for the next month.

At this point, Mary had the stunning realization that she did not want to return to her marriage under any terms at all. It felt "like sitting in a movie theater and watching someone else's life on the screen." Within the week, she contacted a lawyer to find out how legal separations were enacted. When she told Phil, he said it would be divorce or nothing, and so she agreed and told the lawyer to let him file the papers and then respond. When the agreements were finalized, Phil did not need to sell the house unless he wanted to, at which time Mary would receive half the proceeds. Half his savings accounts were transferred to her, and when she retired, she would ask to receive his Social Security benefit, as it was higher than hers. They would be buried in the cemetery plot they had long ago finished paying for, and she would continue to be the beneficiary of his insurance policy (she had none of her own). She was no longer eligible for his medical coverage, so she took it through her job. When she retired, she planned to buy a health policy to supplement Medicare.

Two years after the divorce, Mary was living with Louise and Alma, still working and broadening her circle of friends and activities. Calling herself "happy and contented," she said it was not the way she thought she would "end up" but was careful to say also that "not until I left Phil's house [as she phrased it] did I realize that I had been married almost all my life and yet I didn't really have a marriage."

Phil still lived in the house but was moving closer to selling it. He joined an informal group of retired men who played cards every day at the church, and saw his grandchildren as often as possible. Angie invited him to Sunday dinners, and his two sons took him to sports events in which the grandchildren participated. He made no attempt to date or be with other women, even though Mary heard "through the grapevine" that several women were interested in him. She had no interest in meeting other men, saying she "had no idea how to relate to men after so many years." She was content with her job, her housemates, her family, and her friends. She was truly sorry her marriage had not lasted, but "when you never had one in the first place, what is there to miss?"

CHAPTER FIVE

"CEO-ITIS"

A man at seventy is young today . . . Everybody is on Lipitor and blood-pressure medication, and suddenly you're not looking at the clock toward the end of your life. You're looking at seventeen, eighteen years of living. And that's a long time. And those years could be especially vibrant if you can have a vibrant sex life. The golden pond is now at ninety, not seventy.
—ALEX KUCZYNSKI, "The 37-Year Itch"

IN ONE OF THE MANY versions of this exchange, a character in an Ernest Hemingway novel observes that "the very rich are different from you and me," to which another replies, "Yes, they have more money"[1] And they also have "CEO-itis," said an analyst friend, using the term she created when she realized that most of her clients were the corporate movers and shakers of Silicon Valley They are people (women as well as men) who are surrounded by a retinue devoted to satisfying their every need or want, from their mates at home to their attentive office staffs, and they believe they are entitled to have whatever (or whoever) they want, and *right now*, at exactly the moment they want it. Often, when they have discovered that a steady stream of instant gratification does not bring the sheer euphoria that is supposed to go with unmitigated happiness, they turn to therapy, where, as my analyst friend told me, they resent her for not resolving all their issues in the first session. One client told her he would like therapy a lot better if he could just "dump" his problems on her desk, go off to play golf, and come back later in the day to find that she had everything neatly sorted, filed, and solved.

CORPORATE CHIEFTAINS AND CORPORATE SPOUSES

The list of the incredibly wealthy whose divorces play out in public is vast and continually growing. Infidelity looms large as the cause of those divorces that titillate tabloid readers, who feast upon every prurient detail. From those who have inherited vast sums of money and great business empires to the many more who have created their fortunes themselves, their stories fascinate a public lusting for a peek into the rarefied world where the drama unfolds. Since antiquity, we have had the expression, "No man is a hero to his valet," but in recent times it should probably be revised to "No corporate chieftain is a master of the universe, especially to his ex-wife."[2]

The list of embarrassed, embittered, and downright frustrated CEOs and their mad-as-hell and unwilling-to-take-it anymore cast-off spouses is long and growing. Lorna Jorgenson Wendt refused to accept the settlement General Electric executive Gary C. Wendt offered after thirty-two years as his corporate helpmate. She took her case to the courts of public opinion and used the media throughout a contest of willpowers that took three years to resolve. In that time she forced the courts to consider "the true economic value of a corporate spouse," which had been her unpaid job for all the years of her marriage. She insisted that assets beyond her husband's salary and bonuses be taken into consideration for her settlement, things such as deferred compensation, stock options, and other corporate perks. When the divorce was finally granted, Lorna Wendt received more than $20 million dollars, some of which she put to very good use by founding the Equality in Marriage Institute, designed to help other discarded wives receive a fair share of their husbands' assets.

Jane Beasley Welch, a lawyer herself, was canny in her timing when she sued General Electric's CEO, John F. Welch, Jr., for divorce on the grounds of infidelity. Jack Welch was probably the business world's best-known and most respected CEO, one every other corporate official wanted to emulate. Jane Welch bided her time, waiting quietly until her prenuptial agreement expired. When Jack balked at giving her the settlement she thought she deserved, she, too, went public, revealing all the perks General Electric settled on him for life, starting with the free luxury apartment in Manhattan and ending with satellite TV at all four of the homes he owned himself. With stockholders revolting and his reputation tarnished, Jack Welch quickly settled.

Anna Murdoch Mann threw a giant monkey wrench into media baron Rupert Murdoch's plan to revise a family trust that would dilute her children's inheritance by including children from his marriage to the younger woman who succeeded her. Her lawyers wrote into Anna's divorce agreement that Rupert could not force his four older children (three by Anna, his second wife) to share control of his vast holdings without her permission, which she had no intention of granting.

The details of Joan Stonecipher's divorce from her husband of fifty years, Harry C. Stonecipher, the former CEO of Boeing, have not yet been made public. Boeing hired Stonecipher to be the beacon of ethical responsibility who would restore the company's reputation after a military-procurement scandal. One of his first actions had been to require all 150,000 employees to sign a "code of ethical conduct," but shortly afterward, when he and Joan were celebrating a highly public fiftieth anniversary, Harry's infidelity with a co-worker was revealed. When it became grist for the tabloid mills, Joan, then sixty-eight (as was her husband), cited "irreconcilable differences" and filed for divorce. Her lawyers are asking for a "fair and reasonable sum" from Harry, who was described as having "substantial income and wealth."[3]

Lawyers for the rich and famous tell me that most of their clients try to resolve their differences and divide their assets in mediation rather than in a courtroom, where everything is on display for public consumption (Phyllis and Sumner M. Redstone, who divorced after fifty-two years of marriage, fall into this category, as do George and Susan Soros, who divorced after twenty-one years. Redstone was eighty-one at the time of the divorce, and a year later he married Paula Fortunato, who was then forty-nine). No matter how bitter toward each other the parties are, and with the exception of the most egregious cases, the process usually proceeds discreetly and smoothly.

In the case of Revlon magnate Ronald Perelman and his fourth wife, actress Ellen Barkin, the divorce proceeded so smoothly that she moved out of the Perelman town house on February 9, 2006, and had a divorce five days later, on Valentine's Day.[4] And this in New York State, where divorce law is, to say the least, archaic. Barkin took with her a settlement of (depending on who's talking to the media) $60 million (a friend of Perelman's) or $20 million (a friend of Barkin's). His first wife received $8 million, his second got $80 million, while the third wife's settlement fell back down to $30 million. In happier times, Barkin described Perelman as "a real caretaker . . . a man who will take care of you and everyone you know and love forever, whether he has a hundred dollars or a hundred billion."

EQUITABLE DIVORCING

A divorce lawyer-mediator in Northern California tells me he would put Perelman into the category of many of his very rich clients, whom he describes as "a preponderance of smart people who will put aside their emotions to make practical business decisions. These are people who know how to cut their losses and run." In his practice, 60 percent of the clients who initiate divorce are women, and their usual reason is the infidelity of their husbands. A lawyer in New York agreed with him, adding that the men in these marriages "do not divorce to be alone. Typically, there is someone already out there waiting for them." In the New Yorker's experience, women "may or may not have another partner waiting," but if they initiate divorce, it is because "they want it more than they want the man they married."

This attorney also finds a difference in the divorces of people married thirty to thirty-five years as opposed to those married for fifty or so years. The first group is "usually in their sixties and still working. They see many more years ahead of them to move on and look forward," and this includes both making more money along with finding a new partner who is often a younger version of the one they discarded. Those who divorce after fifty years are in their seventies and are dealing with "what is already there, what they have already accumulated." They may be distressed to find themselves dividing assets that have personal meaning, but in most cases they are not as contentious because they count on the courts to divide the financial assets equally. As for finding a new partner, here again, men usually have one already lined up, while women (as several told me) "are more in love with the money and the freedom it brings with it."

Lorna Wendt paved the way for equitable divorce settlements in Connecticut, but she negotiated hers so that the documents are sealed and the actual details remain private. The largest award in a case that actually went to trial in that state—and indeed, one of the largest awards throughout the United States—went to Susan Sosin, who received $24 million of her husband's $168 million fortune.[5] Howard Sosin was a professor at Columbia University in 1978 when he founded AIG Financial Products, a company he sold for $182 million in 1993. Susan was married to another man at the time Howard founded AIG but divorced him to marry Howard, who divorced her in 2005, citing her infidelities (plural). Their divorce played out in a public courtroom in Bridgeport, where Susan admitted to a single infidelity with a rock-climbing guide and an affair of long duration with a married man she met on a plane to China. Howard learned of the affair when he read hundreds of e-mail messages from Susan to her lover that she failed to delete.

Ironically, e-mail figured in the Welch divorce as well, when Jack (then sixty-eight), was being sued by Jane for infidelity with Suzy Wetlaufer (then forty-four and editor of the *Harvard Business Review*, now his wife), and he discovered that Jane had forgotten to delete messages pertaining to her affair with the chauffeur of a GE board member. However, unlike the Sosins, Jack Welch didn't learn about the e-mail until his and Jane's divorce was well along, and allegedly her affair had little impact on the final settlement.

The Sosins' twenty-five-plus years of marriage became, in the words of Howard's lawyer, "an unfortunate story of a family who, because of the husband's genius, accumulated substantial wealth, and, not withstanding all its effect, happiness eluded them." Howard kept two of their five houses, the $16 million estate in Fairfield, Connecticut, where he and Susan had lived with their three children, and the $5 million house nearby where the servants who took care of them lived. She kept the $3.6 million Manhattan apartment, the $2 million Utah ski lodge, and an $800,000 property in Upstate New York. He also kept ten of their eighteen cars, $960,000 in private club memberships, and $22 million in fine art. She petitioned to keep

$2.9 million in jewelry, including a spectacular ruby she knew Howard had bought for her but had not yet given her.

I asked the New York attorney quoted above for his impression of these two settlements, and he agreed that the enormous wealth involved in CEO-itis divorce cases contributes (consciously or not) to the way judges factor financial information into their decisions. Men often rely upon the defense of "I went out there and did all the work, while you stayed home and sat on your ass and did nothing to earn money. Therefore, I will not share what I busted my buns for equally with you." And the attorney adds, "the more money there is, the less you will find judges making fifty-fifty splits." Judges will factor in the question of need, that is, how much does the ex-spouse really need to maintain the lifestyle to which he or she has been accustomed? What was that lifestyle before the divorce, and how close to living the same way afterward is justified under the changed circumstances? What will be the ability of each ex-partner to accrue assets in the future, and how should this be factored into the financial decisions made at the time of the divorce? Very often the spouse who earned the money will need to keep on working but the other spouse will no longer be required to meet the working partner's personal or professional needs (such as housekeeping or entertaining). Six of the nine lawyers I spoke to on this topic agreed that "if one spouse has no job but does get enough money to live well, it probably isn't fair that everything should be split fifty-fifty. Maybe a sixty-forty or sixty-five-thirty-five split is equitable. If, however, things were put into play by both partners during the marriage that will bring in a steady steam of money after the divorce, then that, of course, should be fifty-fifty."

An interesting case now being adjudicated in New York State concerns a couple who worked side by side for forty years to amass a considerable fortune and whom I interviewed. Even though the wife technically never "worked" because she was raising four children, taking care of ever more spectacular houses as they moved up success's ladder, and ensuring that every support service her husband required was there before he knew he wanted or needed it, she argued that she was an equal partner and entitled to an equal share of the assets. "Technically" (a big word for both their lawyers), he did "run the company," even though he took no action unless she agreed with his every decision. The sticking point in their negotiations puzzles all those who are on the outside looking in as the lawyers thrust and parry: everything is in both their names. Her lawyers want an equal division; his lawyers say she is not entitled, nor will she need half of everything to maintain her lifestyle. At this writing, the case is going into the second year of legal maneuvering, as neither party will budge an inch.

When women have the money in a marriage, how it is divided generally depends on when and how it came into the marriage. Most often, a woman's money comes from an inheritance rather than wage earnings. In a Texas case, a woman had inherited $2 million from her parents during their lifetime and, while she was married, stood to inherit an additional $5 to $7 million after their death. When she divorced her husband of forty-one years, he was entitled to only part of what his wife had inherited during the marriage, for Texas is one of a number of states where "[future] expectancy is not a reality," and an ex-spouse cannot be awarded part of an inheritance that did not come until after the marriage ended. In many other states, one partner has no right to any part of an inheritance received during the marriage.

GENDER BIAS IN THE COURTROOM

One of the more interesting cases concerning money earned by a woman was adjudicated recently in Pennsylvania, where a high corporate executive was directed to pay short-term spousal alimony to her househusband. She asked for and received 60 percent of their assets, and he was awarded 40 percent, arguing that after her day job as breadwinner ended, she assumed a night job at home, with full responsibility to keep the household running smoothly. Her ex-husband appealed, but the appellate court upheld the original decision, saying she had proven her case when she provided evidence that she came home to a filthy house, children who were eating potato chips for dinner in front of television programs they should not be watching, and a husband who was often "knocking off his first six-pack of the evening." The disappointed husband complained of "judicial bias," especially after he received temporary alimony for only five years, during which time he was expected to find a job and become self-supporting.

The attorneys I spoke to around the country all agreed that there was "gender bias in the courtroom" in varying degrees. They share the opinion that some judges find it difficult to relate to older women who have never held a job and who ask for permanent alimony on the grounds that entering the workforce at their age will prove difficult. These attorneys find the judges to be scrupulously fair in dividing the marital assets, but they question the judicial decision to insist upon awarding short-term alimony, perhaps for only five to ten years, with the expectation that women will find jobs and become self-supporting. Unless there is extraordinary wealth to be divided, these attorneys see far too many older women who are unhappy in their marriages and who, once they learn they will get such limited support, "will go back into that marriage and stay in it because it is not financially feasible for them to do anything else." A lawyer in Chicago told me, "the mansions along Lake Shore Drive are filled with miserably unhappy wives and their happily cheating husbands."

The details of Susan and Harold Sosin's divorce were sordid, and to the general public the list of their assets was seemingly endless and endlessly spectacular, but the two parties still managed to keep their personal vitriol mostly contained between themselves. In the case of the multimillionaire former chairman of Goldman Sachs, Jon Corzine, and Joanne, his ex-wife of thirty-five years, everything remained dignified and private until he left the United States Senate to run for governor of New Jersey. Joanne Corzine accused her ex-husband of abandoning "both his family and his principles," and Doug Forrester, his Republican opponent in one of the dirtiest political campaigns of the 2005 political year, used it in a television commercial, attributing to Joanne the remark that Jon had "let his family down and he'll probably let New Jersey down, too."[6] Voters apparently disregarded Forrester's attack ad; they elected Corzine by a substantial margin.

"GETTING CAUGHT" AND PAYING FOR IT

And then there was the anonymous middle-aged investment banker who was living an elegant life in one of Connecticut's richest towns with his wife and grown children when he asked an agent at a prestigious New York real estate firm to find him a pied-à-terre in Manhattan. The banker agreed to buy a million-dollar-plus condo but said he wanted to show it to—Sally—before he made the down payment. Thinking Sally was the banker's wife, the agent phoned his home number to arrange the appointment. Instead, he reached Gerry, who answered the phone in surprise and delight to think that she was getting such an extravagant present for her thirty-fifth wedding anniversary. But why, she asked, did he call her Sally? Was the agent sure he had the right husband and the right number? Recognizing his gaffe, the agent did a fast verbal tap dance to concoct a story about how he'd confused two separate clients who were vying for the same apartment. He ended up showing both the twenty-something Sally and the sixtyish Gerry the same apartment on two separate days. The banker bought it for Gerry, who loved it, and the agent invented all sorts of reasons why Sally, who also loved it, would not want to live there. He showed her others until she found one she liked for a million and a half, which the banker quickly bought to keep her quiet and contented.

"I'm no dummy," Gerry told me a year later, after her divorce was final. Her settlement left the banker "reeling and pretty much cleaned out." Since he no longer had unlimited money to lavish on Sally, she kept the apartment but ditched the banker for someone else, who promised to keep her in the style to which she had become accustomed. When last heard from, the banker was moving in with his secretary, who promised to keep him on a tight financial leash.

A divorce attorney in a midwestern state told me how she has gradually restructured her practice so that it is focused more on mediation than courtroom settlements decided by a judge. The shift was gradual, after more and more of the wealthy clients who consulted her instructed her to "do everything possible" to avoid a courtroom battle over the equitable distribution of their assets. Many of these were men in charge of closely held family businesses, and their wives were seeking divorces because of their husbands' infidelities, "the usual CEO stuff—playing around," as the attorney-mediator described it. These men generally began the attorney-client discussion by saying how "fair" they wanted to be, but then they often added the caution that usually became the deal breaker taking them where they did not want to go—into the courtroom. To them, "being fair" carried the warning "just so long as you don't touch the business." When the lawyer-mediator told them the law would require them to produce information pertaining to the business, "this is where mediation breaks down and both parties engage attorneys."

In a surprisingly large number of such cases, even where there is sufficient money to hire the best and most expensive legal counsel, these couples are so desperate to avoid anything pertaining to the courtroom that they will try to represent themselves in an informal mediation between spouses. Sometimes they succeed, and thus they contribute to the statistic of the more than 65 percent of all divorcing couples who will go to court without legal representation. However, even though rich people may be (according to the lawyer-mediator) "too terrified of divorce lawyers to hire them," it is usually the poor who comprise the greater part of this statistic.

DIVORCED WHILE STILL MARRIED

I found it interesting that, among the very rich who were determined to work out settlements on their own so as to avoid incurring high legal expenses, many had been living separate lives for years, as if they were already legally and officially divorced. I call these couples the "divorced-while-still-married" and found that they came in an interesting variety of guises, all of which involved some form of "CEO-itis."

Jack and Julia were a representative couple. He was a self-proclaimed "golden prince," the darling youngest child and only son of doting parents, who had four daughters before they conceived him. A good student and gifted athlete, he sailed through an Ivy League education and a job on Wall Street, where he quickly rose to the top of one firm and was recruited away by another for an even more spectacular salary. Along the way he married Julia, alumna of a Seven Sisters college and heiress to significant wealth of her own. Together they were the perfect couple; their Park Avenue apartment, house in the Hamptons, and ski lodge in Vail drew everyone who was anyone in the rarefied atmosphere in which they moved. It seemed only natural that Jack should gravitate to private banking, particularly after his appointment to a prestigious policy-making federal commission ended. After heads of state sought his financial acumen for their private fortunes, Jack decided the time was ripe to go into politics, and he planned to start at the top by running for the United States Senate in his home state, where he quickly bought a large house in the capital city to establish residency Unfortunately, his state's political party had someone else in mind, a candidate who had paid his dues as he came up through the ranks. Jack persisted and, with Julia's approval, spent several million dollars of his own money before he accepted the reality that the nomination would not then and probably never would be his. It was the first thing in his sixty-two years of life that he had wanted and not gotten, and it was especially galling because it was the one thing he wanted above all others.

Jack went off to "find" himself, spending several months "writing and thinking" at a college classmate's Caribbean estate. He had never shown an inclination for self-examination and introspection, nor had he ever expressed any interest in becoming a writer. He had also been faithful to Julia throughout their thirty-eight-year marriage. On his own, he began to question many things about himself that he had hitherto accepted, and finding himself "somewhere between despair and depression," he moved into the Southern California guest house of a college roommate and began psychoanalysis. He also began to "date" other women, laughing as he said it and apologizing that "being a man of a certain generation, *dating* is a hard word for me to use." In New York, Julia quietly maintained the life she had always led, filling her days with volunteering for various charities, entertaining a circle of genuine friends (many dating from her college days), and enjoying her two married daughters and three grandchildren.

Jack was entirely honest with Julia, telling her everything he was doing and expecting her to accept it as his "right and due." Jack said, "This does not mean we are getting a divorce; this is the way for people who still love each other to move forward." Dr. William Doherty, director of the Marriage and Family Therapy Program at the University of Minnesota, describes men such as Jack as being part of the "culture of self-actualization: They say, 'Life is more than what I have been living' . . . they are determined to live the balance of their lives in a different way. . . . They take Scandinavian cooking classes, they try yoga. They try therapy to try to understand themselves better. And they're close enough to the boomers to divorce for . . . the 'soft' reasons: 'not happy,' 'not fulfilled,' 'we don't communicate.' "[7]

At first Julia decided to wait it out, to be discreet and keep things private, to go along with Jack until he "came to his senses." She remembered a book she once read about Napoleon's army and compared herself to the French soldiers who marched through the snow during a Russian winter: "It was simply, go forward, Julia, go forward. I am not saying this was a good way to handle the situation; I am saying this is how I am and that is what I did."

Three years passed, and Jack had longish liaisons with two different women that he conducted in public, even taking them to stay with friends for weekends and holidays. He invited his and Julia's daughters and their husbands for dinners in the women's apartments, but the two daughters had such respect for their mother that they would only consent to meet him alone in restaurants. Jack and Julia kept their official marital status so quiet that both daughters told me they did not know during this period if their parents were officially divorced or not. Friends and associates were aware of the "breakdown" of the marriage, but because neither Jack nor Julia spoke of it, most assumed that a quiet divorce had already taken place. Even so, no one seemed surprised that both continued to live in the Park Avenue apartment because it did, after all, have seven bedrooms (each with its own bath) and two separate entrances. Nor did people look askance when the entire family gathered, as they always had, to spend the Christmas holidays in Vail.

When I interviewed Jack, it had been seven years since he entered the ranks of the divorced-while-still-married, and he had no intention of leaving. He always has another woman in his life, sometimes two if he has not succeeded in gracefully unloading the one who no longer interests him. It is not uncommon for Jack to slip his phone number discreetly to another woman when the one he is with isn't looking. Julia knows all this, but she doesn't "care" and doesn't "want him back." She has learned how to "wedge" herself into Jack's other relationships, often telling his women friends what foods he likes best or what colors he likes women to wear. "I kill them with kindness," she boasted, and told how one woman left Jack because "there are always going to be three people in your bed, and I refuse to sleep with you *and* your wife."

Julia has no intention of asking for a divorce because "there is too much money involved and things might get messy." She is on many social A-lists and does not lack for "walkers" to escort her to various charity functions; she has a large list of friends, including most of the couple's friends from the marriage. She "avoids romantic entanglements," again because "there is too much money involved."

In Jack's "serial relationships" with women, he carefully avoids telling them that he is still married until or unless they ask point-blank. Eventually, they grow tired of their vague and indefinite status, and if he has not left them first, they leave him. Each time a woman (in his words) "tells me what I can do with myself," he says he cannot understand why—he thought everything was "just fine." Julia just smiles and tells him better luck next time.

LIMBO MARRIAGES

Just beneath the very *very* wealthy are those who have enough money to set up two separate households, just so long as they are careful. Many of these couples manage to put a great deal of geographic distance between them, in bicoastal or continental separations. When Paul married Yvette fifty-five years ago, he was a British banker on temporary assignment in Zurich and she was his Swiss secretary. His work took them back to London, where they raised three children, whom Yvette took back to Switzerland every chance she got. After they were grown and on their own, she and her widowed sister bought a small house in their native town, where she lived for the better part of every year while Paul stayed in London. Since they had "nothing in common anymore," the arrangement worked fine for both of them and lasted until two of their children relocated to Australia. Paul fell in love with "a place, not another person," and he asked Yvette to join him in a coastal town just north of Sydney. She refused to leave Switzerland, so he went alone. After fifty-five years of marriage, neither had any intention of divorcing even as both admitted they would never live together again.

Teresa wanted to stay on Cape Cod, near her three children and the eight siblings in her large Portuguese family. Will, her artist husband of fifty-eight years, had arthritis in his hands and wanted to return to the warmth of his native Fresno, California. When I spoke to them, he was about to buy a small house very near the one in which he grew up. Teresa said, "he's nuts" and that she had no intention of "even visiting. He knows where his home is."

Will hoped she would change her mind and said he was "open to whatever comes in the future." Teresa just snorted and said she wasn't worried: "He's had girlfriends before, and he always came home with his tail between his legs."

Roger and Wanda had been divorced-while-still-married for five years, when Roger sought to end the marriage legally even as Wanda still hoped that he would "come to his senses" and return to her. "Come to his senses" is a phrase I heard often among those who had these limbo marriages, but rarely, if ever, did reconciliation happen. Once the errant spouse "opened a new door and walked through it," as Roger said he did, that spouse was usually gone forever. Roger told me he was one of them, after thirty-seven years of marriage to Wanda.

They were both born into families of modest circumstances, and every asset they had, they earned together. They met in high school when both were seventeen and married at twenty-one, when they were newly graduated from good western colleges. Both had scholarships to graduate schools, Wanda in Romance languages, and Roger in biomedical engineering. They had been separated for five years when I spoke to them, and if Roger had his way, they soon would become part of the legally divorced.

In the early years of their marriage, both rose through the ranks to become tenured professors at the same large midwestern university. Their attitude toward money was similar, and they shared a strong sense of fiscal responsibility. From the beginning of the marriage, they took advantage of the various investment and retirement plans their university offered. They took on a large mortgage and struggled for a number of years to pay for a huge house in a good suburb because they wanted to raise their three sons in a solid community with good public schools and they knew the property would appreciate. Eventually their salaries and investments increased to the point where owning the house was no longer a strain, and there was extra money for vacations, personal interests, and hobbies. However, everything they did and everything they acquired was done "in tandem, for the good of the family." Theirs was the house where both extended families gathered for every holiday celebration. Friends, colleagues, and even strangers were always welcome, and they took to calling themselves fondly Roger and Wanda's "waifs and strays."

Roger called Wanda "the family switchboard," through whom everything connected with their daily life passed. In the beginning, it was a term of genuine affection; later it became an accusation that she was a "control freak." Wanda admitted that she played the role of "the family's scheduler, the organizer," and Roger agreed that without her doing so, his career might not have prospered as it did. Because she took care of everything at home, Roger was free to devote all his time to the research in his university laboratory. His findings led to several important patents being granted to his university, and also to his being recruited to become the CEO of a major research foundation that was located in their community but loosely attached to a prestigious eastern university. Roger accepted the offer because it allowed him to keep his ties to academic medicine even as it moved him into administration and shot his salary into an "astronomically higher" category. The new position required him to spend one week every month in the eastern city to meet with board members and teach master classes to research scientists. He was so successful in that job that he was soon recruited for another, as CEO of an international research organization, a position that required frequent European travel.

Every new appointment brought with it a much higher salary, until his compensation became greater than he had ever dreamed possible. And each appointment was made possible for a man to whom "family life" remained a high priority because his wife was content to fulfill the responsibilities of being the "family switchboard." Wanda liked her work teaching languages, and because Roger was so busy with his work, she had time to concentrate on her own. All the while, she continued to save and invest her salary wisely, so they had to admit to each other "gleefully" that they were becoming "exceedingly rich!"

In the fifteenth year of their marriage, with their three boys in tow, they went to Switzerland for a sabbatical year. They were in the western part of the country known as the Jura, rugged and mountainous, fairly isolated from the major centers of commerce and culture but close enough to Geneva and France, where there was much to do. They all fit happily into the life of the small village where they lived while Roger spent long days in the research laboratory of his parent company Wanda had trained to teach English as a second language before they left, and she busied herself volunteering in the village school that the three boys attended. They took frequent weekend trips and longer holidays to various villages throughout southeast France, and Roger "fell in love" with the region. He began a serious study of the French language, so family dinners were raucous and happy as everyone brought a mélange of local dialects and languages other than English to the table.

All was well until the middle son, Sam, was diagnosed with a congenital heart condition that ran through Wanda's family Surgery in Zurich successfully corrected it, but there was always the danger that other complications could arise from the original condition at any time in the boys life. From a rough-and-tumble kid who played soccer, Sam turned overnight into a quiet, introspective boy who sat on the sidelines watching his brothers. According to Roger, "the impact on the family dynamic was serious and lasting." No matter how he tried to comfort Wanda, she was convinced that she had brought "something bad" into the marriage. That, along with the changes she sensed were happening in Roger, led Wanda to therapy, which she depended upon for years afterward.

Roger was thirty-eight when Sam's illness was diagnosed, and as he headed toward forty, he began to feel "a personal restlessness." His career was flourishing and he "enjoyed the adulation of women" he met professionally, but he insists these encounters did not lead to "anything sexual." Once they returned to the United States, they resumed life as they had led it before the sabbatical. His work kept him out a minimum of three nights every week, and there were frequent trips to conferences and professional meetings. Wanda went back to her university teaching, and the boys grew and became independent. Roger and Wanda were pillars of their community and to everyone who knew them "an excellent team." He thought she was "terrific in her traditional role," and she was "proud of his brilliance and success." Thus it was not surprising that when Roger eventually left her, none of their friends and colleagues, and indeed not even their children and their siblings, could understand how the most perfectly knit couple among them had unraveled. But this did not happen until long after they first went to Switzerland.

Ten years later, when Roger received another of the occasional "mini-sabbaticals" granted by his company, he decided to spend it in Geneva, where he could observe some work that interested him at the university there, and where he could also have easy access to the part of France he so loved. The family joined him twice, each time for a three-week vacation, and things were as carefree and relaxed as they had been on the earlier trip. But when the family departed, Roger had time for introspection and the recognition that he was "beginning to change in interesting ways" and was "very open to these changes."

One of the directors of the research lab was "a cultured, creative, lovely woman" who engaged him as a consultant, and he went there for several weeks at a time for the next several years. Through this woman he became aware of an "aesthetic world, of art, music, fine clothing, excellent food." The woman was married to a distinguished scientist whose family owned a large estate in eastern France, and Roger (without telling Wanda) bought a small house nearby. Wanda was convinced that he was having an affair, as were Dan and Sam (the two older sons), but Roger insists the relationship was strictly platonic. However, it was through this woman that he did begin an affair, one that lasted for almost two years.

The woman who became his lover was a family friend of the scientist. The divorced mother of a young son in a Swiss boarding school, she came from a wealthy family with holdings in many business conglomerates. Her work was to manage one of the medical-scientific branches, and she moved freely to wherever her work demanded. It seemed natural that Roger would consult for her business as well, and when the affair began, her family accepted it. There was no problem until eighteen months passed and they told him discreetly that it was now time to end his marriage and marry his lover. There would be no financial repercussions because it was assumed they would live in Europe and her family would put him in charge of any of the businesses he wanted to manage. Roger was unwilling to divorce Wanda, so he brought the affair to an end in which "nobody got hurt and everybody parted amicably."

Once he was back in the family home, he was more aware than ever of the "distance" that had grown between him and Wanda. "A door had opened for me with that affair, and by the time it ended, I had gone through it." Wanda suspected this affair from the beginning, but each time she asked Roger, he denied it. She depended heavily on her therapy to help her "keep things on an even keel." Now that he was at home she could feel the distance between them, and she begged him to go to couples' therapy with her. He did, but for him, "by then it was too late. I was already through the door." Nevertheless, he continued with the sessions for another four months, until a number of different crises arose at work.

The board of the company he had run so successfully for so many years decided that a merger was in its best interests, and Roger ran into conflict with the new owners. He threw himself into beating off his rivals within the company and taking the merger in a different direction than was originally envisioned. Having kept alive his academic ties, he also negotiated a sine-cure for himself at the university that gave him the exact division of teaching and writing that he had long wanted but never asked for before. After he had "plowed into work and made everything end successfully, the proverbial lightbulb went off."

Roger realized that this had always been his pattern: when something concerning his family or his work was troublesome, he threw himself into solving or resolving it and making everything right. Usually, the situations he resolved were at work, which gave him an excuse to be absent from the life of his family, for after all, "how could they criticize me when I was doing it all for them?" Now that he had bested his enemies in what was the most intense intellectual engagement of his life, he had to consider whether or not to return to family life as it had always been.

Instead, he had "a clear insight into myself, a clear sense that it was time to go my separate way." He told this to Wanda, who was aghast. "You travel, you have all the space you want or need in this marriage, you have a loving family, you have a wonderful community where everyone loves you. What more do you want!" She did not understand what had happened to him, and he told her he could not explain it to her since he had trouble understanding it himself. After several months of strained silences, of tension, argument, and bitterness, he moved out of the house and into an apartment. The three sons were all living away from home by this time, and so they knew nothing about the problems between their ever-discreet parents. When they learned of Roger's decision, they were devastated. There was acrimony in the "perplexed" community and people took sides (usually Wanda's). Roger became, in his own words, a "fallen icon."

He wanted to tell his sons why he wanted to end his marriage because "they are men and I thought they should put my experience to their own possible future use." He arranged individual restaurant dinners to break the news to them, and Sam's was the first. "Why are you laying this on me?" Sam asked angrily before he stomped out. Dan's came next, and alerted by Sam, didn't stay for dinner. After they ordered drinks, Dan called his father a "first-class shit," and left after giving him (in Roger's words) "a good dressing-down." Tim, the youngest and closest to Wanda, was the most affected. He went to the dinner and sat there throughout with his food untouched, shaking and quietly crying. Roger believed then (and still did when I spoke to him) that Wanda is "too overinvolved" with her sons, especially Tim, who gave up his college dorm room to move back into the house because he thought she "needed" him.

And so, just before the new century began, at the height of the holiday season that had always been so important to his family, Roger moved into his own apartment. Within weeks, he began to "see" other women because friends "fixed me up." That summer, he "reconnected" with a woman he had known for most of his professional life, and he began to see her to the exclusion of all others. Several months afterward, he moved into her house, and as of this writing, five years later, he's still there. He finds the woman "far easier to live with" than Wanda. When asked for an example, he said, "I can wake up now on Saturday morning and know that the day is mine to do with it as I want. With Wanda, every minute was programmed and the bells on her switchboard went off to let me know to the minute when I had to obey the commands." With his new companion, there is time "to sit and read and think, to listen to music, to linger over the dinner table."

Being with her made him realize that everything in his marriage had been "nonstop work, constant striving and achieving, and not having any pleasure along the way." But wasn't he the partner who set the tone and the pace of the marriage? Was the way they lived not only Wanda's decision but also his as well? He admitted that this was true and agreed that "it was fine as long as it lasted," but "now things have changed." He does not know if his current attitude is due to "age" or to "a new depth of feeling." When he was with Wanda, who was an active outdoorswoman, Roger felt that he "always had to be doing something," and most of the time they were activities he did not enjoy. "I used to ask her why she was making me do these things—go ice-skating or race walking—when I was just dragging her down and spoiling her pleasure." Now he relishes that there is "no pressure to do, to achieve; it's just such a good time in my life. Everything is in balance."

To this day, Roger's sons are still chagrined over his departure. (Their story will be told in chapter 6.) Wanda remains in the family home, and Roger is "still surprised" that she has no intention of leaving because it "ties up a significant amount of our family's resources." He thinks that "closure is not there for her. I have been gone for five years, and she still expects me to 'come to my senses' and go back to her." Wanda said he was right about that, that she did live "like someone waiting for the other shoe to drop," in this case for him to come home. But she insists she has a valid reason to live this way because he had never asked her for a divorce.

Roger admitted that it was true, he had not spoken of divorce until the beginning of his fifth year away from home because he wasn't sure until then that he wouldn't return to the marriage. "In the back of my mind, I worried that my new relationship might not work out, and if I got lonely or sick, I might want to go back to Wanda." Now that he was sure that he and his companion would be together indefinitely, he thought he might want to propose marriage and he wanted his freedom in case he decided this was the next best step for him to take.

Wanda has not been alone in the five years since Roger left. At just about the same time as he became involved with his companion, she began a relationship with a recently widowed colleague at the university Although the relationship was a "surprisingly satisfying sexual one," each preferred to maintain a separate home and neither wanted to marry. Both liked things "as they are." Wanda describes her social life as "rich and full." In the third year after Roger left, she decided that it was time to hold a family celebration at Christmas, and that, for the sake of their sons, they must all "learn to live together." She decorated, baked, filled the house with light and music, and invited everyone in the community to join them for Christmas Eve and to come back for Christmas dinner.

"But it was not the same," Roger said. Wanda called it "a big mistake; I was not comfortable with that other woman in my house." Now Wanda has the children on the actual day of the major holidays and Roger makes arrangements to see them the weekend before or the weekend after. When something arises in her sons' lives that she thinks Roger should know about, she phones and invites him to meet her for a drink in a public place to discuss it. He thinks she "flirts" with him; she insists "it is purely business done on a friendly level."

Even though Wanda's refusal to leave the family home eats into the marital assets, Roger admitted that they were both financially secure and she could stay there as long as she wants. Without resorting to lawyers or legal separations, ever since he left he has given her a "very generous" monthly allowance and pays all the household bills. She is still working and her money remains her own; both agree this will remain the case once the divorce negotiations officially begin. Roger says they are "fortunate" that they can "contemplate a secure future after divorce," for had they been poorer, "the bitterness and distress would have been sorely compounded."

Roger thinks that his having become a "fallen icon" to his sons has been good for their relationships because they no longer have to think of him as "perfect." He tells them repeatedly that he is "sorry the divorce happened," because it created "far more sadness and pain" than he expected. Still, he believes he did the right thing. He thinks far too many of his friends "have not gone on to a new life when they could have, have chosen to remain in their old lives." He mentioned a particular friend who had "similar opportunities," to have "a more lustful and sensual relationship but instead retreated into a dead marriage, where he is now a lonely old man." Roger believes that "life is a series of compromises. One has sexual relationships, then one settles, then one is frequently regretful. The choices we make at seventeen are significantly different from the ones we make at fifty-five or sixty." Ultimately however, he believes that "marriage is here to stay; the idea of intimacy and romantic love just needs to be recast—they must be recast—but marriage will endure." He thinks "serial monogamy" will become far more common.

Wanda wonders if she "ever really knew Roger." She said she cannot help but be bitter. "I did everything a good wife was supposed to do. So many other men admired me, told me how they wished their wives were like me. I gloried in this praise. I was proud because it reflected on Roger. And then the perfect life that I made for all of us just got swept away because he didn't want it anymore."

When I asked her if she finds solace in the love that is lavished upon her by her children, her family and friends, and even her lover, she admitted that it "keeps me going." Then Wanda, who is an elegant and cultured woman, a teacher of languages whose language is always perfect, told me that "even so, it's hard to think positive when everything else has been turned to shit."

"WHAT SHOULD WOMEN DO?"

Wanda will have closure forced upon her when and if Roger has his way and they divorce, but Suzanne does not want it and hopes it will never happen to her. She was married for twenty years and divorced while still married for nine, and as far as she is concerned, she will live this way indefinitely. At the end of an interview during which she ranged far and wide over a variety of topics that encompassed everything from her general bitterness toward men to her resentment of having to grow old alone, she abruptly stopped throwing out her thoughts and opinions and asked for mine. "So!" she demanded, "what should women *do*?"

Suzanne lived in a large southern city and our conversation was by telephone. It had been going on for close to two hours, and throughout, Suzanne was in charge. She was suffused with rage toward Raymond, so once I asked the initial questions (how long were you married, how old were you both at the time of the marriage, how long was the courtship, how many children do you have), I let her tell her story as it came to mind, often in a rambling, disjointed, and almost incoherent manner. Just when I thought she was winding down, she fired off a series of comments and questions that represented many I had heard from other women in her situation. First she spoke of the paucity of decent men: "[Men] are not very good creatures. They lie all the time; they try to lure you in; the married ones try to pretend they are not."

Then came the reason women stay married: "It's because there are so few men of good character out there. Women who are still married often feel they need to stay with these guys because there isn't anyone better out there. Maybe they're right to stay—they need to be supported because they can't support themselves, they don't want to grow old alone."

And then what she's looking for: "Not a god, an Adonis, or a multimillionaire. I just want to meet a guy with good character. Someone honest who tells the truth and tries to be a good man in his relationships. It would be nice to find someone [financially] secure as he goes into retirement, but really, what's out there is all so depressing." I ask why it's "all so depressing." "Men want younger women and they get them. Now, I am pretty good-looking and I have a nice body But I am fifty-seven and men want twenty- or thirty-year-olds, or even younger, and they can get them! I ask you, is this an American thing or is it true of the world?"

I tell her I regret to say that from my own exploration, it does seems to be a worldwide phenomenon.

With each question Suzanne threw out, her voice became more strident and shrill. I thought I needed to defuse her anger before I answered the final one, about what women should do, and because she is the mother of sons who have been deeply scarred by their parents' history, I tried for a general response that I hoped would be safe and soothing. I said that perhaps we should concentrate on educating our sons better so that they'll become the kind of men we would want to marry. "Oh yeah?" she replied. "But what about us? What do we do in the meantime?" Furious over the lot of women, she illustrated what she meant by referring to a children's book she despises: *The Giving Tree* by Shel Silverstein, a book well beloved by countless children. Suzanne's interpretation of the tale is that it is "all about a boy who asks the tree for what he wants and the tree just gives and gives, all its roots, bark, water. The boy becomes a full-grown man and he comes back to find the tree is a dying twig." Suzanne's voice rose: "And this is supposed to be a good book? What kind of message are we giving our children—that this is how women are supposed to be—to give and give and give until there is nothing left and they die?"

Suzanne had been living alone since she was forty-eight. At the time of her marriage, she was twenty-seven and Raymond was thirty. It was she who insisted upon a legal separation rather than a divorce, and it is she who refuses to move beyond the nothingness and despair of her nonmarriage and nondivorce.

I asked her why "I have not completely gotten over what happened to me. I have not had the strength or the will to sever the ties." I ask then if the legal separation might be what keeps her from going on with her life. "Yes, this has come up with all sorts of people, not just you."

She told me that she "cannot ignore the possibility" that she is clinging to the life she had," but the legal separation in and of itself "has never been a barrier." She has no hope of ever getting back together with Raymond, although "maybe in the first few years I did, but when things got settled into this rut I guess I didn't go for the divorce because I just didn't want to rock the boat again." But what about Raymond, I asked; doesn't he want some sort of closure"? She laughed and told me she was laughing at my naïveté: "He thinks a legal separation is protection for everybody, especially for him. He can screw all he wants but nobody can force him to marry them."

At this point, I asked Suzanne to tell me what happened to bring two obviously intelligent and successful people as she and Raymond to such a sorry pass. She was still unable to address the subject directly. First she said it was "because of the circumstances." Yes, what were they? She didn't answer the question as she told me she thought "there was a chance to work it out" but she still "needed to file the paperwork." Did she mean documents for the legal separation? Again, no direct answer: it was "because of the evidence" she collected. Evidence of what? She evaded the question and answered with "I still had some hope that we could work it out." And so I returned to my original questions: What evidence? What paperwork? What circumstances? Suddenly she blurted out the word "infidelity" and fell silent. I asked several times if she was still there, and she didn't answer. So I asked many separate questions in the hope that one might trigger an answer, about whether

Raymond's infidelity was serial, ongoing, long-term, short-term, a passing fling. Finally she did answer: "All of the above."

He had one relationship that began before the marriage and lasted throughout, which Suzanne calls "his Charles and Camilla thing." He had "casual flings and many prostitutes" that she knew about. There was a "woman in his main office and others in every branch." For years she was terrified of what disease he might bring home, so she would only consent to "missionary sex with condoms." He laughed at her and eventually they stopped having sexual relations altogether.

Suzanne suspected him from the beginning, but every time she accused him he told her she was "crazy." She was in therapy for eighteen years of her twenty-year marriage, and together they went to four different therapists, but Raymond was so charming and persuasive that "they all believed him when he said I was crazy." The fourth time this happened, Suzanne hired a detective who captured Raymond with other women on both audio and video. She was afraid of what Raymond might do, so she was careful to confront him in a public setting because she "feared violence." She was so afraid that she actually sent her three children away from home so they would "be safe" in case he "tried something after we got back to the house." Suzanne refused to answer my question as to whether she took these actions because Raymond had been physically violent before. She would only say that "when I finally had evidence of his cheating, and I knew how he lied to our therapists, I realized I didn't know him at all. He was a very powerful man out in the world, and I feared how he might use this power at home."

Raymond was the head of an international consortium that stressed (Suzanne snorted when she says this) "family values" and that paid him a seven-figure salary with bonuses and perks. They lived on an estate in the best suburb of a large southern metropolis, in a seven-thousand-square-foot house with a guest house, a five-car garage, two swimming pools, two tennis courts, and a miniature-golf course. All of this was important to Suzanne, and she knew that she was "putting everything at risk" by confronting Raymond, but she still decided to do it. As he was boarding a plane for an international conference, a process server handed him copies of the evidence of his infidelity and the papers telling him that Suzanne was asking for a legal separation on the grounds of infidelity (which was needed in the state where they lived).

Once the "news got out" in Raymond's company, Suzanne learned that "like most wives, I was the last to know." A sex scandal beyond her wildest imaginings erupted. Raymond had not been content with his own sexual adventures; he insisted that every one of his managers in the consortium had to have them as well if they wanted to be promoted. Prostitutes were routinely invited to business dinners, and Raymond's associates were expected to be with them as part of an "initiation ceremony." When he said they had to do this to assure him of their loyalty they were convinced that he had rigged up audio and video systems to capture them in flagrante. One of the men committed suicide shortly after his "initiation," but his colleagues did not reveal the real reason until after Suzanne's allegations were printed in the newspapers of every city where the consortium had a branch.

The board allowed Raymond to negotiate a severance settlement, but it was far beneath his annual salary and he and Suzanne had no wherewithal to cushion their fall from the CEO stratosphere. Everything Raymond made went into maintaining the lavish property and adorning themselves with the finest designer clothing and jewelry. Suzanne knew at once that "everything would have to go." The first thing she had to do was to sell the estate, which she did but after a long time and at a loss when the market was at a low point. What furnishings she could not sell she gave to friends and neighbors or donated to charities. To save face when she took her children out of their swank private school, she told them they would be off to a great adventure in a grand new way of life as they moved into an inner-city space that she "pretended" was a loft, above a series of storefronts. She pretended they would lead an "artistic life" and that she had taken the place because there would be separate "spaces" for each child. When the time came for the actual move, she could not afford a professional mover, so her friends brought their vans and she rented moving trucks. She even sold her car and told the children that riding public transportation to their new schools would be just another adventure.

Because they are not officially divorced at the time of this writing, the only money she receives from Raymond comes from a financial settlement to be paid out over ten years, and she is now in the ninth year of it. She is "floundering" because she never had a career and has not liked any of the jobs she has tried since her legal separation went into effect.

I asked about how the separation has affected her children, and she launched into a litany of Raymond's bad behavior. He "disappeared" for several months as soon as the newspaper stories broke, leaving her and the children to "face the music." When he returned, the children refused to see him, which she "understands, because even during the marriage, he was so superficial with them." Suzanne wanted the children (a daughter now in her mid-twenties, followed by two sons in their early twenties) to go into therapy, but they refused. They told her they were "all right" and said what they were living through was "no big deal because it was always just the three of us kids anyway."

Does she believe that they are indeed "all right" now? I asked. The question was met with another of Suzanne's long silences before she told me, "I really don't know." She paused again and said she'd need to think about it, and this produced another long silence. She said she worries that her daughter "is not that stable where men are concerned. She doesn't trust them." The daughter has had several nasty involvements already. The elder of her sons is "wrestling with the issue of fidelity in his relationships, of which he has too many. I think he may turn out to be his father's son." The younger son "is living a pretty normal life in college, but he is alone too much. He keeps himself to himself." Suzanne thinks he "avoids relationships because they hurt too much."

Hoping to find out what motivates Suzanne to stay in such a desolate state of being, I asked what her daily life is like now, as she heads into the tenth and last year of her support payments. She told me she gets very lonely, that she withdraws into herself, and that she has to set up "patterns of daily life" in order to "keep going." She "gets through each day by being busy," but she is unwilling to describe what she actually does. As the end of her support looms, she has had to "cut out more and more." She has not been able to afford therapy for several years and regrets it; she seeks free entertainment, such as poetry readings or lectures wherever she can find them; she spends a lot of time in her local library; she seldom goes to a movie or eats out and does not buy clothes until she truly needs them. She is "not religious and not a joiner," so church and organizational activities do not play a part in her life. When she went through menopause and hormone replacement therapy played havoc with her metabolism, she refused further medication and believes she righted her system through diet and exercise. She lost weight and came to depend on the physical activity of cycling and jogging, which, she said, "provides a lot of free entertainment." She was an only child and both her parents are dead, and she does not seem to have many close friends, men or women, yet she claims she has had several sexual relationships, which she ended because the men "turned out to be lying bastards."

Suzanne describes her former life as the "job" she "lost" when she was no longer "the corporate exec's helpmate." It was not "a perfect life," but she liked it and did her best with it. Her biggest regret is that Raymond never let them "be a duo" and refused to go "even part of the way" with her in "sharing himself and his emotions." After a sad sigh, she said, "Well, lots of other women shut their eyes and stay in these less-than-perfect marriages. . . ." and then she drifted off again. To break the silence I asked if she regrets not having stayed silent about Raymond's infidelities and remaining in her privileged setting. She thought about it for a while, then once again didn't really answer the question. She only said, "Things just happen, just get forced upon you, and you do them."

COMING TO TERMS WITH DIVORCE

Of all the women I interviewed, it seemed to me that those whose husbands fell into the CEO-itis category had the most difficulty coming to terms with divorce. As we talked, so many kept returning wistfully to the early years of their marriages, calling them "the good times, when we were poor and just starting out." As they described deadening jobs they "endured" for years to put their husbands through medical, business, or law school, they told me without rancor or regret of how they willingly sacrificed educational opportunities of their own, in order to "Ph.T.: put hubby through." They told of how they yearned to have children but delayed starting a family; several spoke tearfully of consenting to abortions because they became pregnant at a "bad moment" in their husbands' career. Some told of how they did not have children at all because their husbands thought children would require too much time and attention and they wanted to "be free to travel and enjoy life." These wives considered their husbands' career to be theirs as well, and they relished it as their "full-time job." Every woman recalled the lives they led once their husbands "made it" to the top as brimful of "delight," "happiness," and "joy." One described herself as a "full-time party planner." Another said the happiest twelve years of her marriage were when she worked full-time with several decorators to furnish their four houses, one of which was a stately home in England.

Many of these couples came from modest or humble beginnings, so the perks and pleasures were often beyond anything they could imagine and in the early years were often a source of mutual glee. "Look at us, two little kids from an Iowa farm town," said one woman who could not mix metaphors fast enough to tell me how "the Big Apple" was their "personal oyster." Those who came from backgrounds where there was some money were pleased to be re-creating the genteel lifestyle of their parents and grandparents as they settled comfortably into the world of charity balls and private clubs to which they had a birthright.

Every one of these ex-wives of CEOs said she thought things were "all right" in her marriage, that there was "nothing wrong that could not be fixed" with "a nice vacation," "a change of scene," or whatever new toy the husband wanted to play with (usually something along the lines of an antique auto, a powerful sports car, a new sailboat, or a private plane). They usually blamed the husband's never-ending quest for "power" as the reason their marriages ended.

Deanna spoke of how "the lust for power" decimated her husband Arthur's medical practice "like falling dominos" when all the doctors divorced the middle-aged wives who had supported them in the years of struggle to marry younger ones. She is convinced "they thought they could get away with anything, that they had enough money and power to do whatever they wanted." But as our interviews progressed and the women digressed, equivocated, or evaded talking about the years when they knew (even if they would not face the fact) that a divorce was in the offing, they eventually blurted out the real reason why their marriages ended: their husbands' infidelity.

In every case it took a while for the women to be able to admit (certainly to me, perhaps even to themselves) that their husbands had "betrayed" them, in some instances "repeatedly" throughout their marriages. Maxine, married to Bobby for thirty years, told me that he "started having affairs, or at least I started to find out about them, ten years into our marriage. After that I never trusted him again, but I always forgave him and somehow we got beyond them." Bobby and two of his college friends started an accounting and investing firm that skyrocketed to financial success. All three men divorced their wives in rapid succession to marry younger versions of the same women. All three wives said they only learned of the "serious serial adultery" after they were "dumped."

Becky, married to Steve for thirty-seven years, said she did not know he had had many "affairs and one-night stands" throughout their marriage until they were divorcing and a "well-meaning friend" (she says this sarcastically) told her that Steve had just ended an affair of seven years with a woman who lived in the same midsized town where "everybody knew each other and knew everything." Becky said she put Steve "on a pedestal, and so I guess I refused to see what was there to be seen." She felt "totally disconnected from reality" when she learned of the long affair in the midst of her battle for an equitable settlement. At first she said, "For an affair to go on that long, he must have loved her." Then she paused for a long time before adding, "Well, maybe not, because there were others, too, during the time he was with her."

As soon as she learned of Steve's last infidelity, Becky confronted him directly, which was her way of addressing problems. He responded in his way, which was to ignore them. She telephoned him at his office, and "he did what he usually does. He refused to talk, and he hung up on me." It would have made no difference if she had waited until he came home to confront him because "he would just put his hands over his ears, his signal that we were not going to talk about something." Becky said she was "really angry" during the phone conversation and that now, five years after their divorce, she remained surprised because "it is a very strange thing; I was really angry with him for messing up our lives, and I still am angry, I have anger. But I have moved on." I asked her to describe her life after divorce, and she said that, first of all, she "found out things" about herself: "I don't have to have a man constantly in my life, but I do miss male companionship from time to time, even though I have had male friends."

Before I could ask her to elaborate, she shifted topics abruptly: "How in the hell do people manage to be in love with one person for such a long duration of time? Is that normal? I think things are changing. By the time my youngest grandchild is an adult, she may not have a marriage in her life. I believe society will change drastically; relationships will change—they will have to. Humans simply do not move at the same rate—how do humans expect to grow at the same rate? Relationships have to change!"

Becky pointed to the recent breakup of her daughter's nine-year marriage, which left her a single mother raising three small children. "She divorced because she was not happy. She faces the same dilemma about relationships as I did, but she's strong enough to stand on her own right now, rather than to wait and have to go through what I have to deal with at my age [sixty-three]. Here she is, my daughter, a beautiful woman, and she can't find a meaningful relationship! What is the answer?"

Like many other divorces among CEO wives, Becky's took several years to adjudicate. At the beginning, when merely getting through the day seemed insurmountable, she told herself "it was either sink or swim, so I started swimming." As soon as Steve moved out of the house, she knew that, as someone who had always been surrounded by people and activity, she had to become involved in new things. Becky was unlike many of the CEO women, who have a strong religious faith and who turned to their churches for guidance and solace. She had been in therapy for several of the last years of the marriage but said she "probably went to the wrong person," for she found little help there. She tried several divorce recovery groups but left each one because "there were so many sad and hurting people, and that was not what I needed. I didn't want to wallow in misery with them."

She said she must have "intuited" that her marriage was "going south," because in its last years she tried to start a couples' dancing club. Steve came once or twice, but he was always late and was usually too tired to dance, so Becky gave it up. Now that she was divorcing, she arranged to take private ballroom-dancing classes, and dancing became her "savior, salvation, outlet, and healer." When she began to go to group classes, she met many others, both men and women, who were experiencing the same need for healing and recovery, all of whom turned to dancing as an outlet for their pain. That was how her first relationship began, with a newly divorced man a dozen years her junior. She found herself "trying to help him heal," but instead they "healed together" through dancing. The affair "ran out of steam," but Becky and he are still good friends who occasionally enter a local competition, especially for the tango, which they always win.

One of the most surprising findings in my interviews with the former wives of CEOs was how many of them told me that some form of dancing "saved" their lives. Dancing was the one constant in all their stories of personal recovery. When they spoke of it, their voices became buoyant, their bodies energized, their smiles broadened, and their eyes sparkled. Some could not help but sway to music only they were hearing as they described how good dancing lessons had been for them.

Maxine tried line dancing, and she, too, found her first male companionship there. He was "pleasant to be with for the first year or so" because unlike Bobby, "he was not hard-charging and obsessed with work. He was just an ordinary guy." Unfortunately the "ordinary guy got big ideas about what he could do with Bobby's money," so Maxine "kicked him out." She wasn't sorry, because like Becky, she has come to enjoy male companionship but on her terms.

There is one common and exceedingly painful problem for all these women who were goddesses of the home and hearth throughout their marriages: the holidays. Be they Christian, Jewish, or other, they all reported some of what Dana, the woman who spent twelve years decorating her various houses, said: "I kept it all together, kept on making the holidays for everybody Thousands of dollars of gifts, decorations, food and drink, and I was the one who had to organize it all. Now I have let a lot of that 'family stuff' go. It's sad and I regret it, but it's necessary for me to move on. Even though a lot of other people are dismayed, I have to think about myself now."

Dana's ex-husband, Evan, an internationally known lawyer, was so determined that she would not share in the assets he had carefully hidden in foreign banks and offshore accounts that he sued her twice to delay her lawyers. The divorce was so acrimonious and complicated that it took five years to complete and unfolded in two stages, mainly because Evan threw up so many roadblocks along the way. Because he was famous in their state, Dana hired and fired three lawyers (who were all in awe of Evan) until she found one who was willing to guide her through the mechanics of the courtroom procedure. Dana did not feel she had the best representation, but her goal was to stop the fighting and get it over with; she ended up giving Evan all the real estate and taking far less money than she was entitled to because at that point, "all I wanted was out."

Dana did not miss the constant hassle of dealing with every aspect of upkeep on their expensive and extensive properties, but she did miss the holiday celebrations she arranged in each of them. In the early years following her divorce, whenever the holidays approached, she felt "like half of me is cut off; maybe even more than half. He was the dominant one who planned our life, and everything revolved around him. I took care of everything else, of paying the bills, making travel arrangements, whatever we needed. I did nothing else but take care of him." Suddenly, she found herself alone and with nothing to do, and she was "vulnerable, shocked, hurt, depressed."

Then, being a "survivor," she "made [her]self busy." For her, ballroom dancing lessons led to professional competitions with a series of partners for the different dances. She sang in her church choir and with three other divorced women formed a "women's doo-wop" quartet, entertaining in nursing homes and children's hospitals. She learned to play bridge and entered tournaments; she revived her tennis and golf. With all this going on, whenever the holidays rolled around, she said, "I had schedules to keep, I had lessons, I had activities. I was too busy having fun to miss the hard work of getting ready for them." That is, until the actual day.

Dana was one of a number of women who told me how for the first several years after divorcing, they tried to re-create the happy family holiday scenes of their marriages and ended up crying over the dirty dishes when they were alone at the end of the day. By the third or fourth year, they were unwilling to go through it again, so they created new ways of celebrating. One woman whose internationally known ex-husband probably battered her (although she discreetly refrained from acknowledging it directly) told me she spent Thanksgiving and Christmas cooking dinners at a battered women's shelter where she had become a volunteer. Another told me she took her widowed mother and an unmarried sister on a "nice vacation, usually to some island." A Christian woman living in New York told me she joined her Jewish friends for "Chinese [food] and one movie after another, all day long."

All these women who, like Dana, "were totally taken care of" during their marriages, said that when the dust of their divorce battles settled, there was one thing they will absolutely insist upon as they face life alone: they will control their finances. Dana said, "I never want to be so blind and vulnerable and blindsided again. I am sure he has money and accounts I never knew he had, and at this point, I can't fester over that. I won't ever again live in the style I had with him, but I'll be okay. I have had to figure everything out on my own, but I did it when I got divorced. And I can do it and keep on doing it."

Money was a significant factor in Johanna's divorce. She was married for thirty-nine years to the CEO of an insurance company. They met when both were on holiday in Honolulu; he was a fighter pilot in Vietnam and she was a nurse in San Francisco. Johanna described Parker as a "survivor, ruthless in business, blessed with a unique talent for making people like and respect him and do whatever he wanted." He was unfaithful to her throughout her marriage, and she knew it; he was unfaithful to the wife who replaced her; and he is now unfaithful to his third wife. Still, the divorce was a blow that sent Johanna reeling. Financially, she said, she "cannot fault" Parker for her settlement, even though he did try to hide assets from her "barracuda of a divorce attorney." He did "try to cheat," but she was "satisfied" with the outcome. Her problem was that she could not "balance a checkbook or pay a bill, and had no idea what a tax form looked like." In the beginning, she was "a basket case, unable to breathe." She was "not a sane person, not a decent mother," and she thought she would have to kill herself until she managed to get to a 12-step program meeting. She chose Alcoholics Anonymous because "there was not enough therapy in all the world to help me" and because she was the child of alcoholic parents.

Johanna had spent her entire life avoiding liquor in any form, but she had avoided so many other things as well. She recognized and freely admitted that in the last years of her marriage she had become "anxious, fearful, almost agoraphobic." She went to 12-step meetings because she could not sleep but was afraid of medication and because after a meeting she "felt safe." She described herself in the aftermath of her divorce as "incapable of holding down a job; I couldn't even take care of myself." She "snapped out of it" after a meeting when she learned that she was "totally codependent" with her husband. "My life revolved around his moods. He controlled our family with his anger. My job was to turn him around, make him happy, and create the myth that we were all one big happy family. I created the myth of how I wanted us to be, and oh boy, did I have to work to do it." Johanna had, she said, to "learn how to rescue myself," and she did so by becoming a "conference junkie." She went to meetings, read books, and listened to tapes; eventually she went back to school for a degree in social work that, with a supplemental degree program and other course work, allowed her eventually to become a family nurse practitioner. Now she is proud that she has a good job, makes her own money, and can take care of herself.

Some of the women abandoned by CEO husbands want to take jobs, whether paying or not. Dana had been asked repeatedly by the wives she knew (original and new) when married to Evan if she would go into the decorating business and work for them. That gave her the idea that she might eventually want to buy real estate to fix up and sell. Becky thinks she will just enjoy dancing and her other interests until she gets tired of them, and then she will be grateful that she'll have the luxury to decide if she wants to work or not. The woman who volunteers at the battered women's shelter thinks she would like to go back to school for further training in social work. Lucy, the New Yorker who ate Chinese food and went to the movies on Christmas Day, thinks she will most likely spend the next year looking for a place to live on the West Coast, because she has found "the East

Coast is far more formal and the couples situation still rules, whereas in the West, it really doesn't matter if you're alone."

Whatever they plan to do, however, they all agree that life after divorce is "an interesting game that you have to learn to play. It is one for which you must invent the rules as you go along."

CHAPTER SIX

ADULT CHILDREN OF LATE-LIFE DIVORCE

Some people grew up during the Depression, some during World War II or Vietnam. That's how they place themselves historically: as children of some great defining calamity. I grew up during Divorce.
—WALTER KIRN, "My Parents' Bust-Up, and Mine"

THE LITTLE BOY who opened the door to a split-level house in a pleasant New Jersey suburb told me that his name was Jared and he was almost nine years old. He and his sister, Amy, were spending the weekend with their father and his father's "friend." I was there to interview his father, Randy, who had agreed to talk about how he felt when his parents divorced after forty-one years of marriage. Randy was so upset about it that he didn't want to be interviewed on the phone but said he would offer me "two for the price of one" if I came to see him on a weekend at his girlfriend's house. He was becoming "deeply involved" with Jennifer (whom he called Jenn), whose own parents had divorced after forty-four years. As we chatted in the family room, I noticed that Jared and Amy (who told me she would soon be five) were parked in front of the television and I assumed that both were engrossed in it rather than our conversation. But when Randy went into the kitchen to help Jenn with coffee and cookies, Jared bounced over to sit down beside me on the sofa.

"My mommy and daddy are divorced, too," he volunteered, smiling and cheerful. "They did it 'cause they don't love each other like mommies and daddies do, but they still love me and Amy best of all."

"Of course they do," I said, taken aback and not knowing how else to respond.

"My mommy and daddy told us they are not going to fight or be mean, because they love us so much." When he told me that his mother and father were often together "in my house," I surmised that he meant the house he and Amy lived in with their mother, where "Mommy and Daddy were always nice to each other."

Everything had gone silent in the kitchen, as if Randy and Jenn wanted to hear what Jared was saying, so I encouraged him to keep talking. He told me how his daddy had come to "my house" every weekend until Randy met Jenn, when he began to bring the children to New Jersey for most of the weekends they spent with him. Before that, he would travel to the Hudson River town where they lived with his ex-wife, Tara, sleeping in Jared's bottom bunk bed in the house where he had formerly lived as a married man. I learned later from Randy that he had a good salary as a master machinist and was able to give the family far more than the monthly child support stipulated in the divorce agreement.

On his weekends with the children, he took them shopping and bought anything they needed. He went to the market and loaded up on organic meats and produce, enough for the week to come, and enlisted the children's help in preparing Saturday-night dinners and something special for Sunday lunch. He baked cookies and made fresh pasta with them, engaged them in projects like building birdhouses in the winter or planting flowers in the summer, and in general devoted his every weekend moment to teaching them new skills or playing games with them. They watched movies and ate popcorn together, played board games or sports. And he telephoned them every night to hear about their day at school, what they had for dinner, and what they wanted to do with him on the weekend to come.

Now that Jenn was in his life, he took Jared and Amy into her home, which they had only recently begun to share. Jenn was in her early thirties and a decade younger than Randy. She had never been married and had inherited the house from her mother, who'd died of a fast-moving cancer less than two years after her own divorce. Jenn told me her mother had asked for the divorce but had become ill so soon after it was granted that she was unable to enjoy life away from a man who had been withdrawn, distant, and emotionally abusive throughout her marriage. Jenn was glad her mother divorced her father but terribly sad that all her post-divorce interactions with her mother and all her energies went into caring for her through a terminal illness. She had not yet begun to process how she felt about her father, who was happy to leave his marriage and move in with the secretary who had been his mistress for the seventeen years she worked for him.

Jenn was a paralegal who wanted to go to law school at some point, and she described herself as "rational and orderly." She cited these qualities as the most probable reason for what she called her "primary undigested emotion" toward her parents' divorce: "confusion." She thought she would like to go into therapy soon in order to "get it sorted out."

But Jared seemed to have none of the emotions I had thought young children of divorce were supposed to have. He spoke of it as if it were the most natural thing in the world. Half his class "was divorced," he told me, and then described how "mean" or "unhappy" so many of his friends were because their mothers and fathers "did bad stuff together." His friend Pammy, for example, was "really acting out" in school and in the disciplinary system used there was always "on the red" (for really bad behavior) or the "yellow" (caution). But her daddy had just left, Jared said knowingly, so she was "still real unhappy." He was sure that when "her mommy lets her daddy see her again," Pammy would surely "get back on the green" (for good behavior). When I asked him to tell me about himself in the classroom, he said he was always "on green" because things were different for him from the beginning; his mommy and daddy told him that even though they did not want to live with each other anymore, they would "always want to live" with him and Amy, and even though his daddy "slept in another house," they knew he would phone them daily and see them every weekend.

As we chatted, it became clear to me that divorce was a common way of life for this eight-year-old boy, as it was for so many of his classmates. It just happened and they all coped with it in their own individual fashion, but one thing that struck me was how they all helped one another through the initial tough time. Jared told me how they talked on the playground or at lunchtime in the cafeteria, and how "the older kids" (and he counted himself as one) helped "the littler ones" to deal with it. I was amazed at the sophisticated insight he showed when he described conversations he had had with some of his classmates. Not only did he comfort and soothe those who were hurting, he also offered advice on how to move beyond pain and blame and other recrimination. He was truly an amazing little boy, and when Randy and Jenn came back with the coffee, I could see the astonishment in their faces at how worldly-wise he had become about divorce.

Children like Jared have been tracked and followed, tested and studied, and the resulting research has been a great help to the many younger parents who end their marriages far earlier than their own parents did.[1] But even as gifted researchers followed so many young children into adulthood, the "adult children of divorce" were, for the most part, neglected.

"I often see adult children who think they are the sun and the parents are only the planets who revolve around them," said a divorce attorney who asked not to be identified. It is difficult for them to realize and sometimes crushing for them to have to accept that their parents have needs, and divorce might be one of them."

The term itself, "adult children of divorce," is a misnomer, but for the life of me, I can't think of a better one to describe the situation of people who were between the ages of twenty and fifty when their parents divorced. On second thought, the term might be the best one to describe adults who suddenly find themselves swept back into childhood as they are forced to reengage in the dynamics of their birth family. Even though they may be adults with their own grown children and some may have already been through their own divorces, they find themselves back where they started, playing the roles the family settled upon them: the eldest son is once again the child who was "responsible for fixing everything"; the middle daughter was always "the family airhead, the one nobody ever expected to amount to a hill of beans," so no one pays much attention to her; and the youngest child is still the one who "gets away with murder" and who will always be forgiven for a multitude of sins. Now the trauma of their parents' divorce is forcing these adults to find a way to combine the roles they played in the birth family with the very different ones they play in their adult lives, and to reconcile them both.

I spoke to eighty-four of these adult children of divorce and gained some interesting insights into their thoughts and emotions. My earliest interviews were with some of the adult children whose mothers and fathers I had already interviewed, after I asked the parents if they thought any or all of their children would be willing to talk to me. The responses from both the parents and children were mixed, as some of the parents did not want me to talk to the children for a variety of reasons.

Usually it was the father who objected, believing that the children had sided with their mother and would not be fair to him in interviews. If the mother did not want the adult children to talk to me, her ostensible reason was that she didn't want to "make them revisit the pain they suffered." These mothers often used the excuse that their children had been so traumatized by the divorce that they must not be asked to relive it, but I learned that in many cases it was simply a screen for the mothers themselves to hide behind. It was certainly true in some cases that the mothers wanted to protect their children from further pain, but it was far more likely (as I found out when the adult children sought me out despite their parents trying to keep them from it) that the mothers had conflicting emotions about their part in the divorce process and their subsequent behavior, and did not want the children to tell me what they thought about it. Many of these adult children were eager to talk about their perceptions and volunteered to do it, even though some of the parents did not want them to participate. I would say that about half my respondents came to me in this manner.

When I told some of these adult children of divorce that I was surprised by how eager they were to talk to me, the majority responded by saying that "a terrible thing" had happened to them, that is, that they had been unwilling participants in their parents' divorce and that nobody before me had come along to express an interest in what they had experienced in the process. One man, age thirty-five at the time of our interview and an only child of parents who ended a forty-seven-year marriage, told me, "I felt like the odd man out, as if nobody cared what I was going through." I repeated the expression "odd man out," to my next several interviewees who were having trouble defining their emotions, and they seized upon it eagerly, saying how accurately it described the way they felt after their parents had gone separate ways.

In general, I found that if there were three children in a family of late-life divorce and I contacted them all, one would usually refuse an interview outright and would not change his or her mind; two might well refuse at first, but one of the two who initially refused would eventually decide to talk to me. The third would often reconsider, usually because of what a sibling reported back after talking to me. I found that around half the children in any marriage, whether from two to six or more, would consent to discuss how they experienced their parents' divorces. Of this half, a surprising statistic emerged: the daughters were more likely not to want to talk, whereas the sons were eager to do so, and at great length. In the final tally of my eighty-four respondents, forty-nine were men and only thirty-five were women. This was exactly the opposite of my experience with their parents, where the women were eager to tell their stories in full detail and with no holds barred, while the men were far more circumspect—if they consented to speak at all. My informal deduction was that, although men were deeply hurt and confused by their parents' divorces, women experienced a far more complex range of emotions, from shame, humiliation, and embarrassment to anger, outrage, and fear. And the fear was not of what their parents had done but about the outcome of their own emotional attachments, whether in legal marriage or informal living together. "What's going to happen to me?" I heard them ask time after time. "Will I be just like her [or him]? Will nothing last for me either?"

"A PAINLESS WAY OUT OF THIS FORTY-YEAR-OLD NEUROTIC MESS"

The Israeli novelist A. B. Yehoshua tells the story of an elderly couple's divorce through the eyes of all the participants in the marriage, including the three adult children and their spouses. One of them is a lawyer who has been charged by his wife and her siblings to attend to "the legal termination of [his in-laws'] hundred-year war," and he is frustrated with trying to persuade everyone to let him handle it:

*I said I'd do it and I will as long as they let me do it my way. Just let the
family keep out of it and I'll hand the old folks their divorce all signed
sealed and delivered. . . . Just all of you keep out of it. If there's an ounce
of sanity among you you'll leave it to me to find a painless way out of
this forty-year-old neurotic mess.*[2]

Like the fractious adult children in Yehoshua's novel, those to whom I spoke
usually had differing perspectives on their family histories. They often began by telling me they wanted to "share" or "express" their "feelings" in the
hope that they would better understand what had happened to their family.
At the end of the conversation many would admit that they were already in
therapy or had begun it specifically because of their parents' divorce. Then
they told me how "therapeutic" it was to have an "informal but in-depth"
conversation, as my questions had helped them to see themselves and their
parents in "surprising" new ways. Many were eager for their next therapy
session so they could share these new feelings with their analysts.

I found that the adult children's responses to parents' late-life divorces
generally fell into three categories, but in each one they used the same word
to describe how they felt when their parents broke the news. The majority
of the respondents reported feeling "devastated"; the next-largest group was
"angry" that after so many years, the parents "could not find a way to keep it
all together"; and the third group, by far the smallest, felt only "relief" that
the parents had finally decided to end the marriage. This was the group who
believed their parents stayed together all those years "for the sake of the
children," and most of these adult children told me their initial reaction was
"What took you so long?"

Joseph Lelyveld, a former executive editor of *The New York Times*, described his feelings, a combination of exhaustion and relief, when his parents ended their long marriage: "My deepest response to the looming end
of the marriage without which I would never have existed was not terribly
deep. This play had already had too many acts, and we were all tired."[3]

Adam, a man I interviewed, mirrored Lelyveld's feelings but with a twist.
He snorted sarcastically and said how much better off he and his two sisters
would have been had the divorce happened earlier: "They stayed together

for thirty years of all-out war and produced three full-fledged neurotics in the process!" His parents married during World War II and stayed together until "the sixties happened and it was okay to split." Neither remarried and each lived alone contentedly for another twenty-five years before they died. Still, Adam and his sisters agreed that they "never entirely got over our resentment that we had to grow up in such an unhappy home."

My interviews with the adult children usually took place after I had heard their parents' stories, and as I listened to each one, I could not help but remember what the man in Switzerland told me of his own marital breakup, that there were five truths involved: his, his wife's, and those of their three children. Of course it was only natural that divorcing couples would want to put the best gloss on the reasons for and the outcome of their divorces, and that they would describe their children as relatively unscathed or, at the very least, coping well in a situation that was unhappy for everyone. Some, however, such as the women I've written about earlier, were perceptive enough to see that the impact on their children had serious unfortunate consequences. Suzanne, for example, described her three children's attitudes about relationships with eagle-eyed clarity, and Mary knew how angry her children were when she left Phil but proceeded with serenity to do it anyway.

THE DEVASTATED

Roger and Wanda (whose history I've given in chapter 5) had three sons who were among the "devastated" adult children when they learned of their parents' divorce, and whose separate truths were indeed far different from those of their parents. Sam, the middle son, was in his late twenties when his father casually admitted during a lull in a family dinner attended by all three sons that there was "a bit of trouble" in the marriage. Later, when Roger took each son separately to a restaurant to break the news, Sam was "shocked," because he had always regarded Roger and Wanda as "complacent, settled into something that would always be there." In his mid-thirties at this writing, Sam realized that Roger was "trying to plant a seed" at that family dinner, but he remained unsure of what: "He told me 'there is a chance,' but he didn't say of what, of staying together or getting a divorce."

Sam said that shortly after that dinner, when Roger said he wanted a six-month "trial separation" and moved out of the family home, it was painful to watch Wanda "hoping for the best as she sat there and watched her life disintegrate." By the time the trial separation ended, Roger was already involved with the woman he would soon begin to live with. Sam talked to me five years after this happened but he still felt the need to explain why he feels "so much emotional devastation": "It has been five years since my father walked out, and to this day I don't know if my parents' marriage is legally over. I don't know if they are actually divorced. He has been with another woman now for more than four years, going on five, and when I ask him if he intends to marry her, he tells me 'there will be a right time.' He thinks he is letting us all down easily, but the point is—he has caused so much anger and pain for all of us."

Dan, the eldest son, did not want to talk about his parents' marital situation. Sam and Tim, the youngest, both believe it is because, as Sam put it, "Dan is the most like our father, the one who has created the same kind of marriage our mom and dad had. We think he is scared now, that what happened to them might happen to him."

Tim, who was still in college when Roger left Wanda, told me that he was the son "who probably had the hardest time of it." He admitted that he was the closest to Wanda and gave that as the reason he nearly flunked out at the end of his fall semester. He took the spring term off and moved back home to be with her, but she convinced him that he needed to return to school and he did so the following fall. Five years later, being in Roger's company was still difficult for Tim, because he is convinced his father thinks he has "chosen a side and it is not his." Tim said this is not true, but because they are so uneasy with each other, there is no way to discuss it. Besides, his father "always feels resentful and guilty," and because communication between them was always so superficial, no explanations are possible. I asked him to explain what he perceives as Roger's attitude toward him. "Resentment because he is in this other relationship and he is happier in it than he was with our mother and us; guilt because he knows he has caused a huge upheaval in our family and has hurt us terribly."

Of the three sons, Sam is the one who presses Roger hardest to explain himself, and the one who has the prickliest relationship with him. When

Roger moved out, Wanda left all his things in place, exactly as he left them and ready for him to come back and use them as if he had never been away. Sam insisted that Wanda pack up everything from books, to clothing, to unused and unwanted sports equipment, and either give it to charity or store it in the basement. When Sam asked Roger what he wanted to do with all the boxes, Roger became furious, saying he still owned half the house and had a right to keep his things where he left them. Sam told him he could not "have it both ways," and in the argument that followed, Roger told Sam, "there were things he didn't know." Sam demanded to be told what they were. "So my father told me one story, and then my mother told me another. And these were very differentfrom the stories they told my brothers. It was very clear to me that nobody was telling anyone else the truth about anything."

All three sons have learned to cope in different ways. Sam and Tim believe that Dan "carries on in the family tradition. When our family was together, everything was always fine: no anger, resentment, no raised voices. Things were always just fine. That's how he's living his marriage now." Tim says he copes by being able to process "only so much information at a time." He still "has problems trying to handle the totality of the breakup, the finality of it." He is engaged to be married and tells me he is grateful his fiancée has agreed "to wait until we have everything talked out about how we want to be in a relationship with each other."

Sam thinks his brothers have chosen marriage as a way to "repair what was broken" when Roger walked out. Sam doesn't "feel the need to repair, but rather, to figure out how to replace what was obviously missing all those years." Of the three, he is the "most skeptical of marriage." He has had several long relationships with "interesting women" since his parents separated, but he cannot "commit" until he can find a way to "deal with the issues, and the main one is honesty." Roger and Wanda constructed a "façade" instead of a marriage, and he does not want to "repeat that mistake." He thought his parents "had resigned themselves to an unromantic life in a placid marriage, but obviously not. After all, my dad did walk out." This makes him wonder about "people who don't change as the relationship progresses. All the years of resentment, disappointment, even anger, they let them all build up until the structure of the marriage breaks." He concluded that "marriage needs both honesty and the acceptance of change." Ultimately, however, he believes everyone should learn to regard all relationships, but particularly marriage, in "less permanent terms."

What Sam "has not been able to figure out is what marriage really means." It was too easy to joke and tell him that when he finds the answer, he can retire as a billionaire, but he remained serious: "Part of me is still very romantic and wants marriage. I don't believe in divorce and I don't subscribe to the 'opt-out-of-marriage' clause it provides. My parents' divorce has caused me to look more critically at marriage. Now I can see that they made a lot of compromises that were not healthy for them and certainly not for us children." He suddenly became so emotional that I thought he might not want to continue after he blurted out: "I cannot fathom how two people who had three kids, owned a big house, and had terrific careers and decades of life with each other and were loved by everyone, could just up and walk away from a marriage."

After a pause and with his voice choking, he told me about his "deepest pain" and the "surprise" he still feels about how much it continues to affect him: "That house was a place of love and warmth. Family and friends were always welcome. All the holidays happened in that house. Now it is all painful, all fractured. I feel homeless. I cannot go back to that house. It takes effort and energy for me to go there. That home was a psychological symbol, a place of permanence where my brothers and I could always go. Now it is gone. I would rather stay with my friends than go back to my mother's house, and I certainly won't stay with my father and his girlfriend."

Sam says he has had his own breakups, but none have affected him as much as his parents' divorce has, because it caused him to "lose his home" and "feel homeless."

Tim expressed the same feelings about the family home. He said he never told Wanda that the reason he accepted her advice to go back to college at the first opportunity was because "the old love-filled house" had become "so unhappy" for him. He, however, points to something positive that came out of the "devastation" of his parents' divorce: "I got to see my parents in human terms, to make strong individual relationships with them. In some ways, it was kind of weird, kind of like me becoming the parent to each of them. Especially when my mother started to date and she'd come to me and ask for advice."

This is not true for Sam, who has to "create distance" between himself and both parents: "I see them, but on my own terms and in my own time. I have to keep distance for my own self-protection."

Tim said that one day, in a fit of anger, he asked Roger how he was to deal with "certain aspects of feelings about his parents' divorce." Roger told him "it always takes children longer to assimilate divorce because by the time the parents tell them, they are already out of the marriage and they have already dealt with their feelings." Sam's only comment to me was "And this is supposed to give me comfort?"

Sam told me about a friend whose parents divorced when the boy was very young, and how emotional this friend was for several years afterward. He remembered this vividly when his own parents divorced, saying he resents it that young children are expected, indeed encouraged, to express their emotions while adult children are expected to take it in stride, which is the equivalent of hiding or suppressing them: "No matter the age, the children should be allowed to mourn if they want to." Sam does not believe his own feelings of "powerlessness and disappointment will ever go away," and he wonders if other adult children of divorce share these emotions. Now that his parents are divorced, Sam mourns that "my brothers and I have nothing to fall back on."

THE ANGRY ONES

Barry and Amanda, the children of Richard and Priscilla, were also among the "devastated" when they learned of their parents' divorce. They added "anger" to their devastation, especially after Priscilla told them she had known about Richard's affair with Evelyn for the last ten years of the marriage. Priscilla told her children she found out about it when Richard said he was "tired of the duplicity" and told her so. Like Wanda and many other women, Priscilla thought the bonds of home and family would eventually be strong enough to win him back and keep him in the marriage, but in the end they were not.

The parents told the children of their impending divorce in the same way they presented everything else in their genteel, well-mannered family life: they had "something important to tell," and they asked Barry and Amanda to come home on a Friday night in time for cocktails and dinner. They were to come without their spouses and be prepared to spend the night in their childhood bedrooms. Getting there was not a problem for Amanda, who lived in the same town, but it was for Barry, who lived and worked two states away. When he phoned Amanda to find out "what's up," she told him to "just come." Afterward, she admitted that she thought it might be "about some kind of separation but certainly not about divorce." As everyone in the family was "always so guarded about personal things," she was not sure beforehand and did not want to worry Barry unnecessarily.

Barry arrived in time for cocktails, and everyone settled into the living room with the ritual first drink. He remembers that Priscilla did the talking while Richard "sat there as if she were telling us about the latest quarterly dividends instead of the news that he was breaking up our family forever." When he was able to assimilate what Priscilla was actually saying, Barry, who calls himself "the verbal one in the family," said he was stunned into "the silence of disbelief." Priscilla told them Richard had asked her for a divorce and she had agreed to give it to him because for the past fifteen or so years he had been "having an affair, no—really, having a second marriage"— with his office manager, Evelyn.

The dinner hour came and went with all four so emotionally exhausted that they couldn't leave the living room and go to the dining room table. Amanda recalled the conversation as "our family's usual stilted avoidance of unpleasant things" until it suddenly turned "uncharacteristically dramatic and angry." Barry's first reaction was "devastation," which soon changed to "anger at my father and a feeling of betrayal for myself and my mother." Amanda was "devastated and hurt, and then in a strange way, relieved. I live in this town and even though nobody ever said anything directly, I suppose I had suspicions."

Throughout the hours they sat in the living room, Richard responded quietly to questions from his children but always managed to return firmly to his main point: that he and Priscilla had grown apart many years before, that he thought he had found a way to answer his emotional needs while remaining in the marriage but had become tired of the "half life, the double life," and wanted "everything out in the open." Priscilla said very little, even though Barry bombarded her with angry questions about her feelings, asking "over and over again how she could have played this lousy game for so many years."

By this time, Priscilla was crying steadily. Richard left to go to Evelyn's, and Amanda said she could not stay the night but had to go to her own home and family in order to "digest the terrible news." Barry was left alone in the house with Priscilla, and from that moment on, he became "the middleman, the unwilling participant," in his parents' divorce. Richard had always been a distant and aloof father; Priscilla had been the "warm parent, the one who expressed feelings and made it okay for us to express ours." Barry and Amanda were always closest to Priscilla, and as she was the one "betrayed and abandoned," both children thought it "only natural" that they should gravitate to her because "she was the one who most needed help." They did not see it as "taking sides," although they felt Richard did and resented them for it, particularly when both children demanded that, in order to protect Priscilla, they should be allowed to pass judgment on the division of the couple's financial assets.

Priscilla had a family inheritance that was to remain hers if she and Richard parted. She also had her income from a museum job she held for many years, which included a pension and benefits. Richard's medical practice was lucrative, and he also had a modest legacy from an aunt. He had inherited some "old family furniture" that turned out to be valuable antiques when Priscilla had it appraised. Richard moved into Evelyn's house the same night he told Barry and Amanda of the impending divorce. He said he wanted nothing from the house but his personal possessions, not even his family furniture. He told Priscilla she was free to dispose of the house and its contents as she wished, and he also agreed to all the terms her divorce lawyer presented, so at first glance she appeared to be financially well situated. They agreed to everything with their usual "good manners and good breeding," according to Barry, who thought "they behaved like two people divvying up Great-Aunt Mary's china and silver rather than the effects of a lifetime together." However, Barry and Amanda both foresaw problems, and it turned out that they were prescient.

"No one ever talks about money, which is so important and so problematic," Amanda said. In their separate interviews, she and Barry raised the same concern. Barry said, "Our parents were married so long, and in this state, their assets had to be divided fifty-fifty. Our mother will have to use all her money just to live out what will probably be a long and healthy span of life. The problem will be what happens when our father marries Evelyn. Evelyn has only her salary to support herself and her children. She'll want some of his money for herself and her kids. And he's reaching the age where his health is going to require lots of caretaking on her part. Will she let us use his money for this? Will she want more from us if it runs out? Does this mean the kids from his first family will get the short end of the stick, or that we'll even get nothing?" In the end, Barry was right, and he and Amanda got very little.

In fact, Richard married Evelyn as soon as his divorce was final. Evelyn did ask for half of his money, and tried, unsuccessfully, to tie it up so his children couldn't touch it. She petitioned in court for more of Richards assets to come directly to her, but Barry and Amanda successfully had it blocked.

These two adult children had been counting on a sizeable bequest coming their way in time to pay for the education of their own children, and now they had to scramble to find the money elsewhere. The lawyer who represented Priscilla in the divorce proceedings told Barry and Amanda that they were being forced to learn a hard truth, that no child has a right to an inheritance from parents; parents are free to do as they please, and in this case, they did.

Priscilla was bewildered by the many decisions she had to make after Richard left, so Amanda phoned her every day and became a frequent visitor. But it was Barry to whom Priscilla turned. She needed "a lot of comforting at first," and if she didn't beg him to come for the weekends, Amanda (who was unable to cope with her) did, having to leave her own family in the process. Her husband, Jim, helped her weather this crisis, but it did not help Barry that his parents' divorce came at a crucial time in his own marriage. He and Claudia had been married for ten years and had two young daughters, seven and five. Claudia worked full-time as a legal-aid attorney, and they were still trying "to establish our own home and our own traditions." Their children were involved in sports and other activities in which Barry, "unlike my own dad, wanted to be a hands-on father and participate." Instead of cheering them on at ball games and recitals, for almost a full year he commuted at least two weekends every month to help Priscilla sort out her life and move forward.

The only positive thing about his parents' divorce was that it brought him and Claudia closer because she, too, was the adult child of divorced parents and sharing that status strengthened their bond. Amanda said the same thing about her marriage to Jim (whose parents remained in an unhappy marriage), that they talked a lot about how they must work harder to "keep the lines of communication open" between them, and how she thought that, "at least for now," they were succeeding.

The hardest part of Richard and Priscilla's divorce for both Barry and Amanda occurred when Priscilla was finally able to bring herself to make decisions, first about selling the house and buying an apartment, then about divesting herself of "things that had been in the family forever." This was difficult for the three of them, but most of all for Barry because "I am the one who adores that house and I am having a hard time accepting that it will not be there anymore." He was the one who did not want to sell or give anything away but "wanted to take everything and store it in my basement." He praised Claudia for helping him to "let go of things, to invite the cousins in to take what we didn't want and give the rest to charity."

For Barry the "next-hardest part" of his parents' divorce was his worry about what he would tell his children. Again, Claudia guided him through it. Her parents had divorced while the children were babies, so they grew up knowing them as separate entities. Claudia told her daughters that Grandpa Richard and Grandma Priscilla would visit them separately from now on, just the way their other grandparents did. Both accepted the announcement without question, but Barry was highly upset that the seven-year-old was sad for several months because she could no longer go to his family home for holidays.

Barry and Claudia think their marriage has "benefited in a strange way" now that both sets of parents are divorced. They "grab on to the subject of divorce eagerly," read newly published books and articles about it, and watch talk shows on the subject. They joke that their tenth-anniversary dinner was "incredibly close and erotic" because they spent it talking about their parents' divorces and how they would not let them have an effect on their personal future: "We both worry that what happened to our parents might happen to us. As we age, and as we approach certain anniversary years, we worry about how or when the dissolution of a marriage begins and what, if anything, we can do to stop it. We hope that taking honest stock of ourselves will be enough to keep us together."

WHEN A MOTHER LEAVES

Marianne, who divorced Michael to marry her lover, Bill, left behind three angry adult children. What the eldest daughter, thirty-year-old Kelly, resented most of all was that her mother left the family home in Dallas for a new life in Tulsa without telling her and her brother, Jason, twenty-eight, and sister, Kim, twenty-four. Kelly learned what her mother had done when she phoned her father to ask why he wasn't visiting his grandchildren as regularly as usual. He made so many excuses that she sensed something was wrong, so she showed up unexpectedly the next day to take him to lunch near his workplace. Always direct and forceful, Kelly eventually got Michael to admit that Marianne had left him "adrift on a sea of confusion." That afternoon, Kelly phoned Jason and Kim and told them what little she knew, which was that Marianne had been having an affair, had gone to live with her lover, and wanted a divorce to be free to marry him. The three siblings agreed to meet at the family home that evening, to see what comfort they could give to Michael but mostly to try to find out what happened and "plot strategy" before they contacted Marianne to hear her side of the story.

Kelly was "unbelievably furious" that Marianne had not only left home without telling her children but also that she had not even left her new address with Michael. She told him to tell the children they could contact her on her cell phone if there was an emergency. Although the three children had agreed that they would not get in touch with Marianne before they met that evening, Kelly was so angry that she could not resist phoning her mother beforehand. Later, she admitted it was "the wrong thing to do," because "as a trained social worker, I should have known better." She lost her temper and "yelled, screamed, and sobbed" into the receiver as she demanded that Marianne "explain herself." When she hung up, she had scant recollection of what Marianne said, remembering only "something like it was now or never so she had to do it, and she was really happy with Bill and she hoped we would understand."

Marianne remembered trying to explain to Kelly why she left, saying she repeated over and over again the same phrase: "I have a right to live my life. I'm a person, too!" That was when Kelly "screamed the loudest," accusing Marianne of "selfishness." In Kelly's mind, Marianne had "destroyed" the family by putting her personal needs ahead of all others. Marianne begged Kelly for understanding, cautioning that relationships change over time and the needs of partners within these relationships sometimes veer in totally unexpected directions. Speaking as a mother, she told her daughter that she hoped Kelly's marriage would always proceed along the tandem path it had taken thus far, but that Kelly should heed her example and "always be prepared for the unexpected." That was when Kelly slammed down the receiver.

That night, Kelly told Jason and Kim that she had made the phone call but did not go into detail about the conversation except to relate Marianne's "selfishness." They weren't angry with Kelly for phoning because "Kelly always does what she wants to do no matter what." They were, however, curious about why their mother hadn't offered an explanation or a defense that they could "accept and live with." They told Kelly they were so bewildered they didn't know what they should do next. They expected her to guide them because they had always bowed to her as being the most like their mother and the forceful and domineering presence within the family. Kelly was so self-confident that they usually accepted her judgment and did whatever she told them was the right thing to do.

Jason thought he and Kim were "too confused to think straight and only became angry" with Marianne after they saw how enraged Kelly was. Later, Kim said, "it sort of sank in, that she had done a very selfish thing, and then I began to hate her for it." Jason used the term "dishonorable" and said he was ashamed to call Marianne his mother. His confusion was magnified when he started to worry that at age twenty-eight and newly engaged, he was having "mixed emotions" that might indicate he had "inherited some [of Marianne's] run-away genes." His fiancée, twenty-six, was a strict observer of a religion that did not condone sex before marriage, and she still lived at home with her parents. After a "rocky year's engagement" full of sexual tension, she had just persuaded Jason that they should get married right away. All of a sudden, "everything was up in the air" for him and he was afraid of where he might "land."

Kelly, the only married sibling, seemed to Kim to be "the boss in her marriage as she was in everything else," what with her clear and firm opinions about everything. It was Kelly who shepherded Michael to a divorce recovery group meeting at a nearby church, and it was she who supervised what she called his "personal recovery from depression." She even made sure he went to group-therapy sessions that were modeled on daily 12-step meetings.

Kim, the baby of the family, was then living with a female roommate. She resented that Kelly tried to "run" her life and that Marianne had always allowed her to do so because "she was too busy with her own interests." After much hedging, Kim told me she knew her mother thought she was gay, and Kelly probably thought so as well. Close to tears, she said she was not a lesbian but was "afraid to get involved with a man" because of how Marianne and Kelly had always treated men with such "callous indifference." She said one of her teachers told her she was a "gentle soul" and urged her to "toughen up," but she found it easier just to "steer clear of involvements."

A year after Marianne married Bill, Michael was finally ready to sell the family house and move into an apartment. Kelly supervised the sale and Michael's relocation and was still urging her reluctant father to "get involved," especially with the singles' group at the local Unitarian church. Jason's fiancée broke off their engagement, and his chief emotion was "relief" that he could "start all over again, on a better foundation this time." Kim got a better-paying job, which allowed her to move into her own apartment and live without a roommate. She had no romantic relationships and wanted none. All three siblings remained "angry" with their mother, whom they had met individually in restaurants on the several occasions when business brought her to Dallas. Each time, she repeated her "mantra," trying to persuade them that "I am a person, too, with my own needs and wants." They were not convinced that she had the right to break up their family, and beyond these restaurant meals, they had no contact with her.

Kelly, Jason, and Kim say they are still angry with Marianne but "even worse" (as Kim put it), they have decided that they are angry with one another as well, because nobody seems able to provide the support and sustenance the others need.

Lauren was also angry with her mother, Virginia, because "she had husband number three all picked out before she got rid of number two, and for the twenty-six years she was with him, we all adored number two." Lauren was the older of Virginia's two children by her first husband in a marriage that she ended after eleven years. When Virginia decided to end her second marriage, to Joe, Lauren was in her late thirties and on her own second marriage. Virginia gave the same reason for both divorces, that she and Joe had "nothing in common" and "it was better to be single again than remain in a loveless marriage." Lauren felt "pity" for Joe, who told her Virginia's decision to end their marriage felt "like a freight train snuck up" on him. He had no idea there was anything amiss, but Lauren said she "suspected all along there was a new man hiding behind the curtains—with my mother, there always was."

The first time Virginia announced that she had "nothing in common anymore" with a husband was when Lauren was nine and Davey was almost eight and the husband was their father. One of Lauren's cousins told her that her mother was divorcing her father and would soon be marrying Joe, a widower with three adopted children. Because their father was always absent from family life and Lauren and Davey hardly knew him, Lauren's primary thought was how nice it would be to have more brothers and sisters, especially Joe's children because both families lived in the same neighborhood and the children attended the same school.

But Lauren didn't believe what her cousin told her about the divorce because her father was "always traveling," so why should her mother want to get rid of a man who was never around "to cause any bother"? In those years, she confided "everything" to her mother, but this time, she thought the idea of divorce was so ridiculous that she didn't even mention what her cousin had told her. Several weeks later it came as "only a little shock" when Virginia told Lauren and Davey that their father would not be coming home anymore. It was their "joint decision," she added cheerfully, so the children were not to be unhappy about it. Dutifully, they obeyed and "stayed happy." Lauren and Davey had "no real sense of loss at all" over their father, who simply disappeared from their lives.

Lauren was looking forward to having Joe as her new father, for she knew how loving and caring he was to his own children and wanted some of that attention for herself. Even though Virginia made no mention of Joe when she told her children their father would not be returning, they knew Joe would soon be a part of their lives and they were eager to have a "real father" for the first time who would let them become part of a large and happy family. "And that's what we were, for almost twenty-seven years," Lauren said, "and that is why I am so angry with her now, for destroying our family."

Lauren was correct that Virginia always has the next husband waiting in the wings before she sheds the one at hand, and indeed, within a year after she divorced Joe, she was remarried to a man in her social circle with whom she had long shared a mutual attraction. He ended his marriage of thirty-nine years at the same time Virginia divorced Joe, and "as soon as convention allowed," they married and moved into a new house in the same old neighborhood. Virginia told Lauren she "was not expecting criticism for what she did" and was "deeply hurt" when the new couple encountered "shunning" by their old friends and neighbors. Lauren called this Virginia's "ability to spin" and resents her for "blaming the neighborhood for bad behavior rather than accepting that she was the cause of it."

She described her mother as "emotionally controlling, able to create the world she wants you to believe is real, although it is not." Repeating that for twenty-seven years during Virginia's marriage to Joe, the five children lived in a large house filled with family, friends, and a motley assortment of pets, Lauren adopted a tone of fake amazement to say, "Now—suddenly—she has this 'epiphany,' and she tells us she has been unhappy for years, and she expects us to believe it." Lauren said Virginia's behavior has left her "personally deeply conflicted" because of how she conducts her life: "I want to stress that my mother is a deeply moral person. Her choices are almost heroic as she defies convention in this very conventional town where we live. But I object to the way she tries to control the perception of what she did in all the others who are unfortunately forced to become involved in her decisions."

All five children were furious with Virginia for how she timed the announcement of her divorce from Joe, which happened at a "pre-anniversary" dinner they were hosting for the children at an expensive restaurant. The dinner was held several weeks before their actual anniversary because Joe was planning to take Virginia to Buenos Aires, where she had long wanted to go. At the dinner, four of the five children sat with long, sad faces, fearing that something portentous was about to happen. Joe's youngest child and only daughter, Sara, demanded to know why everyone was so gloomy, and Virginia blurted, "Oh, what the hell, we might as well get it all on the table." She told them what the elder ones feared, that she and Joe had agreed to divorce. Sara was "deeply resentful that she was the last to be informed." Davey "knew it was coming" but was "so shut down it felt kind of weird." His relationship with his mother had always been distant and troubled, so he "didn't really give a damn what she did." Both Joe's sons, Jamie and Jack, were angry with Virginia for breaking up the only family they ever really knew. All five children said they felt " 'manipulated,' 'mad,' 'hurt,' 'embarrassed,' 'ashamed.' " Although they were all angry with Virginia, Lauren thinks it is she, as the oldest, who was (and still is) the angriest for "how she conned us all those years."

Of them all, Lauren has had the most difficulty accepting Virginia's third marriage. Because she has "a complex snarl of feelings" about Virginia, the third marriage caused her to resume analysis with a therapist she had been seeing since her own first marriage ended. Virginia's "sluffing off husbands she tires of" brought Lauren to a "crossroad," and "like any woman at a crossroad, I need to sort things out." Lauren was seventeen when she first got married, to a man who was thirty-five and divorced. She knew when she married him that it was "an inappropriate match." She also knew early on that she did not love him and was "out the door" at the first opportunity. Virginia was resigned when Lauren married but livid when she divorced: "What I did was inappropriate by my mother's standards. Not the divorce itself, but that I did not create a good departure scenario. She did not give me the emotional support I needed. Only after I was divorced and desperate did she give me financial support. That's when she established her pattern with me: she is always generous with aid but never with comfort."

Lauren married her second husband when she was "coming out of a major depression." He is closer to her in age but was also divorced with children from an earlier marriage toward whom she "feels bad" that she cannot "mother." She describes herself as "happily married now but not without my own baggage. I know I crave security, and I know that it comes from my personal experience." Her strongest feelings about human relationships, particularly about marriage, are "cynicism and skepticism." She explained: "When I am with friends in solid marriages or whose parents have been married forever, I manage to see the cracks in everything. I always point out the downside, and I know I make them unhappy. I think it's because I have been burdened with shame, about my mother and myself, and I am conscious of how toxic shame can be."

FOR THE SAKE OF THE CHILDREN

Allie was the "little afterthought" of elderly parents who began divorce proceedings after forty-seven years of marriage. She thinks they had her after their two older daughters were grown because they wanted to "save the marriage," and despite their behavior after they separated, she thinks they should have ended the marriage years before they actually did. Both Ronald and Shirley were in their late seventies when they separated. Three acrimonious years later, when they were about to be legally divorced, Ron died suddenly of a heart attack. At the time, Allie was thirty-eight and her two older sisters were fifty-two and sixty-four. Both were married grandmothers who lived on the West Coast, where Allie thinks they moved to get as far away from their fractious parents as they could.

Allie thinks her older siblings must have known their parents in a different way than she did, and that there must have been "different stages" in their parents' marriage, but all she can remember is that they were "always fighting, always emotionally overwrought." So much about them remained "mysterious," because her sisters "were of a different generation and they glossed over everything." By the time Ron and Shirley decided to separate, Allie was the only one around, so she became the child who "went back and forth between them with a legal pad—he was in the living room and she was in the bedroom, and it was up to me to see to the arrangements for dividing up the things."

Allie grew up as a lonely child and in effect "an only child" who could never understand why Shirley and Ron could not get along. Both came from a midsized New Jersey town and were of the same social class and similar background: Shirley's parents were a bank manager and a school-teacher; Ron's father was the chief accountant in a factory and his mother gave piano lessons from the home. Allie thought they had everything in common, from people to politics, music, and movies. However, "they were just highly conflicted about each other. They simply could not get along."

Allie was thirty-one and living in New York when she married Mark. Because her parents were so argumentative and because she was "sort of a hippie in those days," she and Mark decided to go to New York's city hall for a civil ceremony, after which they invited her parents (his were both dead) and a few friends to gather in a Chinese restaurant. Shirley swept dramatically into the restaurant and stunned the wedding party by announcing, "Your father is on his way home from Florida with his mistress, and tonight I am going to kill myself." Allie, who was used to such "drama queen pronouncements" and had also "drunk quite a lot of champagne by then," told Shirley not to kill herself but to "go home, pack your things, and move out instead."

Allie described what happened over the next seven years as "the short version: they sold their house and gave up their middle-class existence for Shirley to live on the second floor of a three-family house and for Ron to move in with his girlfriend in a trailer park. According to Allie, "that's when the real trouble began." Shirley "was in such a wacky place" that she accused Allie of taking Ron's side even as she tried to manipulate her into becoming a "superconfidante." If Allie visited Shirley on a weekend afternoon, she would follow when Allie left to make sure that she got directly on the highway leading back to New York and did not stop at the trailer park. If Allie told Shirley she planned to stop at the trailer park to see Ron before driving home, she would follow her and "make a huge scene." Allie got into the habit of visiting Ron first, but Shirley caught on to the ruse and usually spent the morning parked in front of his trailer, on the lookout for Allie's car. As soon as she saw it, she would blast the horn and scream out the window. Ron called the police every time, and soon Shirley was restrained from entering the trailer park. She parked just outside the entrance and glared silently at Allie as she drove inside.

Allie had become pregnant with her first child and was at the beginning of what has since become "nineteen years of a very solid marriage." Mark came from a happy family with parents in a traditional marriage, and Allie gives credit for the success of their marriage to Mark's "standard for family happiness, which has always been much higher than mine." Mark saw it as his "job" to ensure that Allie did not "give in to the kind of behavior that ruined [her] parents' marriage and caused problems for their children." Both her sisters are recovering alcoholics and have settled for "marriages of accommodation rather than affection."

Mark refused to allow Shirley and Ron to upset Allie's pregnancy, so he told them firmly that if they continued to harass each other in her presence, they would not be allowed to see her until she safely delivered the child. For the next eight months until her son was born, "they behaved themselves," Allie said. After that, the harassment began anew, but Allie was "somehow better able to cope with it." Having her own child and starting her own family (she now has three children) made her conscious of something she had not been "super-aware of" when she married: that she came from a truly dysfunctional family and would have to learn how to keep her own little family from becoming another one. Before she married Mark, she told him she thought marriage was "risky business" and how fearful she was that she would "mimic" her parents. He talked her into seeing a therapist, and she spent the first five years of her marriage in intensive therapy, which she credits "along with Mark's generosity of spirit" for helping her to accept that "marriage does not have to be a battleground and does not have to fail."

Ron died in the early years of Allie's marriage, and Shirley died just after her third child was born. I asked her how she remembers her parents so many years later. "Oh my God, what a hard question!" she said. It took her a long time to think about what she wanted to say before she was able to reply: "I think about them all the time. They are very present for me. I was approaching forty when they died, and by that time I had learned how to love them deeply even though I knew every one of their shortcomings. They gave me the example of what to embrace and what to reject, and I suppose they serve as my role model for how not to behave in marriage if you don't want to ruin it."

Alex was twenty-one and a senior at a New England college near his Upstate New York hometown when his parents ended their marriage of twenty-eight years. Ashley was twenty and a junior at a college in Maryland when her parents, both federal-government civil servants, told her they were ending their marriage of twenty-seven years. Both Alex and Ashley were the elder child and each had a younger brother. They didn't know each other, but their experiences were so similar that I decided to recount them together. Both spent a curious Thanksgiving holiday at their respective homes, where each parent was uncharacteristically nervous and edgy. Alex and Ashley were both busy with their own activities, so they didn't pay attention to their parents and returned to their schools unaware that anything was seriously amiss.

Ashley spoke to both her parents on the phone several times each week, but a few weeks went by without them telephoning and with her only getting the message machine when she called. However, there were exams and papers and much to do before the midwinter break, so she was not concerned. Alex's parents seldom phoned, so he wasn't worried about them either. When he got home just before Christmas, he learned that his father had moved out of the house. His primary emotion was "pissed that they ambushed me. I would have liked to know what I was walking into when I got home." They said they hadn't phoned or written because they wanted to tell him in person, but he considered what they had done "deception," and he was angry.

Ashley drove home, laden with presents, luggage, and all the materials she would need for her January work-study project. "Where is Dad and why isn't he helping me?" she asked her mother, who broke the news that he was moving into his own apartment at that very moment, where he would invite her to lunch the next day. Ashley was "too stunned to think." She unloaded her car and went to sleep. Later, she said she must have slept so long and deeply as a way "to put off facing the bad news."

Both these young people said they knew that "something was not right" in their parents' marriages but had no idea that it was anything serious enough to lead to divorce. Alex's mother and Ashley's parents told me that they fell into the category of people who had simply grown apart and decided to do something about it while they were young enough to make a new start in life (both couples were in their early fifties). All had professions that would let them support themselves (Alex's father was a lawyer and his mother a teacher; Ashley's father was a V.A. hospital administrator, and her mother worked at the Pentagon). Both couples agreed to the equitable distribution of marital assets and accepted shared responsibility for the children, and both divorces proceeded without undue acrimony.

Afterward, their children found "major changes in the simple things." Alex said, "Like when I used to call home in one ten-minute talk, I now had to make two separate calls and make sure I told the same things to both so neither one could accuse me of telling information the other didn't have." Ashley said, "Like when they came down to visit me separately." Suddenly their behavior was "more like friendship than like parents. I had to deal with a single mom and a single dad, so that strict sense of parental distance was gone." Alex had a similar experience: "My dad came to visit and I didn't know what to do with him. I took him out to drink with me and my buddies. It was not comfortable."

It was even more awkward when Alex began a relationship and brought his girlfriend to stay for a weekend at his mother's house. By that time, she was seeing a new man, which Alex found "really upsetting. It was as if the 'bachelor instinct' became a way of life for everybody. It was the same behavior for all of us. There were no boundaries for anyone."

Ashley had a more difficult time as she shuttled back and forth between her mother's house and her father's apartment on the far side of town: "My normal routine had been mostly to hang out, sit on the sofa and eat popcorn and watch TV. Now I had to make sure I did that in two places; if I hung out with one parent, I had to do it with the other."

Ashley felt that she had "to parent" her mother, while Alex felt he had to do the same for his father. His mother was "the social secretary" (an expression I heard often) within the marriage, and it was she who kept all the friends afterward. It took his father a while to adjust to being alone. While Alex's mother saw many men in the year after her divorce, his father settled quickly for one woman, which left Alex "free and relieved."

Both agree that their parents' divorces have affected their relationships. Alex said he had always been "kind of guarded," but he always sensed that "the white-knight-horse-and-princess-in-a-castle kind of love that goes on forever would not be for me. The divorce definitely destroyed all that. But my everyday interactions are the same: I don't feel any aggression toward women. I have always seen marriage in my future and definitely children. In fact, I look forward more to having kids than I do to being married."

Ashley said her parents' divorce "left nothing unanswered. It just feels so common nowadays. After the initial shock it wasn't so hard, it just became normal. What may be weird to others has become just normal to me."

In her attitude toward children, however, Ashley is more typical than Alex. Like most adult children of divorced parents, Ashley is "reluctant" to think about "bringing children into a messed-up world and, most likely, a messed-up marriage on top of it." She thinks she will have to be "married for a very long time" before she'll even consider having children.

THE QUESTION OF CHILDREN

Phyllis and Frank were children of divorced parents who "fell in love over the ashes of two burnt-out marriages." They insist that their parents' divorces have been the strongest influence upon their own marriage and, in so many different ways, the major factor in how it has developed. Frank was thirty-six when his parents divorced twenty years ago. He is now fifty-six and has been married to Phyllis for nineteen years. When they got together, Phyllis was thirty-five and had been divorced for a decade after "a starter marriage in college." Her parents had just ended a forty-year marriage, and all four parents were now dead. Both Phyllis and Frank described themselves as "devastated and angry" that after so many years, their parents "couldn't keep it together and got divorced." They cited their own fear of divorce as the major factor in their decision not to have children. They believe it was the right decision for them because it gave them the freedom to concentrate on themselves and their relationship, and they believe that is what has kept them together.

Frank had "years of analysis" before and after his parents parted, and in them he learned how to recall and interpret his dreams. Even today, many years after his analysis was concluded, he has the recurring dream that his family is "back together," but always "something is not right" among the relationships of the parents and their three sons (Frank is the eldest). His father was an alcoholic, a serial adulterer whom the mother always forgave until the time he "literally ran away with a woman younger than his youngest son," who was twenty at the time. The father eventually married the young woman "to do the right thing" because she was diagnosed with a cancer that killed her, and he himself died when Frank was forty-two. Frank's mother also remarried shortly after the divorce, "out of loneliness, but it didn't change anything: all she did before was sit in her bedroom and watch TV, and it's all she did after the second marriage," until her own death when Frank was forty-nine.

Phyllis describes her parents as "all-or-nothing personalities." Her father was a "workaholic, churchaholic, and more than anything else, alcoholic." Her mother was "an alcoholic and bulimic June Cleaver, out in the kitchen in her apron, belting from the sherry bottle." Phyllis cannot remember any good years in her parents' marriage, but she thinks that the trouble between them began "when the children came" (five—an older brother and sister, then Phyllis, then two younger brothers). She never discussed it with either parent, but she is convinced they regarded their five children as a "burden" that made life "restrictive: father always working to provide, mother always taking care of them. There was no time for them to be together and develop a marriage." Phyllis finds it "interesting" that of the five children, only her sister has a child, and that two of her brothers divorced because their first wives wanted children and they did not. Both remarried, to women who had grown children who lived on their own.

Phyllis thinks she and Frank went into their marriage "with eyes wide open," which is why "no wedges" have developed between them. She believes their relationship has grown closer over the years because they both worked so hard to be "different" from their parents, who were "never honest with themselves or their wives and children." Frank agreed that he and Phyllis "are brutally honest with each other." He also thinks that growing up in such fractious households made them both "well aware of what people go through in a marriage." The memory of the failed marriages that produced them is one of the main reasons they have stayed together: "We have become so accustomed to each other that it would be difficult for us to change something we have gotten so used to." I asked if this was his way of telling me that divorce will not become an option for him, and he told me it meant that he often thinks about what his life has become and how he can keep it going in the direction that he wants.

"I never thought I'd be fifty-six years old," he told me as a prelude to wondering if age might cause him to "repeat some of the patterns" of his parents, particularly his father's womanizing. He and Phyllis both admitted to feeling "strong attractions" to others at various times throughout their marriage but insist they have never acted upon them. Both wonder, now that they are middle-aged, if a "midlife crisis" might someday cause them "to stray." They have discussed this and have come to very different conclusions. Frank said that, although he "daydreams" and imagines life with women other than Phyllis, "for a man, it is more of a challenge to really 'be' with someone else. I guess men think 'if I could only change partners, then everything would be okay.' I guess it happens in the years when sex is no longer such a big deal, and a man thinks he could get excited again if he only had a new partner. But then I think of all the other kinds of shared intimacy that wouldn't be there, and I come back to Phyllis. A new partner might rejuvenate the juices for a little while, but I see my father who started again—and again and again—and after a little while, nothing worked for him."

Phyllis said her own reaction to the possibility of "cheating on Frank" surprised her, that she would "do it for the thrill of the experience and not for anything permanent." She insisted she would tell him about it, and if he could not "forgive" her and they separated, she imagines she would "live alone and not be part of a couple. I think I'd be okay living like that."

If they have any fear of a "wedge" coming between them, it is not of another person but rather of their finances. Phyllis is a senior hospital administrator who makes a six-figure salary, whereas Frank is a salesman who works on commission and sometimes earns little more than his "draw." He thinks her financial security is responsible for her "independent attitude," and he said he is "old-fashioned enough" that it bothers him. Phyllis tells him to stop worrying, their retirement is assured and they will go into a golden sunset together, "clipping coupons and eating early-bird dinners."

LESSONS LEARNED, MISTAKES TO BE AVOIDED

It is difficult to generalize about how adults react to their parents' divorces, particularly after only eighty-four interviews with a group of people who were either self-selecting or randomly selected, but I can say that certain patterns did emerge in the stories these people told me. Nearly all of them, men and women, were far less romantic and far more pragmatic about human relationships. They were more guarded about forming intimate relationships and on the alert for "alarms," "red flags," "danger signals"—a kind of code indicating that a relationship might not "go the distance" or "last" or that they would not "be around for the long haul." They all stressed that "honesty" and "openness" were key components of any relationship they might form, and when I asked them to explain what these terms meant to them, they expanded on the theme of "communication."

They planned to be on guard for the first sign that they were not in full and open communication with their partners. Even those who, like Kim, were "gentle souls," told me that they would insist upon "talking things out" and "bringing everything out into the open" before it could become a silent, festering "wedge" that might form an irreparable chasm in the relationship.

Almost every one of the adult children of late-life divorce spoke of how the institution of marriage had already changed so much, and how it would continue to change in the future. Even those of a strongly religious bent who did not approve of gay marriage or civil union said they would no doubt see "such marriages" being accepted and becoming commonplace in their lifetimes. Quite a few said they "hoped" or "prayed" they could "stick it out" with their mate, but if they couldn't, they would not hesitate to leave.

However, because they were so comfortable with the institution of marriage and the benefits it conveyed, they would try to marry again in order to re-create the cocoon of comfort, no matter how fleeting it might be. Only a few said they had gone into their own marriages with the idea that if it did not "work out," they could always be like their parents and "cut [their] losses" and try again.

Walter Kirn, a writer who is the adult child of divorced parents, described his feelings in an article entitled "My Parents' Bust-Up, and Mine":

> *My parents stayed together for the sake of the children. When the children were grown and settled, my parents divorced—for their own sake. . . . Because Mom and Dad had decided to tough it out (29 years in all) we faced their breakup not as vulnerable kids but as self-sufficient adults. You'd think it would have been easier that way; no custody battle, no change of schools, no teenage identity crises, no visitation squabbles.*
>
> *You'd think I'd thank my parents for their decision.*
>
> *Here is what I learned though: when the rug is pulled out from under you emotionally it isn't necessarily an advantage to be standing on your own two feet.*
>
> *NOTHING is quite so shocking, somehow, as news you've been half expecting all your life.*[4]

CHAPTER SEVEN

SPLITTING OR STICKING

[Seymour] Chwast, now 74, married [Paula] Scher in 1973. They divorced five years later—"time off for bad behavior," Mr. Chwast said dryly—and remarried in 1989.

—AMY GOLDWASSER, "At Home with Paula Scher"

PERRY AND PAULINE had been married for forty-two fractious years when they woke up one morning, glared at each other, and decided they could not sleep in the same bed one more night. She was sixty-four and he was sixty-six. Pauline told Perry he would have to move out of their seven-bedroom house in Grosse Pointe, Michigan, because she had too many clothes and shoes and he had only a few moth-eaten sweaters and corduroy trousers and the slippers he shuffled around in all day long. Perry had inherited significant wealth from his family, and his only job throughout the marriage had been to invest it and watch it grow. He did the same with Pauline's modest inheritance, so the two of them were independently wealthy.

Perry had no taste for the trappings of the rich. He drove a Toyota until it wore out and then bought another just like it; he did not have a boat, didn't drink at all so had no interested in putting in a wine cellar, and didn't like to travel. Pauline bought designer clothes and shoes but was selective in her purchases because she seldom went anyplace to wear them. She had no taste for expensive jewelry or fancy furnishings for the enormous house. After they put in some inherited antiques and a few choice pieces they found along the way, the interior remained locked in a time warp, with the curtains and upholstery gradually fading into the genteel shabbiness usually associated with English country houses. If Pauline and Perry had a single extravagance in their personal lives, it was excellent food. She prepared elaborate and elegant feasts for their three meals every single day, and there was always a ceremony associated with eating them. Pauline collected china, crystal, and flatware, and each meal was presented on what was appropriate, be it Royal Doulton with antique Georgian silver or Fiesta ware with equally colorful Bakelite-handled stainless steel.

The only passion they shared that cost money was for collecting anything that caught their fancy, and there were museums throughout the world whose curators wooed them for everything from European silver and Oriental rugs to pre-Columbian artifacts and Roman coins. They liked to tell people that the reason they, a childless couple, needed such a large house was because they "collected collections." They became instant experts on one thing after another as they were offered everything from American primitive paintings to Indian temple carvings, all of which they bought in bulk. They educated themselves afterward, learning which pieces to keep and which to sell (usually at a profit, for everything Perry set his mind to tended to make money).

And so, when Pauline told Perry he would have to move out of the house, his first reaction was "real fear that I would lose some of my collections and then real determination that I was not going to part with any of them." If Pauline wanted a divorce, Perry insisted, *she* not *he*, would have to vacate the house! As for the collections, he was determined to keep them intact, and this became the sticking point in their legal jousting. For the next ten years they argued over who would move out and who would get what, and all the while she remained in the master bedroom suite while he was barricaded in the ground-floor guest rooms at the far end of the house. Neither would budge an inch where the collections were concerned, even as each employed what they called a "gaggle of lawyers" to negotiate on their behalf. As their ten-year battle unfolded, each had lawyers who resigned in hopelessness because no agreements seemed attainable.

Every morning Perry, who could barely measure instant coffee into a cup, woke up to the smell of Pauline's exotic coffees, her Irish bacon or Italian ham, and fresh eggs poaching in the best French butter. He would betake himself to the local diner to "load up on grease," then would stop on the way back to the house to buy some fruit and yogurt for his lunch. Because they only socialized with curators, art dealers, and other people who wanted to sell them something, they had no real social life as a couple, so Perry would go back to the diner for his dinner when the smells from Pauline's exquisite cooking made him too ravenous to stay at home any longer.

Pauline had a great many friendships, most of which she conducted by telephone because she was from the West Coast and her large family and closest friends still lived there. She took to sending them airline tickets and inviting them to visit for as long as they wanted, and most accepted her hospitality. Her part of the house was filled with people, warmth, laughter, and most of all, the divine smells of her cooking. Perry occasionally went out to dinner with people who thought they could break the stalemate between him and Pauline by selling him a new collection, but otherwise he ate at the diner. His part of the house was mostly silent as he did not like to listen to music or watch television, and he preferred to read alone rather than invite people in and then have to make "cocktail-party conversation." Thus it was surprising when Perry became the first to start another relationship.

The woman was a museum curator who came for a week while she catalogued some coins Perry had just bought and ended up staying for several months. She left because Pauline forbade her to use the kitchen and Perry wouldn't let her bring in a microwave and hot plate. When she left, he found it easier to be with a waitress from the diner who stayed for the better part of a year and usually brought food home with her. After that, he had "three or four flings," but by the fifth year, he decided that he preferred to live alone.

Pauline had her first live-in lover at just about the time Perry took up with the waitress. Jeff was in his mid-fifties and a decade younger than she. He was a neighbor she and Perry sometimes chatted with at the occasional neighborhood Christmas cocktail party they felt obligated to attend. Jeff lived nearby until two catastrophes struck in tandem: he lost his job and his wife left him. His house was sold as part of his divorce settlement and he was about to move away when Pauline encountered him in the organic-produce section of the local food co-op. Both were foodies, and so she invited him home for a meal and he stayed for the next ten years. Perry couldn't stand Jeff, whom he described as "cover-boy-model handsome with no brains and no interest in anything but Pauline's body." Despite the fact that Pauline, a sixtyish woman, kept herself in good physical condition, Perry still thought it "amazing" that Jeff was "so happy in her bed." Even more amazing, according to Perry, was that Pauline, who hated anything that smacked of exercise, bought enough equipment for an entire gym and moved it into the great room that abutted Perry's suite. He was a late sleeper who was usually awakened by the grunting and groaning of the two early risers who were using the exercise machines at dawn.

Ten years passed, and Pauline and Perry were now in their seventies. Jeff was still in her life, but Pauline was tired of him and asked him to move on and take his exercise machines with him, providing a generous financial settlement to sweeten his way. She and Perry decided to try again to divorce, this time with a new cadre of lawyers whom both called "sharks." As they sat opposite each other at a conference table after several weeks of fruitless negotiation, one lawyer turned to the other in frustration and said, "Can't we persuade these people that they are never going to divorce, so maybe they should think about getting back together?" Perry said, "It hit like a revelation." Pauline said she was "just tired" and really didn't care what happened anymore; she just wanted "resolution." The lawyers told them to go home and think about "any possibility—no matter what, even staying married"—to settle their differences.

Pauline remembered how, as they walked silently side by side to the parking garage to drive their separate cars back to the same house, she told Perry "in a prickly voice" that she was planning to make coq au vin for her dinner and there would be enough for two. As it was one of his favorites, perhaps he would like some, to eat with her or separately, she didn't care. He said he would join her at the table and perhaps they could talk about what their lawyers had just told them. There was very little talking, however, as she picked and glowered while he devoured his food with relish. Much later, each confessed separately that they were afraid to say anything for fear of "setting off another world war." Perry thanked Pauline for the dinner and went back to his quarters. The next morning, as he was passing through the kitchen on his way out to the diner, Pauline invited him for a cup of her new politically correct organic coffee. He stayed for French toast with fresh raspberries and maple syrup and hand-formed sausage patties from a Vermont farm collective.

As Perry was finishing, Pauline said she was worried about one of the pieces in their silver collection, a Victorian dining-table decoration of elaborate cherubs and fauns, and would he have a look at it? Together, they spent the morning inspecting that one and several other pieces, then reliving the happy way in which they acquired them. By lunchtime, she wondered if he might like some of her freshly made gravlax and the water biscuits she made from scratch.

And so a new era began in their lives, an era of civility, cordiality, consideration, and friendship. Each showed the other the collections they had bought during their years of separation, and together they attended auctions and bought still more. Gradually, mutual kindness became fleeting affection, and on the eve of their eightieth birthdays, affection expanded into the deepest sexual relationship they'd ever had together, one that to this day still surprises them. They are in their mid-eighties now, and they tell me they wish they could figure out exactly what it was that brought them back together so they could "patent it, then bottle and distribute it to every other miserable couple who could use it."

THE TRUTH OF A MARRIAGE CAN BE UNDERSTOOD IN A MUCH SHORTER TIME THAN ANYONE EVER IMAGINED.[1]

Unfortunately, most couples never regain the magical moment that may (or may not ever have been) there when the marriage began. Researchers are giving serious attention to finding out why some marriages endure while others dissolve, and to do so they are studying how newly married couples interact with each other. Among them are Dr. John Gottman, a psychologist at the University of Washington, who has been investigating the phenomenon since the early 1980s by videotaping recently married couples for fifteen minutes each; and researchers at the University of Rochester, who are using twenty-minute telephone interviews with eight hundred newlywed couples, who are then asked to complete online surveys over the next three years.[2]

Gottman's technique depends upon a sophisticated coding system for twenty emotions and behavioral traits that run the gamut from anger to whining to disgust, all of which are correlated with information from the electrodes and sensors each person wears and which measure everything from how fast their hearts are beating to how much they wiggle and squirm in their chairs. When all this information is weighed, factored, and compiled into mathematical categories, Dr. Gottman's conclusions are startling: after he observes how a husband and wife talk to each other for a single hour, his accuracy rate for predicting whether they will still be married fifteen years later is 95 percent (it drops to 90 percent if he only observes the couple for fifteen minutes). However, one of his colleagues, Dr. Sybil Carrère, has gone him one better by lowering the observation time to a scant three minutes.

The Rochester researchers are just beginning their investigations, which do not include direct observation. Through newspaper classified ads throughout the United States, they hope to quadruple the eight hundred couples who have already done the twenty-minute phone interviews and filled out the first of three online surveys. Even though it is still early in their study, they already have one conclusion, that every good marriage "boils down to what we all learned in kindergarten: be nice to each other."

Dr. Gottman's conclusion is another version of the Rochester researchers' ordinary courtesy and kindness, but he couches it in far stronger terms: of all the emotions he factors into his observation of marriages that will ultimately fail, the strongest and most destructive is "contempt."[3] Gottman also cites "defensiveness, stonewalling, and criticism" as the three major signs that point to future trouble in young marriages. He does not deal specifically with long marriages, but it seems to me that all the emotions he identifies in young ones could be classified, as years pass and hurts and slights accrete, under the heading of "indifference," an attitude that has the capacity to meld every other negative emotion into one big festering lump of resentment.

I did hear of some couples besides Perry and Pauline who got together after they divorced and were seemingly happy forever after—the graphic designers Seymour Chwast and Paula Scher (whose brief summation of their marital history introduces this chapter) are one; the writer Joan Anderson is another.[4] In her book *A Year by the Sea*, Anderson describes how she separated from her husband to live alone on Cape Cod, not knowing when she left how long she would live alone or what the outcome for their marriage would be. Toward the end of her book, she recalls seeing a sign in front of a local church that read THE OPPOSITE OF LOVE IS INDIFFERENCE.

It started her thinking, and she asked herself if that was what had happened in her marriage. She "hate(s) the idea of indifference because it denotes not caring, having little feeling, being cold and harsh." Rhetorically she asks if she is like that but concludes that both she and her husband might have been "simply tired souls who hadn't the energy for anything but inertia, both shutting down and keeping our feelings to ourselves." Separating as they did might have been exactly what "two confused people" needed to do. In Anderson's case, the separation coincided with menopause, which, she pondered, might be "hmmm, men-o-pause, a pause from men." Perhaps, she concluded, "all women in long-term relationships should consider it." Well, then, how about men as well? Shouldn't we come up with a term for them to use when they need a marital time-out?

TO STICK OR TO SPLIT

Joan Anderson's story has a happy ending, in that she stayed married after her husband joined her on Cape Cod. For the eight couples I interviewed after Perry and Pauline, the outcome was decidedly mixed and slanted toward the negative. Only two divorced couples were still together five years after they reunited, and of the remaining six, two separated within the first year, one separated shortly afterward, and three others separated between the second and third years. Each of the two couples who were still together after five years gave radically different reasons for why they got back together and what led to their decisions about whether or not to remarry.

The couple that remarried was working-class, from a midsized Rust Belt town in the Northeast. Nick was a machinist and Connie was "just a housewife." Nick had always been the buffer between Connie and the world, even though she feared and resented him in all the years of their marriage. His "silences" were cutting, his criticisms made her feel "useless" and "no good." For years she dreaded the hour when he came home from the plant because she never knew how he would deflect his anger at what might have gone wrong on his job into scathing criticism of her and contempt for everything she had done that day to try to make his homecoming pleasant. She began (in her words) "to doctor," and went to a gastroenterologist who diagnosed all her symptoms as springing directly from the "emotional abuse" she endured every day in her marriage. He told her that she would seriously endanger her health "if things did not change." Connie decided she had to get away from Nick, no matter what the consequences. In what she called "the craziest thing" she had ever done, she filed for divorce and moved out of her house the next day.

Connie told me that she "didn't figure on the loneliness" when she asked for a divorce after their last child (of three) left home to live and work in another state. Nick had worked for one manufacturing company all his life, and when most of the production was moved overseas, he was forced to take early retirement in a buyout. He was bitter about it, saying it "amounted to the same thing as being fired." He had been retired and at home full-time for five months when Connie asked him for a divorce. Nick was angry but (in Connie's words) "never bothered to find out why I was doing it." His only response to her had been "Why should I bother? What difference would it have made?" Nick later told me this was an accurate description of his reaction. As part of the settlement, Nick agreed "against [his] will" to sell their house and split the modest proceeds. Money was going to be tight for them both and so Connie, who had never worked outside the home, moved into an apartment with another divorced woman. Nick found a room with kitchen privileges on the opposite side of town, where he soon got into "a pretty bad way." A man of few words, he evaded most of my questions about what "a pretty bad way" actually meant, but in conversation he revealed that he had no idea how to take care of his daily needs and was "real unhappy about it." He told me he had trouble "feeding myself, finding a clean shirt." Some days, it was too much trouble even to shave or bathe. News of his sad condition reached Connie, and eventually, because she could not "handle" the disapproval of her family, friends, and neighbors, "guilt" brought her back to him.

At first, she said she only contacted him to teach him how to do laundry or shop for simple meals and cook them, but later it came out that she had other reasons as well. Without a house to clean and meals to cook, Connie had few resources for filling her days. Shy and self-effacing, she had never developed any interests outside her home while she was married. Her mother was ill while she was growing up and died when she was a newlywed; she had no sisters and had never taken the time to make any real women friends. She did not go to church and took no part in any community affairs. In her town, there were very few fifty-five-year-old women who ended thirty-two-year marriages, and even if there had been support groups or other resources, Connie would not have known how to find them. Guilt was certainly a factor in her decision to return to Nick, but "loneliness" provided an even stronger reason.

Naturally, she was worried about going back into a relationship in which there had never been talk of "needs or feelings," and in which Nick, "very polite" since the divorce, might revert to being "his same old self." But the guilt she felt was so strong because "everyone" she knew accused her of abandoning Nick "for no good reason." Eventually guilt "got the best" of her and they reconciled, without really discussing why she divorced him in the first place. Nor did they talk about why she was returning to the relationship; she simply asked him if he wanted to move back in with her and he said yes. The first thing they did was to remarry quietly, almost surreptitiously. They went to the county courthouse, not telling anyone in advance and only informing their children during routine weekend phone calls. Together, they found an apartment for which they bought nothing new but melded the things each had taken from the old house. When I asked Connie if she considered the remarriage a "new beginning," she looked puzzled and said she didn't know how to answer. Nick told me, "We just thought it was better to get back together."

They tell me they are content with their lives now, as they see the occasional movie on "senior night," eat the early-bird dinners every Friday night at one or the other of the local chain restaurants, and see their grandchildren whenever possible. They don't have hobbies and they don't read, but they have begun to take long morning walks "for health." Their chief entertainment is watching television, and if there is any one thing they discuss with enthusiasm, it is the afternoon talk shows and evening sitcoms. They agree that they have "made peace" with each other and intend to live out their lives this way. I ask if they have found happiness. Connie turns to look out the window and doesn't answer; later that day when I ask Nick, he just shrugs.

Andy and Jeanine are the couple who decided to live together but not to remarry. The financial settlement at the time of their divorce was complicated because he had been a policeman in an Ohio town and retired with a pension before taking a job (also with pension and benefits) as a private security guard. Jeanine worked in the office of a local building contractor who provided her with pension options and who would have given her health care had she chosen to take it (during the marriage she chose to be covered under Andy's). They told me separately that they divorced because they "fought all the time." The only one of their four children I interviewed told me he grew up in "a house of terror, of raised voices and slammed doors, and the constant fear that one or the other would grab the police gun and start shooting." He said he and his siblings felt "only relief" when their parents divorced.

Andy and Jeanine had significant assets to divide when they divorced. They had CDs and other savings accounts as well as bonds and stocks in mutual funds. The mortgage on their house was paid in full, and they also owned a cottage on Lake Erie where they kept a power boat and snowmobile. They had two cars, a pickup truck, and a Harley-Davidson motorcycle. Jeanine liked jewelry and Andy had given her lots of gold and several "important" diamonds throughout their marriage. Disposing of these assets took time, and both parties incurred significant lawyer's fees as they fought over what each was entitled to outright. It was the first time they had dealt with the legal system, and they were shocked at the cost and wanted no part of it in the future, which is why they concluded that it was easier to keep the assets each was granted in the divorce agreement separate and to live together unmarried. Both were fifty-seven when they reunited and almost sixty-four when I talked to them.

When I asked what brought them back together, each said quite simply, "Sex." Jeanine said she had two "flings" after the divorce and neither one "satisfied" her in the way Andy did; Andy said Jeanine was the only woman he had ever "known," and he didn't want to "know" any others. Eight months after the divorce, they agreed to meet one night "on neutral turf" in a restaurant to "argue about one of the kids." After "cocktails and a bottle of wine," they ended up in bed in Jeanine's apartment. It took the better part of a year of "off-again, on-again sex" before they said to each other (in Jeanine's words), "Oh, what the hell!" and moved in together. They still fight, but they have learned "to go separate ways and cool off," and this is what keeps them together.

I asked both if "sex" was another way of saying they wanted to avoid loneliness, the reason Connie and Nick reunited. Cheerfully, Jeanine said, "Oh, sure!" Then she added, "Hey, whatever works, okay?" Andy just blushed and said nothing.

The other six couples had a variety of reasons for not being able to stay together when they reunited after divorce. In three cases, the couples could not overcome the "pain" and "betrayal" of infidelity (in one case, by the wife, in the other two, by the husbands). In the fourth case, Diane, who initiated the divorce because the marriage had "withered on the vine" and she and Fred had "nothing in common anymore," agreed to reconcile when Fred promised to take a more active part in their life as a couple. However, by the time they reconciled, Diane had completed an advanced degree in social work and set up a clinical practice that consumed all her time and energy. She had little left for Fred, who craved her attention and was willing to stay with her in the hope that the situation would change. Once again, Diane became the driving force that ended the reconciliation when she convinced Fred that it was not going to happen; she liked her new life too much to go back to the old one. Fred remarried eight months later but divorced shortly before the second anniversary of that marriage. Diane remains "single and content."

The fifth couple claimed that they loved each other deeply even as they divorced because the wife could no longer endure the husband's alcoholism. Throughout their twenty-seven-year marriage, he usually "fell down drunk and slept it off," but on rare occasions, he "slapped [her] around." When the violence escalated and he broke her nose, she divorced him. He spent the next three years "getting sober" and convincing her that he would stay "on the wagon." They remarried, and two months later he got drunk and wrecked their only car, which she needed for her work as a night-shift nurse. She moved out immediately, and they were divorced again four months later. He would like to "be in contact" with her, but she refuses to take his phone calls or answer e-mails, and she won't even be in the same room with him. Their children describe them as "the real kids in the family at their eternal war." The woman says, "Twice burned, forever after shy."

The last couple had a complicated relationship, which each described with the same word: "codependency." They were each other's "enabler," and their separate interviews sounded to me like the recitation of psychological jargon and the latest buzzwords from every self-help book about relationships published in the last twenty or so years. They had tried every kind of couples' therapy, from Marriage Encounter to divorce survival groups. They had been on retreats (religious and otherwise); they went to spa weekends and to what they called (but did not explain) "all kinds of twelve-step." Unable to stay together, they were unable to live apart. When I met them, they were in separate apartments in a Chicago suburb but planning to move in together for "one last try." I had the feeling they'd be making last tries for the rest of their days.

THE TERRIFYING UNKNOWN

These couples were among the many who find it impossible to stick together and end up splitting but are afraid to make the final leap into what for many is "the terrifying unknown." Many factors contribute to the fears that overwhelm individuals when they go from couplehood to being single, and by far the biggest fear is the fear of being alone. Both women and men told me how they hesitated to divorce, sometimes for years, because they feared loneliness. Many told me how "things had to get truly terrible" before they realized they had no alternative but to divorce.

The AARP survey shows this as well, that the main fear of what life after divorce might bring is loneliness. Forty-five percent of the 1,147 AARP respondents, both men and women, cited their main fear as having to live alone; in a directly related statistic, another 24 percent expressed the fear of "never finding someone" afterward. Surprisingly, since most divorcing couples found themselves with a greatly reduced lifestyle, only 28 percent of the AARP respondents worried about finances.[5]

Many men and women told me how surprised they were after they divorced by the realization that they were in old age or on the verge of it and had never lived independently, with full responsibility for every aspect of their daily life. They described how they went from life in their parents' house to life in a college dormitory or military barracks, where they lived with a lot of people and had few moments to themselves, and then directly into life as part of a married couple. More women than men told me the recognition that they would have to re-create themselves as a single did not strike them until they were "too far down the divorce road to turn back." More men than women said the realization that they would be living alone was not a major concern because "any man who wants a woman can find one; there are lots of 'casserole ladies' [women seeking male company] out there."

Most of the divorced men who did not have a new partner lined up before their marriages ended told me they were not actively looking for one, but if "a good-looking chick" (or "babe," or "doll"—they didn't seem to be able to say "woman") came along, they would not be indifferent to her charms. In contrast, most of the women told me that they were not actively looking for a new partner and were not able to state definitively how they might respond "if a good one came along." They cited a variety of reasons for why they felt this way, starting with a married life that had been so "grim," "painful," "depressing," "boring," or "terrifying" (to give a few of the most often used terms) that they did not think they could bring themselves to trust another man. Most of the women who had never lived alone were the ones who wanted to "give it a try." They wanted to live somewhere that was, as many said, "all my own."

The word "freedom" resonated loudly in my interviews, just as it did in the AARP survey, where 43 percent of the women—as opposed to 39 percent of the men—used it to describe what they liked best about their lives after divorce. Quite a few said they looked forward to settling down in the evening "with a glass of wine and cheese and crackers and an apple" instead of having to cook "a man's meal." Even more told me it was "such a delight" to know that if anything was dropped or out of place, they had been the one to put it there so they picked it up without the "rage and anger" they felt toward sloppy, messy husbands. And more women than men said they were the ones who told the "nice" or "decent" person they met after divorcing that they enjoyed their company but preferred to live alone.

What men liked about life after divorce was their changed financial situation: 27 percent liked it best, whereas only 18 percent of the women were satisfied with theirs. My own interviews reflected the trend that men were often far better off financially than women, especially after long marriages. Newspapers and magazines are full of articles about "dead-beat dads" who don't support their young children, but these articles seldom uncover the complexity of the financial situation for older persons who end long marriages. Terry Martin Hekker created quite a stir when she bared her circumstances in an article for *The New York Times*'s "Modern Love" series.[6] Just as the feminist revolution was starting in the 1970s, Hekker reversed the trend and wrote a bestselling book in which she crowed about the joys of being a stay-at-home housewife and mother of five children. In 2005, after her husband commemorated their fortieth wedding anniversary by presenting her with a bill of divorcement, she announced that she planned to write a sequel, to be called *Disregard First Book*.[7] Hekker felt "frightening losses and was overwhelmed by the injustice of it all" when her husband took his new woman on a Mexican vacation while she had to sell her engagement ring to pay for a new roof. Her first individually filed tax return qualified her for food stamps, but worst of all, when this sixty-four-year-old woman who had never held a job entered divorce court, the judge awarded her temporary alimony for four years, saying she could always take job training and find a job by the time it ended, when she would be sixty-eight.

FINANCES: DISASTERS AND OTHER TALES

Howard and Eleanor had one of the more interesting stories of coming to terms with a crushing financial reality (for her) when they divorced after forty-one years of marriage. For the last twenty or so years of the marriage, Eleanor, a small-business entrepreneur, made a lot more money than Howard, who held various administrative positions in the nonprofit sector. Even though Eleanor took pains to insist that it was "our money" and that it was "all going into the family pot," it still rankled Howard. In retrospect, Eleanor wondered if her money might have injured his "self-esteem, shaky to begin with," and whether he might have taken refuge in the "sarcasm and contempt" that ultimately turned into the passive-aggressive behavior that led her to divorce him.

Howard came from a religious family in Maine whose women dedicated themselves to living frugally on whatever income their husbands provided. His mother and four sisters were skilled in all the housewifely arts and, in the tradition of their New England forbears, would "make it do, use it up, wear it out." They tended huge gardens and preserved the bounty, made much of their family's clothing, clipped grocery coupons, and found free entertainment for their families. Eleanor's background was also one of modest circumstances, but (in Howard's damning phrase), she "always had big ideas" and refused to pattern herself after his mother and four sisters.

Eleanor waited twelve years after their marriage to become pregnant and deliberately chose to have only one child. She wanted their daughter, Courtney, to have all the things that she herself had always longed for, to go to private schools and enjoy the same privileges and advantages her wealthier classmates had. Courtney wore the same designer clothing as her far-richer classmates and had lessons in everything she wanted, from music and dancing to skating and swimming. She attended an expensive summer camp and partook of cultural experiences in New York or Boston on school outings. When she was seventeen and eligible to drive, she was given her own sports car.

Howard's salary could not possibly cover these expenses, so Eleanor was willing to work, sometimes holding several jobs at a time, to give Courtney this life of privilege. She started with a variety of entry-level jobs in public relations and advertising before striking out on her own as a small-business owner. She had a number of notable and expensive failures, from hand-painted sweatshirts she tried to sell at flea markets to disastrous catering endeavors in private homes, until the day she made a mistake in measuring ingredients and stumbled onto a gold mine. While making cookies for a local bakery, she reached for the wrong spice jar and her accidental recipe became such a success in the small western Massachusetts town where they lived that she was able to sell it to a national company.

It was a straightforward sale, with a one-time payment, but for the next decade or so, Eleanor called herself "the rich lady" as she used the "cookie money" to pay for Courtney's education and an easier way of living for them all. She trusted Howard to take care of the money by investing it properly. Meanwhile, without ever consulting a financial statement, paying a bill, or writing a check, Eleanor spent what she thought was an "acceptable" part of the windfall. After all, she reasoned, the financial sector of every foundation Howard ever worked for had made money, so surely he was making careful and prudent investments with theirs. This turned out not to be the case, as Howard was one of those people who has great success investing large quantities of other people's money while failing badly with his own: his investment decisions provided minuscule returns even as Eleanor was fast diminishing the principal.

She decided she was tired of commuting from western Massachusetts to New York, where she was busy pitching a multitude of new ideas, and she bought an apartment at the height of the housing market just before it crashed in the early 1990s. When the divorce impended, she had to sell it at a loss just as the stock market crashed at the end of the millennium. At the same time, they lost much of the little money that was left because Howard had invested it heavily in high-rolling dot-com mutual funds and didn't withdraw it in time. Eleanor thought they had been living what she called a "modestly lavish life," meaning that if she wanted an article of clothing or something for the house, she could buy it; or if she thought the family should go to Florida for the Christmas holiday, they could afford to go. When she decided that their Massachusetts house needed extensive renovations, she hired a contractor and told him to use the best materials. Howard fumed silently at the cost overruns but said nothing about it to Eleanor. Instead, he took out a second mortgage to pay for them. They went to London almost every summer, were among the first to see the latest Broadway shows, and liked to dine at all the "in" restaurants.

Howard secretly added three more credit cards to the one Visa and American Express Eleanor thought they held and that she airily told people they used only for convenience and paid in full every month. Eleanor thought her cookie money was paying for everything, and she insisted that Howard "was perfectly comfortable" with it. She told people that he kept his "self-respect as the traditional breadwinner" because she let him believe that his guaranteed salary was the "backbone" of their family's financial security. Eleanor, who never wrote a check to pay a bill, who always used charge accounts and credit cards, did not notice how Howard festered when she said this, both of them ignoring the reality that his annual $50,000 before taxes was not really supporting two mortgages, all the related household bills, and their three cars (including Courtney's).

By the time they divorced, Eleanor's money was diminishing rapidly. Howard never revealed how dire their circumstances were, instead, he berated her for not bringing in new income. The strain became so great that neither wanted to be in the other's company—she because everything he said to her was so scathing, he because he was so angry that he feared he wouldn't be able to control what he said or did. They began to live separate lives under the same roof, sleeping in separate bedrooms and gulping down catch-as-catch-can meals in the kitchen when one or the other was occupied in another part of the house.

Eleanor thought the Massachusetts house was too large now that Courtney was away at school and that they should sell it to offset the loss incurred when they sold the New York apartment. Still hoping to "save the marriage," she persuaded Howard that they could buy another, cheaper, house that would put them "ahead of the game." This was no longer true in their area, as housing prices were consistently escalating and Howard, who was supposed to know something about financial trends, was aware of it. Still, he did not stop her because "when Eleanor makes up her mind she wants something, just get out of her way." When I asked if he felt any responsibility for their precarious financial downturn, especially because he did nothing to warn Eleanor that they had to change their way of living at once, Howard turned the question to me, asking if I had not listened to him earlier when he said, "You can't reason with her when she wants something, so I stopped trying years ago." And that, he concluded, absolved him of any responsibility for the divorce: he had "to make her do the divorcing in order to save myself."

Eleanor did not know that most of Howard's investments of her money had "tanked" (her word), and that, to avoid touching the savings he intended to take away from the marriage, he was paying their monthly bills by taking cash advances from credit cards she didn't know he had. They were still living separate lives, but in a new house, which turned out not to be the bargain Eleanor envisioned but more expensive than their old one. Eleanor maintained that the purchase was justified because of her new business—a venture that imported unusual fabrics from South Africa. A number of American designers were expressing serious interest in her products, so she was on the telephone, computer, or fax machine for hours at a time every day, trying frantically to make them commit to buy. It was just at this time that the crisis in their marriage came.

Howard was still going off to his job every day, unaware that his foundation had decided to merge with another one and that half the combined staff would be let go. He was among those who lost their jobs, but as he was eligible for Social Security, he decided to retire early. At the time, Eleanor didn't question him, and it wasn't until after the divorce, when she was faced with the staggering reality of the debt he left her to pay, that she wondered how he could have made such a selfish decision. When she asked him how he thought he could retire when they had no guaranteed income, he said it was because she needed his "backup" around the house. In truth, his decision to retire set the snowball of divorce rolling ever faster down the hill leading to the courtroom.

Howard had become passive-aggressive toward Eleanor: offering to go to the post office, he would "forget" to mail her most important letters; offering to do the grocery shopping, he would come home with expensive items neither of them ate while forgetting the essentials they needed. He would forget to relay phone messages, and when she accused him of deliberately trying to sabotage her efforts to earn money, he called her a "narcissist," and said that "everything always has to be about you."

When we talked five years after the divorce, Eleanor told me there was a certain degree of truth to his accusation that she was "selfish" because she was always the one to determine the family's lifestyle, to bring in the friendships, provide the entertainment, and keep the gracious home. Like so many men whose wives complained of similar behavior, Howard was always happy to enjoy everything Eleanor brought to the marriage, even as he resented her for the ease and ability with which she did it.

Howard's version of how things went wrong was very different from Eleanor's. He said he had gone along with everything Eleanor wanted "every day of the marriage" because he had "no choice." His life "would have been hell" if he had "crossed her," and so he found it easiest "to go along in order to get along." Howard took no responsibility for insulating Eleanor from the financial realities of their marriage, saying, "She didn't want to know and would not have listened if I tried to tell her." So when everything "tanked" and they were down to their last half-million dollars in mutual funds, Howard realized they would be close to broke within the next several years after he made the balloon payment on the new house's second mortgage (taken to buy an SUV and help pay for Courtney's graduate study) and after he paid off the huge credit-card advances (taken to pay monthly bills even as the mutual funds declined in the accounts where he let them sit).

That was when he withdrew completely from the marriage, into the stony silences, carping criticisms, and passive-aggressive behavior that wrecked Eleanor's concentration and caused real damage to her business dealings. When Eleanor lost twelve pounds from her already slim frame and found herself curled up in a fetal position on the sofa in her office for most of every day, unable to do any work at all, she went into therapy. After several months of approaching from every possible angle the "dangerous topic" that her marriage was failing even as she was "unwilling to face it head on," her moment of truth came when the therapist, uncharacteristically for him, made the offhand remark that she knew what she had to do, but it might take her a while before she could bring herself to do it. Driving home after the session, she finally admitted to herself that if Howard did not come back into the marriage as a fully participating partner, she would have no option but to divorce him.

That night, as she was preparing her solitary dinner, he came into the kitchen for something and she was shocked when she noticed that he wasn't wearing his wedding ring. It had been so tight for so many years that Howard joked he would have to be buried with it as it would not come off, so she knew that he must have had it cut. The next day when he was out, she went into his bedroom and looked in his jewelry box, and sure enough, the ring was there in two pieces. When he came home, she confronted him and asked if removing the ring meant he thought the marriage should end.

"That's your idea!" he shouted, and then accused her of "always running away from things" she did not want to face. She was perplexed by the accusation that a divorce was "all [her] idea" and asked him to explain. For the next four months they went through (in her words) "a round-robin of accusation and recrimination with no resolution" and (in his words) "her stubborn inability to change." When she asked what he would have her do in order to keep the marriage together, he said he didn't know how she had to change, she just had to do it. Eleanor had the feeling that Howard was deliberately "backing [her] into a corner," trying to force her into divorcing him, and finally she realized that what the therapist had blurted out was true: she could either remain in a marriage that was increasingly becoming one of "emotional abuse," or she could end it.

In a subsequent therapy session, she told the therapist that she was afraid to be on her own, so she would stay married. In exasperation, he likened her to a person "who is walking down the street with one foot on the sidewalk curb and the other one in the gutter." The vision of herself walking throughout the rest of her life in a slow and crippled manner was so disturbing that it led eventually to her overwhelming desire "to get out of this marriage and walk straight and healthy again."

Before they began divorce proceedings, Eleanor tried one last time to stay married by agreeing to go with Howard to any marriage therapist of his choosing. He said he wanted to go to the first session alone to explain his position because Eleanor "always charmed everyone" and he was convinced that the therapist would "side" with her. He told the therapist that the marriage was in crisis because Eleanor had no sense of financial reality and refused to develop one. The following week, when Eleanor joined Howard for a joint session, the therapist questioned her about her attitude toward money. She explained that she had no idea of their financial situation because Howard would never talk about it, always telling her that he was "taking care of everything." When she said this, Howard stormed into a tirade, accusing Eleanor of "doing what she always does, getting everyone on her side and turning everyone against me." The therapist asked him to sit down and listen carefully to what Eleanor was trying to tell him, that she wanted to start over in the marriage, as two equal partners who would get out of the mess they were in together, but Howard was enraged and insisted that "she says things but she doesn't mean them." He stormed out of the office and told the therapist he would not return.

That evening, because they both agreed that the marriage was beyond salvation, Howard told Eleanor he would give her an uncontested divorce, but only if she agreed to the dissolution agreement he had drawn up. If she did not agree, he said he would "take her for everything she was worth." He said he could do this because the judge would side with him and make a decision favoring a retired man who had no possibility of earning further income, whereas she was still working and her business had the possibility of earning handsomely and for the indefinite future. Howard then presented Eleanor with a fourteen-page document detailing every asset he wanted to take away from the marriage. She was surprised by such a meticulously prepared "Divorce Agreement" (as he had entitled it) because she had not concluded that they needed "to split" until she left the therapist's office, while he had obviously been preparing to do so for quite some time. Without reading the agreement, Eleanor said she just wanted things to come to "a swift and easy end" and would agree to all his conditions. She suggested that Howard consult Conrad, the local lawyer who handled their real estate dealings, wills, and other straightforward matters, during the next week when she was in New York on business matters. She thought that because she had agreed to give him everything in the agreement he'd drawn up, they could save money by having one lawyer handle the divorce for both parties.

When she returned from New York, Howard told her she would have to find her own attorney, for even though the divorce was uncontested, Conrad could only represent one of them. And as Howard had been the one who consulted him, he would have to take Howard as his client. Eleanor, again without reading Howard's agreement, went to the attorney husband of one of her friends. He was shocked by what he read and told her she would have to dispute Howard "every step of the way" because his demands were "punitive and unjust." She asked what disputing it would entail, and he said it meant a thorough investigation of all their assets, perhaps deposing them and their witnesses, and a time frame of "a year or more, possibly two." When she asked how much it would cost, the lawyer said "in the ballpark of ten thousand dollars." Eleanor countered that by the time they were finished, it would cost her "more like seventeen to twenty thousand," and this was not counting what Howard would have to pay. She knew she didn't want to spend that much money, but most of all, she wanted the divorce to be final within the three to four months required for an uncontested dissolution, so she instructed the lawyer to give Howard whatever he wanted. She "almost couldn't believe it" when he told her he couldn't let her accept such a punitive agreement, mainly because she could turn around and sue him for bad representation once she "regained her senses" and realized what she was "giving away." Eleanor said she wanted the divorce and "wanted it fast," but he remained firm that "no decent lawyer" would let a client consent to such an agreement. So she thanked her friend for his advice and said she would go into court without counsel.

"It really didn't penetrate when I read [the agreement] before the divorce," Eleanor told me. "Not until afterward did I realize the trouble I was in, when for the first time in all those years of marriage I had to pay the monthly bills."

Howard's agreement required her to accept full responsibility for their marital debt and to pay it all off, while he walked away from the marriage totally unencumbered. Five years later when he spoke to me, he insisted that he was right to do this because "she made it all, she spent it all, so she should have to pay for it." Eleanor was left with two mortgages totaling $9,000 a month, on top of which she had to make payments of another $1,500 on five credit cards that added up to $70,000 of debt. So she was paying $10,500 every month before she could even think about buying food or gas and paying for utilities. Of their half-million dollars in the investment and retirement accounts, Howard claimed that half was his, even though "to keep things even" Eleanor had contributed more than $ 150,000 of her money to his accounts. He also said that he had incurred debts of $60,000 by using his own savings to support her "cockamamie business schemes," so she was ordered to deposit that sum from her accounts into his, thus leaving her with less than $200,000. She was to assume full financial responsibility for their daughter (who had one final year of graduate study) and to pay off the final $ 15,000 due on the SUV and $12,000 on Courtney's Mazda Miata. He took the Lexus, which was fully paid for.

Howard told Eleanor he wanted very few things from the house, but what he wanted was the best and most valuable, from several Early American paintings to stellar examples of midcentury modern furniture and decorative objects, many of which were one of a kind. He removed what he wanted while she was away on a business trip, so she came home one night to find that all the best things were gone.

Eleanor realized she had no option but to sell the house, and she put it on the market at once. It took a year before she found a buyer, and by that time, only a few of her projects were bringing in money and the rest were hopelessly stalled; she was down to her last $30,000. When she sold the house for a $70,000 profit, which she counted on to keep her head "above water" until at least one of her ventures paid off, she was stunned to receive a letter from Howard's lawyer reminding her that the divorce agreement stipulated that he was to receive a lump sum of $40,000 once the house was sold, whether she made a profit or not. This time she did consult a lawyer, only to be told that she had to give Howard the money because it was in the agreement the lawyer had begged her not to sign. The only good thing about the agreement was that once the house was sold, Eleanor's obligation to Howard was finally and officially over, and she would never have to pay him another penny.

She never did hire an attorney to represent her during the divorce, and she went into court without one because she had been told that if she did not engage counsel, the judge would serve as her advocate. On the day of the hearing, she was still not fully aware of the staggering amount of debt for which she was to become solely responsible, so all she expected from the judge was a swift granting of the decree. He questioned Howard first, and

Howard swore to agree to the divorce as long as Eleanor honored his terms. He explained that he was of retirement age and had always been a salaried employee with little likelihood that he would have any future income other than Social Security and his small pension. The judge asked Eleanor if she would honor the agreement, and she said yes. She thought that was the end of it, but to her astonishment, she heard the judge ask Howard, "Are you fully aware of what you may be giving up if you take only what is in this agreement and nothing more? Don't you want a piece of her future earnings?"

Eleanor was already springing to her feet to declare that she would not consent to supporting Howard even after they were divorced when, to his credit ("the only thing for which I give him any credit at all," she told me), Howard said he would be satisfied to have only the money specified in the agreement and would not want anything further after the divorce was granted.

Since then, the beginning of 2001, Howard's standard of living has risen and he has been faring very well. He rents a town house in a complex that has every possible amenity, from a gym to a social center. He still drives the paid-for Lexus, and he stints on nothing. An opera fan, he frequently takes trips to American and European cities if there is a performance he particularly wants to hear. He enjoys the Southwest and travels to New Mexico or Arizona at least once each year. He takes courses at the community college and helps a local theater group with backstage or business office work during their performance season, often contributing small sums of money to help them buy whatever they need for a performance. He has acquired a taste for fine wine, and he dresses better than he ever did during the marriage.

He tried to keep many of the friendships that Eleanor brought into the marriage, and to her credit, she told everyone that they were free to see both her and Howard as they wished, but she didn't want them to tell her anything about him. One of these friends told Eleanor that most of the friends had already dropped him because of his "ethical cowardice" at leaving her in such dire financial straits. She thought it "sad" that, in their very long marriage, he had made no real friends on his own and that things ended for him in "such a sorry way."

As for Eleanor, so far none of her projects have come to fruition and she finds herself "scrambling" to bring in enough money to survive every year. At the age of sixty-five, she is actively seeking a permanent paying job that will supplement her Social Security and give her "something to fall back on." At the time of the divorce, she needed a big enough space for an office and a workroom, so she thought she would buy a smaller, cheaper house after she sold the big one. She had to give this plan up when Howard sued her for the $40,000, so she rented one floor of a three-family house in order to get the space she needed for what she could afford to pay. She has cut her expenses to the bone. The SUV is long gone and she drives a secondhand Volvo; she buys clothes only when she absolutely has to (having become adept at revamping her existing wardrobe); and she has adopted an almost vegetarian diet, hoping to cut food costs by eliminating meat. She has kept up with her many friends, accepting their invitations to elegant dinners and reciprocating with her "famous noodle casserole and jug wine." They tell her "it's the company that counts," and hers is "the best."

Howard still enjoys friendly relations with their daughter, who did not go to medical school as she had wanted but became a nurse-practitioner and midwife instead. Courtney is married and has a young son, and Howard likes to spend time with the little boy. Eleanor regrets that she can no longer be generous to Courtney and her family, but Howard refuses to give them anything beyond modest Christmas and birthday presents. When Courtney asked him for a loan in order to buy into a medical practice, he told her to go to a bank.

Howard has the "occasional date" but says he is "wary of conniving women" and does not want a permanent relationship. He says it is "important" for him to "protect" his money because "people live a long time" in his family. He likes his lifestyle and says it is a pleasure to buy anything he wants and go anywhere he pleases. As for Eleanor, he thinks she "brought everything on herself and now she has to pay the consequences." He says it was "only right" that he left her to pay off all the debts because "she was the one who made them."

Eleanor admits that she did a lot to bring her "poverty-stricken post-divorce life" on herself and that she probably would have had "a better deal" if she had taken the lawyer's advice. But she is strong in her belief that Howard left her no choice but to divorce, and she is better off for having done so. If she had remained in the marriage, he would have "destroyed" everything within her that she "held dear and was positive about." Even as she "hopes" that she will "strike it rich again," she realizes that such a goal is ever more fleeting and she may have to settle for "barely earning [her] daily bread."

Eleanor would like to have "male companionship" but says she is "too busy trying to keep afloat" to go out and find any. She had one "fairly breathtaking encounter" with a rich and distinguished man in New York who "swept [her] off her feet" and made her "feel like a woman for the first time in years." Charming as he was, he was also "divorced while still married," and she ended the affair when she found out. Since then, she has had the occasional "date—and I mean just that, what the word used to mean when we were young: a little kissy-kissy and touchy-feely but no sex." Mainly, she counts on her strong network of women friends, most of whom are also divorced and worried about their financial survival, and several of whom are widows who live as frugally as she does in the hope that their assets will last their lifetimes. The two she likes best, however, are still married but describe themselves by using the old joke about "the Plotnick curse" ("she wears a fantastic diamond that everyone admires, but it bears the Plotnick curse: she has to stay married to Mr. Plotnick to keep it").

Eleanor, who was never a reader and knows very little about literature, was told by her daughter's husband (a high school English teacher) that she resembles the title character in a Samuel Beckett novel, *The Unnarnable*, who says, "I can't go on. I'll go on." She translates the phrase into her words, saying that when Howard forced her into a divorce she was "almost all the way down but never on the way out." She faces the future without knowing where "the next dollar will come from" but with every confidence that it will certainly come.

CHAPTER EIGHT

THE TRUE VALUE OF A SPOUSE

[The idea] that we can raise a generation of children to "believe that men and women are equal" is wonderful, but perhaps she'd like first to try selling this idea to the men who head corporations and colleges and universities around the country, and that's not even to mention the divorce lawyers and judges who so often contribute to the genteel poverty of divorced middle-aged women.

—PATRICIA HUNT, letter to the editor,
The New York Times

A DIVORCE LAWYER WHO practices in a major northeastern city asked me not to identify anything about her because what she was about to tell me could get her into "pretty big trouble" in the courtrooms where she routinely represents women clients. In her state, more women than men are on the bench and many are "not a friend of divorcing women, particularly those who were stay-at-home moms." The lawyer described the current crop of women judges as usually between the ages of forty and fifty-five, with most having worked steadily throughout their professional lives. "Give me Mr. Judge from another generation anytime," the lawyer said, "because he will be far more sympathetic to a woman in her sixties who was a stay-at-home wife than a fifty-year-old Ms. Judge."

A male attorney who practices in a western state agreed, and he has an explanation for why "female judges are probably not even consciously aware of being tougher on women: they think, if they can go to work every day from nine to five, so can all other women." He insists he is not being particularly ungenerous to women judges, for he adds quickly that "all women are tougher on other women than men." When I press for an explanation, he offers an analogy. He argues that it is a well-known and accepted fact that lawyers for accused rapists prefer female jurors because "they are always harder on the victims. Women jurors are far more likely to ask 'what was she doing at two A.M. in a place like that, dressed like that, et cetera.' " Therefore, he insists, women judges will always hold divorcing women to higher standards than men. I told him that his is an interesting thesis, but I'd wait for the statisticians to prove it before I wholeheartedly accept it.

In the states where I conducted interviews with divorcing couples, I tried to interview at least one family-court judge. I was not surprised when most declined to make any comment on any question at all other than a variant of "I only know what goes on in my own courtroom." Obviously gender bias in the courtroom is a touchy subject for judges, but I did find one constant among them all: women bridled at allegations of unconscious prejudice toward women; men grinned broadly, shook their heads knowingly, and said, "No comment," which itself might well be gender biased.

In an effort to learn how the reforms of the past thirty or so years affected late-life divorces, I spoke to a dozen or so divorce attorneys, equally divided among men and women, in states ranging from New England and the Middle Atlantic to the upper Midwest and Mountain States, the Southwest, and the Pacific States. Except for Florida, I had few respondents in the southern states, and this surprised me because the politically and socially conservative "red states" of the Deep South have the highest divorce rates in the United States.[1] I also talked to psychologists who specialize in counseling couples before and during divorce proceedings, divorce mediators (some lawyers and some not), and lawyers who serve in some Pennsylvania counties as the "masters" who arrange settlements that are then presented for approval to judges who actually grant the divorces. There was a single point all these professionals found they could agree upon: that "everything depends on the state where you live and, even more, the particular district within the state where you file."

One lawyer tried to explain the many differences throughout the American legal system by going back to the nation's beginnings: "California and seven or eight other western states have systems that were originally based on the old Spanish community-property law, which is different from the British-based common law that governs most of the eastern states, and don't forget Louisiana, with the Napoleonic-based community-property law." "Good luck," she told me as I tried to sort through the intricacies of particular cases in different states.

I thought California would be a good place to start because it led the country (and indeed, the Western world) when it became the first state to do away with fault-based divorce in 1970. Since then, the state's family code (which includes divorce) has been consistently revised, and so what might have applied just a few short years ago is no longer valid. Even the term "divorce" is no longer used in California, as couples now petition the courts for "dissolution," and they do so before a judge (no jury) in family courts. If minor children are involved, couples must also go to conciliation court.

ALIMONY

One topic all the courtroom professionals I talked to agreed upon was the vast range of discrepancies in how alimony is decided and how awards vary from state to state. A male attorney in Chicago explained it succinctly: "An older woman who knows she will get alimony is more likely to end an unhappy marriage than one who knows she either won't get it at all or will only get it for a limited time." A female attorney practicing in Rhode Island echoed what many in other states told me, that "economic realities force couples to go back into an unhappy marriage and stay in it because it is not financially feasible to leave."

Divorce laws in most states have changed dramatically in the last thirty or so years, with every reform instituted by lawmakers with the best intentions who thought they were leveling the playing field for both contestants. What they found was that each divorce has its own set of individual characteristics and so there were too many for which hard-and-fast rules of law cannot and do not apply, and that a decision that might be equitable for one couple is punitive to another. Things were supposed to be easier once couples no longer had to prove fault by showing up in court bearing photos of bruises and broken bones or staging phony adultery interludes and hiring investigators to photograph them. Either party was supposed to be able to cite "irreconcilable differences" or the "irretrievable breakdown of the marriage" and leave the other, satisfied that financial justice had been done. Unfortunately, the real-life cases of real people were anything but simple and easily adjudicated.

Connecticut provides one example of how attitudes evolved when the new laws effected in 1973 changed it from a fault state to one of equitable distribution. Several divorce attorneys who were in practice there before 1973 remember how strict the law was about making couples demonstrate "actual fault," which they thought was due to the unconscious (or perhaps even the conscious) attitude that divorce carried such stigma in a state that extolled traditional "Yankee virtues" and "steady habits." The stringent laws made divorcing such a difficult procedure that many couples remained in failed marriages rather than risk having such stigma attached to them. Once the law was changed to equitable distribution, the onus was removed, but even so, things often did not work out to the satisfaction of both parties.

A good historical overview of the changes in divorce law during the 1970s is Lenore J. Weitzman's 1985 book, *The Divorce Revolution*, one of the first to examine the subject.[2] Everyone I spoke to who is even vaguely connected with the divorce process agrees that the book remains valid for the years it covers, but a new survey is needed of the years that have since passed simply because every state is either actively revising divorce law or at least considering changes to it. Lawyers joke that if such a book were written, the law is changing so fast that it might well become outdated before it is even published.

However, Weitzman's initial finding remains as true today as it was in 1985, that changes meant to ensure equality did indeed remove divorce from the realm of "moral questions of fault and responsibility" and relocate it squarely in the category of "economic issues." Marital settlements were removed from considerations of anger, pain, and the related emotions connected with adultery or abuse and put into a far more basic category: that of one spouse's "ability to pay" and the "financial need" of the other. And in so doing, a profound and unexpected change occurred.

Rules that were intended to be "gender neutral" suddenly took on "unanticipated, unintended, and unfortunate consequences." Laws that had been radically redesigned to give women an equal share of marital assets often had an opposite and chilling effect:

> [They] served to deprive divorced women (especially older homemakers and mothers of young children) of the legal and financial protections that the old law provided. Instead of recognition for their contributions as homemakers and mothers, and instead of compensation for the years of lost opportunities and impaired earning capacities, these women now face a divorce law that treats them "equally" and expects them to be equally capable of supporting themselves after a divorce.

When I discussed Weitzman's contention with a divorce attorney in Texas whose practice "evolved naturally" into representing wealthy men, he agreed that what she wrote was true. Then he laughed and told me to put her "hifalutin words into ordinary language: blame the raw deal women get on all those [1970s] radical feminists. You women wanted equality and you got it, so learn to live with it."

DIVIDING THE ASSETS

All states, no matter what original system their basic legal code was founded upon, assign the courts the task of determining the same basic criteria: how best to divide the marital assets; how to divide community property equally; and whether to assign alimony, and if so, how much and for how long. Frequently, an equal division may not happen, as many states still exclude "career assets," all or in part. These encompass everything a couple builds together during marriage, beginning with the principal wage earner's salary and covering a broad range that includes pensions, medical insurance, education (i.e., who got it and who paid for it), the inherent value of a business or profession that may have been started and/or built up by the couple, entitlements to a business or profession's goods and services, and the future earning power of one or both spouses.

When the laws were changing in the 1970s and later, most noncommunity property states did not consider some or all of these to be divisible assets, saying they rightfully belonged to the spouse who earned them. That was usually the husband, who was entitled to keep them, as well as all stock options, bonuses, and other perks that came with his job. His ex-wife usually received a share of his current (at the time of their separation) income and little else. The actual "date of separation" became key in dividing a couple's assets, as one lawyer explained to me by using the example of a client (male) who won a sizeable fortune in a state lottery drawing. The judge allowed him to keep all the money because the date on the ticket and the date on a check he paid to lease an apartment proved that he bought the winning ticket well after he had moved out of the family home and begun divorce proceedings.

One woman in New Jersey whose husband was a physician at the time of their divorce in 1977 accepted an annual alimony of $14,000, which was based on a percentage of her husband's salary. The sum would remain constant and was hers for her lifetime so long as she did not remarry. No consideration was given to her husband's extensive investments, real estate holdings, medical insurance, and even a modest inheritance he received during the marriage and placed in a joint savings account. Nor was any consideration given to the doctor's adultery with the woman he later married. In fact, his lawyers took pleasure in describing his ex-wife's behavior in the open courtroom, so egregious that the local newspaper reported it and the local shock jock on talk radio made a running joke of it.

The doctor's wife knew when her husband was conducting his assignations, and she would park her car outside his lover's apartment building, where she would sit on the horn, letting it blare. Neighbors called the police, who because of her husband's reputation in the community would only caution the wife to "go home and get some sleep." Twenty-nine years later, she still recalled and replayed this incident as if it had just happened.

But twenty-nine years did pass, and the doctor, now divorced from the second wife (and a third and married to a fourth) went on to become a senior executive in a pharmaceutical company where he routinely earns a seven figure salary, plus all the benefits and perks commensurate with it. His ex-wife still lives on the annual $14,000 plus her Social Security and part-time substitute teaching in a local junior high school. She is bitter now, as she scrimps and saves, living modestly while his life becomes increasingly lavish.

She wishes she had taken her husband's future earning possibilities into consideration, but even if she had, she would probably not have had legal grounds for a new petition because judges are charged with making decisions on the facts before them, not on the possibility of future situations. In 1977, her jubilant lawyer told her she had "beaten the system, so be happy." In 2005, three lawyers with whom I discussed the case said something quite different. The first put it discreetly: "Perhaps she did not have the best legal advice." The second was more direct: "Somebody's lawyer screwed up, and big-time." The third said, "This was not a screwup; at the time it was a fair and equitable solution." He noted that she has been paid $406,000 during those twenty-nine years, with more still to come. He thinks she did well, considering the time in which she divorced.

I learned that this woman's protest that she had not received an equal share of marital assets, even though it came years after the divorce, was not unusual. An attorney in New York State said he could describe so many cases in which his women clients actually did not receive an equal share of the marital assets at the time of their divorce that they blurred together in his mind. His comment echoed a remark made by Peter Bodnar, a member of the family-law section of the New York State and Westchester County bar associations, who described judges assigned to preside over divorce cases as "judges who are punished or judges who were just appointed to the bench." Monica Getz, founder of the Coalition for Family Justice based in Irvington, New York, said that although both men and women allege that the courts have a "gender bias," it is more accurate to use the term "power bias: whoever has money has the good lawyer. . . . whoever has the money has the energy and power."[3]

"THE TRUE VALUE OF A SPOUSE"
An attorney in Pennsylvania told me that one of her most bitterly contested divorce cases happened just after the 1980 reforms in that state, when a battered working-class woman who would have been destitute insisted on

receiving a share of her abusive mill worker husband's pension. The husband told the judge, "I worked for it, so it's mine," and the judge agreed with him. The case went to appeal, and several years later the decision was reversed and the woman did receive 30 percent of the pension.

The most famous case of a wife who sued for what some attorneys called the "intangibles" of a couple's "career assets" is Lorna Jorgenson Wendt, whose case was discussed inchapter 5 and who in 1994 began a three-year battle with Gary C. Wendt, the CEO of General Electric. Legal scholars agree that the Wendt settlement has become the landmark case in determining "the true economic value of a corporate spouse,"[4] and when they go to court on behalf of "ordinary women," they ask that it be applied to "the true value of a spouse," no matter what the woman's economic status and social position may have been during her marriage. Lorna Wendt's long battle ended when she accepted a $20 million settlement that reflected her many contributions to her husband's career. She used some of it to found the Equality in Marriage Institute, which educates women to become "more attuned to what is theirs in the partnership of the marriage."

A case not nearly so high-profile and without the positive settlement (for Lorna) of the Wendt divorce involved a California college professor and his wife, who ended their thirty-year marriage several years ago, before the 1985 reforms.[5] They met in graduate school, but while he earned his Ph.D., she earned her Ph.T. working by day as a secretary and typing his papers at night. Once he began his climb up the academic ladder, she gave up her own plans for a business career and devoted herself to raising children, giving dinner parties, mothering his graduate students, and entertaining his colleagues. She still typed his books, for which she generally did much of the research and all of the editing, becoming, in effect, his co-author. In the divorce settlement, the judge awarded her $700 a month for three years, after which she was expected to get a paying job. With justified bitterness, she complained: "Never mind that I am fifty-one, never mind that I had a job and did it well and am old enough to be entitled to a pension. It's not that I regret my life or didn't enjoy what I did. But it was supposed to be a partnership, a fifty-fifty split. It isn't fair that he gets to keep it. It isn't fair for the court to treat it as his. . . . I earned it just as much as he did."

The same lawyers with whom I discussed the New Jersey woman's case agreed about the settlement in this one: "This would never happen today, but because of how the law was written in those years, she didn't do too badly."

"OLD AND USED WIVES"

In the initial years after the California Family Code was changed to no-fault, some judges deplored what they saw as the unfair adjudication of the alimony statute. An oft-cited reversal was made by appeals court judge Robert Gardner in 1977, when he ruled that a woman who had lived her long married life as a homemaker was unlikely to find gainful employment, so "the husband simply has to face up to the fact that his support responsibilities are going to be of extended duration, perhaps for life"[6] Judge Gardner added that it had "nothing to do with feminism, sexism, male chauvinism, or any other trendy ideology. It is ordinary common sense, basic decency, and simple justice." He concluded that, although "[no-fault divorce] has been heralded as a bill of rights for harried former husbands who have been suffering under prolonged and unreasonable alimony awards . . . the act may not be used as a handy vehicle for the summary disposal of old and used wives. A woman is not a breeding cow to be nurtured during her years of fecundity, then conveniently and economically converted to cheap steaks when past her prime."[7]

Marital assets are often the cause of the most bitterly contested divorces. Helen and John, who divorced after thirty-eight years because of irreconcilable differences, spent a fortune in legal fees disputing theirs. John was a physician in Connecticut, and Helen had never worked outside the home. At the time they divorced in the late 1980s, Helens mother had recently died and her father was gravely ill and not expected to live much longer. When he died, Helen, an only child, thought she stood to inherit between $3 million and $5 million, but because her father had always been so secretive and cagy, she didn't know if the money would come to her directly, be dispensed through a trust, or, with the exception of a small annual stipend, even skip her and go directly to her four children. She had already received half a million dollars from her parents earlier in the marriage, which she and John had commingled and used for a down payment on a larger house and their children's education.

Helen was in her mid-sixties, and because the inheritance was uncertain, she felt justified in asking John for long-term alimony, to be paid until the end of his or her life. Also, because her earlier inheritance had paid for many of the numerous investments he had accumulated over the years in his name alone, she wanted a share of them. John specialized in facial and reconstructive surgery, and his professional reputation was as high as his income. Helen wanted the courts to take his future earnings into consideration, arguing that she would have nothing to fall back on if her fears that her father would set up a generation-skipping trust that gave the expected inheritance directly to the children turned out to be true. John countered that he should be entitled to half of whatever inheritance Helen might receive because he had been her sole support during their long marriage.

Once they began divorce proceedings, they were confronted with a truth that was bitter to them both: in Connecticut, "expectancy is not a reality." Connecticut is an "all property distribution" state, thus an inheritance, treated as separate property in all common-property states and in many others as well, could be assigned in Connecticut to either or both spouses. The one thing the court could not do is speculate—in this case, to look at possible inheritances that may or may not come to pass. This meant that when and if Helen did receive the inheritance after the divorce, it would be hers and John could not share in it. That was the good news, at least to Helen; the bad news came with the division of John's investments.

These were assets that still possessed the ability to accumulate money in the future, but future earning possibilities had no bearing on their value at the time of the separation. John had made those investments during the marriage and therefore they counted as marital property that had to be equitably divided. Unfortunately for Helen, the division coincided with a sharp drop in the various markets where he had invested them, and so their value was far lower than when he bought them. Each would reap any profits from future earnings if their values rose again, and within six months after the division, they did rise steadily, greatly surpassing the value they held at the time of the divorce. Helen did not share in the windfall, however, because she sold her shares as soon as she received them. John held on to his, which gave her one more reason to resent him.

A law professor who did not represent either party but who uses their case in her teaching told me, "the courts don't do 'if,' 'as,' or 'when.' " She said difficulties always arise in divorce negotiations when one person decides to ask for a larger share of the total assets at the time of the divorce in order to balance out what the other might earn in the future. Often, "the road toward achieving a balance can be highly contentious." Whenever the wife wants lifelong alimony from the high-earning husband, "things can get especially complicated. Husbands get very resentful if they have to keep working to support an ex-wife, and many are very clever about finding ways to slither out of it."

Helen and John's lawyers eventually worked out a resolution that left both parties "disgruntled," which the law professor interprets to mean that all community property was probably divided as fairly as possible. However, Helen and John refused to accept their lawyers' advice to let the matter rest, and each petitioned the court for a "modification." The judge who heard the petition was a man (as was the original judge who granted the decree), and when the law professor who teaches this case read their decisions, she thought each had acted responsibly and fairly She pointed out how the appeals judge factored a very important concern into his decision: the future needs of each party In this case, he based it upon their lifestyle before the divorce and their ability to maintain it in the future.

John, who earned their income throughout the marriage, planned to continue to work but to cut back on his long, stressful hours, which would mean that his income would be significantly reduced. Helen was no longer running their home, overseeing the physical condition (decor and upkeep) of John's offices, entertaining on John's behalf, or fulfilling the charitable obligations that went along with his work and that required substantial monetary donations as well as clothes for her. The judge decided that, as she had never held a paying job and as these duties would no longer be required of her, she would not need as much of John's income in the future. He decreed that the original 65-35 split was fair and that it should not be changed to 50-50, as Helen wanted it, or 80-20, as John wanted it. Helen was given ten years of alimony based on the 65-35 percentage, after which, when she would be in her mid-seventies, the judge said she could "always find something to do."

It turned out that Helen's suspicions about how she would receive her inheritance were well founded. Although her situation was never going to be dire, her income was still going to be much less than what she had during her marriage. Her father locked the money into a trust that gave her a modest annual income for life, with the rest dispersed to her children periodically at their significant milestone birthdays, starting with age twenty-five. Helen railed against a legal system that she swore would someday soon reduce her to "clipping supermarket food coupons," but her children rightly pointed out that her house was paid for and her annual income was enough for her to live in it for as long as she wanted. They assured her that she would never want, but she dismissed their assertions, saying, "You never know who they will marry and how they will feel about me, and then what will happen to the money!"

EQUITABLE DISTRIBUTION

Forty-one of the fifty states have adopted "equitable distribution" as the criteria for dividing assets when a couple divorces. The nine remaining "community property" states are Arizona, California, Idaho, Louisiana, New Mexico, Nevada, Texas, Washington, and Wisconsin. In those nine, any property acquired by the couple during the marriage up to the date of separation is considered "community property" and must be equally divided between the spouses. Equitable distribution, which was adopted by the other forty-one with the intention that it would be exactly what its name describes—equitable—is often far from it. Equitable distribution is *not* the equal division of a couple's assets but rather, it depends largely upon the judge's decision as to how best to divide any assets a couple has amassed that fall under the heading of "marital property."

The law was intended to ensure simplicity, but it has often had the opposite effect, resulting in complexity and contention. In almost every equitable-distribution state, even in the most straightforward divorces where minimal assets are at stake, couples become mired in animosity and antagonism as they argue over what they believe is their fair share. Lawyers all seem to agree that equitable distribution usually requires divorcing couples to have far more contact with the legal system than they expected, and "the greater the contact, the more bitter the divorce."

One of the saddest disputes occurred fourteen years after a bitter divorce when Russell Hendrix and Renee Amick went to court to battle over which parent had the right to bury the remains of their son, Staff Sergeant Jason R. Hendrix, killed in Iraq.[8] It took the parents three years to become divorced, as they argued over alcoholism, money problems, accusations of domestic abuse, and the welfare of their three children. When their son was killed in Iraq, the fight over burial rights began. It became one of several similar cases (the others are in Nevada and Michigan) inadvertently created by legal loopholes and other shortcomings in divorce law relating to equitable distribution of community property. When a soldier does not leave a will or otherwise name a person who will have the right to claim his remains, Pentagon policy grants custody to the elder of his or her parents, in this case, the father, Russell Hendrix. Renee Amick disputed this decision, insisting that her son told her verbally where he wanted to be buried, and it was not in the place his father chose.

Representative Sam Farr (D.-CA), who is spearheading a change in the Pentagon's policy, asserted that the original document was created under the assumption that "everybody was coming from an *Ozzie and Harriet* background." The policy has to be changed, Farr continued, for there are now "a lot of soldiers coming in from dysfunctional families." Because of these cases, a soldier's "emergency contact form" is being rewritten to ensure that a specific "person [is] authorized to direct disposition" of the soldier's remains.

In the Michigan case, the body of Lance Corporal Allan Klein is temporarily in a crypt until the "custody battle" between his parents is settled. The battle over the body of Staff Sergeant Hendrix is a sad one, as he lies temporarily interred beside his grandfather's grave in Tulsa, Oklahoma, because his parents cannot agree about his final burial. His two surviving siblings and one stepchild have chosen sides, and members of the extended family have been enlisted to testify on behalf of one or the other feuding parent. During recesses in testimony, "members of the family congregate in a parking lot, sometimes exchanging rude hand gestures and accusing each other of lying." The judge told the parents they would have "the court's bless-ing" as he appealed to them to settle their differences and compromise, but they were unable to do so.

The judge in the Hendrix-Amick case suggested a possible compromise that is becoming a growing trend among divorced couples. To give an exam-ple from an unrelated case: when a child long estranged from his divorced fundamentalist Christian parents died of AIDS, they agreed to divide his ashes. The Hendrix-Amick couple refused this option as well as all others.

DIVORCE INTERNATIONAL STYLE

No matter what the country, equitable distribution is basically the same concept albeit under different names. In New Zealand, the Relationships Property Act of 2001 aimed to make it easier to divorce for women who had never worked, had no money of their own, and depended financially on their husbands. Under this law, assets are no longer split fifty-fifty, but the courts are required to compensate for economic disparity. For example, if a husband and wife agreed early in their marriage that she would stay at home, raise the children, and cater to the needs of his career rather than forging one of her own, once they were divorced, her standard of living still had to equal his.

In France, where 40 percent of marriages end in divorce and it is an openly accepted fact of life that women's salaries will always be at least 20 percent lower than that of men who do the same work, a sweeping set of changes were instituted in 2005 to allow for greater equality. Couples can now divorce in two years instead of six, and a woman's right to sufficient spousal maintenance is all but assured. Some opponents of the changes said it would surely lead to "societal disruption," but politicians with an eye on reelection have pledged to deliver salary and divorce equality within the next five years. Also, France has long had the reputation of being a country where couples might lead separate lives—sometimes openly taking a lover or lovers or even having children in a second family—but stay married to keep the assets intact. Things are changing now, with divorce among the older generations almost on a par with the younger ones as the rate rises steadily every year.

Chile was the last country in South America to allow divorce, when the country's 1884 marriage laws were finally overturned at the end of 2004. It still took nine years of legislative debate before the law permitting divorce was passed, but in the two years since it has been in place, women's groups have monitored the courts and agree that its greatest benefit is that it permits women who initiate divorce to "live a new life with dignity, without fear [of male reprisal or punishment]."

In China, until the reform laws of 2003, divorce was anathema and infidelity so widely accepted that men who could afford to do so stayed married but set up their mistresses in "concubine villages."[9] Since the new laws were enacted, the stigma attached to overthrowing "traditional values" is no longer enough to keep a couple together, for "individualism has taken over." Because male infidelity is the main reason cited in Chinese divorce cases, it is probably not surprising that women are asking for them in record numbers. More than 70 percent of the divorces in a single province, Guangdong, were initiated by women, while throughout all of China the overall rate of divorce, though still well below that of the United States, climbs each year by at least 20 percent.

Before the reforms, divorce was such a complicated process that few Chinese couples had the physical and mental stamina to deal with the many insulting requirements, primary among them that the employers of both parties had to approve it. Many older couples stayed in loveless, abusive marriages because of the shame involved when they had to seek permission from a spouse, an employer, and a host of government officials. Now older people are divorcing in the same number as their younger counterparts because it is easy to get an uncontested "flash divorce." They need only show up at a government office with a marriage certificate, identification card, photographs, and an application for divorce. If all goes well, a marriage can be dissolved in thirty minutes or less, the same amount of time it takes to get married.

In fact, divorce is now so easy in China that 98 percent of the married couples in one village, Renhe (population 4,000), stampeded to separate early in 2006.[10] The oldest couples were in their nineties, "and barely able to move," while the youngest were newlyweds with infant children. The rush to enter SPLITSVILLE, CHINA, as a headline in the *Los Angeles Times* story put it, had nothing to do with falling out of love and everything to do with getting a bigger and better apartment through what the peasants believed was a legal loophole. When the government seized farmland to build houses, the farmers were told that a married couple would be relocated into a two-bedroom apartment, whereas a divorced couple would receive two one-bedroom apartments. Everyone seized upon divorce as the better option, thinking they would live in one apartment and rent the other until the deal was safely sealed, after which they would remarry. The race to the local divorce registry was "practically jolly" as the suddenly-singles contemplated their expected windfall.

"Everyone divorces," said one of the farmers, who described it as "now a local custom." People were foolish if they did not, he added. "Divorce gives us a chance to sit on a longer bench. Don't get divorced and you sit on a small stool or in the dirt."

Like most get-rich schemes, this one hit a major glitch as soon as Chinese authorities realized what was happening. The compensation package was changed so that divorced farmers had to pay market prices for the second apartment and to wait, often for years, for it to be built.

Meanwhile, the village's social fabric is in shambles. Many ex-spouses have drifted off into new relationships and won't return to their former mates; many more have decided they like being single and independent and refuse to remarry. Many others can't see their way clear to remarry even if they want to, because of the lifelong financial insecurity they face after surrendering their farms and finding they have few prospects for other jobs.

Villagers in Renhe no longer offer the traditional Chinese greeting of "Have you eaten?" Now the customary greeting is "Have you divorced?" No one would have divorced had it not been for the enticement of two apartments, said one elderly grandfather whose wife refuses to come back to him. "At our age, what's the point?"

SPOUSAL MAINTENANCE

In all the countries discussed above as well as the United States and so many others, the question of spousal maintenance—alimony—looms large in all courtrooms, and many judges do not look too kindly upon it. Today people have the option to plan ahead with prenuptial agreements that usually do mitigate settlement disputes over who brought what possessions, money, and property to the marriage.

Pennsylvania provides an interesting example of what happens when a "fault" state adopts equitable-distribution codes, as it did in 1980, a decade after the California law was changed. Until then a divorce required proof of wrongdoing, and a truly equitable division of property usually happened only when one person was an egregiously "guilty party." Property was divided according to who held title to it, so if a house was a couple's only asset and it was registered in a husband's name, the wife got no part of it. The person who had the pension was entitled to keep it, and this usually meant the man. Lawyers, mediators, and psychologists who practice there all agree that pre-reform laws were so punitive that many women endured marriages of abuse and terror because they had nowhere else to go.

Now Pennsylvania is an equitable distribution state in which four major concerns are paramount:

1. How long did the marriage last?
2. What is the disparity of income between the two parties?
3. What resources did the couple accrete?
4. How should they be equitably divided?

Alimony is a "secondary remedy" in Pennsylvania, granted only after all the marital assets have been equally divided and the court deems that one person could not survive financially without it. However, as in so many other states, alimony is not something to count on permanently, as judges almost always award it for a minimal period. Ten years is usually the maximum, but five years or less is increasingly the norm.

Although there is a statewide system that is supposed to oversee alimony awards, there are differences from one county to another, particularly with those that use the "master system," that is, a court-appointed lawyer who is put in charge of equitable distribution. Divorce lawyers who practice in counties that rely heavily on masters agree that, with the evolution of divorce law, judges have taken a secondary seat in the proceedings and "everything depends on the masters," who settle 90 percent of all Pennsylvania divorce cases. Judges decide the remaining 10 percent, only stepping in to do so if one or both parties claim the master has committed an "abuse of discretion." And in nearly all cases where the judge has to adjudicate, alimony is paramount.

There are statewide guidelines but no systematic formula for determining alimony, so masters generally make the award by using a simple formula: for every year of marriage, they award a certain sum of money. Even so, women who have been married more than twenty years are often shocked to find how little they have been awarded and then for only four or five years. Far too frequently, judges have been upholding the masters' decisions that women in their sixties who have never worked outside the home should still be able to find a full-time job and become self-supporting, even as their husbands, who are nearing retirement age, can looked forward to a fairly comfortable life after divorce.

WHERE DIVORCE IS NO SLAM DUNK

New York is still a "fault" state, with laws so complex and convoluted that many lawyers (even those who don't even practice there) agree it ranks first among the fifty states in throwing obstacles at couples who have every justified reason for wanting to divorce. A famous case of how capricious the law can be began in January 2003, when Cathy and Robert Jacob went to court to end their twenty-six-year marriage. The divorce was granted but Robert appealed because he did not like the financial settlement. Both parties were stunned when the appellate court ruled in June 2004 that neither Cathy nor Robert had shown "proper grounds" for being granted a divorce in the first place. The divorce was overturned, ruled invalid, and the astonished couple was told they were still legally married. As of 2006, three years after the original divorce, the couple remains in marital limbo. The lawyer who represented Robert said she had no idea "that the court would say, 'A pox on you both,' " and she cautioned other couples who wish to divorce in New York State "that getting a divorce [there] is not a slam dunk."[11]

As of 2006, divorce in New York can only be granted in cases where both spouses consent. State legislators and jurists are considering a change of law that would allow one spouse to cite grounds such as irreconcilable differences, incompatibility, or irretrievable breakdown as reason to divorce without first having to secure the agreement of the other. Because mutual consent is required, often one of the parties must agree to what is most likely a charade, pretending to be the victim of cruel or inhumane treatment, adultery, or abandonment (either physical or sexual).

The only way a couple can divorce without proving fault is to agree about everything from the division of financial assets to child custody, and they must certainly agree on spousal maintenance or alimony. They must then live apart for one year, during which they are no doubt on tenterhooks, for each spouse has the right to change his or her mind and profess to want to return to the marriage, or to claim that the other has not lived up to the terms of agreement and therefore no divorce should be granted. There are, however, ways around the law, as in a recent high-profile New York divorce that has everyone from lawyers to gossip columnists wondering how it happened so fast. On February 9, 2006, the actress Ellen Barkin moved out of businessman Ronald Perelman's town house, and on February 14, a judge finalized their divorce. A writer for *New York* magazine was discreetly parenthetical when he wrote, "(It's not clear how the couple divorced so quickly)."[12]

Judges who don't want to deal with the claims and counterclaims of marital disputes, such as that of Cathy and Robert Jacob, often advise couples to cite "constructive abandonment," in which one spouse asserts he or she repeatedly asked for sex and was denied, at least for a year. Even that doesn't always work, as it, too, becomes "he said, she said" and is difficult to prove.

In another oft-cited case, an unnamed woman who wanted to end a thirty-year marriage on the grounds of "cruel and inhumane treatment" was denied a divorce by a judge who decided that her husband's latest threat, to cut up her sofa with a chain saw, did not meet the legal requirement for cruelty, which had to be so severe that the couple could not live together. Apparently, this judge thought it was still possible for them to share an apartment and a life, even though the woman might have to live with the constant fear of finding her furniture in a shambles.

When John DeFrancisco, the state senator who is chairman of the Judiciary Committee, heard of this decision, he said, "It may be time for New York to get back to reality rather than legal fiction." Early in 2006 a state commission was convened to investigate matrimonial law and recommended an overhaul that would permit no-fault divorce. The state's chief judge, Judith S. Kaye, said the possibility of change "unquestionably will be front and center for us in the coming months."[13]

As for Robert and Cathy Jacobs, the couple has been separated long enough that Cathy can now file legitimately for divorce on the grounds of abandonment and have it granted. However, she is sitting in the catbird seat because the court awarded her "indefinite spousal support" and she does not have to sell her home. Her lawyer agreed with a reporter that Cathy could indeed "commence another action for divorce, but why?" Other lawyers agree that in this case "the legal ramifications boggle the mind!"

PET ROCKS AND HOUSEHUSBANDS

Lawyers in four states—California, Illinois, New York, and Pennsylvania—told me that judges have a term for women who have never worked outside the home and therefore believe they should receive lifelong alimony equal to the income they had during their marriages: "Pet Rocks." Judges who are this unsympathetic to the plight of these women, who are usually in late middle or old age, usually express "the overall feeling: you are healthy and you can work, so go out and find a job." Women who may have worked part-time throughout their marriage and who settled for taking jobs rather than forging careers so they could put the needs of their husband and children first discover an equally harsh reality when they enter divorce court—that even part-time work may count against them when it comes to alimony. Judges grant them limited alimony and expect them to turn part-time work, no matter how insignificant it may have been, into a full-time profession.

There is an interesting new wrinkle in how alimony is awarded now that so many women have spent most of their married years in the workforce.

Women in their forties and fifties who came of age during the feminist revolution of the 1970s have generally always worked outside the home. Many women in their sixties looked at their example and joined the workforce once their children were safely situated in school, so they also have a history of working. Many of these working women were more financially successful than their husbands, who played differing roles within the marriage. Some were stay-at-home dads from the beginning of the parenting years, while others chose this option early in the marriage whether or not they had children. Roles for middle-aged married men with working wives changed when an increasing number lost jobs in recessions, layoffs, and outsourcings. Many chose not to reenter the working world or else had to take lesser jobs that turned their wives into the family's principal wage earner. Some men were disabled and forced to rely on disability compensation and the salaries of their wives. There are still others who were victimized by an unspoken age discrimination, who wanted to find jobs but could not, thus becoming an unwilling statistic among the permanently unemployed.

When divorce happens to some of these couples, it is the women who howl in protest when men ask not only for an equal share of the marital assets but for alimony as well. Women complain that they had to hold two jobs throughout the marriage and should be compensated accordingly because they were not only the family breadwinner but also the primary caregiver. They argue that, once their paying job ended for the day, they went home to their "second job on the second shift" as they took over most of the household responsibilities.

In several of the Mountain States, where "traditional values" is the dominant mantra and divorce is highly frowned upon, lawyers who represent women hint that judges often slant their rulings to favor men. Even if women cite financial inequity, based on the clear claim that they earned more than men throughout the long marriage, many judges ruled that marital assets had to be equally divided, with the men receiving half of everything the woman earned, as well as a generous alimony to be paid until the man found a job or remarried. The women in these cases believe strongly that if the situation were reversed, they would have received a reduced share of the assets and minimal alimony.

A California attorney explained that this would not happen in her state, which still follows community-property law: "Each spouse owns half of what the other earns jointly, et cetera." And she added, "woe to the spouse who commingled an inheritance from good old Uncle Fred! Although an inheritance should constitute separate property, once commingled in the joint account, the money is no longer the exclusive property of the spouse who received it."

In Texas, lawyers say that judges are far more reluctant "to give men money, even when they are clearly entitled to it." Interestingly, Pennsylvania, which often holds women to more stringent standards than men, recently upheld the interests of a working woman against her house-husband: she was awarded 60 percent of the couple's assets, and he received 40 percent. He appealed the decision but lost when the appellate court cited "no abuse of discretion" on the part of the master.

In other states, attorneys marvel at the "gall" or "stubbornness" with which some men pursue the assets of working wives. A California divorce has been in limbo since the couple, Ernest and Eva, separated in 1996. He has not worked since the separation and lives on government disability payments (SSI), while Eva has continued to work for a company that will grant her a pension when she retires in 2018. As he finally files for divorce in 2006, Ernest wants half the money she will receive then—and he wants it *right now!* He refuses to accept the reality that he will be entitled to only a portion of the value of the 401 (k) plan as it was valued at the time of their separation, and that Eva will not have to give him this money until her pension begins in 2018.

Another interesting wrinkle to the alimony situation involves couples who did not begin their families until both were older, or in some cases, who are ending a second marriage in which an older man has fathered children by a younger wife. Most states have wage-attachment laws that garnish salaries for child support, but child support usually ends when the child turns eighteen or graduates from high school. The state does not concern itself with the education of an adult child, and so couples often make their children's college expenses an issue of "negotiated settlement." Sometimes a wife will forgo alimony in order to force a husband to pay for the children's higher education, but far too many women cannot afford to do so and the children are usually left to fend for themselves if their fathers refuse to help them. Lawyers advise some of these divorcing couples about the importance of negotiating all sorts of terms while settlement decisions are still in play, among them such things as orthodontia, music lessons, school fees, and higher education. Child support, however, cannot be negotiated and is between the noncustodial parent and the state.

Even fathers who want to remain a part of the children's lives and insist upon sharing custody are often "driven by money" during the divorce process. When they protest the amount of support a judge decrees they must pay, they will often try to have it reduced by arguing that "if I have to keep the kids part of the time, then I should pay her [the ex-wife] only part of the money." In states such as Pennsylvania, lawyers have to advise them that if a husband does not share custody equally, a divorced wife's expenses remain constant whether the children are with him for an afternoon or a weekend, or in her house or not: the rent is still due, the utilities must be paid, and the children must be clothed and fed. Often, lawyers say, this is a difficult argument to convince an angry father to accept. However, even though joint custody often means that one parent does not have to pay the other spousal support, support payments are still the bone of contention many couples cannot stop chewing.

REALITY CHECKERS

A divorce lawyer in a western state who works solely as a mediator described what he does as "tripartite: one part law, one part accounting, and one part therapy." He described how he settled into his current career through a "roundabout route" that began thirty years earlier when he joined a prestigious firm and was assigned to practice family law. He found it so emotionally distressing that he left it as soon as he could: "Except for the loss of a child, divorce is generally the hardest thing a couple has to go through. They are distraught, bitter; they want revenge. It was too intense for me."

He practiced other kinds of law for twenty years until, in his mid-fifties and with "age and experience," he became so intrigued by the intricacies that brought couples to the brink of divorce that he returned to family law as a mediator. He explained the change of mind by saying that, as a young man, he tried to dissuade clients from divorcing and would look for reasons why they should "make one more effort" to stay together. Now that he is older, he is an advocate for divorce if he thinks the dynamic that held the couple together is no longer working and the marriage is well and truly over. When both parties have been miserable for so long, "what they need is peace. They might as well separate and start over." He believes that "people do become happier after divorce. It takes anywhere from six months to two years on the average, but the mood does lift and people really do get happier. Divorce helps them to pull their lives together."

This mediator finds that more women than men seek his services, which means that although he must meet with both partners in order to work out a mutually satisfying agreement, women are more likely to make the initial contact because "they are the ones who want divorce the most." Also, women are more likely than men to want to gather all the available information they can to guide them through the process, which dictates that they may come to him with the mistaken impression that the mediator will be their ally. In reality, both spouses must agree to go to the same mediator, which dictates that they must meet together with an impartial third party who will help them resolve their differences before they set foot in a courtroom. In this mediator's experience, "when a woman makes the decision to divorce, the marriage cannot and will not endure. By the time she comes to me, she has been processing divorce information for some time. This is what she wants and this is what she will do."

He practices in a wealthy county where divorcing couples are encouraged to resolve their differences through mediation so that the judge has merely to approve what they have decided. Mediation is "big" in his county but not in the three others that border it, a discrepancy he explains by saying that his is wealthy and the others are not, and his clients prefer to have everything settled privately rather than to broadcast their differences in a public courtroom where spectators can watch the proceedings as if they are in a movie theater. In his practice, "a preponderance of smart rich people put aside their emotions to make practical business decisions. They don't want to sit in a courtroom where their names get dragged in the mud. And besides, their lifestyle does not change after divorce because there is plenty of money to go around."

A woman lawyer-mediator in a midwestern state tells a far different story about her practice. "I am the reality checker. For my clients, ending a marriage usually comes down to economics. Most of my work consists of telling people, almost always women, that they won't be able to survive if they divorce. "

Her clients represent a trend that is increasing every year. Sixty-five percent of divorcing persons go into court pro se, that is, representing themselves without legal counsel, because they fear, often rightly so, that they will not be able to afford a lawyer. This is why so many poor people who are desperate to divorce generally start by consulting a mediator if they think they need someone to guide them through the process. They may have heard somewhere that mediators must act as the neutral third party, which indeed they are legally bound to do, but their main reason for contacting a mediator rather than a lawyer is "for one simple reason: people hear we are cheaper." This is often not true, she cautions, as mediators in many states, especially those who are also lawyers, charge hourly rates that are on a par with divorce attorneys.

Mediators usually ask divorcing couples for an initial retainer to be paid at the first meeting, a fee that can vary widely depending on the mediator's qualifications and location.[14] After the retainer fee is used up, the mediator will bill the couple on an hourly basis for the sessions, which generally number between four and ten. There is never a set number, and because mediation is often complicated, there is no limit to the length of time (in terms of months or years) it might take to prepare the couple to go into court. Mediators almost always recommend that each party to the divorce retain a lawyer, but in complicated settlements where large assets are involved, they insist upon it. The additional cost of a retaining a lawyer is often what drives divorce litigants into pro se representation.

When poor people learn what costs and commitments mediation can entail, and because they have nowhere else to go, they often look for advice and guidance from family-service counselors who are employees of their state system. As one such counselor in Connecticut put it, "We are the ones who negotiate cases and assist clients (lawyers, too) in trying to compromise and reach agreements that all can live with. . . . We help settle cases, assist pro se clients, and inform them of their options. We make the process far less intimidating."[15]

However, family-services staff members in several states told me that what is described above is "the ideal, and often very hard to do." Most are so overburdened with caseloads that poor people who do manage to secure an appointment generally leave disappointed with the scant amount of attention they receive and are befuddled by the oft-confusing information they are given.

In California, for example, mediators who work in courtroom situations are generally social workers with a license in marriage and family counseling, LCSW being the initials they hang on their shingles. "If we were Ph.D.s," one told me, "we would never work for the low salary the state pays us." He says this cynically, even as he describes the care and attention he tries to give to couples who cannot afford to hire lawyers. He has to tell them, usually in blunt language: "Either you go with the standard division of property or you devise your own. Otherwise [he points down the hall to a courtroom] you go in there and the guy in the dress will do it for you, and you won't like it."

The "reality checker" mediator (who is also a lawyer) has seen many changes in the twenty-five years she has practiced. She finds that people today are both "informed and ill informed" about how to divorce. Even the poor have access to the Internet, and almost everyone who wants to divorce as cheaply as possible begins online, which she says is "not necessarily helpful or even legitimate." People become angry or upset when she has to tell them that the information they copied from Internet websites is "so generic as to be totally useless because everything varies from state to state." But just as state laws differ, so, too, do mediators and what they are legally permitted to do.

Mediators "come in so many colors that we are a motley, variegated lot," as one in New Jersey told me. They may do their work in court-ordered situations or in private practice. Depending on the state, they may or may not need to be lawyers first. Some states do not even require licensing, while others require mediators to complete a rigorous training course through organizations that are state-authorized to provide certification. Some states might also offer mediators the option of taking related courses for adjunct certification, such as those given by agencies specializing in domestic violence (to name just one example); others may require them to take such courses annually if they wish to keep their certification.

Some states require mediators to hold an advanced degree in one of the mental-health professions. Others stress how important it is for mediators not to act as therapists during negotiations with couples but to address only the legal or professional issues pertaining to divorce. Judges in some states told me how they "hate" (the word used by quite a few) to be presented with divorce agreements drafted by therapists who are also mediators because "they are often convoluted touchy-feely documents that don't deal with legal realities." A California publishing company sells a video/DVD that cautions attorneys to be wary of clients who may "expect and demand that you inflict pain and punishment on the spouse new!" The tape purports to show lawyers how to fulfill their legal role without having to act as the client's "therapist."[16]

All the mediators I spoke to agree that it takes a certain type of personality to be able to do work that demands delicate negotiating skills. They must be willing in every case "not to win, but to conciliate and compromise." Lawyers who do not mediate praise those who do even as they explain why they could not. A West Coast attorney described mediating as "always [being] stuck in the middle. No authority. No power. Trying to get square pegs into round holes all day long." Two mediators who responded to this comment begged to differ, and as one said, "Yes, but when we get those pegs into the right holes, nothing can compare with the satisfaction we feel."

WHY MEDIATION? MEN'S REASONS

No matter where in the country the mediators I talked to worked, they shared some general common experiences. Most agreed that clients who come to their offices have already decided that divorce is their only option, and they are there for two reasons only: to work out an equitable distribution and to try to avoid having a judge do it for them. Not surprisingly, men and women have different reasons for consulting mediators. Men are most eager to go to mediation when there is a closely held business at stake. They may consult a mediator hoping for an ally who will give them a "better deal," and before they even begin to discuss how other marital assets should be divided, they will declare that they'll agree to "almost anything, just so long as you don't touch the business." Mediation frequently ends right there, as soon as the mediator tells them they are in the presence of an impartial observer and they must produce all documentation pertaining to the value of the business. Most refuse to "open up," and the mediator has the unfortunate task of telling them she can no longer assist them and they must consult separate lawyers.

Another reason men consult mediators is when they have been "caretaker husbands" who "can't take it anymore." They want to shed the wives who may have been a burden for many years, either due to chronic illness or mental conditions ranging from bipolar disorder to depression. Others have wives who have been diagnosed with fatal diseases for which they need constant care and attention. In most of these cases, the men want so much to be relieved of their wives that they try to be as generous as they can even as they are embarrassed or ashamed of what they are doing. They want their generosity to unfold in the privacy of a mediator's office rather than in a courtroom, and they leave it to the mediator to work out the terms of agreement.

All the mediators I talked to agreed that when men consult them, at least 70 to 80 percent already have a new partner waiting in the wings. They also find that the men who want new partners are in their fifties and at the "younger end" of the late-divorce age spectrum, while the women for whom they want to shed their wives are almost always much younger, generally in their twenties or thirties. Mediators say it is rare to see older men who consult them about ending long marriages because they have found a new love interest, but several were able to tick off fairly long lists of men in their seventies and eighties who "rekindled old flames" and wanted to be "reunited" with them. The most popular places for such rekindling to happen are high school or college reunions, when one spouse or the other encounters an "old sweetheart." A mediator told me he was surprised when he counted up how many divorces instigated by "rekindling the old flame" he has negotiated in the past decade and found a dozen. Of the twelve, he has so far so negotiated second divorces for four and thinks at least one other may soon be in the offing. Unfortunately, he said, "the rekindling fizzles out fast," which confirms the statistic that second marriages entered into with high emotion often end on a note sad and low.

Men also go to mediators because they "just want peace." Mediators can sense that this will be the reason men finally admit to when they cannot make eye contact and "blush and stammer and beat around the bush." Eventually they admit that they have come to a mediator because they are too embarrassed to go into a courtroom where it might come out that they were "nagged and henpecked" throughout their marriages. They want mediators to protect them from embarrassment and get them out of the marriage "fast and easy." One mediator told me that when he tells these men they must bring the wives they want to shed to subsequent sessions, he often never sees them again. He doesn't know if they engage a lawyer and go into court or if they just resign themselves into staying in a miserable marriage.

WHY MEDIATION? WOMEN'S REASONS

Most of the women who consult mediators begin by saying they are "so tired, tired of what it takes to keep the marriage going." Then they describe what "sent them over the top" and brought them to the mediators office. This is usually some variation on how "generally clueless" their husbands have been about decades of unhappiness. When their husbands hear this, they tell the mediator how perplexed they are to be there, saying, " 'We don't fight. . . . she makes my dinner . . . what else does she want?'—or words to that effect." Mediators say much of their practice consists of counseling couples who are "out of sync: what may be fine for one spouse may be what triggers the other to fall over the edge."

It is usually this "male zone of comfort and familiarity that enrages the female," and these are the women who tell mediators "they just want to do something different with whatever time they have left." The specter of old age and the possibility of incapacitating illness often push women to divorce. One woman whose husband was a farmer told a mediator in a western plains state, "I haven't liked him for thirty-five years, and now he is getting old and taking a lot of pills and I don't want to have to care for him when he's sick. He wouldn't be able to take care of me if I got sick, so why should I stick around to nurse him when I still have time to do the things I want to do?" She is among the approximate 60 percent of women who don't want to care for an aging or ailing spouse and who seek divorce because they want to find a new companion. They want to be the one to choose a new partner and decide how the relationship will develop.

Other women consult mediators to learn how to divorce "the whole damn family, not just the husband!" This reflects the dissention older children sow between their parents as the "boomerang generation" keeps bouncing back to the family home. Sociologists and psychologists have gussied up the behavior of adult children by calling it "emerging adulthood" and excusing them as "not teenagers and . . . not really adults." When asked if there was a "specific age" when adult children might be expected to become independent of their parents, psychologists and economists "point to the early or mid-thirties."[17]

Josephine, who "walked away from forty-two years of marriage just so I could get away from my kids," snorted when I read these quotes to her. I told her I could see steam coming from her ears when she elaborated: "I went to college when I was eighteen, married when I was twenty-one, had my first kid at twenty-two, and never took a nickel or anything else from my parents except for birthday gifts and Christmas presents. Where in the hell do these kids get off, mooching for half their lives? What is this generation—the child from one to forty?"

Others I interviewed described adult children who live independent lives elsewhere and make excellent salaries but who still expect their parents to help them buy houses, pay for the grandchildren's education, or procure the lifestyle they had as the children of affluent parents and cannot afford to buy for themselves. Jerome, who sold his small business and retired when his wife left him, says he can understand why she "wanted out." He moans that his son "makes eighty thousand a year, and that's still not enough for him. I'm supposed to kick in enough for him to live like he makes a quarter of a million, and if I don't give when he asks, I don't get to see the grandkids."

When these wives and mothers instigate divorce, mediators attribute it to the overwhelming desire to "wean the thirtysomething generation." The mediators worry about the "serious societal impact" of the children's demands and the husbands' incomprehension of the plight imposed upon so many elderly women by these adult children. These women are fed up with having to mother their children, and they become even angrier when their husbands don't understand why they object to becoming full-time caregivers to their grandchildren. One mediator used the description offered by one of her woman clients because it could stand for what so many told her: "like [Ibsen's] Nora, she walked out and slammed the door forever on her marriage when her husband said he didn't understand what she was so upset about: Didn't she mother her own children, and isn't helping to raise the grandchildren just a continuation of a woman's life's cycle?"

In countries like Switzerland, where married women with children are only just entering the workforce in large numbers, therapists and analysts find their practices burgeoning with young mothers who resent that their own mothers will not provide steady day care for the grandchildren. The grandmothers remember that they could not enter a profession or pursue a career and say, "I raised my children and now it's my turn to be free to pursue my own interests." Divorces happen more and more frequently in the older generation, when the grandfathers side with their daughters and insist that the grandmothers assume responsibility for raising the new generation. The grandmothers respond by quietly walking right out the household door and into their own independent lives. The grandfathers only permit this to happen because at all costs in such male-dominated societies, they want to avoid "scandal."

In Germany the problem is starting to affect the marriages of older couples, as their daughters no longer fear the hostility that comes with being a *Rabenmutter* (whose literal translation is "mother of a raven"), a woman who chooses to marry and have children but to work as well. In a country so hostile to working mothers that child-care centers routinely shut down at 1P.M., most women who can't afford a nanny find they have an unpleasant choice: grandmother takes care of the kids, or the mothers don't work. These grandmothers are caught in a painful bind: if they do care for the grandchildren, they face the disapproval of a hostile society; if they refuse, their children resent them. I am told by many therapists that older German women are quietly seeking counsel in record numbers, just to deal with this unfortunate situation.

In England, Australia, and New Zealand I encountered long marriages facing problems created by the demands of adult children. In the United States, mediators describe elderly couples arriving at their offices with grandchildren in tow. The harried women say they simply want "out from under," referring to the expectation that they raise another generation of children, while the puzzled men say they think "she just needs a little vacation to help straighten her out." Both mediators and therapists describe these couples as the "husbands and wives whose kids made them forget how to be a couple, how to nurture their marriage." It is sad, but having to raise their children's children makes this starkly apparent, and many can't bear to face it. Divorce became more than an "option," as one grandmother told me—it became her "salvation."

EQUAL BEHAVIOR, UNEQUAL TREATMENT

For many women who have been in the workforce the better part of their adult lives, a growing reason they consult mediators rather than divorce lawyers is their own infidelity. Mediators say that women "are just as likely to succumb to the same temptations that are out there as men," but women fear the social stigma that might bias their divorce proceedings. "Equal behavior doesn't mean I'll get equal treatment in court," one woman told me. Others also fear that lawyers may not "fight as hard" for their rights and that judges "might take out their innate prejudice" on female spouses who stray.

Often a woman who has had one or more affairs will initiate mediation in the hope of persuading her husband that she has reformed and will recommit herself to the marriage. Mediators do see a significant number of couples who confess to previous infidelities and still manage to go back into a marriage and make it work, but many more say that when these couples consult them, they are "going through the motions without any real desire to fix the marriage." They are the ones most determined to avoid the "fear and embarrassment" of the courtroom and are most likely to agree to a division of assets in the mediator's office rather than submit to a judge.

There are, however, serious "sticking points" that impede mediation, and one of the most contested is medical insurance. The issue of who will pay for it after divorce looms large unless both are working and each can get it from an employer, but most of the time this is not the case. In years past, many older couples consulted mediators to arrange for legal separations instead of actual divorces because the need for such things as Social Security or continuing medical coverage was so crucial to their well-being. Some insurance companies tried to eliminate the separated spouse from the policy, and in many instances they succeeded.

Money is key in mediation, as it is in so many aspects of divorce. Couples have to prepare a postdivorce budget when they enter mediation, and many women are terrified of having to take responsibility for their own finances. However, mediators find they can often empower women whose only contact with money was what the husband doled out if they make women realize how successfully they balanced their household budgets all through their marriage. They often need to do this when a couple does not have enough money to fight over. In divorces where the major asset is the jointly owned house, negotiations are simple and direct: the couple must decide whether to go into poverty, genteel or desperate as it may be, or to stay together to keep the lifestyle they have.

In many cases, mediators have to beg women to look realistically at what their lives will become after divorce, but their advice to "focus on the money"[18] may be ignored because "the marriage was too bad; they just want out." A woman, it seems, always pays a higher price than a man for financial cluelessness. After divorce, her standard of living will probably drop by 27 percent while his will rise 10 percent above what it was during the marriage.[19]

In far too many cases women are unwilling to make the necessary financial sacrifices, so they return to the marriage, but they also return to the mediator, sometimes for years afterward. One woman arrived at the mediators office when she was seventy-two, and returned annually for the next fifteen years until she was finally ready to make the financial change she knew from the beginning she could make if she wanted but could not bring herself to do. At the age of eighty-seven she "grew tired of waiting for [her husband] to die" and was so desperate to be rid of him that she finally decided to sell a small house in Maine that had been in her family since 1749 and had appreciated greatly in value. With that money, she divorced and lived comfortably in an apartment outside Boston until she died at the age of ninety-four.

Besides making couples prepare a postdivorce budget, mediators who cannot convince their clients of the financial realities that will befall them sometimes insist that their clients go to financial consultants who specialize in divorce. Many of these clients are the women who refuse to see the reality of what divorce will mean for them, those whom the judges call by the unfortunate nickname "Pet Rocks." These are women who believe they are entitled to lifelong support and will not listen to anything else the mediator tries to tell them. The husbands who refuse to face the financial reality of divorce are generally those who are preparing to retire—and comfortably— but believe that their wives, who may never have worked or may only have worked part-time off and on, should be able to get a full-time job.

Mediators recognize how impossible these situations often are, but neither party will accept reality until a financial divorce consultant spells it out for them. Like mediators, financial divorce consultants agree that the hardest part of their job is the "dilemma/conundrum" where they have to tell people they will not have the wherewithal to separate and their only recourse is to "stay married." However, all the lawyers, mediators, and financial consultants I spoke to firmly insisted that they have never recommended a couple should stay together if they suspected spousal abuse was at issue.

FINANCIAL DIVORCE COUNSELING

Women who have not been in the workforce are the ones who most need financial divorce counseling because they enter the process with so little confidence in their abilities. Even if they wanted to, many could not return to jobs they once held because technology has changed their professions dramatically. For these women, retooling is not enough and total reeducation is the only recourse. One mediator described a graphic designer who had done commercial art in the early years of her marriage but had no knowledge of the intervening changes computers brought to her field. To her chagrin, she learned that "design is a young person's game" and as a "gray-haired, glasses-wearing, sixty-year-old granny" she was unlikely to be hired. She calls herself "one of the lucky ones," for she took training in computer design and landed a job as an administrative assistant in an advertising firm where her new knowledge, coupled with her old experience, stands her in good stead. She "answers the phones, makes the coffee, and keeps the calendar." "It beats being on welfare," she says.

The mediator who encouraged this woman to settle for a lesser job told me that mediators will often press their clients to apply for and become accepted in some form of vocational or educational training before they ever have to face a judge because the courts have been generous about awarding support that allows them to retrain or retool as part of their settlement. If they can prove they need alimony for a specified period of time, they will usually get it.

TWO COUPLES, COPING DIFFERENTLY

Floyd and Brenda, who live in Maryland, were able to resolve both reeducation and medical issues through mediation. Both were in their sixties when they divorced, and Brenda had never worked. She had been a volunteer in a hospitals women's auxiliary throughout the marriage and liked the environment. She decided the quickest way to become qualified to work in a D.C.—area hospital was to enroll in a medical technicians course that lasted eighteen months and cost $5,000. Floyd, a midlevel civil servant, was ordered to pay for Brenda's education and to provide COBRA medical coverage while she was in school. Both were satisfied when the judge approved the plan.

Most mediators deal with the very real problems of people desperate to resolve them and get on with their lives. However, according to a New Jersey mediator, almost all have a "*War Between the Tates* story" (alluding to Alison Lurie's novel about a couple whose divorce literally killed them). A West Coast mediator told me he had many such stories to tell because he sees so many couples who refuse to "take responsibility for the problems they have created." He marveled at people who "always blame the other side and refuse to admit they had anything to do with the situation that led them to divorce."

A mediator in Dallas said she is continually fascinated by those who insist "its always his—or her—fault, never the fault of the 'blameless one' who is talking to me." She said her clients almost always begin by saying, " 'I just want to be fair,' which usually translates as 'I want things to be fair for me; I want things the way I want them.' " These are usually the clients who tell their mediators, "I know I could straighten everything out if I could just talk to his [or her] lawyer." She has to convince them that the lawyer for the opposition has the ethical obligation to fight for his clients rights and cannot possibly listen privately to claims from the other side.

And then there was the mediator in New Jersey mentioned above, the one who went to court in a dispute over photo albums. Jerry worked on Wall Street in a high-pressure trading job, and Alice was a high school English teacher. They met in college, and because both were poor and knew they were getting married they bought one set of yearbooks to share between them. In mediation, Alice asked for them all and for the family memorabilia as well, because she had been the one to collect and arrange it. This consisted of photo albums, movies, and videotapes for each of their four children, plus all sorts of sports trophies, awards from work, and everything else that could come under the heading of family souvenirs. Alice claimed she should have them because Jerry was always "too busy working to have any interest in his family" She was the one who initiated the divorce after thirty-four years and four children, citing "irreconcilable differences and the irretrievable breakdown of the marriage—in other words: his complete and utter indifference to family life."

Dividing the marital assets went relatively smoothly, but the sticking point became "the memorabilia." Alice fought for the yearbooks and Jerry let her have them. He proceeded to "get even" (an expression both used when I spoke to them individually) by agreeing to give her half the memorabilia and then withholding what she really wanted, the photo albums. Alice took Jerry back to court to try to persuade the judge to enforce the original order, but the judge said he could not possibly do so because he had no idea of what constituted "a fair half of four photo albums." When Alice's lawyer said there was nothing further he could do, she went back to the mediator, who told her the same thing.

The New Jersey mediator used the case to illustrate "how hard it is to come up with an appropriate response when your client says the system is not fair." He said he usually tells his clients "the system cannot solve all your problems. You must take some responsibility for what has happened your-self." He told Alice, "You just have to tell yourself that Jerry is a jerk, and you have to forget about the memorabilia, and you have to move on."

Did she? I asked. "No," he said. "People don't learn. They keep making the same mistakes over and over again. We have to face the fact that they are going to do this, and we have to put these incidents aside and keep on trying to do our work as best as we can."

NO BLACK AND WHITE BUT LOTS OF GRAY EDGES

Women may initiate divorce in greater numbers than men, and may also consult mediators more than divorce lawyers, but the largest percentage of couples who will stick with mediators until everything is settled are gay and lesbian. They may initially consult individual lawyers, but they often go through mediators because of disagreements over how to divide assets accumulated during a long relationship. Gay marriage and legal civil unions are new to some states, under consideration in others, and banned by constitutional amendment in at least fourteen others. Thus, when same-sex couples want to end long relationships, they usually seek private legal expertise because, whether their concern is justified or not, they fear ending up in court before an unsympathetic or openly hostile judge. Even though their property is constrained not by law but by how they took title (that is, in whose name it was registered), they often decide that it is far easier to keep it together rather than try to separate it. It is a decision that is imposed upon them not by the legal system (because it falls under contract rather than family law), but they believe it will be in their best interests to try to settle it there.

A gay lawyer-mediator in San Francisco whose clients are preponderantly from the gay and lesbian communities said fear of what might happen to shared assets in a courtroom "keeps many gay couples together—at least on the surface—because its often economically better than splitting." He spoke of how recent changes to marital law have created many "gray edges" in relationships that were neither black nor white to begin with, and he introduced me to Thad and Derry as an example.

They have been together since they met in the 1960s at a party on a Sausalito houseboat. Thad was an administrator for the City of San Francisco, and Derry had just "tuned in, turned on, and dropped out" of medical school to become a carpenter. In their forty-four years together, they made a good living in their professions and an even better one through real estate investments, as they bought and restored derelict or run-down properties, which they then sold or rented. They lead an extremely comfortable life now that both are retired, living part of each year in their San Francisco "painted lady" house, their Mexican hacienda, and their beachfront apartment in Hawaii. However, they are never in the same place at the same time, as they have not lived together as a couple for well over a decade.

Derry was the first to want to "opt out" of the relationship, consulting their lawyer about five years before the couple began to live separate lives. Derry was tired of monogamy and wanted "to experiment." Thad reluctantly agreed to an "open marriage" because he was sure their long, shared history was so strong that Derry would soon lose interest in other men. Instead, Derry met Marshall, fell in love, and wanted a permanent new partnership with him. Derry and Thad were preparing to separate and needed to determine how to divide their assets. Everything was in both their names when Derry and Thad went back to the lawyer-mediator Derry had initally consulted, who explained that it would be difficult but not impossible to separate the joint bank and savings accounts, health and other insurance policies, and—most intricately tangled of all—the assets from real estate that they had routinely combined in their (then) thirty-some years together. Both men balked at what they were told with each insisting he was not receiving a fair share, but the biggest obstacle to a reasonable settlement was that each man thought he was entitled to sole ownership of the San Francisco house. The stalemate endured for the last two years they lived together and became so acrimonious that they decided to separate without resolving it.

Thad and Derry were both approaching seventy, and they knew they had to find a "safer, quieter" way to live out their lives. They refused the only recourse left, to go into court, and agreed instead to live apart while maintaining the façade that they were still a couple. Derry moved Marshall, his new partner, into the house by creating another entrance so they could live on a separate floor from Thad, who insisted on keeping most of the rooms from the original living space he had shared with Derry. Ten years have since passed, and Thad and Derry continue to socialize as if nothing has changed. They act as co-hosts for the elegant dinner parties and Sunday night suppers for which they are renowned in their circle, but they live their emotional and sexual lives outside the relationship. It is unspoken but accepted by their old and trusted friends that Marshall is Derr's new partner, and they never comment overtly about Thad's occasional dates.

Thad and Deny have created legal partnership agreements to ensure that inheritance will be unencumbered, no matter who survives the other. As neither man has siblings or other family members, they have also prepared living wills with each the others designee for health-care decisions. Thad told me that he is still "blindsided" by Derry's "desertion" because he thought they would be together "forever." In his experience, "old gay men don't split; one or the other partner just ups and dies."

This view was reflected by most of the other gay men I interviewed, all of whom were "stunned" (a word used by many) by the breakup of their long relationships. Anson, an accountant in Philadelphia, was among those who attribute the increasing number of long-established gay couples who are calling it quits to "multifold decisions." He cites the increasing openness and ease with which same-sex couples set up housekeeping, and blames this for allowing them to separate with the same ease. He speaks of the states that permit gay marriage or civil unions as providing a legal framework in which to build assets together and, in many cases, to divide them equitably as well. "When things are not under the counter or hidden, you don't need to be afraid or ashamed to bring them into the open," Anson said. Alluding to himself, he thinks it is "far more liberating to be able to leave a relationship because it doesn't satisfy anymore than to have to stay in it because you don't think you have other options."

In his own case, Anson was thirteen years older than Tripp, his partner of thirty-seven years. He describes himself as "always the stable and understanding partner, always hoping Tripp's little upsets and temper tantrums would blow over." Anson insisted that the age difference never seemed to matter, for he was always the father figure who enjoyed the antics of his more "childlike, impetuous" partner. And like many gay men, he was proud of his body and worked hard to keep it in shape until several crucial changes happened in the last years of their partnership, which Anson compared to "the things that break up straight marriages as well."

Tripp's mother, a wealthy woman who settled large sums of money on her only son during her lifetime, died and left him "close to a fortune." At the same time, Anson was diagnosed with a slowly progressing muscular degenerative disease that doctors told him would not "kick in" for several decades. The diagnosis horrified Tripp, who dreaded having to become Anson's "nursemaid," and he called Anson "a chain around [his] neck." They still stayed together, which Anson said resulted only because he "trained [himself] to become more forthcoming emotionally." Never one to express his feelings, he learned to say "I love you, and to say it a lot!" Unfortunately, he said wryly, he didn't learn to "say it in time."

Tripp worked as an arts-and-crafts teacher in a private school, where he had a long and close friendship with Patrick, a married history teacher who finally admitted that he was gay and divorced his wife. Patrick's wife knew it throughout their marriage but thought she could "reform" him. After the divorce, she and their three children accepted his new partner, so Tripp conceived the idea that they would all form an "expanded family" Anson included. Anson was horrified, wanting no part of what he dubbed "promiscuous polygamy," and suddenly, money and property became major issues. They owned a house in the city and a cottage on the Jersey shore, and they had pooled their money to buy stocks and bonds, all of which were conservatively invested and steadily lucrative. Because everything was merged and it was difficult to discern who owned what part of any single asset, they consulted a lawyer. She sent them to a mediator, who labored for several months to arrange an equitable settlement. That was almost six years ago, and the separation is still unresolved and most of the assets are still disputed.

Anson thinks he will soon have to agree to whatever Tripp wants because he can't afford any more legal fees. He has already sold his share of both properties to Tripp, whose inheritance was tied up in trusts so that he had to take complicated second mortgages and personal loans to buy them. Feeling the "first twinges" of his muscular degeneration, Anson moved into a retirement community that will provide assisted living when he needs it, and where many of the men are gay and the women are "lots of sad widows and lots more merry ones, all trying to put the make on us poor old guys, gay or not." He doesn't join the neighbors who go to gay bars because "the rejection is horrible" for older men. His gay friends who are still in couples have let him drift away, as they feel more comfortable being with Tripp because he has a steady partner. Anson understands why they have chosen Tripp over him: "Gay couples have strong emotions of jealousy, of the fear of invasion, so you must always be on guard all the time, in fear that somebody will come along and steal your partner." For this reason Anson is a strong believer in gay marriage, arguing that "marriage vows cement relationships far more deeply than simply choosing to live together. Gays can (and do) just walk out now, whereas if they were married, this would be so much harder to do."

The lesbian couples I spoke to agreed with him. Among them were Sharon and Barbara, who had lived the first twenty-four years of their relationship in Vermont and were among the first to participate in a civil union when that state first issued them in 2000. Now, after twenty-nine years together, they have decided to separate. Both fear it could "get a little messy," as they struggle to separate benefits they fought so hard to gain, everything from being accepted as each other's "next of kin," to the group insurance and public assistance they counted on to sustain them in their "alternative lifestyles" as a potter and a weaver.

Sharon and Barbara both admitted that when they applied for a civil union, they "grasped" the opportunity as the "last gasp" to save a dying relationship. They entered into it "for all the wrong reasons," thinking if they did "just one more thing to make it last, then perhaps it will." They both regret that civil union was not the panacea they hoped for and agree that separation is necessary. Sharon said, and Barbara agreed: "Just because we are married in our own eyes doesn't mean we have to stay together forever. If you close off the possibility of moving on, you close off the possibility of going on to live good lives,"

Both women were sixty in 2006, and neither had another partner in mind. Sharon thinks both she and Barbara are "probably relieved" that "the split was so amicable"; Barbara said she felt "intense grief" for several months, "and then it dissipated." Now she lives alone contentedly but is not sure how long she will enjoy a solitary existence after so many years as part of a couple. Sharon, a buxom woman with large appetites and a booming laugh, is the more lighthearted of the two, but she still claims to be the "worrier" who wonders what they might have done to keep the relationship intact. They have parted "in friendship, probably because there's nothing to argue over," says Barbara, who jokes that they should have moved to Massachusetts if they wanted to "stay married." She is referring to statistics showing that Massachusetts, known politically as the bluest of the blue states, and the most liberal, has the lowest divorce rate in the country, while the bright-red conservative Bible Belt states, home to many born-again Christians, have the highest (in Arkansas, Kentucky, and Mississippi, voters in 2000 and 2004 almost unanimously supported constitutional amendments that banned gay marriage even as their divorce rate climbed to become the highest in the nation).

"And we're supposed to be the ones who thumb our noses at moral values," Sharon said with a snort, as Barbara laughed with her.

FORGING ACCOMMODATIONS

In Richard Ford's story collection *Women with Men*, a character muses about how "other people forged" the accommodations that allowed them to justify the continuation of a relationship or a marriage:

> *His parents, for instance. It was possible they hated each other, yet hating each other was worth more than trying to love somebody else,*

somebody you'd never know in a hundred years and focus on whatever good was left, set aside all issues they would never agree on, and call it marriage, even love. How to do this was, of course, the predicament.[20]

He might have added that how to divorce is an even greater predicament.

CHAPTER NINE

THE WAY WE LIVE NOW

*My brother had an attack of hysteria and began screaming at my mother
and hitting himself . . . my sister tearfully implored her . . . but she still
wouldn't sign. So on Thursday my father . . . finally grasped what he
should have understood long ago . . . that is, if he wants his freedom he
has to let her have the whole apartment.*

—A. B. YEHOSHUA, *A Late Divorce*

*"You always wanted me to sell the house. I always told you, 'I will leave
the house only if I am dead.' You ridiculed me. You should have taken it
seriously. When you read this . . . your life will change forever. You will be
transformed from gold digger to ash and rubbish digger."*

—DR. NICHOLAS BARTHA, quoted in ANTHONY RAMIREZ,
"Doctor Dies from Wounds Suffered in East Side Blast,"
The New York Times, July 17, 2006

IT WAS ONE OF those steaming hot July days that settles like a thick gray
pea soup over the upper Midwest and hangs on day after day, driving otherwise reasonable people to do almost anything to get cool and be comfortable. It was just such a day when Gloria, Carl's wife of twenty-four years,
met him in the kitchen when he came home from work to tell him he was
the most boring man alive and she wanted an immediate divorce. Carl was
"surprised, to say the least," and thought "maybe the heat got to her" because

it was the first time she had ever expressed any discontent, let alone unhappiness. She surprised him even further when she said she had packed up everything she wanted from the house and her suitcases and boxes were in the front hallway, waiting to be loaded into her car and taken to her new apartment, after which she would never cross the house's threshold again. He could do whatever he wanted with everything she left behind, but she did want her share of the equity, and so he should sell the house as soon as possible. She told Carl his dinner was in the microwave and there were papers on the hall table that would tell him how to reach her through her attorney. Gloria thought it best that they did not otherwise communicate because there was "nothing left to say."

Carl said he always knew Gloria had a "sarcastic streak," but when she called him the most boring man alive, he thought she was "going far too far." While she methodically packed her car, he stood in the kitchen stunned, bracing himself against the counter as if "hit by a truck," unable to process anything she had just told him. Several years later, he remembered how, even though his mind was racing erratically and he was deeply hurt, he was still angry enough to wonder if he could countersue her for "emotional abuse." It wasn't true, he thought to himself; he had been "the best husband and father" he knew how to be and didn't deserve such treatment. He may have "bored Gloria to death," but what she was doing to him was indeed "cruel and unusual emotional abuse."

His head was spinning, and by the time he regained his bearings, she was barreling down the driveway spinning her wheels as if she could not get away to her new apartment fast enough. Carl was convinced Gloria was leaving him for a lover, someone she might have met in her new job at the state board of education. He told himself that if she had stayed on as the assistant principal of the local junior high school, she would never have had the time or the opportunity for such "foolishness." Actually, he was dead wrong about why Gloria was leaving him; she didn't have a new lover and really didn't want one. Now that both her daughters were away from home attending the state university and she had a new job in the state capital, a forty-minute drive from the house, it struck Gloria "almost like lightning" that this was the perfect time to leave a stagnant marriage and move on to a new life.

Gloria described her personality as "self-contained," "composed," "maybe emotionally distant," and she thought it probably had a lot to do with how her marriage played itself out. Carl did nothing to encourage "connection" because he thought the best aspect of his personality was the "live and let live" attitude that "always let people be who they wanted to be." He liked to think of himself as "a good feminist husband" and was proud that he had always supported her ambition. Gloria had worked all through their married life and was happiest when concentrating all her energies on rising in the state's educational administration. At first she appreciated Carl's understanding, but very soon she simply "took home and family for granted" because she could devote herself to work and he never complained. She liked their house, but as far as she was concerned, Carl could stay there until he sold it, for he was more attached to it than she had ever been. She liked their two Irish setters and the old tabby cat, but in truth, they were more Carl's pets than hers, and so he could keep them as well. It was the same with the garden, the neighbors, and the entire neighborhood. Carl was the one who came home early from the university medical-research lab, where he was in charge of writing grant proposals, to fuss in the garden and take care of the animals and their daughters with "more devotion than Gloria ever showed." She was clear-sighted enough to know that she wouldn't miss any part of her old life, whereas Carl would be bereft to lose even a fraction of it. So she packed her clothes and the few possessions she cared about and found herself a furnished apartment near her new office and left him to figure out how he would handle the rest of his life.

Carl ate the dinner Gloria left in the microwave, rinsed his dishes and stacked them in the dishwasher, then gathered the leashes and took the dogs for their evening walk. Halfway down the block, he met some neighbors who were watering their lawn. When they asked him the usual neighborly summertime question—was it hot enough for him?—he burst into tears and blubbered that Gloria had abandoned him. They took him to their porch, sat him down, and made him drink a glass of cold water. After Carl regained his equilibrium, he knew that before he went to bed that night, Gloria's leaving him "would be all over the neighborhood."

He left for work early the next morning, and when he returned home, the phone message light was blinking frantically and the in-box was full. When he checked his e-mails, he had triple the number he usually received on any given day. Every one of them was from someone in the neighborhood who clucked and tsk-tsked in words they genuinely meant to be comforting before they got down to their real business for calling: to offer advice. A man who sold real estate told him to sell the house while the market was "hot," and he just happened to have several apartments, or condos, or town houses that would all be "right up [Carl's] alley." There were messages for dinner invitations from others, including a widow, a divorcée, and the one gay couple on the street, who called themselves the "unofficial mayors."

That evening, Carl listed all the messages by subject category in his usual precise, methodical manner. He noted that the majority were about real estate, as most people assumed he would sell the house immediately More than one told him that his ordinary split-level was a "hot" house in a "hot" neighborhood in a "heated" market so he should "strike while the iron is hot." One neighbor predicted he would be "gone by Halloween."

Instead, trick-or-treaters had to weave their way past a curbside wall of detritus, piled high with the things Carl and Gloria had amassed while living in the same house for twenty years. Carl had arranged a bulk-trash pickup for several days later, but he thought there was enough "good stuff" that some of the people who were out on Halloween night might want it, and indeed they did. Most of it was gone when the trashmen came.

And now, people asked, would Carl finally be putting the house on the market? No, he said firmly. Now that he had removed the junk and clutter, he was looking forward to cooking Thanksgiving dinner for himself, his daughters, and some of their friends. He was going to do everything he could to keep intact the only home his children had ever known. He was going to find a way to stay in his house.

Gloria didn't want the house, but she did want half the equity and she wanted it fast, even before the divorce. From the day she left the house she made it clear she would not contribute the half share she had always paid toward household expenses, and there was still ten years left to pay on a thirty-year mortgage. The only expense she agreed to assume was payment on her one-year-old Toyota. She would not continue to pay half the monthly payment for the Honda bought for the daughters who needed it to navigate their sprawling campus, and she expected Carl to shoulder the entire burden of their education expenses. He agreed to do both. They had never used credit cards, so there was no debt to speak of, but he had three more years of payments on his Volvo. He and Gloria each had medical coverage through their jobs and the two girls were covered under Carl's, so there was no argument in that quarter. Each had a life insurance policy, and Gloria reluctantly agreed to pay for hers only after her lawyer told her the judge would never let her get away with foisting the payments onto Carl. On the surface, it seemed that the divorce would proceed smoothly because, as each had maintained separate pension and retirement accounts, there were no contested assets to fight over.

Carl admitted that as the divorce proceeded, he had been "drifting along, thinking everything was okay." He thought he could handle all the extra expenses and still afford to live in his house—until he "crunched some numbers" and suddenly realized that without two salaries paying for the family's upkeep, he could not afford to pay for the house on his own, especially since Gloria insisted that she wanted her half of the equity before they went into divorce court. Also, he did not realize how much money was needed to keep two daughters in college.

His lawyer said the sensible thing to do was to "unload" the house, but he resisted until the lawyer prepared a spreadsheet laying out the grim reality. He also helped Carl make a postdivorce financial statement for two possible budgets, one that showed how well he could live if he sold the house, the other showing how he would soon lose it if he tried to stay there. Carl credited "the budget revelation" with "pushing [him] over the edge." He had always been a quiet man, content to come home to his family, his garden, his pets, and "puttering around the house." He got on well with his colleagues at work, and all the neighbors were fond of him, chatting with him when he walked the dogs morning and night. If he had a social life, it was at neighborhood gatherings, for Gloria didn't enjoy them and seldom went with him. She always went alone to any social event connected with her work, saying it was "all girl stuff anyway" and he would have been bored. She was not much of a "social animal," didn't enjoy those occasions either, and found excuses to go late and leave early.

Carl realized that even though he had often been alone in his house, he was quite lonely without Gloria and their daughters. He also realized that he was "upset," "confused," and "terrified" about what to do now that his future was "turned upside down." He and Gloria were "loosely Protestant," but neither was religious and they had not attended any church during their marriage. He heard about a men's support group at the local Unitarian church and went to it because he had no idea what else to do.

A dozen men were there, and when it was his turn to speak, he blurted out his entire story, returning again and again to the fear that he would lose his house. The group helped him to explore his reasons for wanting to stay there. Although he gave "maintaining a home for [his] daughters" as his primary reason, they helped him to see that it was more than that: Carl liked the life he led in that house and he wanted it to continue. He and Gloria had never had a "passionate relationship"; their courtship had been "two people approaching thirty who didn't want to be alone anymore, and so they married." The men's group helped him to see that they had "never done the necessary work to become a couple," and so it was probably not so surprising that one or the other would eventually want to live a separate life. Carl said that once he realized the truth of this, he felt "such a sense of relief." Even if he really was the "most boring man in the world," he was still not entirely responsible for the failure of his marriage. However, although this was a "liberating" truth, it was also "deeply depressing," for he was still going to lose the life he loved now that he had finally accepted that he had no recourse but to sell the house.

However, just at that moment, several of the men in the group asked if he had ever thought of taking in roommates to help with expenses. It had never occurred to Carl, but he thought it a good suggestion and well worth a try. He remembered that a visiting scholar was on his way from India to spend six months working in the medical lab and needed housing. The next morning he e-mailed the doctor, who said he would be delighted to rent a room. The most immediate problem for Carl was how to set the price, but his lawyer helped him there as well, suggesting an equitable sum that covered a share of the rent, utilities, and use of the kitchen; Setandra, the visiting scholar, accepted without question. Several days later, Carl received a phone call from Dan, one of the men in his support group, who had to vacate the studio apartment he had been subletting. Was Carl still looking for a roommate? The house was big enough, so Carl presented Dan with the same figures and he agreed eagerly, as it was less rent than he had been paying. With the equivalent of Gloria's share of the mortgage assured, Carl refinanced the house, paid Gloria her share of the equity, and settled into his new life.

Carl kept his daughters' rooms just as they were and moved Setandra into the fourth bedroom, formerly the family's "junk dump" where they put anything they had no other place for. Most of what was in there had gone out to the curb at Halloween, so the room was clean and comfortable, with easy access to a hall bathroom. Carl asked Dan if he would be satisfied living in what used to be the basement "rec room." Dan was delighted with what he saw as a mini-apartment with its separate entrance, full bath, and a small bar with a sink and under-the-counter refrigerator. He brought his own microwave oven and coffeemaker and planned to be fully self-contained and self-sufficient.

However, an interesting dynamic arose among the three men. Although they all kept different schedules on weeknights, they found themselves gathering on weekend evenings for meals. It started when Setandra volunteered to cook his native dishes and they returned the favor with "ail-American comfort food." None of them liked sports, but they rented movies and spent companionable evenings playing cards and chess. When Dan "entertained female company," Carl and Setandra "made [themselves] scarce."

Carl and Gloria were divorced thirteen months after she left the house. Setandra returned to India, and his place was taken by another visiting scholar, who rented the room for an entire year. Dan is still there, and he and Carl have become fast friends. Dan has a succession of "dates"; Carl has them occasionally and reluctantly. He continues with the men's group and also sees a therapist, who has persuaded him he is not "the most boring man alive" and whom he credits with helping him to understand his "part" in "allowing his marriage to unravel." He does want another relationship, but not until he can "do it right and make it last."

WHEN "OURS" BECOMES "HIS AND HERS"[1]

Once the trauma and distress of dividing the accumulated assets and possessions of a long marriage are finally over, divorce lawyers say the most difficult thing they have to do is to convince many of their clients that they must sell their house or lose it in foreclosure.

In July 2006, New York was rocked—literally—by a gas explosion that destroyed a town house in one of the city's richest areas, the Upper East Side, when an ex-husband allegedly chose to blow himself and his house up rather than sell it to satisfy the court-ordered financial settlement to his ex-wife. Dr. Nicholas Bartha, sixty-six, and his ex-wife, Cordula Hahn, sixty-four, ended their twenty-six-year marriage with five years of legal wrangling over a property that was worth several million dollars while intact and worth far more once it was a pile of rubble that could be hauled off to make way for a new and far more expensive building. According to Ms. Hahn and both their lawyers, Dr. Bartha was obsessed with the house to the point that he meant it when he said he would blow it up or burn it down rather than sell it. And while many angry exes often rail and rant about how they will destroy a property rather than give it up to satisfy the claims of their former mate, they eventually calm down enough to go on with their lives without carrying out their threats. Dr. Bartha was the exception to this rule of thumb.

Dr. Bartha survived the explosion, which he allegedly planned to include his suicide as well as the destruction of the house, but was so severely burned that his initial treatment included a medically induced coma, and he died several days later. It was a tragedy, but newspapers nevertheless had a field day with the story. The *New York Post* irreverently called him "Dr. Bomb," as it described his "scorched earth response to their split."[2] *The New York Times* was more circumspect with a headline that equated DIVORCE, REAL ESTATE AND RUBBLEwith WHEN MARRIAGES GO REALLY AWRY. That story was content to quote Donald Trump's first wife, Ivana, as saying, "Don't get mad, get everything," before going on to give details of how couples may fight for years over the most unlikely possessions.[3]

The articles about the Bartha divorce used some of the same examples that I heard in my own interviews and conversations with lawyers who tried to settle bitterly contested divorces. As one in California put it, "whether apocryphal or not, we all have heard the one about the dog that got microwaved and the cat who went through the entire wash cycle and survived." However, everyone I talked to who dealt with the process of divorce, from lawyers to battling spouses, all seem to agree that the one possession that inspires a gamut of emotions, running from rage and rancor to sadness and depression, is the house, which all too often one spouse is desperate to keep.

After a divorce in which they have to give up their home, women are twice as likely to buy a smaller, more affordable house than men, even though they generally end up poorer after divorce. A study by the National Association of Realtors showed that in the decade beginning in 1993, single women outpaced men 21 percent to 9 percent in buying homes.[4]

Everyone wants to be the analyst who comes up with the definitive reason for why women choose to be nesters while men are content to live in fraternity-style shared housing, but they generally accept the same answers: women have more control over their finances now that so many are in the working world, and they are savvy about the advantages involved in home ownership. Women usually gain custody of minor children after divorce, but whether the children still live at home or not, women view home ownership as offering stability during an unstable time in their lives. Whether a woman is divorced or has never married, she is no longer content to sit around waiting for Prince Charming to fit the glass slipper on her foot. The prince may never come along and glass is uncomfortable anyway; many women say they would rather find sensible footwear on their own, which often means buying a house.

If a divorcing couple already owns a house (or two or more), it is usually the woman who is desperate to keep it, and women, far more than men, have gone to all sorts of lengths to stay put. Sometimes their efforts pay off; sometimes they don't. After her divorce, Maureen wanted to stay in her three-hundred-year-old house near the best ski areas in New Hampshire.

She petitioned all the local banks that had begged her to accept their credit while she was married for a modest home-equity line of credit, but now that she was divorced, they all found reasons to turn her down. When no financial institution would give her one, she borrowed from friends, family, and one of her children to get the money to reconfigure the rooms in the house and restore the barn into a "highly exclusive" bed-and-breakfast. She advertised it on the Internet and in posh travel magazines as a "destination" setting and soon had more business than she could handle. She never thought she would retire from her job as a secretary in the town hall, but the B and B is fully booked year-round and is doing so well that it is now her full-time occupation. All her loans are repaid, and not only does she still live in her house, she is thinking about constructing a guest house behind the barn.

Anna was not so lucky. After years of living separately in the same house as her husband, she recognized the toll it was taking on her health and asked Daniel for a divorce. He agreed, but only if she would meet his terms, which he told her meant that he would "walk away unencumbered" from the marriage. She thought it meant that he wanted none of the household furnishings and that he would let her keep the house, and so she agreed because theirs had always been a simple, "on the fringe" way of living. Anna was an architect by training who worked as a freelance set designer for smaller theaters in the tristate area surrounding New York and, whenever she could get the commission, for theaters anywhere in the country. Despite the sometimes precarious life of a freelancer, she was the main wage earner in her family, and as she put it, "If I don't work, we don't eat."

Throughout their twenty-four-year childless (by choice) marriage, Daniel was involved in one vague entrepreneurial endeavor after another, none of which ever seemed to pay off or "hit it big." What they were, actually, were bad investments in pre-computer days and later, in the age of the Internet, bad "trades" he made from the "office" he was allegedly renting in their New Jersey town (in actuality, a booth in a local diner and a corner of a "buddy's construction-site trailer." Anna knew nothing of this when she agreed to let him walk away from the marriage, and so she told him to go out and get a lawyer who would guide them both through what she thought would be a simple and straightforward divorce process.

She was tied up for the next three months on several major design projects in the Midwest, and she wanted the divorce to be over and done with by the time they were completed. Unfortunately for Anna, Daniel went to a lawyer who had the divorce agreement all but finalized by the time she returned, and to her horror, she discovered that her casual acceptance of Daniel's demands required her to pay off bad investments he'd made and gambling debts she didn't know he had. She had full responsibility for a first mortgage on their house plus a second she didn't know he had taken and for which he must have forged her signature. There were also debts on credit cards in both their names that he had taken out without her knowledge, as well as smaller debts to various business and tradespeople connected with house repairs that she thought Daniel had paid off long before. Most alarming of all were several debts to unidentifiable "holding companies" she could only describe as "shady." Confronted with this staggering debt, she decided she could not afford a lawyer and, in her words, "penny-wise and pound-foolish," went into court unrepresented, "to get it over with."

Anna knew from the beginning that the only way she could meet the obligations Daniel left behind was to sell her house, but for several months she tried to keep it by setting up a budget and a schedule of payments to all the creditors. In defeat, she finally put her house on the market, but it took almost two years to sell. By the time of the closing, she had spent all but $35,000 of the money she had wisely saved for retirement in a fund Daniel could not touch during their marriage. The profit from the house's sale paid all the debts in full, leaving her with $10,500 to her name. Anna was not "completely down and out" because she had commissions lined up for the next year that would give her a decent income and had signed contracts to prove it, so she was able to buy a much smaller house on a "risky" interest-only mortgage that she hoped to convert as soon as she was "back on [her] feet."

She had lost almost everything she cared about when she sold her original house and most of its furnishings, but she was content with the new little house and was getting on with her life. All was tranquil until the day several months after she moved in, when the postman asked her to sign for a registered letter. It was from Daniel's lawyer, reminding her that, according to his "settlement agreement," she owed him an additional $30,000 from the profit of the sale of the house they had owned together. Anna consulted an attorney, who told her what she already knew and didn't want to hear: how foolish she had been to go into court without legal representation. He also told her she had no recourse except to give Daniel the money and get it over with, which she did. In order to do so, she had to put her new little house on the market, and fortunately, it sold for enough to pay the Realtor and get back her down payment. She now lives in a rental apartment in New Jersey and continues to work. She has been able to save and so far has a grand total of $38,000 in her retirement account. She is determined not to touch it until she has no other option, and for now, she lives on a "strict cash economy."

Other women have looked for creative ways to circumvent various legalities that might keep them from staying on in their homes. One who owned a three-bedroom co-op apartment in New York quietly bypassed her building's board to list it with agencies that cater to tourists who cannot afford hotel prices. "Everyone in the building knows I'm running an informal B and B," she admits, "but they like me and I'm a quiet tenant, so they pretend not to see." Women throughout Silicon Valley rent rooms in their houses or turn their garages into separate apartments, while others, like Bonnie in Southern California, move everything out of their houses because they can rent them for extraordinary amounts of money.

Bonnie agreed to rent her beach house to a European executive for a year at $15,000 a month and a grand total of $180,000, with the option to stay on month-by-month, should his job require it, at a higher rent of $18,000. Bonnie had lived in the rambling Spanish-style hacienda for twenty-five years and had refinanced her mortgage to stay there after her divorce; even so, her total house expenses were so high that she knew it was only a matter of time before she would have to sell it. A real estate agent who hoped eventually to be the one to get the listing phoned to ask if she had ever considered renting it, and Bonnie was overjoyed with the unexpected windfall. However, there was just one stipulation: the man's wife did not like anything about the interior and wanted it entirely redecorated. She wanted Bonnie to empty the house of all her possessions, to paint every room a different color, and to replace the granite countertops in the kitchen with a different-colored stone. Bonnie agreed to hire a mover and put her household goods in storage but told the renter she could change the wall colors at her own expense and only if they were repainted back to their original colors when the lease ended. Changing the granite countertops was a tug-of-war that almost canceled the deal, but Bonnie finally convinced the woman that she couldn't do it. Eventually the renters agreed to all the terms, everyone signed the lease, and Bonnie was ecstatic.

At first she thought of renting a small studio apartment in the same area as her house but was astonished at the high rents they commanded. A friend jokingly suggested that she advertise her services as a sitter for houses and pets, and within a week she had more offers than she could accept. She lived the entire year rent-free. It was coming to an end as I write this, and she is hoping to find someone else to rent her house for another year and for a much higher rent, after which her finances would put her "in fat city" and she could live there herself "forever." Meanwhile, she was delighted with her year of itinerant life, saying it was a "well-earned vacation" that was also physically good for her: she lost weight from walking dogs three to four times a day, made friends with other dog walkers, and went out on dates with two of them.

INVITING ANARCHY

Liz Seymour and her husband of twenty-eight years had "come to the end of the line, as married people sometimes do."[5] Both realized that their "hopes and goals for the next couple of decades were diverging," and the day after they separated in 2002, she started the process to pursue hers. She turned her three-bedroom house into a "seven-person anarchist collective, run by consensus and fueled by punk music, curse-studded conversation, and food scavenged from Dumpsters." It was still going strong in 2006, when she wrote about its ups and downs. "It is not utopia," she wrote. "What it is, though, is fun. . . . As messy as it is, to my mind, it is a lot more interesting than utopia could ever be."

"AT MY AGE—IN A COMMUNE!"

Rosemary, the eldest daughter, had always been "the shy sister" of three when they were growing up on Cape Cod. Caroline, the middle child, was "the live wire," and Nancy, her "Irish twin" (ten months younger), was "the ice princess." Rosemary married Ben the day after she graduated from college and stayed quietly and unhappily married to him, though he was an alcoholic, for forty years, until he pushed her down the stairs in a drunken rage and she broke her leg. Caroline was twenty-six when she married the first time and thirty-seven when she divorced "amicably." Two other brief marriages were followed by two more "amicable" divorces. By this time Caroline was in her mid-fifties and convinced she was not cut out for marriage and happy to be a "confirmed single person." She liked her job as a cardiac intensive-care nurse in Texas and intended to keep it until she could "no longer stand up." Nancy, the third sister, disappeared from her sisters' lives when she was twenty-four and married an upper-class Englishman she met on a skiing trip in Switzerland. They are still married but live separate lives in a London apartment and his ancestral country home. Both her sisters are convinced that Nancy always found them "noisy and vulgar," so they have not had any real contact with her for years, which is how all three want it.

Rosemary divorced Ben after he had been fired for his drinking and had not worked for several years. When he began to gamble on top of it, Rosemary tried to go back to teaching kindergarten, but there were no positions where she lived, so she settled for a low-paying job as an aide in nursery school. Ben had gone through their meager savings and owed back taxes to the IRS, so there was no option but to sell their house even before they divorced. It was so run-down that they realized very little profit, not even enough to pay off the government. Caroline wanted Rosemary to relocate to Texas, where it was much cheaper to live, but Rosemary could not stand the heat and stayed on the Cape, living in a succession of barely winterized cheap rental houses, all that she could afford. One day in the middle of a blizzard, Caroline phoned to tell Rosemary that her legs had finally given out, and after knee-replacementsurgery, she was moving to a small town in West Texas where she would be an administrator in a nursing home, the only one for miles around. A large house came with the job, and she was planning to live there. Would Rosemary care to join her? She explained that other personnel from the nursing home lived in the house, and visitors from out of town were often put up there for varying periods. It was "kind of a commune," Caroline said, with a lot of activity "coming and going," and mostly the residents were "fun." Caroline begged Rosemary to think it over.

Rosemary was appalled by the idea, comparing it to "riding the T [public transit system] in Boston," and rejected it at once. Caroline told her to think about how precarious her life was in Massachusetts and how much easier things would be in Texas, a state with no income tax and low energy costs. "Think of your heating bills," Caroline told her, and added that if Rosemary was uncertain about making a permanent move, she should come for a visit as soon as the blizzard let up. She could escape the cold for a little while, and Caroline needed help to get settled after her own move. There was a sale on flights from Boston to Dallas, and when Caroline offered to pay for half the ticket, Rosemary agreed to go.

The house was a huge rambling farmhouse that had been added on to helter-skelter over the years and so had nooks and crannies and curious additions, such as the one that had been an attached stable, unusual for Texas. The horse stalls had been converted to interesting living quarters, and that was the part of the house Caroline would be moving into. There was room enough for partitions to be added for a separate apartment, which Rosemary could have if she wanted it. She did, and as of this writing, she has been there for almost three years. She blushed as she said she stayed because Caroline, who "never takes no for an answer, bowled [her] over." Caroline admitted that she did "a heck of a selling job," but even so, Rosemary was "always the practical sister" and she knew instinctively it would be a good move on her part.

Two men rent other parts of the house—one is the accountant for the nursing home, the other a divorced man, "gay and quietly in the closet," who works in the town. The other permanent resident is a widow, a retired social worker for the county. Several rooms in a separate wing are reserved for relatives of the patients, and they are almost always full. Without any specific effort on anyone's part, the five residents began to gather informally for dinner once in a while. Eventually it became a tradition that whenever possible, they would eat the evening meal as a group. That led them to draw up a rotating schedule for food shopping, preparation, serving, and cleaning up afterward. They contribute to a "food kitty" every month, and if it does not cover all the general kitchen expenses, they add to it. Transient residents are given the option to join them for dinner and are expected to pay for their meals.

Rosemary says she relishes the privacy of her own quarters but is delighted to know that every evening she can sit down at a dinner table with friends and afterward have company for as long as she wants to enjoy it. There is a communal living room separating the kitchen and dining room from the guest quarters that holds a television, game table, and a good selection of paperback books that keeps growing as visitors leave new ones behind. There are a lot of houseplants, which Rosemary, with her green thumb, has taken over, and there is always someone with whom to make the long drive to the nearest movie theater, shopping mall, or pharmacy. Rosemary lives on Social Security and disability (from the accident to her leg, which never healed properly), plus the occasional stipend she receives for special services from family members who pay her to provide various kindnesses for their relatives in the nursing home. Caroline says she will keep working until she "drops in [her] boots," and they both intend to stay in Texas and, hopefully, in the house for the rest of their lives.

THE FIRST (AND BEST) WIVES' HOUSE

Communal living is catching on among divorced people. A group of women who call themselves "the first (and best) wives" of well-off men who divorced them for "arm candy" and "trophy wives" have pooled money from their divorce settlements and banded together to buy a four-story brownstone in New York City. There are two apartments on each floor, including the basement level, for a total of eight. Each has a separate bath and a tiny kitchenette, but there is a large communal kitchen/dining room and living area in the center of the main floor. Residents may be as private as they like during the day but are required to dine together unless they have other engagements, a rule that was put into effect "by necessity," when one of the group became too depressed to get out of bed, let alone leave her room. The women insist that an important part of the "mission" of living together is to keep one another in good health and good spirits. They also share household costs, but they are wealthy enough to employ people to cook and clean, and so their only responsibility regarding the evening meal is to show up.

A group of nine friends from Southern California, including two retired married couples as well as two divorced men and three women, bought land in the Texas hill country and had a "compound" built to their specifications. They all had enough money to pay for the living quarters they wanted as well as to ensure that they could stay there if they became ill and needed assisted living. They have now been together for six years, "ironing out differences along the way," and think they will most likely stay together for the indefinite future.

In Florida, *The Golden Girls* television program reflected the life of many widows and divorcées in the ultimate retirement state. As soon as the program aired, it inspired people to create their own kinds of communal living. Among them were divorced men and women who took up group life in imitation of Bea Arthur and her cohorts, offering different reasons for doing so. More women than men cited finances, and the majority of those told me they would prefer to live alone but probably won't ever have enough money to do so. They find it far more pleasant to share a large and comfortable house than to submit to the alternative, living far below the standard they enjoyed in marriage.

However, among those who insisted they would much prefer to live alone and on their own, I found that when they described their daily schedules and activities in detail, I had to tell them it appeared to me that they were enjoying life far more than they might have if they were living alone. They thought about this carefully, and the greater number admitted that they hadn't realized it was true until I asked them to think about it. They said they could not otherwise afford such a high standard of living and "do the things [they] do." An even more important consideration occurred to them—that although there are "irritations and stresses" among them from time to time, they would "miss the company." They laughed as they agreed that the company kept them "young."

More men than women told me that "to have company" was the primary reason they lived in groups. One man who actively sought a group living situation was Albert, a retired auto-body-shop owner in Brooklyn whose wife of forty-four years left him because of his "coldness" to her and their children. Albert said he didn't understand what he "did not do right," for he was only imitating his father and older brothers, who provided him with the example of "how the man was supposed to behave."

Like many Italian men of his background, Albert lived in his mother's house until he went into the army, then returned there until he was married and in his own home. He said he "always lived in a house full of people" and needed to be surrounded by "noise and family." Steve, also Italian and a widower from Albert's old neighborhood, owned a house in Fort Lauderdale, and Albert originally went there to visit. He ended up staying, and soon after he settled in, he and Steve invited Louis and Sam, two divorced Jewish men they met at the local community center, to join them. The four men josh about which of them is Felix and which is Oscar from *The Odd Couple*, but they are a congenial group, well adapted to one another's needs.

THE FAMILY THAT LIVES TOGETHER . . .

When relatives share a home, the situation is decidedly mixed. The difficulties that confront adult children who take a divorced parent into their homes are almost too numerous to mention, as are the mixed emotions the parent feels about having to be taken in. A divorced parent (usually the woman) who may not have enough money to survive alone has to face the loss of autonomy and the possible reversal of roles, where the child becomes the authority figure and the parent has to conform to new rules of behavior. Often the adult child has no other option but to take in a parent who has become sick or incapacitated and who needs care and shelter. Further, more and more adult children who work are finding that they cannot afford child care, and so they take in a parent to provide care for the grandchildren, which may or may not work out satisfactorily for any of the three generations. Far too often in situations such as these, when a parent moves into an adult child's house, the move is dictated by necessity and nobody is happy.

The same is true for many siblings and other adult relatives who end up living together. Lena, who was divorced, and Delia, who had never married, were sisters who inherited their parents' run-down house in an Ohio mill town that had seen better days. Jeanette was their widowed sister-in-law whose husband had been killed in a mining accident in West Virginia. She and her sisters-in-law pooled their meager resources of pensions, Social Security, and disability, which, all together, added up to barely enough to keep them and the house afloat. No one was happy but they saw no other option and were grimly resigned to living out their days together.

Men and women enter into other living arrangements for practical reasons that sometimes turn out to have surprisingly happy results. After Elaine, Denny's wife of thirty years, left him for another man, he couldn't decide what to do with their pleasant two-story Garrison colonial house on Long Island. He told me "inertia" was the reason he kept on living there, mainly because he could afford to and he "didn't know what else to do." He could have retired, but inertia also kept him going to his job at a research facility in a neighboring town, and because he "didn't know what else to do," he intended to keep on working for as long as he could.

The statement "I didn't know what else to do" was a major refrain in Denny's life since his divorce. One day over lunch in the cafeteria, he said it to a group of friendly young women, "girls really," who worked in his department. They thought of him as a "great boss," and he enjoyed their "teasing and joshing" because they reminded him of his two married daughters who lived across the country, whom he missed and with whom he had an excellent relationship. One of the young women asked what Denny planned to do with his house and told him she would love to rent a room but her parents would never permit her to live alone with a single man. The group teased Denny, telling him he should advertise for "a harem" and then they could all move in with him. Everyone laughed, and that afternoon during the coffee break, the girls repeated the story of "Denny's harem" to Sarah, their supervisor and a widow who had had a very happy marriage of thirty-eight years. They joked to Sarah that living alone was not good for her and that she should join them as their chaper-one. Sarah joked right back that being "housemother to a harem" was a fine idea, since she had just put her own house up for sale and was not sure how or where she wanted to live after it was sold. It began as a joke, but the more she thought about living in Denny's house, the better the idea seemed.

Several days later, she approached him with her proposition: that she would move into his house, and unless he really wanted "a house full of kids," perhaps he should think about advertising for one or two others their age to join them. Denny told Sarah she could move in, but neither thought of it as anything more than a "business deal" beneficial to both because of the difference in their respective ages. Denny was in his early fifties and looked younger because he was in such good physical condition, while Sarah was a buxom, matronly sixty-three who described herself as "feeling forty but looking seventy."

Somehow, they never got around to advertising for other boarders, probably because once Sarah moved in, they discovered they had so many things in common and so much fun enjoying them together. They went bird-watching on Long Island beaches. They rented action movies at which they laughed raucously as they consumed huge bowls of popcorn and six-packs of beer. They went to every basketball game they could get to, whether it was the Knicks or the local junior high school team. Soon they were spending all their spare time together, and soon after that, were surprised to see how mutually dependent they had become as a couple who shared a "solid emotional life." Despite their deep need for each other, both agreed that they didn't want to remarry.

Sarah's husband had been a doctor who arranged his assets in a series of trusts that would support her in comfort for the rest of her life and still leave a handsome estate for her two adult children. He was a wise and compassionate man who had encouraged her to marry again, but she does not feel the need for "that little piece of paper." Neither does Denny, who said he "got taken to the cleaners" by Elaine. He would "happily" marry Sarah if she wanted him to, but he is also quite content to live with her.

Just down their street are their neighbors, Gretchen and Palmer, both of whom are divorced and living together but also reluctant to marry. They were introduced by a mutual friend shortly after their divorces, which occurred within months of each other. Both agreed that they moved in together because each "needed somebody to help [them] cope," but coping meant something different for each of them. Gretchen's divorce from a corporate lawyer was bitter; she is convinced that her ex-husband "bribed the judge" because of the terms of her alimony, which she will receive only as long as she does not remarry. She has little sense of her financial situation and shows scant interest in understanding it, preferring to insist that in and of itself, her settlement is "not enough" for her to live independently. She blames the judge for colluding with her ex-husband, both of whom told her to "get a job" if she needed more money. Palmer has "plenty of money" and would "love to support Gretchen," but seven years after her divorce, she refuses to remarry. She is still so angry that she intends to make her ex-husband pay alimony "until he draws his last breath."

Palmer is a retired CPA who invested carefully, both his money and the sizeable inheritance he received when his parents died. He is far more relaxed in general than the high-strung Gretchen, but whenever they talk about money she almost always says scornfully, "Oh, sure—with his money, he can afford to be." Palmer blushes every time, but he has heard it so often that he just shrugs, looks into the distance, and says nothing.

Gretchen said they were initially drawn together for very different reasons, and Palmer agrees. She needed "a place to perch" and could not "make it" on her own; he said he was immediately attracted to her because he liked her "vitality" and the way she "brought color to [his] otherwise dull life."

And so, two recently divorced couples who were initially drawn together by matters of convenience have developed new relationships that appear likely to last but for very different reasons. Denny and Sarah worked carefully to establish a partnership of "two equals" as they live by a "cost-sharing" plan that works well for both. After Sarah sold her house and moved into Denny's, she bought half of it so that both names are on the title as joint-owners with right of survivorship, so that whoever is the surviving partner will inherit the entire property. Everything else they own will go to their respective children after their deaths. They maintain separate bank and investment accounts but split all household expenses, from utilities to food, equally. Both have hobbies that they use their own funds to support: Denny is a home brewer who takes his beers to national competitions; Sarah buys expensive fabrics for hand-sewn quilts of her own design, and she goes to a Broadway show at least once a week. To ensure that they have enough money for their hobbies, Denny does all the gardening and property upkeep, while Sarah cleans the house. They have two cars registered in both their names, but they maintain them separately. Both marvel that, although they often disagreed with their spouses about how to use money, they have never yet had a financial disagreement with each other.

Palmer and Gretchen say that if Denny and Sarah have a relationship of "two equals," then theirs is probably one of "two very unequals." Their financial disagreements are frequent, and usually it is Gretchen who erupts in unfocused anger and Palmer who tries to calm her down. He pays all their household expenses, from food and utilities to a twice-weekly cleaning woman, while Gretchen provides the "fun money" for the entertainment she likes and he could live just as well without. Her tastes are expensive and run toward frequent vacations and cruises, weekends in New York hotels for dinner and the theater, and shopping for designer clothing. Palmer says Gretchen usually gets "very testy" after one of these "sprees," because she knows she doesn't have the money to pay for them and he will have to do so. Palmer says her way of admitting she has spent too much of his money is to "pick a fight over nothing," after which he has to "calm her down and tell her it's okay." He insists that "it really *is* okay" and he doesn't mind "paying for her little pleasures" because she brings "so many big ones" to his life. He wishes she would "worry less and enjoy it more. After all, it's only money."

"AND THEN WHAT HAPPENS?"

Irene and Jett were both fifty-two in 2003, lawyers who had been together since they met on the first day of law school. They married on graduation day and had been in a shared practice for twenty-eight years, until she decided one day that they had "not been a couple" for more than half the marriage and she wanted a divorce. They lived and worked in a Wisconsin town just north of Chicago, where they had gone to law school and married, and where their two children were now in college. Theirs was a life of comfort, relative ease, and community service. Separately and together, they pursued cultural interests, contributed to (different) political parties, and always took an active interest in their children's school-work and extracurricular activities. They never fought, never raised their voices, and as Irene said, "never really engaged emotionally." Jett admitted that "on the surface we were a really great couple, but we never learned how to do more than scrape that surface." Their divorce didn't surprise either of them, and neither contested it. They dissolved their legal partnership, and Irene took a job with a large firm where she began a successful practice of appellate law; Jett went into partnership with the owner of a real estate agency and within a year was taking only cases that involved residential-property sales. He was also married to the owner of the real estate firm, boasting proudly that she was his "new partner in life and work."

Jett was ecstatically happy with his new life, exhibiting a vitality Irene had never seen in all their years of marriage. Although she was "miffed" that she had never been the one to "turn him on," she was still sure that she had done the right thing to divorce him. However, she had never lived alone and did not like it, and was determined "to find a new man ASAP." And she didn't just want a lover; she wanted another husband.

Irene spent all her spare time looking for one, through online dating services and chat rooms to social occasions for older singles sponsored by churches she had never heard of, let alone attended. She went to legal conferences and seminars, reconnected with her college sorority sisters, and went to her high school reunion in the hope of seeing her old boyfriend—who was there, fifty pounds overweight and beaming at his equally heavy wife. Several months after Jett remarried, Irene was invited by a client to his son's bar mitzvah, where she met Jesse, a divorced man whose hotel room she went to within the hour and whom she married three months later.

Irene said she had never experienced "such passion" as she had with Jesse and thought it would be the "perfect foundation" for many happy years to come. Two years passed, and the physical passion remained but, said Irene, "not much else." At the time of this writing, she and Jesse were in the process of separating, and although he hoped it would only be a "trial," she already knew she wanted a divorce. Irene described him as "a nice man," whom she wanted "to let down gently." She was confident that she had at least fifteen more years of working life ahead of her and was sure that she could take care of herself because she had always earned a good living as a lawyer. She still wanted to be married because she liked "being part of a couple," but she saw "no sense in staying in a marriage just to say you are married."

"I am not a feminist, but . . ." Irene told me repeatedly before launching into a catalog of the many benefits women her age owed to the feminist revolution of the 1970s. First among them was the opportunity to work and earn a good income on her own without being stigmatized for being unmarried and independent. To Irene, marriage was only one of the many factors that went into "figuring out a woman's existence." She saw no reason for a woman to remain in a marriage that was not satisfying. "If you stay married, what happens? You get old, you get mean and miserable. And then what happens? You end up miserable and alone anyway. Better to get out while you can."

Irene was just approaching her mid-fifties, and if the AARP survey is accurate, her attitude is typical of her age group. Women in their fifties (and men as well), are more open to admitting that their second (or third) marriages are in trouble and more likely to do something to end them, whereas women who are older will often claim just the opposite, that their remarriages are "on solid ground" or "working pretty well." Irene is typical of the former, and several other women I interviewed bear out the latter.

Jean, a woman in her sixties, was one of them. "I knew the minute I got divorced that I wanted to get married again," she told me during a coffee hour convened by a therapist friend of mine in the Pacific Northwest in early 2004. My friend's clients were divorced or divorcing women, all of whom had the option, in addition to their individual sessions, to join one of several discussion groups she conducted every week. This particular group was composed of women who were sixty or older and had been married for around thirty years, give or take a few. Five members of the group were firmly committed to being single for the rest of their lives, but two were eagerly contemplating remarriage.

Jean was about to marry Adam, whom she first met as "the husband in the family next door" when both couples were newlyweds living in military housing at the Great Lakes Naval Air Station. After the husbands finished training, the two families were posted to different parts of the country and didn't see each other again, although they kept up the ritual exchange of Christmas newsletters. When Jean wrote in hers that she had just been divorced, Adam replied from Ohio to tell her that he was too. For several months, he and Jean exchanged letters, e-mails, and long telephone calls before he agreed to visit her for a week in her new town house. It was the first time they had seen each other in thirty years, and both admitted they were "nervous wrecks." Jean went on a crash diet and colored her hair, while Adam worried about what she would think of his bald spot and prominent paunch. After their initial uneasiness, they had a good time together, enjoying each other's conversation, and after the first two nights in separate bedrooms, they even had "decent sex." Before the week was over, they decided to get married as soon as possible. Adam went back to Ohio, fired up to make a permanent move to Washington State.

The other women in Jean's group were worried that she might perhaps be "jumping" at the first man who came her way, but she insisted that she and Adam had been attracted to each other from their days as newlywed neighbors, and their marriage would be "just fine." Becky was the other group member who was about to marry for the second time, and the five others used her as an example of why they thought Jean was "bound for trouble" if she "married on the rebound," which they were convinced she was doing.

Becky had been divorced for almost six years; for the first three, she'd lived happily on her own, without male companionship but with two large and active mutts she adopted from the local animal shelter. She had a specific reason for choosing such energetic dogs: she was overweight and thought she'd be more likely to get back in shape if she had to exercise two rambunctious dogs every day. They needed to walk as much as she did, and that was how Russell came into her life.

She met him at a dog run in a local park. He was carrying Daisy, his old and arthritic cocker spaniel, to let her lie beneath the benches where owners congregated to socialize after they walked their dogs. Becky often joined an informal group who gathered around the picnic table where Russell read the newspaper while Daisy dozed at his feet. After several months of seeing him daily, she noticed he hadn't come to the dog run for several days in a row. All the regulars were curious to know if something had happened to Daisy, and Becky volunteered to phone and find out. Russell told her Daisy had died, and he choked up when Becky told him how concerned everyone was; on behalf of the others, she invited him (as a gesture of friendship, for she didn't think she was attracted to him) to walk with her and her dogs the next morning. Russell showed up, but their conversation was awkward and sporadic. He did tell her afterward that he enjoyed the walk and hoped to do it again because he, too, needed the exercise. He told Becky he had no intention of getting another dog, so she invited him to walk with her, but he didn't do so until a month or so had passed.

When they did start to walk together, walking and talking was all they did for several months. Becky knew that Russell had been divorced for "quite a while," but that was all she knew about him. She never asked personal questions and he never volunteered any information about himself. They never saw each other away from the dog run until the other regulars talked about the movie *Best in Show*, which they had missed in theaters and wanted to see on DVD. Becky suggested they watch it at her apartment and share a potluck supper beforehand. Russell brought a chocolate cake, and everyone wanted his recipe. When he shyly admitted that he had taken cooking lessons after his divorce, Becky suggested a group session where he could teach what he had learned, and he agreed to it.

Even though other dog owners were always with them and they still hadn't officially been on a date, and even though she still knew nothing about his personal life, the casual low-key friendship gradually developed into a relationship. At her mutts' checkup time, Russell accompanied Becky to the veterinarian's to help her manage her hyperactive dogs, after which they shared a fast-food lunch in the park. She invited him to a lecture; he invited her to a concert. She included him in a group of friends who were going on a hike, and he invited her to be his guest at a friend's birthday barbecue. When almost a year had passed, they realized they were "getting pretty serious" and marriage was becoming a distinct possibility. They had taken weekend trips together down the coast to the Oregon beaches, but they had not actually lived together and they rarely slept at each other's apartment. Both had been "badly burned" in their first marriages, and they were determined to "get this marriage right," so they were "going slowly."

Becky's first husband was "a philandering computer genius" who she thought would most likely have stayed married to her "forever" because she was "the protective coloration who turned a blind eye to his cheating."

However, when he impregnated a woman "younger than our younger daughter," Becky told him she didn't care if he married the woman or not, but she could no longer stay married to him.

Russell's wife asked him for a divorce shortly after their thirtieth anniversary. She said throughout their childless marriage she had been attracted to women but had never acted upon it until recently, when she formed a "deeply loving friendship" with a woman she met at her church. Russell told Becky he was "embarrassed and ashamed" to admit that his wife left him for another woman, but she assured him that only he mattered to her, not his past history.

Both Jean and Becky married for the second time in late summer of 2004, and I spoke to them again in early 2006. Jean said, "Things are just fine" with Adam, but she wished they had spent "a little more time together before marriage." If they had, they would have "sorted out the small stuff," which often led to long cold silences and to one of them (usually Jean) storming into the bedroom and slamming the door behind her. All their disagreements were over "silly little things" like not folding the sections of the newspaper back in order after reading it, or not hanging up trousers so they wouldn't wrinkle, or leaving makeup spread out all over the bathroom counter. These seemed like trifles to me, so I asked Jean if they were perhaps excuses that masked larger differences pointing to more serious consequences. "Absolutely not," Jean insisted. They were going to stay together, for after all, they had just bought two four-cup coffeemakers so she could drink hers strong and black and he could make his "weak as dishwater." Living together was "not easy," but they were "learning." Neither wanted to live alone, and each was determined "to make this marriage stick."

Becky was more succinct when I asked about her marriage: "We had a lot of time to get to know what the other was like, so it's not as if we went into this marriage like two high school kids blindly in love. We knew what we were getting, and I think we're content with what we got." Theirs is a quiet relationship with "a lot of distance" between them. Becky sees this as a "positive," in that they allow each other "time and space apart." She said they also plan to stay married.

"A MARRIAGE IS LIKE A CAR . . ."

Agnes and Wade were approaching their eightieth birthdays when they met after moving into the same retirement community. Wade spoke disparagingly of his former wife, Lillian, who had divorced him fifteen years earlier "for no good reason; she just wanted 'her own space.' " He was in his midsixties at the time, a handsome and outgoing man who had no trouble finding other women with whom to live because he wanted someone to take care of him. He moved into the homes of three different women, living with the first for six years, the second for four, and the last for three. According to Wade, who had been a salesman for a roofing company, none of these relationships lasted because all the women had more money and property than he did, and they "lorded it over" him.

When he moved into the retirement community, he had a pension and a decent amount in savings, plus Social Security and a small army disability pension from an injury to his foot when he was a soldier in Germany. All this enabled him to buy an apartment in a pleasant community where he could live until he was ready to move to the next two stages, assisted living and hospice care if he needed it.

Agnes was already living in her apartment when Wade arrived. Her first divorce was long behind her, after her newspaper-reporter husband left her for a slightly younger colleague with whom he had had a long-term relationship that produced a child. Less than two years passed before Agnes met a man at a Unitarian singles' coffee hour and married him. That marriage lasted less than two years because "he [she refused to say his name] turned out to be something other than what he claimed to be," and this, too, she refused to explain. Agnes then went to live with her sister in their family home, but after her sister's death, she sold the house and used the proceeds to move into the retirement community. Both she and Wade admitted that they were "on the prowl for somebody," and soon they were "romantically involved."

They were about to have a wedding when I first spoke to them at the end of 2004 and were looking forward to moving into Agnes's apartment because it was larger than Wade's. I asked him if he was not just a little uneasy about giving up his home and moving yet again into a woman's house, but he said not this time because he and Agnes were "on a par" where money was concerned. Agnes was convinced that she and Wade had known each other long enough "before getting hitched" so that there would be "no surprises" afterward. I spoke to them again in separate conversations in 2006 and asked if they were still "satisfied" that marriage had been the right choice. What they relished most of all was the "companionship" of always having someone to talk to, even though they often disagreed with each other. Wade said it was "as simple as this: I'm a Democrat and she's not." Agnes said she willingly "puts up with his beer and his TV sports," just so long as he "sits down at the dinner table and makes polite conversation." Had they "settled," I asked? Was the fear of loneliness keeping them together in a marriage of convenience? "Probably," each said separately. "Everybody needs a reason to get out of bed in the morning," Wade said; Agnes said, "Loneliness can be a killer." Both agreed that living with another person was well worth "the pesky troubles" it entailed. Still, when I asked them—as well as Jean and Becky—if they regretted ending their first marriages, all insisted they had made the right decision.

Wade thought marriages were like cars: "Some just plain don't work and you need to get rid of them, turn them in for another model. The new one might have glitches, but you can straighten them out, you can fix them."

MOVING ON WHILE STAYING PUT

Carl, whose story began this chapter, was determined to stay in the house where he had lived for most of his marriage, as was Bonnie, who moved out of hers temporarily in order to be able to live in it permanently. Even though Bonnie had to admit that her renter had "fabulous taste" when she redecorated, Bonnie liked things the way they were and when she returned to live there, she wanted everything as it had been when she moved out, which is exactly how it was all during her marriage. "I divorced my husband, not my house," Bonnie said. Carl, on the other hand, changed everything he could afford to change, which entailed doing most of the work himself.

He thought about why he wanted "everything different," and decided that it was because Gloria had always made the "design decisions" even though he was the one who truly cared about the house. In effect, she had done little or nothing to make the house pleasant. She wanted plain white walls, had no interest in window treatments, no taste for decorative objects or art. There was nothing on the walls except a few family photos, and except for an ashtray on a coffee table in the living room and a pair of badly tarnished silver candlesticks that had been a wedding present, there was nothing in the dining room. Once Gloria was gone, Carl realized that he loved color and wanted to be surrounded by it. The walls of the entry hall became a cheerful apple green, the dining room a soft apricot, and the living room a pale dove gray. His study was chocolate brown and the bedrooms all became various shades of "soothing blues." He bought several large prints for the dining room, an African mask and other tribal artifacts for the study, and framed some posters for the living room. The kitchen became a brilliant saffron yellow with flashes of color from the Fiesta ware dishes he bought en masse at the local discount store. He replaced several kitchen-cabinet doors with glass-fronted ones, so the color of the dishes would show.

In short, Carl was keeping his past life intact by staying in the house even as he made himself comfortable, secure, and happy to look forward to the future by turning the house into what he wanted it to be.

Noel O'Malley, a Los Angeles psychotherapist, explained what Carl was doing: "[New] furniture, remodeling, asserting your will upon the things around you, is central to healing. Redecorating can be the psyche's way of rehearsing for emotional change."[6]

The psychologist C. G. Jung believed that "a house depicts a situation in life. One is in it, as one is in a situation."[7] Carl's situation was that he loved his house and wanted to stay in it. He was lucky that he could find a way to do so, but in some parts of the country, to stay or to move is not a viable choice simply because it makes better financial sense to stay put. In many cities, New York paramount among them, apartments are often rent-stabilized and it is far cheaper to keep them.

Patty found this to be true when she divorced Ben after twenty-seven years of living in New York's "Alphabet City." When they were newlyweds, they moved into the top floor of a redbrick tenement overlooking Tompkins Square Park, in an area known as "Loisaida" (a Spanglish approximation of the "Lower East Side"). Then it was a hotbed of homelessness, drugs, and crime; now it is the increasingly gentrified East Village, where nannies wheel English prams in the park and chic shops and destination restaurants abound.

Patty worked on Wall Street, first as a secretary, then as a senior computer programmer, while Ben designed and illustrated book jackets. Along the way, they bought a ramshackle farm in Upstate New York, where they spent weekends and summers. Their divorce began as one of "mutual consent" when Ben decided he wanted to live on the farm all year round and Patty said she preferred to stay in the city. It soon became bitter when she learned that he was moving to the farm to be with the man who had been his long-term lover, for both were now HIV-positive.

Patty was so furious over Ben's deception that her first impulse was to turn the key in the lock and walk out of the apartment forever. But then she remembered that the rent for her four large rooms was $675 a month (including utilities) and she could not find a tiny studio in the same area for less than $1,800, so she curbed her anger and looked for another way to "clean [herself] of the stink of Ben." First she got herself tested and was relieved to learn that she had not been infected with the virus. Then she lugged everything of his that he had not taken from the apartment down five flights of stairs and put it on the street. She threw out all the furniture, including the bed, and for several weeks she slept on the floor until a new mattress was delivered. Once she got the bed, she "sat on it and cried a lot," asking herself over and over, "How could you live with someone for so long and not know him?" She had no children to console her, and she initially rejected the friends who wanted to offer comfort.

Patty spent almost a month doing what she called "wallowing in self-pity," but "having to eat is a powerful incentive," and so she got out of bed and went back to work. She walked the several miles to and from her job on Wall Street each day, hoping the exercise would tire her out enough so that she could sleep at night. On one of her walks home one pleasant spring evening, she paused frequently to look into the Chinatown store windows that displayed stacks of cobalt blue and white temple jars, dragons, and dishes. On Orchard Street, she found herself relaxing and smiling as she looked at bolts of fabric draped in the windows, and as she strolled up the Bowery, she paused at all the restaurant-supply shops where everything from stoves to stockpots were piled along the street. A copper skillet caught her eye, and on an impulse, she bought it. Heading across Sixth Street on her final lap home, she saw a large red tin foot-locker in front of one of the Indian restaurants, battered and covered all over in colorful paper stickers with Indian writing and floral designs. Someone had put it out for trash collection, and Patty picked it up. At the Korean grocer's on her corner, she bought armloads of tulips and daisies, and when she got home, she put them in every container she had not thrown away. She phoned for Chinese takeout, lit the stubs of two candles, and put them on her street-find footlocker, then sat down on the floor before the little chest to enjoy her first meal in her new life.

That weekend, she invited friends to help her paint the walls. A trip to Ikea provided basic furnishings, which she supplemented with "mongo," all the perfectly good things New Yorkers have no room for and put out on the street for anyone who wants to take them. Patty has turned what used to be "our place" into "my home," and she has learned to savor the beauty and comfort she has created.

Patty is one of the women who agrees that Katharine Hepburn's idea about how men and women should live is a very good one indeed: "Sometimes I wonder if men and women really suit each other. Perhaps they should live next door and just visit now and then."[8]

Interestingly, more and more people in committed relationships are doing just that, not only in the United States but throughout the world. Sociologists and staticians have dubbed the phenomenon "Living Alone Together," and it is now a recognized demographic category, abbreviated to its acronym, "LAT."[9] These are couples in committed relationships who are often divorced (sometimes twice or more) and who want to share their lives with a significant other, but only to a certain extent and on their own terms. Each partner maintains a separate residence, and they only live together when it suits them both.

Because the United States Census Bureau does not count such households, researchers have found it difficult to come up with hard and fast numbers of how many there actually are, but a survey conducted in Great Britain in 2005 estimated that there were more than a million in that country, with the figure escalating yearly. Recent studies done in Canada, France, Norway, and Sweden have all found this to be a steadily increasing trend in those populations as well.

Some of these LATs are couples who actually marry but make the conscious decision to live separately from the beginning. San Franciscan Robert White was fifty-four when he and then forty-six-year-old Elke Zuercher-White were married in 1991. Fifteen years later, he says they have never questioned the decision, which for him makes it "kind of like the first date" every time he sees her. Usually, however, LATs prefer to stay single rather than marry again and are, as Daina, age fifty-seven and living in Northern New Jersey, told me, among the ranks of "the once or twice badly burned." Her partner, Morrie, age seventy-one and living in the Bronx's Riverdale section, enlarged her statement to include "the slightly bruised and the walking wounded." Each was twice divorced, the first time after long marriages, the second after short "rebound" ones that put them into the statistical category of the 60 percent of second marriages that fail (as opposed to 50 percent of first marriages). When they met at a millennium New Year's Eve party, each had reluctantly consigned themselves to (in Daina's words) "life as a pathetic singleton," and (in Monie's) "a guy trying to avoid old ladies on the make." Each owned a condo apartment near where their grown children lived, and early on, both agreed they did not want to move. Daina had never worked outside the home but was financially secure with the "guilt money" settled on her by her wealthy first husband who "ran off with a bimbo younger than [her] two daughters." Morrie had retired from a small manufacturing business that he sold to the son of a cousin, and he is very friendly with the new owner, who welcomes him when he drops in several afternoons each week to "kibitz." Morrie did not want to give up this tie with his old life. He liked to "check things out" to make sure the business was being well run, after which he liked to go back to his condo, cook a simple dinner, and eat it while watching a movie on the television. He liked to be asleep by 10 P.M. Daina wanted to play bridge several nights each week with her girlfriends, and she had a standing date for a "sleepover" with her twin teenage granddaughters every Wednesday that she never missed.

Daina and Morrie spend most weekends together, dining at her country club or his, and they usually go to Florida or the Caribbean for a winter vacation in the month of January. They keep all their finances separate and each pays for half of everything. Neither likes to give or receive costly presents ("What for? We have everything we need," both agree). "We're both happy living like this," Daina says, and Morrie nods his head in vigorous unison.

But there are other reasons committed couples are reluctant to live together, and their reasons parallel the ones people give for deciding to divorce when each partner brings dependent children into the relationship. Children are often the bone of contention that plays a huge part in the decision to live in separate households. If the children are young and still at home, the tension of trying to meld two separate families into one is often more trouble than the partners find it to be worth; if the children are older and living on their own, and one or both partners has substantial money and property, the adult children often worry so much about inheritances that they throw up huge roadblocks when an elderly parent shows romantic interest in a new partner. There are statistics indicating that only one out of three stepfamilies lasts, and the tabloids are full of stories about elderly sons and daughters of the first marriage battling the beautiful widows (often younger than they are) of their deceased fathers.

It's not surprising that the baby boomer generation comprises the largest segment within LAT statistics. Their tendency to divorce for the "soft reasons" is exemplified by Chloe, a fifty-year-old banker in Chicago who told me she was forty-four when she "cut [her] losses to get out of a boring eighteen-year marriage that was going nowhere." Still, she did not want to be single and alone but "wanted to have it all, to have [her] cake and eat it, too." For her, this meant having male companionship on her terms. After the divorce, she vowed never to give up her freedom even though (and here she giggled and blushed) she "started looking around the courtroom for a new man the minute the divorce was final." She found Kenny, a divorced co-worker and father of three teenage boys of whom he shared custody, keeping them two weeks every month. From the beginning of their six-year relationship, Chloe refused "to play wickedstepmama" and almost never sees Kenny when his sons are living in his house. She thinks "it works best for us if Kenny plays grown-up with me when they live with their mom."

The verdict is still out on whether LAT living will become the wave of the future for older adults. Some therapists see setting up separate households as a tragic loss, diminishing or perhaps even negating the possibility of true intimacy. A marriage counselor in Detroit told me that "real togetherness" can never be attained unless there is the sustained interaction between two people that comes only from living with each other every day. Others, such as the group of family therapists who practice in northern California and who invited me to sit in on one of their round-table discussions, told me they see living in separate households as "a viable, probably very good alternative" to what so many people cite as the reason they end up in divorce court: the lack of (yes—here are those words again) "communication" and "the overwhelming desire for freedom."

The LATs who fall into this latter category cling to their independence, refusing to surrender the often painfully hard-won sense of selfhood that came when they walked away from marriages in which they had had to cater to someone else's needs or depend on another person for every aspect of their daily lives. Time after time, I heard both men and women say, "I'll never live that way again," when they described the marriages they had ended and how they are conducting their new relationships. They insisted that I could not possibly imagine the sense of exhilaration they felt every time they turned the key and walked into their own place, no matter if it was the proverbial stately home or humble flat. They swore they would never again surrender the tranquility and independence that came from knowing this place was theirs alone and that no one would be waiting inside to "harangue," "harass," "kvetch," "moan," or "bitch" at them.

Julianne Foley, a financial services executive who lives in Mount Kisco, New York, described a "suffocating marriage" to a man who expected her to arrange his shoes in his closet with all their laces tied in perfect bows. Now that she is in a five-year relationship with a divorced banker who lives near her, she admits that living alone rather than together is far more expensive. Even so, "the emotional costs of living with someone are too high. You can't put a dollar value on being your own person."

Ultimately, that seems to be what matters most.

CHAPTER TEN

THE PASSIONATE LIFE

Before I turn 67—next March—I would like to have a lot of sex with a man I like. If you want to talk first, Trollope works for me. NYR Box 10021

—JANE JUSKA, *A Round-Heeled Woman*

He didn't know. The change. The stop. He didn't know. The partnership. Fuck it, the marriage. And it wasn't true about the sex, either, exactly. They still had it, did it. Now and again. The odd time . . . he didn't know when it had stopped. . . . And it had been a long time. Twenty-six years. What had happened? He didn't fuckin know.

—RODDY DOYLE, "The Joke"

PERHAPS IT IS NOT SO unusual that even as people were open and honest about revealing the most intimate details of their married life and why they felt they had no option but to divorce, they were reluctant to talk very much about sex—within the marriage, with other partners while it lasted, or after it ended. I always asked the people I interviewed about their sex lives, and almost always their answers were embarrassed, evasive, and equivocating. So I learned quickly how to change the kinds of questions I asked, removing them from the directly personal and phrasing them impersonally through some of the statistics in the AARP survey. When I told my respondents what the survey found, they were quite likely to become relaxed enough to talk about their own experiences and to put me in touch with friends and acquaintances whose postdivorce sexual encounters paralleled their own.

The AARP survey found that 77 percent of divorced women who did not remarry said they *never* had sex, but only 49 percent of the men said the same. If they did remarry after a late divorce, the frequency of sexual activity was about the same for both, as 57 percent of men and 54 percent of women admitted to having sex at least once a week. The largest age group to enter into a sexual relationship either within two years of their divorce or before it was even granted was the fifty-year-old baby boomers: 85 percent of women and 81 percent of men in this group admitted to having a sex life that was serious, exclusive, and intense.

In my own interviews with 184 women and 126 men, no matter what their ages, about 80 percent of both told me they were either in such a relationship or insisted they could have one if they wanted it. And about 90 percent of that 80 percent told me they found it far "easier" not to have one. More women than men told me it was "too much like hard work" to establish new and lasting intimate relationships, so they decided instead "to do without" or else "to have a little fun and then go home to sleep in my own bed at night" (a phrase I heard repeatedly in many variations). Here again, the AARP survey provided a confirmation of my informal findings and paralleled what my respondents told me: of persons in their sixties or older, the majority of women (over 52 percent) did not want to remarry, whereas approximately 67 percent of the men did.

Most men were like Ted, the man whose story I told earlier, who went on three cruises and was "exhausted—wink, wink, nudge, nudge," until he found a woman who would "take care [of him]" physically, emotionally, and "occasionally, sexually." Another man like Ted was Henry, a distinguished scholarly gentleman in his mid-eighties whose second wife divorced him after twenty-eight years. He told me he wanted to marry again because he needed a woman to take care of him, and he had "one simple test" a woman had to pass. He was dating three divorced women between the ages of sixty-two and seventy-three at the time, and he put his test to them: Would they be willing to bring a cup of tea to him in bed every morning before he got up? All three refused, but he did find a fourth who said not only would she do it, she would buy him a new mattress because the one he had hurt her back. They were married within the month.

AFFECTION VERSUS PASSION

I did most of the interviewing for this book from late 2004 until early 2006, just before the recent spate of books was published about older women seeking out sex.[1] As they garnered reviews (particularly Gail Sheehy's *Sex and the Seasoned Woman*), articles appeared by writers who scoffed at, disputed, or strongly disagreed with the conclusion that older women were out there pursuing what Sheehy calls "the passionate life."[2] Many readers, older women both married and divorced, wrote letters in response to the articles and reviews, and most of them snorted in derision at the idea of older women lustily searching for a sexual partner.

One exception was Helen Gurley Brown, the legendary former editor of *Cosmopolitan*, whose letter to *The New York Times Book Review* both defended Sheehy's thesis and hinted coyly at her own happy sex life with her husband, David (he is ninety and she is in her eighties).[3] Unlike that happy couple, most writers of letters, reviews, and articles were more like the septuagenarian couple who wrote into their prenuptial agreement that they would be required to have sex only once a month.[4]

Then came Erica Jong with her new memoir, *Seducing the Demon: Writing for My Life*,[5] a rollicking romp of sex among the chattering classes. Jong, who famously boasted that she "smelled of sex" back in the seventies when *Fear of Flying* was selling more than eighteen million copies around the world, now says "the zipless fuck could not interest me less," but "mature sex, committed sex, with all its zippered encumbrances," interests her plenty.[6] Jong is now in her mid-sixties, and sees "something nice about the freedom of getting older." She told a reporter for *The Washington Post* that sex in her sixties is still "delicious," even though "certain body parts might not work as well, but a willing spirit makes up for weak flesh."

Because of these books and the fuss they created about sex and the older woman, who is having it and who is not, I decided I had to go back to the men as well as the women in my original interviews to ask if time's passing might have caused them to change any of their views about sex. I asked if they were aware of the buzz about these books and if they had read any of them, and if so, whether any of their experiences parallel those of the authors and the people who wrote letters and articles in response.

In my original conversations, I had asked if they missed not having a regular sexual partner after they divorced. Most of the women said they missed "affection" in a general sense rather than the sexual act in and of itself, but they also reminded me that "lack of affection" within the marriage was a strong reason (and often the only reason) why they divorced. When they described what they "yearned for," I heard words like "hugging," "kissing," and "touching" far more than I heard anything connected with "sex," "passion," "intercourse" (some were formal in the language they used), or "fucking" (some were direct).

One of the women to whom I returned for follow-up conversations told me she wanted to introduce me to one of her oldest and dearest friends, who had just decided to end her thirty-eight-year marriage "while she still had time." Time for what? I asked. "To find love," the woman replied. Jenny, her friend, had just read an article by Calvin Trillin in *The New Yorker*[7] in which he poured out the love he felt for his late wife, Alice. Jenny told me, "As I was reading it, I was okay with realizing that Dave [her husband] had never once felt that way about me. And then I came to the place where Trillin quoted a letter somebody wrote to him after Alice died, about how she sometimes looked at her boyfriend and thought, 'But will he love me like Calvin loves Alice?' It just took my breath away. Nobody had ever felt that way about me, and I knew then I had to get away from Dave to see if there was someone out there who could."

When I asked if she would be looking for a passionate sex life, she replied quietly, "No. I will be looking for love, and I don't know, but I think they might be two different things altogether. I'll have to find out."

Jenny's response led me back to Doris for the third time. She had been one of my more formal respondents when I first spoke to her but who talked about her sex life far more freely the second time. A quiet woman who struck me as prim and proper, Doris had blossomed in the fourteen months since I first met her. Now she told me how she and her friends often talked about sex when they got together and volunteered to get a group of them to tell me what they encountered when they found themselves "suddenly single." Doris was divorced after forty-four years by "mutual agreement: we just bored each other to death and decided to get out while we could still navigate." She was about to turn seventy and finally ready to retire from a job she enjoyed as an office manager for a small business in northern New Jersey, and so she sold her house for a handsome profit and moved to Florida.

She had been faithful to her husband throughout her marriage, and now, after years of "occasionally wondering what [she] was missing," she was consciously looking for a new partner "to find out." However, she knew from the beginning that she wanted one who would be more of a "companion" than a "lover." "This is what I've been finding since I talked to you before," she told me: "My divorced friends wanted a lot of sex, especially if they were the dumpees. I was more of a dumper, so I was interested in what was out there but not so intense about it. But my married friends—hah! One of them told me she has 'high school sex' a lot, hand jobs in the shower because of [vaginal] dryness. Otherwise, I can't say any of the women I know are doing a whole hell of a lot on the sex scene."

I pressed Doris for "details" about her divorced "dumpee" friends: Were they *really* having a lot of sex with a lot of different men? Were there that many available "out there" (as she put it)? She said she'd get back to me, and a week later she phoned.

Doris played bridge every week with seven other "single women," three widows and five divorcées. They always played in the morning, after which the hostess served Bloody Marys, lunch, and lots of white wine. At this particular luncheon, they filled their glasses, talked about sex, emptied their glasses, and filled them again and again. Doris said it was "one of the best lunches ever," as "wine is the great lubricator" that made her friends "come clean."

All agreed that Florida was not the best place for a woman alone to relocate because there were too many men who had had "only one partner all their lives—wives who may or may not have even liked it [sex]—and suddenly these old farts are acting like kids in a candy shop. I'll have this one, and this, and this one, too."

Doris thought Marcia, a widow in her early sixties, put it best when she said, "Men differ only in their degree of selfishness." Marcia, a "self-pro-claimed dumpee," described her "humiliation" at "having to do what men want" and was scornful of "how little they give back and how arrogant they are about it." She decided it was "too much work" to help all these "condo cowboys" to orgasm and "too frustrating" not to be helped to her own. Worst of all, these men took pride in their "one-night stands." She either never saw them again, or if she did, they sheepishly avoided having anything to do with her, from making eye contact to engaging in conversation. Marcia still wanted something she had not had for all the years of her marriage—"someone to go to the movies with, to eat dinner with and watch the sunset, and maybe kiss and cuddle." Time was passing and she was growing "more certain by the minute that this is not going to happen."

Two of the other women in Doris's bridge group told a different story. Both were divorced and had been in relationships for the past four or five years. One woman was in her late sixties when she met a widower during a "senior social hour" at the Unitarian church in her Oklahoma hometown. They had moved together to Florida but lived in separate apartments in the same building. Neither wanted to remarry because there were "children and a bit of money" involved. They were "grateful for the companionship" and enjoyed "all kinds of physical touching" even though they had not had intercourse since their first year together because "it was too much trouble for what we got from it." They were content to "hug and hold hands" and expected to end their days together.

The other woman met her companion at the local Jewish community center after she had relocated from a small Canadian town where she felt "ostracized" by her fundamentalist Christian community after her divorce. She was sixty-two and he was eighty-four when they met about three years before I spoke to Doris. In the beginning "the sex was good—infrequent, but good." Since then, they describe themselves as having fallen into the "high school sex" category and were quite happy to be there. They lived together in an apartment she owned but now that "[his] health problems were start-ing to kick in," she worried incorrectly, actually, that his children (who have power of attorney) might remove him. He and she always had "so much to talk about," until his mind started "to wander," and she said she must learn to resign herself to the day when his children may take him away from her. But for now, sex was "far down the list of priorities" and the most important thing for them both was to enjoy every minute they had together.

"IT'S EMBARRASSING, BUT . . ."

Liam, a dapper little bantam of a fellow whose seventieth birthday was "around the corner" when we first spoke, told me that he took full responsibility for the breakup of his "first and only" marriage, to Joyce, of "thirty-nine years and five children." He had never set foot in Ireland until his fifty-ninth year but had spent his lifetime cultivating an Irish persona, which he was firmly convinced was the reason he prospered in all his business dealings. He worked his way through law school at night but never practiced, choosing instead to become an "entrepreneur." "I never got an idea where I could not make a buck," he boasted, and indeed, everything he touched did seem to turn to gold. That is, until Joyce grew tired of his endless philandering and enlisted her three older children (two of whom were lawyers) to help her divorce Liam and tie up a large chunk of his assets.

He was surprised when she "kicked [him] out" but chuckled with a combination of astonishment and pride that "she had the chutzpah to do it and the kids had the balls to help her." Liam had not been idle in the year between our first and second conversations: he invested in several theme-park shopping malls in the Midwest and made a tidy profit; he bought a failing vineyard outside Bordeaux, France, and was revitalizing it; and he had already lived with two different "zaftig babes" and was about to invite a third to move into his high-rise condo in downtown Houston. There was only "one little fly in [his] otherwise very fragrant ointment."

When his characteristic staccato tough-guy speech disintegrated into a bout of coughing and stuttering, Liam said, "I'm glad I'm talking to you on the phone. This is really embarrassing to admit," he started, then stopped, and then there was a throat-clearing pause. I waited, having an idea of what he would eventually confess, for I had been hearing it, or something like it, from other men fairly often in the last several days. "I have to take those pills," he blurted.

"Do you mean Viagra?" I asked.

"Yeah, them. Something like them." He laughed nervously before launching into an explanation of how it was not uncommon among men his age, and how he knew a lot who "pretend to be big-time studs but I see them in the drugstore and I know they aren't picking up Rolaids."

We laughed together, and then Liam grew thoughtful. He told me he "liked sex," he "liked women's bodies," he liked "all the stuff you can do in bed," and he wanted "to keep on doing it." He liked sex with Joyce ("and we did it a lot, fer crissakes, we had five kids after all"), but he liked to have sex "all the time," and this meant having other women "on the side." He insisted that Joyce knew and was not upset about it because "it gave her a break from me." When Joyce finally called a halt to the marriage, it was not because of his serial adultery but because she worried about his escalating extravagance. Liam explained that, as he "got older, the playmates got younger," and the "gifts and things" he gave them became truly expensive. Liam regrets this "bad judgment," saying if he had not "scared Joyce and the kids about the money," he would still be married.

He liked being married and confessed that he so missed having a woman in his home that he had offered one of the two he had been with, the one who had lived with him the longest since his divorce, a half-million dollars if she would consent to live with him for a minimum of one year. "To her credit," Liam said, "she told me she didn't know if she could put up with me that long, and besides, she wasn't a whore and couldn't be bought. She said she'd move out when the time came, and it came a couple of months later." He asked me if he should offer the same amount or more to the third woman whom he was now considering; I told him he would have to make that decision on his own.

Liam had chosen some interesting women as possible replacements for Joyce. Unlike many men in his position who gravitate toward "twenty-something arm candy," he had chosen three women who were divorced and in their mid-to-late fifties, and all three had professions. One sold commercial real estate (which was how he met her), another was the executive secretary to a lawyer with whom he had business dealings, and the third worked in the public relations firm that promoted some of his investments. They were "old enough that [he] could talk to them," and "young enough that you would expect they still liked sex." He was puzzled by how they responded when he took Viagra. He expected them to like the fact that he often had an erection for twenty-four hours or so ("Never longer," he said. "What's this crap about thirty-six hours? No way!").

He was willing and eager to have multiple encounters and was always considerate enough to take the time and care to bring his partners to orgasm, but the women "couldn't keep up" with him. He described the "bushels" of jellies and lubricants they used, but to little avail, as they were "always complaining they were dry and they hurt." The first woman left him because she was convinced he made her prone to recurring bladder infections, while the second complained of soreness. With the third, "the jury is still out," but he hoped she would be "different."

Liam's experience with women may or may not have been typical, and I'm not sure how appropriate it is to generalize, especially because what both men and women told me often changed in the telling. The things they said reminded me of something from what I call "another life," when I was a university professor of literature, teaching students how to "deconstruct" a text in order to get to the "real meaning" that often lay hidden beneath the written language. In this case, most of the women in their fifties and sixties who gave me follow-up interviews insisted that they could have "as much sex as [they] wanted" and had "few, if any" of the symptoms of Liam's partners. Yet as the conversations continued, they did say they either "couldn't do it more than once" a day, or no longer "wanted to do it" with anything like the frequency of their younger years, which they said was "two, three times a week." A few admitted that "these days," they could "easily forget about doing it altogether."

About a half-dozen women told me they had taken Prempro or related estrogen therapies in order (as one put it) "to get some juice back in the old box," but they all agreed it didn't give them the hoped-for results. They described how a cocktail or two with women friends might well turn into a "giggle fest about sex and which vaginal jelly provided the most comfort during the act," but none of them would be rushing out to buy them anytime soon.

"What about these sex-toy parties?" I asked a small group of women who invited me to join them for drinks after an afternoon reading I gave on my last book tour. "Are they really the new Tupperware? Do you go to them? Do you buy them?" These women had traveled from the retirement community where they all lived to hear me speak. They described themselves as mostly in their sixties and "veterans of the dating scene." They told me that there is "always somebody out there trying to make a buck" by selling sexual aids, so they go to the parties not to buy them but for the opportunity to "get together and socialize." They made a point of stressing that they "go for the gab, not for the goods."

"Most of us already own a vibrator," said one. "Or two," said another, laughing. Edna was the oldest member of the group, a woman who looked fifty-five but confessed to being seventy-two. She told me she attended her first sex-toy party when her forty-five-year-old daughter (also divorced) invited her to "bring some pals and join a group of PTA moms" for a demonstration of "edible underwear and other toys." Edna gave us a vivid demonstration, complete with hand gestures, of these "goods" and how to use them. Her descriptions of "the goods" (a term I heard often) sent us all into gales of laughter, which some of the women said was "better than sex." Edna said if "talking about sex" was what it took to connect with her daughter's generation, she had "never before connected so well" and hoped to go to a lot more "bi-generational parties" just "for the fun of it."

At that point the laughter quieted and the conversation grew serious. Edna, the seventy-two-year-old, said her daughter's friends were women in their mid-forties to mid-fifties, at the tail end of the baby boom generation. They "took sex toys seriously" and were "obviously unhappy" that they had to resort to them, for they were all interested in marrying again and were "in the market for a lot of good old-fashioned sex with a real man." Her daughter was a member of what Edna called "the gym generation," women who were often exhausted from the double life of holding down full-time jobs that made it possible for them as single moms to raise their children alone. Still they found time to go to the gym to tone their bodies and to the plastic surgeon for all that the gym could not fix. This, too, is what Edna calls "the Botox generation," women who plump their lips, diminish their wrinkles, and rid themselves of unwanted cellulite and belly fat. She and her friends are especially shocked by the spate of articles about the newest surgery to reconfigure the vagina, vaginal rejuvenation. "Who looks?" they asked, almost in unison. "Why would anyone want to?"

Lakshmi Chaudhry, a writer for the online magazine inthesetimes. com and a young woman of Edna's daughter's generation, questioned the recent books and articles that heap praise upon aging women who are out on the sexual hustings. She has wisely recognized a connection between older women who seek sex and the reality of their lives:

> *Underneath all this talk about staying sexy is the stark reality of the loneliness of old age in America. At a time when women live longer than ever, they often find themselves single in their old age because of death or divorce. . . . Of course they should be encouraged in their efforts to find intimacy, companionship, and yes, even romance. . . . But surely after a lifetime of toil, these people are entitled to sex that requires less work—must they really endure long hours at the gym, extensive hormone treatments, and the petty humiliations of online dating just to get laid?*

Edna described herself as "luckier than most women her age" because she was "dating" several men concurrently but infrequently. Her friends teased her by pretending to be "shocked" that she did not practice "serial monogamy" because she routinely slept with more than one man. Then they confessed how they would "like to try some of that" and asked Edna to talk about what it was like. What she had with men now, Edna explained, was "a different kind of sex." She still liked "good old-fashioned missionary sex" best, performed oral sex "only when I really have to," and said she "always" found a way to "help" her partner bring her to orgasm. But she stressed that she generally had "real sex" (vaginal penetration) on the average of once a month or less, more likely every six weeks or so. In between times, there was "an awful lot of hugging and touching." She liked it when she and her "dates" stayed in on a Saturday night to watch a movie and was particularly "thrilled" with one who liked to put a hand on her bare breast. She liked to hold and stroke her date's penis as the movie progressed, but "just as often as not, that's as far as it went." It satisfied them both.

Edna introduced me to Joan Anderson's memoir, *A Year by the Sea*, the story of the author's time living alone in a family cottage on Cape Cod while she considered whether or not to end her marriage. Edna particularly wanted me to "read page one fifty-two," where Anderson wrote about "the myth around sex in this culture . . . that we should want it, that we are abnormal or repressed if we don't have it." Anderson wondered if "perhaps I stopped being available for lovemaking simply because I didn't like it. It seemed fine for helping to pin down a man for marriage, even finer when I wanted children. Then it became a chore—a duty to perform after the dishes were done and the kids were put to bed. Pleasuring her man was what I had been taught a good wife simply should do."[8]

Edna said she "identified" with Anderson during her own marriage when she wondered what, if anything, she had "been missing." It was the catalyst that spurred Edna to "get out there and date," and she considered herself fortunate that she had met several men who were "kind and generous throughout the sexual act." She used Anderson's examples to describe "the reality" that applied to some of her other women friends: of a husband whose lovemaking was akin to "any keyhole would do," of another "whose idea of romance" was lying in bed with the *Sports Illustrated* swimsuit issue, expecting her to become aroused while he played with himself. I thought of these examples as a replay of Doris's friend Marcia's judgment that "men differ only in their degree of selfishness."

The conversation faded into quiet as the women at the table busied themselves fussing with napkins, twirling glass stems, or consulting their purses. "What are we *really* talking about here?" I asked. "Is there some intangible in human relationships that we are trying to define and can't?" No one seemed to know what I was getting at—actually, I didn't either—until one of them said, "I just don't want to feel . . ."—and here she hesitated. Another volunteered, "Do you mean dirty?" Another said, "Ashamed?" Another offered, "Embarrassed, maybe?" Edna, who sat there so serenely, yet so deeply engaged with her friends, asked: "Do you mean something like 'self-respect' "? This seemed to be the concept they were looking for, and it set them off. Soon they were offering other synonyms for "self-respect," with "dignity" strong among them.

One woman described herself as of the generation that "did not call boys; they called me." So she found it "hard" to take the initiative about dating. Once when she "cooked a nice dinner" for a widower, she was "insulted" when he asked if she wanted "to get the sex over with before we eat." She was "humiliated" when he walked out without eating after she told him she had really just invited him for dinner so they could "get to know each other." He said he already "knew" enough women to talk to; he was interested in "getting to know" some who wanted sex.

Another said she gave up trying to find "companionship" when she grew tired of "waking up in the morning wondering how to ask if they still"—here she chuckled—" 'respected' me." These friends agreed that a third woman seemed to express it best: "Men assume such arrogance toward women after divorce. They could never get away with such nasty behavior during marriage, and I doubt that most of them could have gotten away with such callous cruelty to women before they were married."

We ended our conversation with decidedly mixed conclusions about the sex lives of older women, and as she usually did, Edna seemed to sum it up for everyone: "You could get lucky, but probably not. You can always hope to find a nice guy, but it's not likely to happen. Something crazy happens to these men once they're single again, and I can't figure out what it is."

THE "WRONGLY ACCUSED"

Well, then, what do men expect sexually from women? Surely, they could not all be like the selfish boors Joan Anderson described. Even Edna and her disappointed friends thought "some men *must* be good guys." When all the evidence and information about how men behave toward women is tossed into the hopper, does everything funnel down to the lack of communication that so many couples give as the reason why they divorced?

Deborah Tannen, in her bestselling book *You Just Don't Understand: Women and Men in Conversation*, describes how couples talk but don't connect: "Women feel men don't communicate," while men feel "wrongly accused."[9] The political scientist Andrew Hacker makes a similar observation, that women frequently blame lack of communication as the cause of their divorces, while their husbands seldom do.[10] In *Men on Divorce: The Other Side of the Story*, editors Susan Spano and Penny Kaganoff observe that many of the male writers who contributed essays "describe lives filigreed with long chains of relationships [as they] move serially from one woman to the next, repeating the same mistakes over the course of each involvement and arriving at the same failure."[11]

In his essay "Bedroom Tapestries," Tim Parks seems to prove the editors' point when he writes how "unfaithfulness never fails to rejuvenate."[12] Even so, he is wise enough to caution that "if we start again too often, nothing will be brought to completion."

Parks's description of men who continually strive to "start again" struck a note that came up in many of my second-round conversations with men. Whenever they were willing to talk about their postdivorce sexual behavior in something other than vague generalities, they admitted to being "on the lookout for something new" even before the divorce. Andrew, who had just turned sixty, told me he left his wife after thirty-five years because "the world is full of successful men and the women they married when they were very young." He had "outgrown" her years before but, like many other men, stayed "for the sake of the children." Now they were grown and gone, and he knew his marriage was "well and truly over" because he could only have sex with his wife if he dreamed of "pursuing other women, of meeting someone wonderful." He expressed a fairly uncommon theme among men, that he was more interested in "finding a loving and caring relationship than in finding a woman to take care of me." He admitted that he was fortunate because he had enough money to make it possible to find a loving relationship.

Of the men I interviewed, Andrew was one of those who were most successful in finding a new and satisfying sexual relationship. No matter how or where they met the new partner, and no matter where they fell on the age spectrum of late-life divorce, they were the ones who told me that they were "happy." I asked how often they had sex with the new lover, and the replies were fairly consistent: they had a lot more sex because they were far more "romantic" with the new partner than they had ever been with their wives. Sex was "far more spontaneous" and "far more gratifying" whenever it happened: "We could be making the bed in the morning and she'll throw a pillow at me in a mock fight, and the next thing you know we'll be in it and making out," said Alvin, age sixty-nine. Bernie, age seventy-two, said, "Sometimes I just watch her while she's moving around in the kitchen, humming to herself, and I can't wait to get her into bed."

Andrew, Alvin, and Bernie all told me they married their first wives when very young because their religions forbade sex before marriage, and so they "got married to have sex." Bernie called himself "a hormone-driven conservative Catholic who got married for life at twenty-two rather than burn in hell. We were both virgins, and it didn't work out from day one." Andrew said of his first marriage, "Somehow romance got left out of the equation." Alvin, Bernie, and many other men agreed with Andrew, that they were engaged in a "romance" for the first time in their lives and they were "very happy."

Other men who divorced after long marriages looked for romance in a different way and with less successful results. While they were married, they fell into the category of men who used "work" or "the children" or "hobbies" as a shield to distance them from their wives. Eventually, the children grew up, work led to retirement, hobbies no longer consumed them, and they could no longer avoid the sterility of their marital relationships. In this group, it didn't seem to matter whether the husband or the wife initiated the divorce—both admitted freely that they were "in the market" for something that was missing in their marriage: "sex, and a lot of it." This group placed personal ads, went to online dating sites, agreed to be "fixed up," and suddenly found themselves joining groups and becoming involved in everything from ballroom-dancing classes to elder-hostel lectures and excursions.

Daniel was one who found it "all very thrilling in the beginning, but it soon paled." The women he met "expected too much" of him. When I pressed him to explain, he would not be more specific than to say searching for a sexual partner was "not worth the game." It meant that he had to "indulge in behavior suitable for guys half my age," and he no longer had the energy "to get out there on the dating scene" more than once a week. Also, he didn't think he had enough money to pursue an active dating life in the

Long Island community where he lived. Like many men his age (late sixties), he regretted the number of nights he spent "with a bottle of beer in front of a lousy TV program" because he was too lethargic or too shy to do anything else. Recognizing that he "had to do something," he had just volunteered to help out at the twice-weekly bingo game at a nearby church in the hope that it "might lead to something."

Daniel was a working-class man lucky enough to have retired with a decent pension but was representative of many like him who nonetheless resented "rich guys who can screw around as much as they want." Daniel spoke for the rest when he said, "Everything comes down to money, and if you don't have it, you can't get anything else, especially sex." There were, however, others in his social class and age group who disagreed entirely. "He doesn't know where to look," they said. "Horny broads are a dime a dozen"— or words to that effect. As one boasted, "You can always find a woman who wants to get laid, and it won't cost you a dime."

Many of these men exuded a deep, seething anger, sometimes focused against the wives who initiated their divorces but even more against women in general. They had been bewildered by social change and were quick to blame "the bra burners" of the feminist movement for "filling her head with a load of bullshit." The man who said this pulled a well-worn news clipping from his wallet in which the evangelist Pat Robertson was quoted in *The Washington Post* as saying: "The feminist agenda is not about equal rights for women. It is about a socialist, anti-family political movement that encourages women to leave their husbands, kill their children, practice witchcraft, destroy capitalism and become lesbians."[13]

He believed this to be true. Okaaay, I said to myself, take a deep breath and smile. I found his anger frightening, but sad to say, I also found it typical of so many others like him, who thought they had "played by the rules" all their lives and somehow, when they were distracted or weren't paying attention, the rules were suddenly changed and they were in a new ball game they didn't understand.

And then there are the men for whom sex is not a major goal, need, or pursuit, but who do crave female companionship. "I'm too old for that stuff anymore," said one man who was sixty-two, a surprisingly young age among those I talked to who no longer wanted sex. He could not understand why his wife, age fifty-nine, was unwilling to go on living in a sexless marriage. Most of the men I interviewed who no longer wanted sex were a decade or two older than this man. Whether a correlative or not, the one thing they had in common was that many of them had been unfaithful to their wives throughout their marriages. They had had numerous sexual partners, both "one-night stands" and "long-term liaisons," but all of a sudden, as one, named Howell, put it, "sex wasn't all that important anymore."

Howell cheerfully admitted to a "life of CEO-itis" and, as our conversation unfolded, to having "tried Viagra when it first came out," but he insisted (repeatedly) that he "didn't really need it." He said he was fortunate enough to "move in a world where some good-looking woman always needs a walker,' " and if he wanted sex, it was his for the taking. He was, however, "tired of all the chasing and the game playing" and was finding "new pleasures in other things," like the condo he and his "long-suffering wife who always looked the other way" had just purchased in a gated community on an Arizona golf course.

During my second round of interviews and conversations, I felt freer to ask men if they ever had any negative physical sensations during or after sexual intercourse similar to those that troubled women, from penile pain to bladder infections. If so, I asked, did this have any bearing on why they no longer wanted to have sex at all or to have a different, less frequent kind? Several admitted that the "tip" of the penis "got sore" and so they "gave it a rest." One confessed to getting "a rash" from "a really respectable lady." Another man whose only sexual partner was his wife until he was divorced was so bitter he could hardly spit it out when he told me the first woman he slept with infected him with the herpes virus; he had no experience, and so he believed her when she told him it could only infect him when she "broke out," and as she was "clean" at the moment, he didn't need to use a condom. Most said they "objected" to having to use condoms because it "took all the fun out of it." Quite a few said condoms decreased their interest in sex because "it's hard to get it up with a rubber." Straight men said there was "always the fear of AIDS" and they were sheepish about being with women who may have "slept around." Gay men said they were "conditioned to be open" about asking new partners their health status; older gay men who had been in long-lasting, monogamous relationships said, "You can get used to anything" when I asked if they used protection.

The men who consented to discuss their physical reactions to sex surprised me by falling into a category that was otherwise relatively prudish. They were noticeably uncomfortable talking about sex and, when I asked them why, were unwilling to go into specific detail except to confess that they had never talked to a woman "this way." After I urged them to take my gender out of the equation and to think of me as "just a reporter," they became slightly more open. That's when I heard the following or its equivalent: "Women are so aggressive these days; they don't make it easy to get it up." They blamed the blatant sex on television and in the movies for "giving [women] ideas." They insisted, despite all other evidence to the contrary, that women more than men visited Internet pornography sites the most and were more likely to rent X-rated videos. I heard this from several men, one of whom told me he did not "grow up in a world like that." Another joined in, blaming women for the male reluctance to have sex because today's woman is "not nice in bed." Why did they think this was so, I asked? What did a woman have to do to be "nice in bed"? Could they be specific? The reply was always the same: "They are too demanding. They expect too much."

"WHO WANTS IT MORE?"

You can imagine my surprise when the man who sat next to me in business class on a red-eye flight from Los Angeles to New York asked me this question. We had just been seated next to each other for fifteen hours on a flight from Sydney, but as we had Qantas's wonderful podlike bed-seats, we flew the whole way without saying a word to each other. When we found ourselves once again assigned to sit side by side in ordinary seats on the last leg of the flight, we greeted each other and exchanged a few pleasantries. My jet lag made me ready for sleep, but Torrance ordered several drinks, and as he drank, his jet lag made him want to talk. He said he thought I looked familiar, and it turned out that he had attended one of my talks at the Sydney Writers' Festival earlier that month. He was deliberately vague about his profession and I didn't question him beyond what he told me: he had a doctorate and did research into "human behavior." He was also a divorced man whose marriage ended by "mutual consent" after thirty-eight years, during which (this came out later in the conversation) he had been "routinely unfaithful." He said he had thought about contacting me after my talk when someone in the audience asked what I was writing next and I described this book and invited people to get in touch and tell me their stories, and so he thought it was fortuitous that he found himself sitting next to me.

I ended up staying awake far longer than I wanted, taking copious notes and asking questions, as Torrance told me about his marriage. Just as I was nodding off, he asked a question that jerked me wide awake: "Who wants it more?" I must have looked puzzled because he asked it again quite emphatically, before repeating the word several times: "Sex. Sex. Who wants it more after divorce—men or women?" I was propelled into wakefulness by the question because, although I was more than half through with my interviews at that time and I had always asked general questions about sex and sexuality, I had to confess that I had never thought about sex in terms of who wanted it most.

How does one codify desire, I wondered, "desire" being the word I used as shorthand for "wanting to have sex." I had only been asking people whether or not they had been dissatisfied with their sexual activity during marriage, and whether or not they wanted to change it after divorce. I had not really asked how frequently they desired sex, although many of them volunteered this information. From then on, I made sure I found a way to ask questions about "desire and the frequency thereof," and what I thought were perfectly ordinary questions took many aback.

"Wow, that's getting pretty personal!" was just one reponse among so many women who said I "amazed" them by asking. Men often told me my questions shocked them because they "never" had a woman "talk [to them] like that before." I only asked questions like these, which I thought were fairly straightforward and harmless:

- Did you seek a new sexual partner before you were divorced, or did you wait until after?

- How did you approach him/her?
- Describe what the first encounter was like, that is, where did it take place? Who undressed whom? What did you do? How long did it last? How did you feel when it was over? What did you do then? How did you leave your partner (or how did your partner depart)?
- Did you see this partner again? Did you have sex only with him/her, or did you have sex concurrently with others? How long did the relationship(s) last? What did you actually do (sexually) during the rest of your encounters? If they ended, what was the reason?
- How often (that is, how many times weekly or monthly) did you have sex with any or all of your postdivorce partners?
- When you say you "had sex," describe exactly what you mean and what you did.
- While you were having sex with partners, did you have sex with yourself, through masturbation, with or without the aid of sex toys, or both?

These were only some of the questions I asked routinely; others occurred spontaneously when something the individual was telling me triggered them. Most of the respondents answered fully, but I still found it difficult to create statistics or patterns of behavior that would codify desire—for example, to put a group of men who all told me one thing in column A and all the women who told me another in column B. There were just too many intangibles, too many individual responses that neatly defied every table or category I tried to construct or create. I will have to leave that for the sociologists who come after me.

As I was trying to codify and categorize, I was reminded of Ted Solotaroff's essay in *Men on Divorce*, in which he wrote that "most marriages do not separate equally."[14] He had been through three "separations" (was this his euphemism for divorce, I wondered), and each time he was better off than the wife he left behind "in the dismembered household with the troubled child or children." While she had to deal with "the isolation of the single woman" and make sense of "a new and difficult life," all he had to do was "pick up the phone to become an available man."

So here, then, was one possible way of looking at desire: through availability and opportunity. If men do fare better financially after divorce, does this give them more opportunity to make themselves available for new and interesting experiences? If so, what of the man who said "horny women are a dime a dozen" and are always available to "get laid"? Is he arguing that the same degree of opportunity is available to women no matter what their personal or financial situation, and if sex is the only thing they want from a relationship, it is theirs for the taking? Like so much else surrounding late divorce, this, too, bears thinking about.

"KEEPING TRACK" AND "NOTCHES ON THE BEDPOST"

Kenny told me he liked "to talk in numbers." Adding things up helped him "to remember" and "to put things in perspective." He was a man in his mid-sixties who lived a fairly comfortable "alternative lifestyle" by taking jobs at various Washington and Oregon college campuses, churches, or cultural institutions, providing whatever form of technological support they needed. He recorded lectures, set up PowerPoint presentations, showed films, and when the janitors were busy and "the unions were not looking," he turned on the lights and turned up the heat or the air-conditioning. When he got tired of one location, he moved on to another.

He was happy to contribute to the discussion of "who wants it more" and, without pause, launched into his numbers. His "living-together-longer-than-a-month relationships to date total eight." He told me he wasn't boasting, nor was he counting "notches on the bedpost," but he had had sex with "at least two hundred and fifty women—so far." He "keeps track" of these numbers not because he wants to "brag," but because it is his way of "honoring and respecting the women I have known." He considered every one of them a "friend, even though there are quite a few who do not look upon me as their friend." Kenny said he is an "incurable romantic who falls in love easily." He expected to fall in love "a few, maybe a lot, more times," and he promised to keep me "up to date" with his numbers.

Adeline was the daughter of middle-level bureaucrats in the State Department who spent much of her adolescence in foreign countries. Her parents were both posted to London when she was sent to boarding school in Switzerland, which is why she earned the nickname "the British Open." Her sex life began when she was eleven and "got groped by a kid my own age." She liked it and consciously sought other experiences, all of which she "probably made happen." She insisted there was no abuse, no coercion, "nothing bad," in her early experiences, and when she went to college on a midwestern campus in the "Swinging Sixties," she continued her "happy free sex life." For a few years, she lived with the man she eventually married in a commune in Northern California and for a few years after that on a houseboat in Sausalito. They moved back to a Northern California town near the Oregon border where Adeline had two children and her husband worked at whatever job sustained their "laid-back life." Throughout the "open" marriage, both had other lovers, and eventually, after "twenty-nine years, give or take a few," they "split." He was always "more settled" than Adeline, and he "found a lady he wanted to be with," which was quite all right with her. She moved several towns to the south and took a job as an activities director in a tri-stage living complex for seniors, where she has continued to have a "lusty life" with the men who live there. She has not kept track of all her partners and said she could not possibly count them all up, but she has "thoroughly enjoyed the act of loving" and hopes to be able to do it "for a good long time."

Kenny and Adeline were far from typical of the older people I talked to, and if the statistics kept by everyone from AARP to various family-research groups are to be believed, they are in the distinct minority. When I was trying to answer Torrance's question, I thought of them at once, just as I thought of Edna and her sexual partners and how content they were with the mere act of occasional touching. Andrew, Bernie, and Alvin were thrilled with the new romance in their lives, while Liam was still willing to pay a woman half a million dollars to stay with him for a year. Joyce, his ex-wife, loved her "new tranquility" and would not trade it for another relationship, no matter "how attractive the man." The Canadian woman merely wanted her companion to ward off the afflictions of old age for as long as possible so they could share the companionship of life together, while Doris's friend Marcia still believed there were nice men out there and she wanted to find one.

"Longing for satisfying sexual companionship is the great malaise of the moment, is it not?" Marnie asked me. She was Marcia's twice divorced friend who had just decided not to marry for a third time and was telling me why: "To be sixty-seven and alone is to know that there is not always an easy social life out there. I would be bothered to think that I would never have sex again, but at the same time, it just doesn't excite me enough to want to get naked in front of yet another man."

A woman who echoed this sentiment wrote a letter to AARP's magazine describing her life after being widowed several years earlier. She had remarried but thought that if given another chance to remarry, she would prefer to remain single. She would advise all unmarried women, no matter what their age, "to teach yourself to build fences, retile floors, and landscape yards. Buy a body pillow to hug and a heating pad to keep yourself warm. That way if you ever do choose to get married, it will be because you want a man in your life, not because you need one."[15]

I thought about all these responses, and so many others I heard or read throughout my year and a half of interviewing, and I decided that Torrance had asked me the wrong question, to which I had still managed to find the right answer. The question really isn't *who* wants to do it the most; the question is *what* do they want to do the most. And the answer, like humanity in its infinite variety, is—just about anything.

CHAPTER ELEVEN

THE QUEST FOR HAPPINESS

Boomers grew up as divorce rates surged, making the exit door more of a right than a taboo.
—CLAUDIA KALB, "Marriage: Act II"

NORA, THE HEROINE of Ibsen's *A Doll's House* who slammed the now famous door and walked out on her marriage, has inspired debate and stirred emotional upheaval ever since the play was first performed in 1879. Everyone has weighed in, from dedicated scholars to occasional theatergoers who may have thought they were out for an evening's harmless fluff but ended up with something else entirely.

Torvald, Nora's husband, was unable to fathom why she could not accept the serenely comfortable place in the world that her marriage to him made possible. He was prosperous and secure, and she was supposed to be his contented little wife in a well-appointed home, cosseted from the unpleasant realities of life outside it. She was beautifully clothed; she had servants to spare her the duties of keeping house, plus family, friends, and children who loved her. Torvald was a better husband than most, for he indulged Nora with more personal freedom to pursue whatever interested her than other women were given in that time and place. Unfortunately for him, his generosity in giving Nora just enough freedom made her realize with what an extremely tight leash he kept her tethered to the marriage.

Torvald was puzzled; he could not understand why Nora didn't appreciate the fortunate circumstances marriage granted her, or why she was (so it seemed to him) so ungrateful. He was confounded by her unfocused yearning for something new and different and, most important, for whatever it was that was happening outside the house. He could not envision the void she struggled to fill, a void that tortured her; he had no idea what it was, why she yearned for it, or how or why it ever came to be.

Throughout the play, Torvald questions Nora from the position of male superiority and power that his place in society bestows upon him because he exemplifies all the qualities it has decreed right and proper. Although they are in Norway, the English and American system of law that began in medieval times and lasted well into the nineteenth century explains his society's attitude best: "Husband and wife are one, and that one is the husband." He holds the power and she is his property; he calls the tune and she is expected to dance to it. These are the basic rules of behavior, but Nora refuses to play by them.

When Torvald asks questions, Nora's answers shift society's ground rules and in so doing, she renders him both frustrated and powerless. He cannot understand what she is trying to tell him because she is trying to create a level, more equal playing field that will require new and different rules for the social contract that is their marriage. They become two people who talk at cross-purposes, an earlier version of the contemporary "Mars and Venus" speech patterns between husbands and wives who "just don't understand" each other. By the end of the play, when each is exhausted by the inability to make the other comprehend what it is he or she wants and needs, it is inevitable that Nora should walk out that door. Audiences are sad that she has to do it, but even if they don't approve, they accept that if she is to survive, she has no other choice.

THE QUEST FOR HAPPINESS

Nothing much has changed since the end of the nineteenth century when Nora walked out on Torvald. The Scandinavians—theatrically at least— were well aware of marital unhappiness and were trying to deal with it long before the baby boom generation turned calling it quits into such a startling statistic. Hedda Gabler was another of Ibsen's deeply frustrated housewife-heroines who raged and seethed with unfocused and ultimately self-destructive anger. Marianne, Ingmar Bergman's heroine in *Scenes from a Marriage*, was suffocating in her forty-year marriage to Johan and saw divorce as her only way to escape from "prison." Much of Bergman's own autobiography is a stunning indictment of the sterility and hatred his parents felt for each other, which film critics think is directly reflected in the marital conflict in so many of his films.

Even today, the Scandinavian version of the fiction phenomenon dubbed the "chick-lit pandemic"[1] is strongly dependent upon the same old existential anxiety and yearning that, if it didn't start with Nora, certainly claims her as one of its premier examples. It is the same throughout the world in every one of these novels, from (to name two of the best-known) the British *Bridget Jones's Diary* to the American *Sex and the City*. They all share the same underlying motif: the exploration of human relationships and how they have changed in the years since the feminist wave of the 1970s brought women greater educational, financial, and, some would say most important of all, sexual freedom.

Nothing points out more strongly the profound difference in the literary evolution of marriage than the names of some of the most tragic heroines: Nora and Hedda certainly, but also Anna Karenina, Emma Bovary, and the noble Isabel Archer, whose depiction in *The Portrait of a Lady* peels away the layers of an ironically unfair marriage. Unfortunately for all of these women, as it was for most others no matter where they lived in the world, there were few other options than to remain in loveless marriages or to die trying to get out of them.

And that's how it remained until the end of World War II, when a lot of returning soldiers looked at the wife they left behind several years before and didn't recognize her. A writer who lives in New Mexico told me his GI father stayed married for twenty-five years to the girl he met on a Texas air base and married a week later, "long enough to get the last kid through college, and then he was out the door." A woman in Los Angeles said she met her first husband at the Stage Door Canteen and after that "he was in the Pacific for the first three years of the marriage so it was all lovey-dovey in letters until he came home and there was sheer hell for both of us for the last eighteen."

Mary Wesley, that wicked old Englishwoman who writes scathingly devastating novels about human relationships, has the postwar parents of one nubile young lady fear for her prospects of staying married when they recognize the "loosening of morals during and since the war among their contemporaries, [and] wished time for their daughter so that she could avoid making mistakes."[2]

Their wish is useless, of course, and the marriage they think will be just the ticket to her happiness turns out to be a quietly boring disaster. All of Mary Wesley's couples stick it out, at least for a goodly number of years and with the comfort of lovers, but their children are exactly like the American baby boomers as they cast a cool, appraising eye on how hard their parents tried to justify staying married. They don't hesitate to declare that their own marriages no longer work, and off they go, to have a lot of sex in unmarried bliss or to go it alone as soon as they can get a divorce.

"CARMELA SENT TONY PACKING WHEN SHE WASN'T HAPPY"

The comment is from Steve Slon, who edits *AARP the Magazine*, and he uses it to illustrate how attitudes toward divorce have changed.[3] When the statistics are broken down by age, no other single group has more readily embraced the concept of ending a marriage gone sour than the boomers, who are "shedding their marriages" in record numbers as they embark on "the quest for happiness."[4] The 2003 government census shows a dramatic rise in the number of unattached persons between the ages of forty-five and fifty-nine: in 2003, more than 28 percent of this age group was single—an increase of 10 percent since 1980, when it was 18.8 percent.

Because divorce is on the rise among boomers, the pundits and prognosticators fear that all these single people will have no one to care for them when they are old and thus they will become a mammoth burden upon the states that have to provide health care and social services. But something unexpected happened as the first generation of boomers approached its sixtieth birthday: these predictions did not hold up. The gloom and doom was dispelled when a surprising new set of statistics emerged to prove them wrong. Contrary to the dire warnings of how burdensome the boomers will be, quite the opposite is true. They are in better physical and financial health than any previous generation. They eat well, don't smoke, drink designer waters rather than hard liquor, slim themselves at the gym, and carefully fatten their portfolios. The scary prognostications had to be revised to show that if a large percentage of boomers from almost every social class cannot take care of themselves, they will have more than enough money to pay someone else to do it for them. And in the meantime, they don't need to marry or stay married to have financial security; they can live alone in the style they enjoy because they can pay for it themselves.

Having enough money makes so many things possible, among them overcoming the fear of the unknown that formerly played so large a part in keeping the pre-boomer generations locked into loveless marriages. When there are two incomes in one family, with two retirement funds assured, it is so much easier and far less painful for one partner to tell the other that the marriage is over, and for the other partner to agree that it is probably a good thing, and high time and not a moment too soon.

THE "CLASSIC" BOOMER DIVORCE

Mark and Melinda were among the very first generation of boomers, and so the twenty-five years of their marriage encompassed most of the major dramas that occurred in the last three decades of the twentieth century I interviewed them together at length and had several separate follow-up conversations with each. In one, Mark said ironically that if I wanted to write "the classic story" of how the baby boomers came of age, married, and "routinely divorced," he and Melinda would provide my "classic examples." When I sifted all the accounts I had heard from other boomers, I had to admit he was right.

Mark was born in 1946, to a soldier who came home from Germany at the end of 1944 taciturn and deeply scarred by his wartime experiences. "Ours was not a cheerful house to grow up in," Mark remembered. He thinks his parents, who were "otherwise conservative Protestants," might have divorced if his father, a heavy smoker, had not died of throat cancer when Mark (the oldest of three) was a teenager. Melinda was born in 1949, the last of five children, to a farmer whose bad eyes, flat feet, and "essential civilian occupation" disqualified him from military service. Hers was "a happy, churchgoing, 4-H home," where everyone worked at whatever task needed to be done: "There was no mans work or woman's work on the farm; there was only work, and all us kids pitched in and did it."

They were both from one of the Mountain States, and they met at the state university where Mark was pre-med and Melinda was in—"What else?" she said with a shrug—"home economics." There was a demonstration supporting the Vietnam War on the main square at lunchtime, and they were two bystanders on the fringe of it who struck up a conversation. Melinda wondered why there were no protest speakers to balance the war supporters, but neither had any strong feelings about it except for Marks worry about his draft number. (It was never called.) He was able to graduate and go directly to medical school, and he wanted to become engaged to Melinda, who was reluctant "to get tied down." She was only a sophomore but an increasingly "politically active" one who had come out against the war, so she suggested they stay "pinned" until her senior year. She was also enrolled in an English class taught by "an uppity woman who did not get tenure" when she read two books "back to back, that blew [her] mind": Betty Friedan's *The Feminine Mystique* and Simone de Beauvoir's *The Second Sex*.

When she finished the books, the first thing Melinda did was to change her major to political science; the second was "to join every hippie, feminist, antiwar, anarchist, communist—whatever—commune and/or demonstration." Mark said he had no time to deal with her "foolishness" and took back his pin because she was "embarrassing" him. They went their separate ways during her last two undergraduate years—she indulging in "free love, flower power, and making love and not war," he "keeping my nose to the grindstone to get through med school." They reconnected when Mark took a urology residency at a hospital in the California city where Melinda was enrolled in law school and were married shortly before she graduated, mainly because she was pregnant with their first child. If she had not been pregnant, Melinda would have been content to live with Mark rather than marry him, but this was the seventies, and there was "still too much stigma for unmarried mothers." She loved her parents and did not want them to bear her "shame" in the community where they lived, and so she and Mark were married on a hillside overlooking the sea at sunrise in an "alternative ceremony" for which she wrote the vows and he "reluctantly mumbled them out."

Roe v. *Wade* was in the offing, but not for Melinda, who later became an outspoken pro-choice advocate: "I was young and healthy and I expected to deliver a baby just like all the lambs and calves I helped birth when I was a farm kid. And the next day, I expected to get up and go back to work. A farm girl is used to doing everything, and I expected to keep on doing it all my life." She was fortunate that the birth happened as she envisioned, and "even more fortunate to get it all over with at once," for she had twins, Leanne and Lawrence.

Mark joined a practice in urology and Melinda found a job with a mid-sized law firm where she was assigned to corporate litigation. She hated the work and after a year of "total burnout," when she thought she would have to stop practicing law until her children were older, she received a "lifesaving call from the blue." A law school in a town that was just barely within commuting distance of their home offered her a temporary teaching position to replace a professor who was going to Washington to work in the Carter administration. She grabbed it eagerly, thinking it would be so much easier than what she was doing. "Hah!" she said, snorting. "I loved it, but it was the start of all my troubles."

The commute took two hours in each direction, and she had to drive because there was no public transportation. That meant she had to spend much of her time at home not with her toddlers as she had envisioned but in her study preparing her lectures. Because she and Mark had two salaries, they could afford two cars and a big enough house for an au pair as well as a cleaning woman twice a week. They were also paying for expensive year-round yard maintenance and anything else that needed to be done to the house because neither of them had the time to do it. Because they were committed to paying legal wages and benefits to their help, they were barely able to put the minimum from their salaries into Mark's firm's retirement plan and her university's TIAA-CREF account. There was no money for any extras, and even if there had been, they were too tired to think about enjoying them.

Meanwhile, Melinda was "raising [her] consciousness" on her campus. The temporary job had turned into a permanent appointment, and she felt free to speak out whenever she thought it necessary. She helped to institute a program in women's studies for undergraduates and to incorporate specific programs in the law, medical, and business schools that were tailored to women's needs. She helped write sexual-harassment statutes that were adopted in the undergraduate school, worked for Title IX to ensure equal funding for women's athletics, and was instrumental in founding a rape-crisis hotline. She demonstrated for the Equal Rights Amendment and, when that failed to pass, turned her attention to any organization that supported women's reproductive rights. She was in the state capital so often that she joked about how her local representatives "ran the other way when they saw [her] coming." All this took time, and it meant that she frequently stayed overnight on the campus several times a week, at first "crashing" with various friends and eventually, fearing she was wearing out her welcome, in a studio apartment of her own. She was away from home routinely every Tuesday through Thursday during term time.

To make up for her absence, she spent every weekend shopping for her family's food for the week and then cooking it. She was a farm girl who knew how to cook, and she made meat loaves, stews, casseroles, and spaghetti sauces by the gallon, and filled the freezer with pies that needed only a quick baking or cakes and cookies that only needed defrosting. She did most of this at night because she spent the days with her children, as these were the years for music lessons and ballet, baseball, and soccer. Having grown up in a family where there was not men's or women's work but "only work," she expected Mark to do his part, and for the most part, he did. Or so he claimed. If she did all the cooking, he would do the defrosting or microwaving, and he did try to be a good father and eagerly attended his children's activities whenever his schedule permitted.

However, now that the children were in school they no longer needed the au pair, so they made do with an after-school sitter and a weekly cleaning woman on Friday. Thus, if Mark ate ice cream in the living room on Tuesday, the congealed remains and the dish itself would still be there when Melinda came home on Thursday. If he dropped his socks on the bedroom floor, he expected that she would pick them up and put them in the clothes hamper because she or one of their help had always done so. And he really did try to put out the garbage for the Wednesday-morning pickup, but mostly he forgot. It was the same thing with the dry cleaner or the drugstore: he really meant to run those errands, but he was too tired, too frazzled, and he often forgot.

This was the first crisis in their marriage, when they had been together a little over twelve years. Melinda was so exhausted that she spent the entire spring vacation in bed and feared she wouldn't be able to get out of it to finish the semester. Mark said something had to be done and suggested she "go to part-time." She was furious. If anyone went to part-time, why couldn't he? They lived in his town, after all, and she was the one who bore the extraordinary strain of commuting on top of everything she did at home. The fights magnified as insults were hurled, accusations leveled, and threats made.

When Melinda got herself out of bed and returned to her teaching, she did so without preparing a single meal, doing the laundry, or organizing the weekly schedule of the children's activities. Mark would just have to manage, she told him; she was simply too tired to cope. All was well for the first several weeks because there was still enough food in the freezer and he left the laundry for her to do on weekends. Also, he threw himself on the mercy of neighbors, who carpooled the children but soon let him know they expected him to take his turn. After that, chaos set in briefly until such calm descended on the household that Melinda suspected that something was up, that Mark was having an affair.

He was in a fairly large practice comprising five physicians and a large supporting staff. Joan, one of the records administrators who worked part-time, "volunteered" (said Melinda derisively) to help Mark with his scheduling problems. She was separated but not yet divorced, with two children the same age as the twins. She told Mark it was no trouble for her to pick up his dinner fixings when she did her own marketing. Sometimes she prepared one dinner for the two families in Mark and Melinda's house. Joan drew the line at laundry but was a willing driver to all the after-school activities, which is how Melinda soon sniffed out that she was "an even more willing bed partner" for Mark.

It was a terrible shock for Melinda because Mark had always been the "traditional one" in their marriage and she thought of herself as the "loose cannon most likely to go off." Because of their history, when he was a studious "nerd grind" and she was "into free love," she always thought that if one of them were to be unfaithful, it would most likely be she. In her usual blunt manner, she asked him straight out if he was sleeping with Joan, and he broke down in tears and confessed to it. Melinda said she "cursed, screamed, threw things. How could he do this to me? I was the one who had lots of opportunities to cheat and I never did. I figured our marriage was the one secure thing we both had. How could he mess it up this way?" Mark swore he would never sleep with Joan again, and she departed from their lives as swiftly as she had come in. Fortunately, it was summer and Melinda was at home full-time. She was supposed to finish the book that was intended to secure her promotion to a full professorship and put her "on the legal map," but instead she spent the summer wandering around the house, eating, and gaining weight. She asked Mark to go with her to a marriage counselor, but he swore his infidelity had been a "onetime aberration" that would never happen again, and besides, because of his position in the community he could not risk having anyone find out that he was seeing a therapist.

Melinda had two good friends who were already divorced and who claimed that the ubiquitous consciousness-raising groups of the seventies and eighties had given them the necessary "permission" to go out and "find themselves." They urged her to join a group, or several groups ("whatever works for ya, baby," as she recalls), and she did. "I joined everything," she remembered. "I tried EST, Esalen, speed, Valium. I screamed and rebirthed, and learned to love my vagina, and went on retreats and meditated and"—here she stopped and her voice drifted off. What she said once she could trust herself to speak again without breaking down was: "I did everything but have an affair with a man." Her pregnant pause was so fraught with unsaid meaning that I asked: Did that mean she had had an affair with a woman? "Several," she replied. "I wanted to get even but I didn't want to hurt my marriage and I thought women didn't count. All it taught me was that I didn't enjoy being with women."

September came, and with it stability in the household. The children went to a private school from 8 A.M. to 4 P.M., after which they did compulsory athletics. They got home at the same time as Mark, shortly after six, so they still ate family dinner together even on the nights Melinda was away. Instead of cooking on weekends, she bought simple foods that Mark could steam or grill as soon as he came home, while the children fixed the salad and set the table. The washer and dryer were outside the children's bathroom, and she taught the twins how to use them. "Everything came out pink or gray at first, but they learned to separate clothes," Melinda said proudly. They also took turns feeding the dog and two cats and putting out the garbage for weekly pickup. Melinda was determined to instill in her children the self-reliance and participation in family work and life that she had learned while growing up.

When she was at home, she was "really at home" because "the tenure wars were over" and her place was secure. These were the last years when they could do things together as a family, as the twins were entering "the terrible teens." Melinda made sure there was something scheduled every weekend, even if it was only popcorn and a movie in front of the ancient nineteen-inch TV screen. She and Mark should have been "happy," but both remember that instead they were mostly "relieved" to have weathered a crisis. They were solicitous and polite to each other, but the sex had become "occasional and routine."

By the time they were heading toward their eighteenth year of marriage, the second period of crisis occurred, but at first neither recognized it was happening. The children were in their junior year at a "pressure cooker" school and left for their rooms as soon as dinner was over to fill out college applications and attack mountains of homework. Mark developed two consuming interests: reading about the Civil War, and stamp collecting, so he went off to his study while Melinda, who always had work to do, went to hers. Months went by, and the only interaction they had with each other was when some activity of the twins required it.

They had never been "in the dinner-party set," and they never entertained.

Mark often attended medical conferences alone, and Melinda always went to legal meetings without him, so they didn't even share their professional interests. Vacations consisted of two weeks on a beach or in the mountains in a rented house. All their parents were dead and they had little contact with their siblings, so, as Melinda put it, there was "no extended-family interaction; everything with us was nuclear."

Mark thinks it was around this time that he became "depressed due to sheer boredom." Melinda said it was "only a midlife crisis" and "stubbornly, he would not let anyone help him get through it." He remembered an "overwhelming sadness" that he was powerless to lift. She claimed they had been "too busy to have sex for years," but as both declared themselves throughout the marriage as "not particularly erotic," neither was especially unhappy about it. In an attempt to jolt Mark out of his depression, she bought "sexy nightgowns and perfume," but he was "not moved" by her gestures. He said—to himself, not to her—that he doubted that he still loved her, or that he had ever really loved her at all. He confessed to me that he was sexually inexperienced when they married, and she was the only woman he "really knew" (he would not elaborate). When she became pregnant, there had not been "a hell of a lot of options out there." Even though he was a doctor, both rejected abortion for themselves even though they supported it for others.

Melinda could not provoke a response of any kind from Mark during this depression, even after several "magical weekends that turned out not to be so magical at all." She became belligerent. "I needled him," she recalled. "I said all kinds of terrible things." Still, Mark remained withdrawn, and at this point Melinda left him.

The children were away from home, spending their winter break between semesters in a work-study program sponsored by a consortium of private schools, so Melinda moved permanently to her campus apartment. She told Mark she would come home when the children returned, but only long enough to see if they could get back together. Otherwise she thought they should consider a permanent separation if not an actual divorce. She hoped her action would shock him into "a sense of what was at stake here," and she hoped he would want to resume the marriage. Mark did realize that the marriage was in crisis, and he was determined to force himself "to feel something." He still rejected therapy of any sort, believing that as a physician, he could pull himself "out of the blue funk."

Midway through their ten-week separation, even though he still could not relate to Melinda emotionally, he invited himself down to her apartment for a weekend. He bore flowers and wine, and when she saw them, she embraced him, dumped them inside the doorway, and pointed him toward the bedroom. The weekend passed in a "haze of sex" that surprised them both. Both said they were astonished that they could "feel so much," especially because it had been years since they "felt anything at all." Melinda became (in her words), "gushy and garrulous, fluttering around, chattering, making plans for the future." Mark was his usual quiet self, but he did remember (in his words) that he "worked hard to smile a lot." Melinda resumed her commuting life, and the rest of the weekends while the twins were away were as "raunchy and sexy" as the first one was. She thought they had weathered the crisis.

But the children returned, life resumed its daily patterns, and the "heat and lust" returned to "normal, which is to say, nothing much." Mark insists that he tried to maintain the level of desire but could not do it to the extent that Melinda seemed to require. Melinda said she could not help "watching him from the corner of [her] eye" every time they were together. She compared him to "a bright red balloon, slowly deflating right in front of me." She told him he needed therapy, and he responded that it was she who needed it, that she was the one who had to "change." He said it was finally clear to him that she was a "narcissist" who wanted everything to be "about her, around her, for her benefit, for her needs." There was a standoff, as both tried to retreat from an abyss neither wanted to fall into, so they attempted to be cordial and friendly even as they found excuses not to be together.

By this time, the twins were off on their high-achieving ways, recipients of scholarships to prestigious schools on separate coasts. And this time it was Melinda who turned to other men for solace. "It is easy in a university community," she said quietly. "There is always some egotistical man out there whose wife doesn't understand' him or whose students adore him. A few of them prefer to seduce a mature woman, and I was willing to be seduced." She did not "broadcast" her affairs to Mark, and he did not question her, but she "knew that he knew." Still, he said nothing, and they continued to live in the same house but go their separate ways.

Neither can recall which of them first brought up the idea of divorce this time, but Melinda believes it was she. She put it in very practical terms: they did nothing together, had no friends in common, shared no interests, and had been sleeping in separate bedrooms since the twins left home, and so there was really nothing to keep them together unless they wanted to be with each other. As usual, it was Mark who vowed "to change, to make things different," and as usual, he did try. For a while he attempted to make conversation at dinner. Several times he suggested they rent a movie and watch it together. Once he even suggested they buy two copies of the same book and read it at the same time so they could discuss it when they went out for a celebratory anniversary dinner at an expensive restaurant. "This way, we'll really have something to talk about," he told Melinda, who was horrified that they "had to resort to artificial communication so as not to be like all those silent couples you see sitting in restaurants."

"We probably could have gone on forever as we were," Melinda remembered. "We may not have been happy, but we were not unhappy either. There were a lot of good things about the life we lived, and except for the fact that we didn't have much in common, there was nothing truly bad about our marriage."

But then she asked herself, "Why stay in a situation that is neither fish nor fowl? We were married but we were living alone together." She realized that she was miserable being alone in her own house and quite content when she was alone in her campus apartment. If that was the case, why stay married? Still, she was reluctant to end her marriage.

And yet she could not help but think how much more time and energy she would have for her own interests if she wasn't always jumping into a car to go from one place to another. She could concentrate on how much she liked her teaching and everything that went with it, from the lectures she was invited to give to the articles she was asked to write. She was "middle-aged and very tired," and exhausted by her fractured life "where it was raining in one place but both the umbrellas were in the other, where there were two gallons of milk spoiling in one fridge and nothing to eat in the other." At this point, all she wanted was "stability."

For Mark, there was an awakening of a different sort. His practice had evolved into one of caring for terminally ill patients, and he had just attended a man who died tragically young, of cancer. The man's widow was a social worker in the hospital where Mark practiced, and he had known her professionally before her husband's illness. From time to time, they encountered each other in the coffee shop, and an initial cup of coffee had blossomed into a professional friendship. Now that she was widowed, it was developing into a romance. What attracted Mark initially was Rita's touching devotion to her husband. He marveled when she described how they had been so deeply in love from the first day of their marriage to the last and found it "painful" to realize that he had never shared such feelings with Melinda. He wanted to feel them before it was too late.

Melinda said she was "more amazed than anything else" when Mark told her of his feelings for Rita, for she had always thought of him as an "emotional zombie." Describing herself as a "realist," Melinda said she had shrugged and thought about "moving on to the next step. Cut your losses and run." She had her job, her income was assured for as long as she wanted to work, and her retirement was secure and would be comfortable. She could have "a man or two" whenever she wanted "company or sex," which was "not that often." She had developed a network of professional women friends who shared her political interests, and she was even thinking about running for the state assembly. She told me, "I wished us both well, and we seem to be doing okay."

"YOUR BASIC BABY BOOMER WHINE"

Mark and Melinda were a lot more fortunate than many divorcing baby boomers. Both had professions they enjoyed and other interests that gave them pleasure; most of all, they had the financial security that gave them the freedom to change their lives. They also had two highly independent children who had happy memories of growing up in a stable household, where they ate dinner with one or both parents every night and where they were encouraged to be independent in all things, from doing their own laundry to going on foreign exchanges through their schools. Their parents presented the divorce to Leanne and Lawrence as the necessary next step in their lives, and although the twins were sad to think they would no longer be together as a united family, they accepted it because more than anything, they wanted both parents to be "happy."

I spoke to them together on a single occasion, when they were approaching their mid-twenties. Leanne had a "steady beau" but was not planning to marry "anytime soon." She liked her job at a university research laboratory and thought she might eventually go to graduate school in chemistry, so she wanted "to keep [her] options open." Lawrence described himself as "your standard Gen X or Y or whatever I'm supposed to be—the guy who 'can't commit.' " He had been in two long relationships with "good women" but insisted on living in his own apartment throughout them both. When we spoke, he was trying to decide whether to stay in his job in the financial sector or to enroll in a program in social work that would lead to a career as a therapist. He, too, wanted to keep his "options open."

When it came to marriage, neither bore any "scars or wounds" because of their parents' divorce, but neither expected to be married "forever." It would be "nice" if it happened that way, but they did not expect it. Lawrence explained: "In the old days, people died when they were in their fifties, so I guess they stuck it out for all the obvious reasons: religious and social disapproval, no money to pay for two households, all that kind of stuff. Nowadays people live into their nineties and they are active and healthy for most of those years. Who says they have to stay in love with the same person for fifty to sixty years? Who can do that? Nobody does that anymore."

Leanne agreed with him. Whereas some of the people in their parents' generation, and almost all of those in the generations that preceded the boomers, saw late-life divorce as a trauma, tragedy, or failure, she insisted that their generation sees it as an opportunity for reinvention and renewal.

While some scholars and writers believe this hopeful attitude about leading a fulfilling life after divorce belongs only to older women in late-life divorces,[5] I found that younger men held it as well. Lawrence was one among the dozen or so I talked to who fully accepted the possibility that they would have more than one marriage, and that each one would be what they needed at that particular period of their lives. He and his male contemporaries hold the same view as their sisters: when a marriage no longer satisfies, they are ready to end it and move on to another, whether a relationship of equal partners or a legal marriage.

WHEN LIFE SHIPWRECKS MARRIAGE

Lawrence, Leanne, and their contemporaries believe this sanguine attitude toward human relationships will stand them in good stead as they face the uncertain future of the new millennium, even while so many others in their parents' generation hold a decidedly negative and pessimistic view. Many are like Debra and Colin, who feel "cheated" by the marriage they ended after twenty-one years.

Both projected an aura of bitterness, which Colin expressed through the word "gypped." Debra agreed that it was a good description of how "life shipwrecked the marriage." She explained further: "There were so many things we wanted to get, to do, to be, and none of them happened. When we were growing up, we were told that everything we did was wonderful. We were made to believe we were exceptional. Nobody ever told us we were ordinary because all we got was praise at home. At school there were no grades, just 'excellents' and 'satisfactories.' Even in Little League everybody got to bat and in ballet everyone got to dance. We got everything we wanted, from getting into college to getting the right boyfriend to making the right marriage. And then we found out we were just like everybody else; we were only average and only going to go so far in life and get so much out of it, and then when the reality sets in, guess what, it stinks! So we get out. We break up. We find something else. We think we're starting over but we're just turning over the same old crap and nothing changes."

A letter writer to *The New York Times Magazine* called this way of thinking "your basic baby-boomer whine that the boomer girls didn't get everything they wanted."[6] It's an apt description, but it has to be applied to men as well, for they feel equally disappointed by the way their lives have evolved. One day they wake up to find themselves middle-aged and unlikely to get out of the cubicle that confines them in a thankless job, and even more, they resent knowing that they must consider themselves lucky to have this cubicle to go to every day, for the specter of unemployment is worse.

Colin is typical of many men who thought that they were on the "fast track to the top" until economic uncertainties derailed them. For the last five years of his marriage to Debra, he was an art director at a midsized advertising and public relations firm in Chicago. He rose slowly but steadily through the ranks after graduating from the Art Institute, and he also taught design courses at night at the local community college. Occasionally he participated in group shows at local galleries, where his collages of "found objects" were popular and sold fairly well because he priced them at around $100 and "people can afford real art at that price." Colin knew he was "never going to be Picasso," but he did expect to be at the top of the game in advertising, and indeed, he did win several regional prizes for his designs.

Debra wanted to be a lawyer but she came from a working-class family in Detroit and there was no money for college, let alone law school. After she graduated from a commercial high school, she worked as a secretary-typist in a suburban law office that encouraged the staff to enroll in educational programs. Debra took paralegal training and was very good at it, but she still harbored dreams of going to law school. She and Colin had one child, Susan, and they spent the rest of their married life using every form of contraception to guarantee there would be no others. Susan was nineteen when they divorced and was just ending her first year at a four-year state college.

All through the marriage, "the dreams got put on hold" for both of them. Susan had a difficult childhood with several illnesses doctors had trouble diagnosing. Debra and Colin took turns sitting for interminable hours in various consulting rooms as specialists debated about how to treat her. She had dietary restrictions and needed special therapy for a chronic bone condition. Both parents had good medical insurance through their work, but there were still many bills that weren't covered. Susan needed orthodonture, which was expensive and which their health plans didn't pay for, and when she was twelve, she was operated on for scoliosis. Afterward, she needed physical therapy, which was not covered either.

They scrimped and saved and denied themselves any outside pleasures in order to buy a house in a good school district, but all they could afford was a fixer-upper, which had many more things that needed attention than they had counted on. They had one "good car," which Debra used to get to her job in a suburb "two freeways away," and one "junker," which took Colin to the train station for his commute into downtown. One of the cars was always "on the fritz." Also, they both had old and ailing parents, whose expenses they and their two other siblings had to share, and who required a fair bit of time.

Years passed, "happy enough," both agreed, but at the same time this statement came up repeatedly in their conversations with me: "All our dreams got put on hold." There were no infidelities by either one, for as Colin said, "When would we have the time and where would we get the money?" He joined the men at work for a Friday-night beer, and he and his brothers liked to watch basketball when it was in season, but otherwise, he spent his free time at home doing his artwork. Debra had her "girlfriends from Susan's school and the office," and they went to the mall on Saturday afternoons or held lunches or potluck suppers to mark occasions such as birthdays or children's births. Debra and Colin's lives were centered on work, family, Susan's health problems, and the little house they thought would be their "starter" but that they had come to accept might be their "ender" as well, for real estate values where they lived were not appreciating.

The fissures in the marriage began to appear in early 2003, three years before they actually called it quits. Colin lost his job when his firm merged with another and half the staff was no longer needed. He expected layoffs and firings, but not for him, since he was in a fairly senior position as the art director of several of the firm's most important accounts. He was shocked to learn that the new owners had their own ideas about who should manage them, and even more demeaning to him, they had not even considered keeping him on in any other capacity. Still, he expected to land a new job within the month, for he was well thought of in the little world of local advertising and he had many good friends as well as professional contacts. However, his dismissal coincided with a general downturn in the field, and a lot of the people he counted on to help him had become his competition for any job that was out there.

Colin was unemployed for "a full-blown crack-up year." He found other ways to bring in income, but nothing to compare to the salary and benefits he no longer received. He taught at several community colleges, racing between them and fighting traffic to be able to meet all the classes on time; he placed his collages everywhere he could, from coffee-shop galleries to craft shops, but they only sold sporadically; he offered to fix ailing computers for neighbors and friends but gave it up because he was embarrassed to charge them what he really should have been paid.

He found another job fourteen months after he lost the first, but it paid a little more than half what his old one did, and the benefits were scant. He described it as "routine scut work" and resented that he had to "feel grateful to have it." Debra said that everything about Colin changed when he got the new job. He became bitter and frustrated, and she was equally frustrated because nothing she did could "jolly him out of his permanent black mood." She had just been assigned to a case that was one of the biggest her firm had ever tried, and she was thrilled to be a part of "the first team" of lawyers and support staff. All her energies were going toward her work; she could not wait to get to the office in the morning, and she came home late at night, only to sleep.

They had seldom eaten the evening meal together even when both were working and Susan was living at home. Colin often grabbed something on his way to teach an evening class, and Debra and Susan were in the habit of ordering fast food or making do with a bowl of cereal or an apple and some cheese. So Debra could not understand why Colin was suddenly so upset by her work schedule until she put his situation into a truly insightful perspective: "He used to be the one to bring in the major bucks, and now I was the one on whose income and benefits we depended. He was unhappy with himself and his work and his life, and the only thing he could change about it was to try to change me. But the sad part was, I didn't want to change because I really liked what was happening in my life."

Debra expressed these feelings to Colin, who rejected them outright. He was furious with her for "implying" that he could no longer "cut it as the breadwinner" and told her she was turning into a "castrating bitch."

"I suppose I should have tried to convince him that this was not true, and I suppose I should have tried to help him find some way to get his self-respect back," Debra said, before adding that "hindsight is always twenty-twenty."

Instead, she turned inward, toward her rewarding work, which she felt had revitalized her. She felt herself "growing" as she had never done before and was so excited by her participation in the court case that she was more determined than ever to enroll in law school: "I am going to die a lawyer, even if I have to get there by taking one course a year for the next fifty years."

Colin observed the changes in Debra, and they "started [him] thinking." She was doing exactly what she wanted to do and was happy and excited about her life. Why couldn't he do the same? He said: "I thought about all the things I wanted to do but, as a working-class kid, didn't think were possible for me. I had a lot of dreams and I put them all on hold, and now I wondered if I could get them back."

One morning he woke up and went into the bathroom where Debra was putting on her makeup. He could hardly believe the words that came from his mouth: "I don't want to be a middle-class husband and father anymore. I want a divorce."

Debra said she put down her eyeliner for fear she would smear her entire face, stood looking at his reflection in the mirror because she was afraid to turn around and face him, and said, "Okay, if that's what you want to do."

"Good," he said. "Maybe you can come home early one night this week and we can start working on it."

Which is exactly what they did. They agreed to put the house on the market, and to their surprise, it sold quickly and for a modest profit. They split the proceeds and each kept the individual retirement funds amassed during their years of employment. Dividing the household goods was easy because Colin didn't want anything, so Debra sold what would not fit into her two-bedroom apartment and they split the money. Debra wanted a large apartment so she could re-create Susan's bedroom and make her feel that she "still had a home" when she was not at the university. Susan had never been "close" to Colin but depended on her mother and was now hinting that she wanted to transfer to the local community college and live with Debra. Debra told her quite firmly that she was "very proud" of how Susan was conducting her life at the university, where she was making friends and doing well, and that she must stay there and prepare for her own independence. "I am beginning my new life, and I want her to establish hers on a solid grounding," Debra explained.

Colin sold the "junker" and bought a decent car. When the semester ended, he packed his painting supplies and his few personal belongings and drove to the Southwest because he had long been fascinated by the landscape and color and had never been able to see it for himself. He ended up in Arizona, where he got a job in a frame shop and fits comfortably into the local artistic community. Besides collages, he now does watercolors and is proud that people who come into the frame shop ask to buy them. He lives modestly and finds his greatest pleasure scavenging the desert on weekends for natural objects he can use in his collages. He has "woman company" when he goes to gallery openings or other community events but is happy being on his own and thinks he will probably stay that way

True to her burning desire, Debra is enrolled at a local law school where she takes two night courses each semester. Her employers tell her they look forward to welcoming her to their ranks, and they are encouraging her to find a way to take a full semester off to go to school full-time. She sees her life as "the start of a second chance" and thinks she is lucky to live at a time when "such possibilities are out there for women like me."

I told this to Colin, who, with an expression of surprise on his face, said he had to "stop and think about what she said." After a short pause, he said Debra was right. "I don't think my parents were particularly happy, but they had no options. My father held a factory job and my mother was a housewife. I'm sure they stuck it out because there was nothing else they could do."

Colin broke into a smile and said, "I guess this [his divorce] makes me a feminist," and I asked him to explain: "Feminism made women do a lot of crazy things, but it also made it possible for them to go to work and support themselves. What a relief it is for men to know that they don't have to stay with a woman because she can't take care of herself. I never could have left Debra if she didn't have the means to provide for herself. This makes my generation of men luckier than the ones that came before me.

In his own way, Colin was expressing what so many other baby boomers have discovered, that divorce is one of many options for making a life gone sour sweet again. They see it as an opportunity, even as outsiders looking in on so many terminated marriages (I deliberately do not use the adjective "failed" here—I prefer to give the sense of an ending, followed by a new beginning) ascribe divorce to the boomers' overweening need for "instant gratification." So then—is it that?

Mark and Melinda and Debra and Colin were perhaps luckier than most boomers because they were able to end their marriages with civility and consideration. Certainly, far too many end in bitterness and recrimination, with one party determined to chase an elusive happiness while the other struggles to maintain the status quo, whether it's a good one or not. But the word they all use, in one form or another, is "happiness." They speak of the "quest" for it, the "pursuit" of it, the "desire" for it, and usually, a statement like this one follows it: "I am entitled to have it."

Deborah Barrow, a New York City writer, was musing on a needlepoint kit she lusted for that cost $1,100, when she asked herself if she was truly entitled to it and out of her mind to want it.[7] It led her to ponder a series of questions that all came down to one: "Just who am I, anyway?" At the end of the self-examination she asked why she must be "forever . . . analyzing and questioning [her] life's purpose." She called it the "WILD syndrome," her acronym for Women in Mid-Life Disorder, and said she coined it for all those women who were "raised on the ridiculous pap that we can have (and do) it all." She hoped that younger women would learn from her generation, to "chill, baby, lest you get WILD." WILD women want it all, and Barrows writes amusingly of their frenetic quest to find it, have it, get it, do it—whatever will assuage the desire and end the quest.

Jane Glenn Haas, who founded an organization called WomanSage to support women in midlife, remembered her first divorce, now twenty-seven years in her past, as she contrasted her options to end an unhappy marriage with the options available to women of her mother's generation.[8] Her family asked Jane why she was divorcing her first husband, and she told them, "I'm not happy." Her mother demanded to know, "Who told you you were entitled to be happy?"

The baby boom generation, having grown up with a profound sense of entitlement all their lives, would no doubt reply, "We told ourselves. We are entitled. And we are going to be happy."

The profound effect they will have on marriage and divorce remains to be seen.

CHAPTER TWELVE

STARTING OVER

Divorce is like a death. In reality, it is the death of hope.
—Protestant minister-marriage counselor

Better by far to be alone than to face daily the intolerable loneliness that one experienced in the presence of the absence.
—VIVIAN GORNICK, *The Solitude of Self*

THE TART-TONGUED DIVA Bette Davis thought there was "nothing lonelier than a turned-down toilet seat"[1] and called herself a "four-time loser" who could not manage "to make divorce work either." Davis claimed to be miserable when her fourth and last divorce left her with "a life sentence, a life of loneliness without possibility of parole." Hers is an emotion shared by a vast number of divorced men and women who, no matter how relieved they are to be out of untenable situations, still find themselves passing through a predictable pattern of grieving.

Ours is a society that likes to qualify and quantify, and we name and number everything from Erik Erikson's division of life into eight stages of psychosocial development to Elisabeth Kübler-Ross's insights into how we approach death while we are in the process of dying. It does not seem all that unusual, then, that going through a divorce almost always evokes a particular set of emotions, and that most people experience most or all of them as they wend their way through the highs and lows of it.

At some point in each of my conversations with the people whose stories fill this book, almost all of them talked about the range of emotions they felt as they went through the process of severing the legal ties that bound them to one another. I heard these stories from those who were pondering divorce and from those who had already gone through it. I heard it as well from the professionals whose guidance they sought, from therapists to ministers to lawyers.

One phrase surfaced repeatedly when people described the initial feeling they had when they first sought a divorce: the overwhelming *feeling of failure*. They described how the feeling of failure engulfed them at this moment when they contrasted their early history with their partner, the rosy glow of optimism that accompanied courtship and marriage, with the sadness of the present.

So many of my interviewees related feelings that go along with those of failure, but the way they described those feelings tended to differ because, quite simply, people are different. For example, people who describe themselves as "churchgoing Christians," no matter what their denomination or level of devotion, often told me they felt "shame" along with failure. In many instances, they said they stayed married far longer than they should have because in their communities, being divorced meant they would be disgraced for breaking their marriage bonds. They feared being "ostracized" by their peers and shut out of activities they had formerly engaged in as part of a couple, and when this did indeed happen to them, they were ashamed of how humiliated they felt and how they could not get over feeling they "deserved" to feel both humiliation and shame.

It didn't seem to matter how relieved people were to be free of a marriage they could no longer endure—they still kept second-guessing themselves, and at this point all the emotions that coalesced around the feeling of failure were overtaken by two related emotions: the sense of *loss* and the feeling of *guilt*.

ALL THE WHAT-IFS

A woman in a northern Rust Belt state described the sense of loss by using the words "what if?" She held herself "responsible" for the divorce, even though her husband was the one who spearheaded it through the courts so he could marry a younger (pregnant) girlfriend. She told me she felt so "guilty" for not "trying harder" that for well over a year she thought she would have to engrave WHAT IF on her tombstone. Every day, from the moment she woke up in the morning to her last waking moment, her mind would roam unfocused over the twenty-five years of her marriage and she would ask herself "what if" she had "done this or done that, different or better," and whether it would have kept her marriage intact.

A man in Florida used the same expression to describe the end of his twenty-eight year marriage: What if he had not been so prone to sudden outbursts of unfocused anger? What if he had apologized for them once in a while? What if he had told his wife "just once" how much he appreciated her patience? Would she still be with him? He, too, felt "guilty" for "lettings things get to the point where they could not be reversed."

This man was one of the more than fifty people—men and women alike—who told me they experienced actual *physical pain* at this stage of the divorce process. Many described a depression so deep they could not rouse themselves from bed, and most described symptoms that struck me as similar to those of a genuine heart attack, and certainly akin to panic or anxiety attacks: shortness of breath, lightheadedness, fear of fainting, dizziness, and tightness in the diaphragm. Others talked of simply sitting in a chair, hugging themselves, rocking, crying. It was difficult to force themselves to eat something, and many otherwise fastidious people talked about how they couldn't even take care of their routine personal hygiene. One woman said she had to force herself to bathe and, when she finally got around to it, had to lower herself gently into a bathtub because the "sting" of the water coming from the showerhead hurt her skin.

They all described related feelings that can be summed up under the heading of *worthlessness*. One common among them was "No one cares if I live or die." Men complained that ex-wives turned the children against them; ex-wives were ashamed that they were dumped for women they perceieved as being younger versions of themselves; both men and women used the expressions "I don't matter to anyone anymore," or "Nothing seems to matter to me."

Around this stage of the divorce process, *grief* intrudes. Even those who say their primary emotion is *relief* that they are escaping the trauma of a disastrous marriage admit to feeling grief. When I asked them to explain why they grieve and for what, I got these answers:

- "I will never forgive myself for the way I treated her. I feel so bad I would do anything to change it."
- "Everybody said we were the 'perfect couple,' and I tried hard to live up to that. It was never true, but I still cry all the time just thinking about how hard I tried to make it work and why I wasn't strong enough to do it."
- "We were so good together. We started from nothing and built everything ourselves, and then he decided he didn't want it (and most of all, he didn't want me) anymore. I mourn the magical life I lost. It's like death, like dying every day."
- "He walked out on twenty-five years with me for a twenty-five-year-old. I could kick myself for crying over him, but I still want him back. I am in mourning and can't see how I will ever get over him."

After people express emotions such as these, they confront the new card divorce has dealt them, and grief gives way to *fear*, which some women told me "kicked in big-time." Fear may coincide with grief, but if it doesn't, it almost always follows hard on its heels. Even as men and women grieve for what they have lost, they are starting to think about what will happen to them in the future, how and where they'll live, and what they will do to keep body and soul together.

A large number became focused on *revenge* during this period, and they were bitter and angry as they concentrated their energies on "getting even." It was almost always followed by some variant of "I'll show [him/her]!" A man who was divorcing his wife by mutual agreement because their nineteen-year marriage had been "one long battle about everything" suddenly found he had another reality to deal with: her sudden death from anaphy-lactic shock after a deadly spider bite. While cleaning out her office, he came upon a curious journal that she wrote in a semi-code he had no trouble deciphering. It spelled out her every infidelity throughout the marriage, "so many" that her widower "gave up counting." He was so angry that he walked around for weeks "punching walls and breaking anything [he] could throw at her picture." Two years after her death, he told me, "I wish my wife were still alive so I could kill her." One year after we had that conversation, he telephoned to say, "Okay, I'm over it. I'm not angry anymore." He wanted me to know that he was "moving on."

But most people aren't like this man and are forced by circumstances, such as the need to support themselves and find a place to live, to concentrate on moving forward and put the divorce behind them much sooner. In these instances, fear takes over much earlier. It can be fear of the future, fear of the unknown, and in some unfortunate instances even the fear of physical or mental harm the ex-spouse might try to inflict.

Women told me how they were terrified at having to face life alone because they were financially unprepared to care for themselves. Their only money had been what their husbands gave them; they had never balanced a checkbook, paid the taxes, made a budget, had a car serviced, or called a plumber or an electrician.

One woman in a New England state could laugh five years later about what happened to her on the day of her divorce, but she was certainly terrified and in tears at the time. First she had to drive home from the courthouse in a January blizzard, in a car whose tires were bald because her ex-husband (who had always taken care of it) had ignored the garage's maintenance reminders for well over a year and maintenance was way overdue. Once she made it up the last unplowed hill and into her driveway without skidding into a ditch, she was confronted by the frozen geyser of a burst water pipe in her front yard.

"But wait, there's more," she said, laughing in imitation of the television commercials where one thing after another is on offer if you just buy the first one: her basement was flooded by the broken pipe and the old furnace had finally rusted out and died. It took the better part of a week, but she took care of everything from getting the pipe fixed to replacing the furnace. When she picked up her car with its new tires, she was so proud of how she had coped that she "tooled around the neighborhood singing how I was woman and I was invincible."

Men face a more basic fear, one they are sheepish about admitting: "Who is going to take care of me?" More than one described buying "seven Hungry Man dinners, one for every night of the week, and maybe one or two extra in case I was really hungry." In big cities, they described "OD'ing on pizza or Chinese takeout," and in the suburbs they spoke of the "shame of sitting on the same stool in the diner, alone night after night." These were men who had never done laundry or picked up after themselves, who had been taken care of by mothers and wives and who suddenly found themselves "ankle deep in crap," as one put it. "I had the feeling nothing would ever be right in my life again," said one man who admitted that his wife left him for "emotional abuse" after enduring twenty-seven years of his alternating temper tantrums and taciturn silences. He was one of many who expressed *regret* that he had "not done the simplest little things that might have made all the difference."

It's hard to pin down where regret fits into the emotional spectrum of divorce, for it seems to "come and go" or "flit in and out," expressions used by quite a few people who experienced it. Even those who wanted the divorce most told me they "could not explain why it wells up and where it comes from" when they felt the pangs of regret. "I think it's all tied up with how I couldn't make the biggest thing in my life [marriage] work," one man said. I found myself using what he told me as I tried to help others explain why some of them felt the crushing pain of regret when they were the ones who initiated the divorce. So many said something like "All I wanted was *OUT*" to explain how bewildered they were when pangs of regret engulfed them and left them breathless. As they talked about it, most agreed they felt regret for what once was there in the marriage, or for what they thought it might have been, or even for what it never was. No matter what the truth of the marriage as they lived through it, getting divorced induced many responses on the spectrum of regret.

"SHEER JOY"

Eventually, in almost all divorces, a sense of *relief* does set in, and with it there is often surprise at the feeling of "sheer joy" that sometimes comes with it. One woman said that on the third anniversary of her divorce she felt "happy for the first time in years" and had to ask herself, "Where did this lightheartedness come from?" She described sitting at her kitchen table that afternoon, drinking a cup of coffee in a "toast to the freedom ceremony" and watching birds on the feeder in her backyard, when she felt as if a "two-ton weight had been lifted." She said to herself, "'It's over; it's finally over,' and indeed it was."

The woman who had to take baths because the shower spray hurt her said one morning she had the "sudden urge to get all dressed up and go out," and from that moment on she knew she was going to be "okay." Men told of sitting on a commuter train or walking glumly down a street when they would stop short and say to themselves, "Wait a minute—I *wanted* this divorce; I'm so happy to be rid of her, what am I doing moping around like this?" A man who asked himself that question got off the subway at his usual stop in Washington, D.C., walked into the first bar he came to, sat down, and did something he had never done before: he began a conversation with the person sitting next to him. Several drinks later, he had made two new friends, one on either side, both also divorced men. The three began to meet regularly several times a week for drinks, then to have dinner, and until Washington got a baseball team, they often went to Baltimore to see a game. He said his wife had been the "family social secretary" (another common expression among men) so he had never bothered to make friends of his own. Now he was brimming with a sense of independence and self-confidence he never had during his marriage and "felt really good" about his ability to "have a good second half of life."

C'MON, GET HAPPY

When a California lawyer-mediator told me that "people do get happy" after divorce and that he thought it took "about two years," I began to ask others in the legal and mental-health professions, among them psychiatrists, clinical social workers, and family therapists, how long they thought it took to get over a late-life divorce. Mostly, they thought it took "a bit longer, between three to five years." I think I would agree with them, for when I asked the people I interviewed to talk about their "life now," I discerned that feelings of optimism seemed to surface somewhere between the third and fourth years after the divorce. By the fifth year, unless they were beset by dire poverty or unrelenting illness, most of them were "relieved" that it was behind them. Even though there may have been terrible trials and traumas along the way, they believed they had "come through" and were now "doing okay."

There is one group who believed they "found a new happiness" much earlier in the divorce process: those who had a new partner lined up before or during the divorce, or who met someone fairly soon afterward. In most of my interviews, these people were "still happy" as long as a decade afterward, but there were some for whom the initial happiness with the new partner (or partners) had fizzled, as one man said, into "the same old thing." He told me he could not understand why he "kept going for the same kind of woman," but the three with whom he had been involved in the almost ten years after his divorce "all turned into newer versions of the same old bitch." In my interviews, divorced men who entered new relationships that didn't last gave reasons for why they "dumped" the new partners that all boiled down to the same one: the women did not lavish the care and attention on them that they felt was their due. One man said it for all of them: "There are a lot more women out there looking for a man than vice versa, and they should be grateful when they connect with a good one." "They should be grateful?" I queried, and asked him to explain. "We take them in, give them a nice life; they are supposed to take care of us, not run around with their girlfriends or take care of their kids and grandkids. We should come first."

Women who entered new relationships expressed different reasons for eventually "dumping" unsatisfactory partners. One met her new lover on the treadmills at the gym in the southwestern state where she lived. They were soon taking long exercise walks, riding mountain bikes in the desert, and running half-marathons together. "At first it didn't seem to matter that I had a lot more money than he did," she said as she described a substantial settlement from her former husband, a successful businessman. The new man in her life "was divorced and his ex had her own job and there were no kids, so he had no one to spend money on but himself, and he had a good job and a nice apartment."

But all too soon, he was telling her how to invest her money—especially in a business he wanted to start. "If I learned anything from my divorce," the woman said, "it was that I was never going to let another man dictate how I should live my life and spend my money ever again."

She broke off the relationship and went through a period of depression over "another failure," as did many other women who told me how "low" they felt when they became dissatisfied with new partners. When I pressed them to explain what had gone wrong, it all seemed to come down to the same thing: the men expected to "move in on me and take charge of my life," or as one woman added, "Translation needed here: take charge of my money." None of these women were about to give up their newfound independence to become, once again, "a spoke on some boss man's wheel."

One other group who entered a relationship after divorce bears mentioning here: the 2 percent (according to the AARP survey) who remarried the same spouse. The survey gave no information about how long they stayed married the second time or how happy they claimed to be. I can't contribute very much here, for I knew only two couples who "got back together." One had been remarried for three years when I spoke to them. The husband shrugged and said things were "okay" and he was "glad" they reunited. The wife said she initiated the contact that led to the remarriage because the insecurity of being on her own had been more than she could cope with; she was "relieved" to have "him" (she seldom used her husband's name in our conversation) "around to deal with things again." Neither expressed any particular degree of happiness, and out of kindness (misplaced or not), I did not press them.

The other couple had gone through fairly complicated arrangements at the time of the divorce to divide their life's savings, approximately $400,000, and they had paid significant legal fees to do so because they fought over it. They decided not to remarry because of the expense of dealing once again with the money, so they remained divorced but lived together as if they were husband and wife. The man said he was glad to have her back because "she makes the place nice to live in." The woman said he was "far nicer [to her] than he had ever been before," but what she liked best about "the second time around" was "being with someone I already know, and best of all, knowing that whenever I need to, I can always walk out again."

"I DID THE RIGHT THING"

The greater number of people I talked to decided that they were "happy" after the divorce because, as so many said, "I know I did the right thing," not only for themselves but (surprisingly) for the well-being of the ex-spouse and (not so surprising) for any children who were young and unfortunate enough to have been involved in their parents' divorce. A slightly smaller number said they could not describe themselves as "happy" but were "certainly better off" being out of an unhappy marriage. Only a small percentage described themselves as "unhappy," "not able to get over it," or "downright miserable." Usually these were people who called themselves the "dumpees," women whose husbands left them for another partner or men whose wives gave "no good reason" for "walking out on the marriage."

The AARP survey found that the degree of happiness expressed by divorced people had a lot to do with their age, but this did not seem to hold true for my interviews. Their statistics showed that sixty- and seventy-year-olds "appreciate life after divorce most" because they enjoy the person their newly-found independence has allowed them to become.[2] Forty-year-olds worried most about finances, which the survey concluded was because they wanted to prove that they could "get on with their lives." I found that when forty-year-olds worried about money it was because of the fear that comes with the realization that they are on life's downhill slope toward retirement and they are not mentally prepared to accept it. The generation in their fifties, according to AARP, had the "most difficulty" after divorce and was the most likely to say that learning to deal with it was "more difficult than a major illness." Only here did the AARP statistics parallel my findings, for we both found that what this age group liked best about divorce was "not having to deal with another person."

But in every instance, and no matter their age, my findings crossed the age boundaries that AARP delineated. I found that what women, no matter how old, liked most after divorce was being "independent," "in charge," and "having control" over their lives, all of which they cited far more than men did. What women feared most was "being alone forever," "never having someone to do things with," "never finding love," or, as several women said, "I won't say never finding love *again* because I never had it the first time."

Very few men expressed the fear of being alone. When they said they wanted to be with a woman again, they seldom described the woman they wanted as one they could "care for" but rather, as "a woman who will care for me." When I asked these men if they were equating a woman caring for them with "getting their meals cooked and their laundry done," quite a few laughed sheepishly and said something like "Well, not exactly, but it would be nice." Or, as one who was offended by my question put it, "What's wrong with wanting a woman who can cook as good as she can fuck?"

Not surprisingly, given the hard statistical reality that women are worse off financially after divorce, men put "having more money of my own" at the top of the list of things they like best about divorce. When men told me why they liked the extra money that came from not having to be the sole support of a wife and children, they said it was because they had "a lot more freedom to play." I always asked them how they liked to play with this bonus income, and the answers ranged from installing a home gym in a newly purchased bachelor condo to putting in a wine cellar to engaging in expensive hobbies or traveling to exotic places.

"When I was married, we could never afford to go further than Cape Cod or the Jersey shore, and I always wanted to go to Antarctica or on an African safari," said one man from Long Island who had just returned from the Galápagos Islands. "Now I can do it." I asked about his ex-wife and he told me she shared a one-bedroom apartment with their high-school age daughter. When I spoke to his wife, she told me she was living so frugally because she hoped the girl's father would contribute to her tuition when she went to college in a year, but she wasn't counting on it.

This is where I found the only difference according to age in the attitudes of the women I interviewed: women who still have children in high school or college are often saddled with most, if not all, of the responsibility for the children's education. This is particularly true when children become eighteen and the courts consider them adults, for that is often when fathers cut off support "cold turkey." The mothers of these children resent the financial inequity that allows their ex-husbands to enjoy "the playboy lifestyle" (an expression I heard a lot). They say it is "unjust" and are bitter about it.

One woman described how enraged she was when her ex-husband, who had never complained about paying for their older son's expensive boarding school and private university for the six years immediately after the divorce, smilingly told her he would not pay anything at all for their younger son and daughter: "I wanted to smack that smug grin right off his face because I knew what he was doing: he was getting even with me by turning my kids against each other and making them resent me." When I asked other fathers if they felt even the slightest guilt about leaving their ex-wives to cope with the full responsibility for their children, most shrugged and said nothing as they looked at me in blank-eyed amazement at my even asking the question. But when I asked this particular father why he was willing to pay for one child and not the two others, he responded angrily, "Why should I? She wanted the divorce, so let her pay."

BAD RELATIONSHIPS ARE BAD FOR YOU

A group of researchers at Ohio State University have found that "hostile interaction in a marriage may slow the healing of [physical] wounds," such as the blisters they deliberately raised in order to measure how much time it took to heal them.[3] Dr. Janice Kiecolt-Glaser, the lead author of the study, described "bad" marriages as "particularly risky" in how fast one's body heals "because your major source of support [your spouse] becomes your major source of stress." Her group found that blisters induced on partners in hostile marriages heal only 60 percent as quickly as those induced in nonhostile ones. Even more alarming, they found that hostility causes battling couples to have a much higher risk of heart and other diseases.

Divorce, which many men and women see as their salvation from the daily draining, sapping, and debilitation of a hostile marriage, brings its own kind of stress, but one that arises from different issues. Chief among them is financial inequity. No matter what the age group of my respondents, worry about money was almost always coupled with increased "stress," and women were the ones who suffered most from it. Among the hardest hit were women whose husbands walked away from the marriage free and clear while leaving them saddled with staggering amounts of credit-card debt, first and second mortgages, and other bills they never knew existed, never mind having to sell their homes to pay the ex-spouse his share of the equity. They described physical breakdowns that ranged from clenching their jaws so tightly in their sleep that they actually cracked molars to having to pull their cars to the side of the road and phone for an ambulance because their anxiety attacks were so severe they thought they were having a heart attack.

If men worried and became "stressed out," they were reluctant to admit it and even more reluctant to talk about what caused it. Those who did admit to excessive worry or stress offered generalizations about fears for job security or not having saved enough money to last their lifetimes, but otherwise, my asking if they experienced increased levels of stress after divorce usually produced a puzzled expression and the answer "Not really."

Women, on the other hand, described disturbed sleep patterns, insomnia, and anxiety, especially, as one woman most graphically phrased it, "the four A.M. galloping insecurities." Even women who were financially well-off after divorce told me they "worried" most about money, which produced so much stress they thought it affected their general health. So many said something like "I never took pills before . . ." as they described the medications from Ambien to Valium to Zoloft that now cluttered their medicine cabinets. Those whose former husbands had a lot of money and who received generous financial settlements that were meant to keep them for the rest of their lives worried that the men would make bad investments or "bad deals" that would render the legal agreements worthless and end their payments. Even those who enjoyed the independence and self-control that being divorced brought to their lives worried that chronic ill health would "ruin everything" they wanted to gain from it. Last, the unfocused anxiety about not being able to care for themselves, as well as the fear of becoming a burden on their children, worried mothers far more than it did fathers.

NEW LIFE—NO DOWNERS!

Still, when men and women finished telling me about the fears and anxieties divorce unleashed, they then changed the subject to something positive because they did not want our conversations about their "new life" to end "on a downer." They wanted me to know that their present-day lives were pleasant and satisfying, and they were eager to talk about their hopes and dreams.

"I have had to learn how to 'live in the moment,' " said one woman who claimed she suffered greatly from anxiety and worry for the first three years after her divorce. She had gone to various support groups but said she did not "do well" in them, whether they were "divorce recovery" or "consciousness-raising." She had tried therapy but rejected it after several sessions, saying, "I could tell myself the same thing the shrink said and save a hundred fifty bucks an hour." What helped her most, she said, was "so silly" she blushed to describe it. When pressed, she said all she did was to concentrate on "every trite truism out there, from 'smelling the roses,' to thanking a god I hardly believe in for 'a lovely day,' even if it was pouring down rain and I didn't have an umbrella." She laughed at herself and said, "Maybe it's silly, but it works for me."

"It works for me" was another statement I heard often, along with so many different explanations of what it was that "worked." The woman just quoted was one of many who learned to take pleasure in "little things." Because she had so little money to keep her going, she named everything from "free movies at the public library" to "free tastings of gourmet foods and wine" she could not afford to buy at the upscale grocery in her neighborhood. Others who had led secluded lives in their homes while waiting for husbands to come home at night had to "work hard" to make themselves "establish contact" with people, or "to interact" on many different levels, from chatting with neighbors in casual encounters over the back fence to telephoning children more frequently than before. They described how much courage it took for them to invite friends to join them for everything from potluck suppers and rental movies to excursions or vacations.

Many of the women who had been content to center their lives on caring for their homes and catering to their husbands described how difficult it was for them to "reach out" to others but how "vital" it was for their physical and mental well-being. These are the women who spoke of the "courage" they needed to make the initial contact and the "pride" they felt after they had done it.

Men seldom went into detail about how they had restructured their lives after divorce except to describe volunteer activities they participated in for the first time ever. As they listed everything from community-service projects to political campaigns, they described the "sense of connection" that "joining something" gave them. What pleased them most was, as one man whose wife left him because he was "boring" put it, "the sense of relief that comes with knowing that I do matter and there is value to my life." Men far more than women, told me they needed "validation" after a divorce, which might be related to what many ex-wives told me their "job" had been throughout their marriage: "to tell him every day how wonderful he was, how handsome, important, sexy, good-looking, smart, et cetera. To buck him up and bolster his ego in whatever way he needed at that particular moment."

Many of these same women told me how much they "resented" that it was so much easier for men after divorce to "go out in the world and find whatever they want," while they had to struggle much harder to make their way in a brand-new world in which they had not chosen to live. Nevertheless, women who complained of having "to learn how to do everything for myself because there is nobody out there to catch me when I start to fall" still insisted that our discussion must end on a positive note, as they spoke of the satisfaction and well-being that suffused them once they knew they were capable of doing whatever needed to be done. Becoming divorced had not been easy for any of them, whether they initiated it or had it forced upon them, and they wanted to make it known that in the first instance it was the right decision and in the second they were (in the words of one Californian who spoke for a group of divorced women) "not only surviving, but thriving."

The women in this group reflected the research done at UCLA by Drs. Laura Cousin Klein and Shelley Taylor, who recognized that over 90 percent of all the research on stress had used male subjects, and that women respond to it far differently.[4] They found that "women respond to stress with a cascade of brain chemicals that cause [them] to make and maintain friendships with other women," whereas when men become stressed, "they holed up somewhere on their own." The researchers concluded that friendships and social ties reduce blood pressure, heart rate, and cholesterol, which "may explain why women consistently outlive men." At Harvard Medical School the highly respected Nurses Health Study showed that women who had the most friends were the least likely to develop physical impairments as they grew older and were most likely to be leading "a joyful life."

The people who told me their stories may not have used the phrase "a joyful life," but in almost every instance they were looking for one and most were finding it.

THE SILVER-HAIRED SINGLES

A man in the D.C. area told me, "I'm fifty-nine years old and single again, and I haven't a clue about what to do next." A woman in Upstate New York asked, "How does a fifty-five-year-old woman let the world know I am out there again?" A woman in Philadelphia said, "I don't go to church, I don't go to bars, I don't like sports, and I don't go bowling—so where am I going to meet a man?" And a man there told me he didn't think he was "ready to be out there," but his two daughters had signed him up for "one month on JDate" (an online dating service for Jewish singles) and made him get "all dressed up" for an evening of "speed dating" at the Jewish community center. It left him "reeling," but even though he didn't "connect" the first time, he "liked it" and planned to go to the next speed-date meeting several weeks hence.

A little farther south, divorced singles are flocking to Maryland's Eastern Shore, where groups catering to the social life of older people are burgeoning. Eight of the nine counties that comprise that part of the state have more people over sixty-five than all the rest of the state's population put together, and retirement communities are booming. These vital and dynamic divorced elders are generally of retirement age, and most of them say they are not interested in hosting the traditional dinner party, are bored by church socials, bingo, and early-bird mealtime gatherings. They are looking for things that engage their enthusiasm, so it's no wonder, then, that this segment of the population has cast a curious eye on how younger singles try to meet future partners and have decided to use the same tactics themselves.

Some of the older singles who tried online dating told me it was "lots better than sitting in a bar waiting to be picked up." On the Eastern Shore, Mingling Singles, a speed-dating group that catered to younger people, had its membership triple in two short months after older people saw how well the younger set was connecting and enrolled in it. When membership in Ocean City's Beach Singles reached 150, more than the chapter could successfully accommodate, the directors decided to open a new branch in nearby Salisbury rather than let the original one grow to the point of unwieldiness. At this writing, another Ocean City group, the Merry Widows and Widowers, is also oversubscribed and considering what to do next.[5]

Interestingly, the phenomenon of senior online dating simply grew by itself, without any marketing or advertising, when those who had a lot of time to play with their computers decided that, if their children were doing it, it was socially acceptable for them as well. What they found, however, was that if there was any "aggressive marketing" out there, it was directed only to younger singles. "They did not come courting me; I had to go find them" was how a lot of men and women explained it to me.

But as soon as the older set found the online dating companies, they realized what a huge market was out there waiting to be tapped and older singles became the "hot target" they all wanted to hit. The dating website Match.com, for example, found that since 2000, registration among singles over fifty climbed more than 340 percent, and some companies in the matchmaking industry set up special seniors-only sites. Spark Networks, a Los Angeles online dating service, created SilverSingles, which grew to more than 600,000 members in less than a year, and another of its websites, PrimeSingles.net, has so far attracted more than 13,000 members.

Older singles may need to get their grandchildren to show them how to program any number of new electronic toys, but when it comes to finding companionship, they know how to navigate the net with alacrity.

GROUP SUPPORT VERSUS INDIVIDUALISM

One of the factors that makes the phenomenal rise in online dating most interesting is how it contrasts with the way older singles have generally avoided, evaded, or ignored other kinds of groups set up specifically to help them cope with divorce. The AARP survey found that only 5 percent of late-life divorcers used a support group of any kind, from community organizations to government agencies or other organizations that represented older people.[6] The other 95 percent may have relied upon friends or family for emotional support, but otherwise they coped on their own. I found a different perspective in my interviews, for over half of those who talked to me said they did initially seek some sort of group support, even though most soon gave it up as "not for me."

In my interviews, some form of talk therapy topped the list for both men and women, as well as for their adult children. In general they all began with individual consultations, and many supplemented private sessions with group encounters. Family therapists told me how they "ran groups" several times each week and would invite their private clients to join. Most, they said, would "eventually drift in on their own," and some of those who did would end up staying, as they found companionship and comfort in sharing their histories with others who had gone through similar experiences.

The other half of my interviewees either rejected therapy at the outset or never sought it at all, or they left shortly after they started because it didn't bring the satisfaction or consolation they hoped to find. A large number within this latter category told me that when therapy "failed" them, they tried other groups that "succeeded." High on this list, as quite a few expressed it, was "any kind of twelve-step group I could get into." People who did not classify themselves as alcoholics found comfort in attending Alcoholics Anonymous meetings; adult children told me they went to Al-Anon or Alateen meetings, even though they and their parents were not alcoholics but only "social drinkers." Some heard of informal groups in their communities that were "self-founded" (that is, by people who felt a need for them) along the lines of a book-discussion group. They met to discuss the writings of "self-help gurus" (their phrase), among them Dr. Phil, Wayne Dyer, Barbara De Angelis, Jean Shinoda Bolen, Clarisssa Pinkola Estés, Deborah Tannen, and John Gray. Others told me that they themselves organized such groups when they felt the need for them and that they got a lot from them.

Many more women than men told me they found comfort in their churches. They often changed their membership, not only from one church to another in their Protestant denomination but from one denomination to another. In many cases, they were looking for female ministers, who they thought were more understanding than men, and in other cases, they found certain denominations to be "more welcoming," "more forgiving," "more caring," or "less judgmental" and "less punitive" than their original faiths.

I found that the greatest number of men who turned to their churches for support declared themselves Roman Catholic. They often attended daily mass and trained to become deacons and assist in religious and social services now that the number of parish priests is in decline. Several of these men described going through the long process of a religious annulment after they divorced because they wanted to continue to receive Holy Communion and the other sacraments.

I also found that men of all faiths or of no faith at all joined what they loosely call "men's groups," which, from their descriptions, struck me as similar to women's consciousness-raising groups. These groups are catching on and growing so fast that they will soon number as many as women's groups. Many of their founders said they studied how women's groups operated and deliberately patterned theirs after them, hoping to "learn something" from "how the women did it." The men in these groups were predominantly the ones whose wives left them "for no apparent reason" and who were hoping to understand how and why their marriages ended.

All the groups I've described above are different from the formally constituted divorce recovery groups that are found in most regions of the country. Most of the people I interviewed may have tried some of these but did not stay involved with them for a significant period. I was puzzled by this, for my understanding of how divorce recovery groups function came from an explanation given by Dr. Adele Hurst, a Dallas psychologist and marriage counselor, an explanation I thought would have made them invaluable to late-life divorcers: "The crux of [divorce recovery] therapy focuses on helping the person fill out the parts of himself or herself that the other person functioned for."[7] Dr. Hurst explained that long marriages become "institutionalized," wherein, for example, one partner takes care of the house and children while the other pays the bills, doles out the money, and makes the major decisions about how the household will function. Neither partner feels capable of doing the other's job, so that when divorce happens, each has to start from scratch to learn how to do all these things he or she had done little of or had never done before.

When I recognized that the people who contributed to this book put more faith in their own individual ability to cope with any obstacles put in their way than they did in joining groups, I set out to determine why this was so. In many instances, I telephoned the contributors and asked follow-up questions to see if anything had changed since we spoke last. I was almost always told that very little in their lives had, and that they still found "what worked" for them was "picking and choosing" what they thought they needed, which in almost every instance centered on "laughing" and "having fun."

PUTTING "A LITTLE FUN" IN LIFE

What seemed to work best was finding something "far outside the daily mainstream," as Gwen, a woman in New Mexico, put it. She was depressed and lethargic as she headed into her second year of being divorced, when she gave in to a friend who lived in "the people's republic of Austin," Texas, who insisted that if Gwen did not come to visit, she would drive to New Mexico and "kidnap" her. Gwen's friend took her line dancing at a club where older divorcées congregated and refused to let her sit on the sidelines. The reluctant Gwen joined in and discovered that she loved it, even though she was "overweight and out of shape" and "huffed and puffed like an old warhorse." She danced every dance and made her friend take her back to the same club every night for the entire week of her visit. When she went home, she found several groups in Albuquerque and joined them all. Heading into the fifth year after her divorce at this writing, she was still attending weekend dances, enjoying a new and satisfying social life, and experiencing an enthusiasm and vitality that she credits to an improved diet and lots of exercise from dancing.

Several women described transformations similar to Gwen's but with ballroom instead of line dancing. They reported that once they began taking lessons, their depression lifted and their general health improved. In conjunction with ballroom dancing, many among them began to practice yoga as a way of "controlling the body" to make the dancing "smoother and more powerful." Doing yoga gave them a general sense of well-being, especially because those who experienced the most stress and worry during their nondancing hours were able to practice positions that induced "positive meditation."

Ballroom dancing enhanced their lives in other ways as well. Several women spoke of finding their first new postdivorce partner at the lessons. All agreed it was a "terrific ego boost," even though the relationship was lasting for only a few of the dozen or so women who took up dancing. Interestingly, in every one of the relationships formed through dancing that did not last, it was the woman who ended it, mostly because, as one put it, "he not only wanted to lead me in the dance, he wanted to lead me in life, and I had had quite enough of that, thank you."

Two women who took up ballroom dancing as a postdivorce cure were delighted when it led to a new business. They met in dancing class and discovered that both were excellent seamstresses who liked to copy designer clothes for themselves. One had actually worked before her marriage for a mass-market clothing designer in New York's garment district, so she had a sense of how a business should operate. Together they began to design and sew costumes for the dancers who engaged in competitions, and soon they had a thriving business in their home state. As I was interviewing them, they were trying to decide whether to keep their business local or to sell it to a national costume designer, and both were thrilled that their lives were "richer and fuller" than they had ever been.

I asked men what activities they found rewarding in their new lives, and many were unable to think of anything other than "mostly doing the things I did before." Some said the divorce had brought them closer to their children but especially to their grandchildren, with whom they shared outings to museums and ball games. They often told me they did things with their grandchildren they had never done with their children, with whom they regretted not having been more involved. Some men said they joined a gym where they did solitary activities like walking a treadmill, swimming laps, or lifting weights. Quite a few told me they had formerly "scoffed at the sissies" who took yoga classes but had "dropped in" on a class and found it so rewarding that they'd been doing it "religiously" ever since.

Unlike women, who had no qualms about walking into a group or an activity (like ballroom dancing) on their own and alone, men tended to be more comfortable as part of a group whenever they made their initial foray into the world of singles. Many Jewish men told me they joined their local Jewish community center to find company and signed up for group outings such as bus trips from their Pennsylvania towns to Atlantic City's casinos or spending a week attending lectures and performances at the original Chautauqua Institution in Upstate New York. Several men joined the Italian community center in their Michigan town; having grown "tired of the same old ziti" the women cooked for the monthly dinner and poker night, they took over the kitchen on a dare and produced a meal so good that it became a recurring project as they and the women alternated cooking every other month. Women also found it easier to go to the movies alone and to eat in restaurants by themselves, while men said they were "too uncomfortable" sitting at a table for one, so they seldom dined alone.

Men also explained that they "had it easier" than women, because "the casserole ladies beat a path to [their] door" the moment word got out that they were "back on the market." Most liked the attention, "not to mention the food," and many new relationships and second marriages were forged in this way. Here, in the "casserole" situations, as in so many singles groups, women far outnumber men, so men have greater opportunities to "take [women] or leave them." Kathleen Roldan, a spokesperson for the San Francisco branch of Match.com, noted that "fifty-five and older" is the fastest-growing segment of people looking for partners. She also noted that as this group gets older, "the pool of eligible people [that is, men] we have to choose from gets smaller and smaller."[8]

This did not bother Lois West, age seventy-one, of the Ocean City Beach Singles. Like others in her group, she doesn't worry that she may not find the new partner of her dreams; it's enough to find pleasure in doing the same things that her children's generation enjoys. "If romance comes later, they'll be ready," Lois said of those in her age group, for "hope springs eternal."

THE MARRIAGE REVOLUTION

Dr. Stephanie Coontz, a leading scholar and writer who studies the family, said in an interview that the institution of marriage has "changed more in the past thirty years than in the previous three thousand."[9] She attributes this to many things, from doing away with the "legal and political requirements that women be subordinate to their husbands," making it easier to end unhappy or abusive marriages; to the economic independence that the feminist movement of the 1970s put into play, allowing women to enter the workforce in large numbers; to lessening of the stigma attached to children born to single mothers.

In a related article, Coontz argued that marriage has been in a constant state of evolution since the dawn of the Stone Age. However, part of this evolution has ensured that while it has become "more flexible," marriage has also become "more optional." She also noted that when laws were changed to give married women an "independent legal existence," these changes did not "destroy" traditional heterosexual marriage. Rather, they gave husbands and wives the freedom to choose the role they wanted to fill, "where a wife can choose to be the main breadwinner and a husband can stay home with the children." Coontz was among the many who did not agree with the prediction of "the far-right opponents of marital equality" who believe the end of traditionalism will "lead to the unraveling of marriage." Reflecting upon their fear some years later, she agreed that "as it turned out, they had a point," even though the point was exactly the opposite of what they intended. Quite simply, "it opened the door for gay and lesbian couples to argue that they were now equally qualified to participate in marriage."

Coontz recognized the many people who do not like the truly earth-shattering changes of the last thirty or forty years in how families conduct their private lives, but she calls it "magical thinking" to believe that acts such as banning gay and lesbian marriages will "turn back the clock." Among those who decry her support for "whatever works in human relationships" is Glenn T. Stanton, director of Social Research and Cultural Affairs for the group Focus on the Family.[10] Writing in response to Coontz's article, he sent a letter to *The New York Times* dismissing what he interprets as her contention that the "genderless family" is merely "the next change so just deal with it." Having to "deal" with it, he wrote, "denies the importance of wife and husband" within a family and does not "represent change" but rather "represents a bad change."

An eighty-two-year old woman, Roslyn Fallick, responded to Coontz's article with a letter published at the same time as Stanton's.[11] Coontz, Fallick wrote, "has hit the nail right on the head." As for the idea that traditional marriage is "holy and sacred," Fallick argues that if this were indeed true, "there would not be so many marriages that end in divorce." Speaking of her long lifetime, she wrote of the many "dramatic changes" in human relationships she had seen, among them "the legal, social and psychological factors affecting the institution of marriage." These, to her, were "all for the better. Women are no longer possessions. They are equal partners."

All these writers left unsaid the idea that "equal partners" in marriage also have a related option: to dissolve unsatisfactory unions. Divorce is now as viable an option for a marriage as is the dissolution of a business agreement that no longer works for the parties involved.

STARTING OVER

Throughout this book, I have written about how men and women cope with the extraordinary changes that late-life divorce brings to their lives. As I listened to their stories, what impressed me most was the resilience with which they went through the often painful process of having to reinvent themselves before they could even begin to think about how to start a new life. A high school English teacher tried to describe what she was feeling after she ended her twenty-nine-year marriage to a cold, withdrawn, emotionally abusive husband. She was packing to leave the comfortable suburban home outside Milwaukee where she had raised her family, to start anew in a modest city apartment, and she told me she could not help but compare herself with Huckleberry Finn when he " 'lighted out' for a brand-new territory." She was among the many who described with wonderment all the changes that had to be made once a person who was part of a couple for so many years became suddenly single, and how dealing with so many changes "sometimes felt like standing on the sidelines watching another person go through the motions."

"Everything is different now," said an Irish Catholic father of five whose wife told him that with the children grown and on their own, she refused to live her "last decades" with a bullying alcoholic. "It's different for me, too," she replied huffily when the subject of new and different ways of living came up in her interview with me.

These two both called their marriage a "failure," an expression used by so many others to describe what brought them to divorce. Both men and women may make statements that range from "It wasn't my fault" to "I really fucked up," but they still see their future in strikingly different terms. Women embrace whatever is to come and whatever may befall them, whereas men are far more cautious, hesitant, and reluctant to embrace change.

"I have had to learn a whole new way of operating out there in the world," a man from Ontario told me. He was not yet sure that he "liked it," but he was "determined to make the best of it."

"I've learned from my mistakes," said a philandering Californian, who deeply regretted losing his wife but still wondered what made her leave after she "put up with all my little affairs for twenty-eight years." He told me how, after the divorce, he tried to get her back by insisting, "I can do better now," but she would have nothing to do with him. This was a man who was used to getting his own way, which is probably why he countered that what she told him only meant that he would have to keep trying to persuade her that he was "a changed man" until she gave up and returned to him. He listed all the things he had been doing to "impress" her, from community involvement to having more interaction with their grown children.

"He's dreaming," his ex-wife told me. "It's my time now." She went on to describe the many things she hoped to do, to accomplish, to enjoy, now that she was no longer "covering up his philandering to protect the children." She hoped he would "move on," as she had "finally found the courage to do, after so many years of wondering if I should or even if I could."

These former spouses saw their future in strikingly different terms—he being hopeful to reunite with her, she happy with her new independence—but both, like most of the people who contributed to this book, gave off an aura of positive energy when they spoke about their "postdivorce lives."

There is also a related honesty in the way most late-life divorcers appraise the marriages they ended (or that were ended despite their desire to keep them). The marriage may have ended badly, but they have scant regret about having married the ex-mate in the first place. Often they said, "He/she gave me [fill in the number] children, and I cannot imagine being without them." Or, "We had [fill in the number] good years together, and I am grateful for the experience." Even those who think their marriage ended as "mostly disaster" will justify their choice of a mate with something like "My hormones were raging and he/she was perfect for me when I needed him/her." Others will say, "I knew from the beginning it was not going to last, but I wanted him/her, and at least I have the satisfaction of knowing how hard I tried to make the marriage work."

They brought this same honesty to bear on how they intend to live their future lives, even though this was more difficult for them to explain. Quite a few seemed embarrassed to talk about what they hoped to find and would apologize for having to use "touchy-feely" or "New Age" "jargon." A woman in Florida who was having particular difficulty trying to express herself accurately finally gave up in exasperation and said, "I need to find a new way to live my life, and more and more I find myself turning inward to look for it." She was expressing what a man said after he left Los Angeles to begin his postdivorce life in northern Idaho. He found that "church," in his case the LDS or Mormon church, "didn't do it anymore," and he was looking for "a more personal, individual kind of spirituality." People did tell me they found comfort and solace through organized religion, but many more were like the woman in Florida who found herself "turning inward" and the man in Idaho who needed "something personal, individual."

The Florida woman explained that whatever she was looking for, she knew she wouldn't find it "anywhere but within herself." Her "personal connection" to herself first and only afterward to the world outside came through yoga and meditation. I attended one of her classes and spoke to several other women, each of whom described the process of seeking and finding "something different" that "worked" for them. One said it was reading *Daily Word*, the monthly handbook of spiritual meditations published by the Silent Unity Prayer Service. Another spoke of joining a Bible-study group, and still another said she and two divorced friends (both men) were reading "great philosophers of the world." The rest told me that the yoga class itself and the friendships they formed there "worked best" for them. This last response seemed most typical of the women I interviewed, who credited an external activity with triggering internal satisfaction, especially when it coincided with new friendships among people who shared the same experiences.

FORMING NEW FRIENDSHIPS

One of the more fascinating tales of how women formed female friendships after late-life divorce was told to me by Joan, a Jungian analyst who used Jung's word "synchronicity" to describe the individual random acts that have meaning only after they are all put together. Joan told me how "the synchronicity story" began when she was approaching her fifty-fifth birthday and wanted to do something she had always wanted to do and never had the time for—to tap dance. Joan's husband of twenty-eight years had recently divorced her to marry another woman, and she was looking for an activity that would tire her body after her long days of seeing patients who tired her mind. She phoned all the dance studios listed in the yellow pages until she found a teacher who had never taught adults before but was willing to try, especially because Joan was the second woman in the past several days who had phoned to ask for lessons.

When Joan arrived at the studio, she found that the other woman, Lydia, had brought a third, her neighbor Celeste, and both were also recently divorced. Over the next several weeks, Joan said, "something must [have been] in the water," for they were joined first by Caroline and then by Carmen, who were also divorced. They were five total strangers from different backgrounds with different levels of education and social standing, and they became fast friends who still take tap lessons four years later, and who celebrate with one another all the milestones in their lives.

Men were more likely to describe their search for how to live in a postdivorce world and to find new friendships very much in terms of their education and social station. The greater their education and financial standing, the more they credited authors like Emerson, Thoreau, Voltaire, or Montaigne with helping them find "something inside" themselves that "spurred" or "inspired" them in the creation of a new life. Working-class men told me they found what they needed by "getting together with the guys," "talking to my parish priest," or "reading some stuff my kids gave me." Only then did they describe how they interacted with new acquaintances.

"The kids" often provided a lifeline for late-life divorced men. They were the ones who encouraged their fathers to go to various group meetings, to speed-date, or even to read some of the "touchy-feely stuff" the men swore they would never have "picked up" on their own. In many cases, these men had been the traditional patriarchal father, the head of the household who was far removed from the daily life of the children. Now that they were divorced, they were becoming a part of their children's lives in ways they had never been before. A great many of these fathers described how "getting close to the kids" helped them "learn so much," about themselves and their human relationships, in ways they had never thought about before. Many times I heard them say something like "I'm turning into a real philosopher here," as they blushed with pleasure over the new and meaningful relationships they were forging withtheir children and the "new insights" they were gaining about themselves. These new insights often involved meeting new women, and only seldom was the term extended to cover new friendships with other men.

THE "CORRECT" RATE OF DIVORCE

Harvard law professor Janet Halley made an interesting observation about divorce in an article entitled "The Future of Marriage," published in the university's alumni magazine:

> We don't know what the "correct" rate of divorce is. We don't know whether the right couples divorce. We think that women who are being beaten up by their husbands should surely divorce, but people who have just developed a seven-year itch ought to "stick it out." We don't have a good baseline. If half the people in the seventeenth century weredead by the time they were 45, we don't know what they would have done if they had . . . still [been] living with the same person at 65.[12]

Here we are, living in the twenty-first century well past the age of sixty-five, often going strong into the nineties and still looking for many of the same things we wanted when we started out in our twenties to forge our first (and often most lasting) human relationships. What is it that we wanted then, and is that what we are still seeking? An elderly man in Washington State who divorced the first time after fifty-one years and the second time after three was about to embark on his third marriage. What was he seeking? I asked. "Oh, well, I guess just your basic life, liberty, and the pursuit of happiness,' " he told me, with a wink, a nudge, and a grin.

Now that we live so long and remain healthy well into old age, shall we learn to call our first marriages, even those that lasted fifty years or longer, the "starter"marriage? Professor Halley argues that the constantly rising divorce rate has created a "new ideology," in which the "starter" marriage is often followed by the "encore marriage," and taken together, they give new meaning to the concept of "serial monogamy."

I can't help but wonder if this is this how human relationships will proceed to unfold throughout the new century, and perhaps throughout the new millennium as well. Will we find that we need a series of companions as we go through life, rather than the one single "to death do us part" person whom society, culture, and organized religion have conspired to make us believe is the *only* acceptable companion?

THE DIVORCE-MARRIAGE MIRROR

Margaret Mead thought every woman needed at least three men in her life: one to give her passionate sex and children; one to help her protect and nurture those children to a safe adulthood; and one to be the boon companion of her declining years. The conservative movement would list Mead among those who advocate the demise of the traditional family, for they interpret her decree that every woman needs three men as basically advocating "divorce, cohabitation, 'illegitimacy,' and the demise of the traditional family [leading to] moral decay and the destruction of the American way of life."[13] Its no wonder, then, that the Republican Congress enacted the Defense of Marriage Act (DOMA) of 1996, in which marriage was defined by law as "one man, one woman" (and notice who came first here), and that the Democratic president Bill Clinton signed it. Most Americans sighed, shrugged, and ignored DOMA, going their individual ways espousing same-sex marriage, cohabitation without legal ceremony, and the right to have children born out of wedlock.

Two researchers who study the effects of divorce on children, Judith Wallerstein and Sandra Blakeslee, prefigured the public's post-1996 determination to maintain individuality in relationships when they published their book *Second Chances*, in what now seems like another lifetime way back in 1989. The book assessed the lives of men, women, and children ten years after divorce and described in part what the authors call "the divorce-marriage mirror." They argue that it is "time to take a long, hard look at divorce in America"[14] because it is the "mirror image of marriage." Wallerstein and Blakeslee maintain that divorce serves two purposes. The first seems obvious and a given: to "escape the marriage, which has grown intolerable at least for one person." It is their second assertion, however, that resonates for me as having the most importance for the many people who contributed to this book: "to build a new life."

Everyone who initiates divorce is seeking to build a new life. All are hoping "fervently" that life after divorce will bring them "something better." Most would insist that they have found it, no matter how long since their divorce was final or how their situation might appear to those on the outside looking in. Just as the reality of a marriage is known only to the two people who participate in it (and perhaps they don't have the most objective view of the relationship during or after having been in it), so, too, is the reality of life after divorce really known only to those who are living it every day.

The French use the expression "I wasn't holding the candle," meaning literally "I was not standing over the bed observing the two people in it," and it provides a metaphor for how much an outsider can really know about any marriage or why it ends. I am inclined to believe all the men and women who told me "things are better now," never mind how much I saw them struggling to keep body and soul together, to control the loneliness that sometimes overwhelmed them, to hide their grief and their feelings of loss for a beloved home or a cherished possession that had to be sold because they needed the money.

Divorce may not be the be-all and the end-all, but it is often (and perhaps always should be) just the beginning. It is the start of a long-distance march whose finish line is a destination so far in the future it cannot be seen at the outset. Joan, the Jungian analyst who took up tap dancing, told me she envisioned life after her divorce as standing on the edge of an Olympic-size swimming pool, knowing she is a mediocre swimmer but that nonetheless she has to dive in, hold her breath, and keep on paddling until she gets to the other side. Carmen, her dancing friend, who was born in the United States to illegal immigrants (now citizens), told me she had "no education" so it was "not easy to talk as well as Joan," but she also had a metaphor for what she "had to do" after her divorce: "I was like an airplane and the weather was bad, and I had to go into a holding pattern and circle round and round until the clouds broke, and then I knew I could land safely."

They and all the other people who told me their stories were so brave and so determined to find in their postdivorce lives the happiness and contentment that eluded them in their marriages that I could not help but be impressed by their courage, dignity, and the strong sense of self-value they gained after going through what was often a painful and traumatic process.

My role was to be the outside observer who dipped briefly into their lives to listen to their stories. All the while we talked, I tried to maintain the necessary distance that would allow me to write about them objectively. And yet I cannot help but end this book by stepping outside that objectivity to say that, as they embrace whatever the future has in store for them, I'd like to be holding that candle and looking down at the new bed in which they lie. I have every faith that they will turn late-life divorce, in so many respects the end of a dream and a certain kind of failure and loss, into the beginning of a new and successful endeavor. They are off to a good start, and I wish them well.

ACKNOWLEDGMENTS

THIS BOOK COULD not have been written without the testimony of the men and women who divorced late in life, and of the adult children who observed their parents' experiences. I am grateful to the 184 women, 126 men, and 84 adult children who volunteered to share their personal histories, and I thank them for letting me write about them. I am also grateful to the many persons who engage in the divorce experience through their professions and who, with enormous patience and unfailing courtesy, gave their time and shared their expertise. I thank the judges, attorneys, mediators, and other courtroom personnel, as well as the therapists, social workers, group leaders, counselors, and other clinicians who work in fields related to family law.

If I were to include the names of everyone who helped me, these pages would be at least as long as the longest chapter in the book. I would like to thank them all personally, but they spoke to me because I guaranteed them confidentiality, and so I shall respect their collective wish for anonymity. They all confided in me candidly and freely because I agreed to disguise their identities within case studies or composite portraits, and I have taken great care to honor their request. I hope they will feel that I have respected them in every instance.

There are others who provided all sorts of personal guidance, comfort, and sustenance as I wrote the book, and I take pleasure in acknowledging them by name. As always, I must begin with my children, Vonn Scott Bair, Katney Bair, Niko Courtelis; and especially my granddaughter the Wizzerbel, Isabel Anna Courtelis. My brother, Vincent J. Bartolotta, and my sister, Linda Rankin, are, quite simply, the best, as they guide me through all things legal and medical. My sister-in-law, Judy Bartolotta, is the glue who holds our family together, and I speak for us all in expressing our appreciation to her. My nephews and nieces come to my rescue at interesting times. On the Bartolotta side, Vincent III holds my hand at crucial moments; Nicholas straightens me out; Garrett feeds me the best fish tacos in San Diego; and Brett and Heidi gave us little Katie and Rebecca, who bring such joy. On the Rankin side, John and Kim know how to drive a mean truck through the streets of New York, and little Sydney gets her purse when she thinks we need to go shopping. My mother, Helen Bartolotta, graciously puts up with us all.

Two of my dearest fans were with me when the book began but, I'm sad to say, are not here to see it published, my beloved aunt and uncle Catherine Montecarlo and Armand Bartolotta. We all miss them as we rally together to honor their mormory: Aldo, Joan, Camera, Bruce, Lorayne, Dora, and Robin Bartolotta; Leah Balliard; Toni Jo and Archy Allridge.

Friends do so much for the writer, who sits in a room all by herself, day after day, putting words on paper. To describe such friends in the detail they deserve would be to write another book, and so I list their names without their many distinguished titles but with affection and gratitude: Lina Alpert, Peter Anton, Joyce Ashley, Mary Beasley, Richard Benge, Diana Cavallo, Jane Denning, Claire Douglas, David Doyle, John Ferrone, Guy Fitzhardinge, Hans and Marjorie Gunthardt, Phyllis and Thomas Hoehn, Barbara Katzrothman, Jean and Thomas Kirsch, Leonie Kramer, Jesse and Sylvia Lavietes, Liliane Lazar, Caro Llewellyn, Patricia Louis, Herbert and Virginia Lust, Mandy Martin, Jane Messer, Sophia Messore, Susan Mitchell, Deirdre Morris, Roberta and Kenneth Nesheim, Sylvia Brinton Perera, Jill Rawnsley, Leon and Myrna Bell Rochester, Mild Rosen, Karen Ross, Patricia Rossi, Andrew Samuels, Joan Schenker, Othmar and Lissa Schmidlin, Shirley Secunda, Christina Slade, Sydney Ladenson Stern, Allison Stokes, Ghillian Sullivan, Rosemary Sullivan, Maggie Tabberer, Mary Lawrence

Test, Patricia O'Toole, George and Suzanne Wagner, Aileen Ward, Barry and Beverly Wellman, and Mary Wong.

Drs. Kenneth Catandella and Salvatore Florio provided the offices and the magazines that gave me the inspiration for this book. Ileene Smith was the first editor to believe it should be published and Caroline Sutton oversaw the process with grace and goodwill. Christina Duffy provided the assistance that made turning manuscript into book a pleasant experience, as did Margaret Wimberger, whose thoughtful copyediting is much appreciated. I thank the two designers—Lisa Sloane for the book itself, and Anna Bauer for the jacket—and I am grateful to the Wadsworth Atheneum for permission to use Milton Avery's painting *Husband and Wife* on the cover. My agents, Elaine Markson, Geri Thoma, Gary Johnson, and Eva Koralnik were, as always, staunch supporters, good friends, and my biggest boosters.

Of all my books, it is not an exaggeration to say that, with this one in particular, people bared their souls to contribute to it. No writer goes it alone while a book is under way, and when it is finished, the only way to recognize what others have contributed is to tell them all: Many thanks.

June 21, 2006

NOTES

INTRODUCTION

1.*AARP the Magazine*, July/August, 2004.

CHAPTER ONE: THE THIRD AGE

1.AARP, *The Divorce Experience: A Study of Divorce at Midlife and Beyond*, May 2004, p. 4.

2.Joanna Wane, "Before Death Do Us Part," *Sunday Star Times Magazine* (Auckland), May 29, 2005, p. 28. The article reported that 40 percent of divorces in New Zealand happen during the first ten years of marriage, but the ratio is rising sharply for late-divorce statistics. In 1999, 16.8 percent of divorces were of couples married twenty-five years or more, compared with 11.8 percent a decade earlier. In 2005, one in four divorces was granted to couples married twenty years or more.

3.Margaret Drabble, *The Seven Sisters* (San Diego: Harcourt, 2002), p. 148.

CHAPTER TWO: INFIDELITY

1.Lillian Ross, *Here But Not Here: My Life with William Shawn and the New Yorker* (New York: Random House, 1998).

2.Nathaniel Kahn's film *My Architect: A Sons Journey*, Movietone, 2003.

3.Steven Kuchuck, 'Till Therapy Do Us Part," *The New York Times*, April 26, 2005, letter to the editor, p. F7. Kuchuck, a psychotherapist, wrote: "Odd as it may sound, success in couples therapy is not always determined by whether a couple stays together . . . Therapists . . . must also recognize when it is better for a couple to separate . . . Though a last resort for most clinicians, helping a couple separate with integrity and self-esteem intact can also be a successful outcome of therapy."

4.Kristin Kauffman, "Divorced After Decades," Divorce Recovery.net,

December 16, 2004. The article describes one of the longest-running programs of its kind, held at the Northway Christian Church in Dallas.

5.John van Tiggelen, "The Wife Stripped Bare," *Sydney Morning Herald*, Good Weekend section, May 28, 2005, pp. 20—24. All quotes are from this article.

CHAPTER THREE: ABUSE TAKES MANY FORMS

1.Penny Kaganoff and Susan Spano, eds., *Women on Divorce: A Bedside Companion* (New York: Harcourt Brace, 1995) and *Men on Divorce: The Other Side of the Story* (New York: Harcourt Brace, 1997).

2.Kaganoff and Spano, *Men on Divorce*, p. xviii.

3.Matt Richtel, "Past Divorce, Compassion at the End," *The New York Times*, May 19, 2005, pp. 1-2.

CHAPTER FOUR: THE "LAST CHANCE" DIVORCE

1.Jane Gross, "Its Cold on Mars," *The New York Times*, July 22, 2004, pp. Fl and F8.

2.Andrew Hacker, "Divorce a la Mode," review of *Husbands and Wives: A Nationwide Survey of Marriage*, by Anthony Pietropinto and Jacqueline Simenauer, in *The New York Review of Books*, May 3, 1979, p. 24.

3.Catherine Kohler Riessman, quoted in Deborah Tannen, *You Just Don't Understand: Women and Men in Conversation* (New York: William Morrow, 1990), pp. 40-41.

CHAPTER FIVE: "CEO-ITIS"

1.Ernest Hemingway, *The Snows of Kilimanjaro* (New York: Charles Scribner and Son, 1936).

2.The first phrase is generally attributed to Mme. De Sévigné; the second phrase is from Geraldine Fabrikant, "Divorce, Corporate American Style," *The New York Times*, August 14, 2005, section 3, p. 1.

3.The first quote is from Leslie Wayne, "Executive Involved with Chief Has Resigned, Boeing Says," *The New York Times*, March 19, 2005; the second is from "Ousted Boeing CEOs Wife Files for Divorce," AOL online news, March 13, 2005.

4.Geoffrey Gray, "Tough Love," *New York*, March 27, 2006, pp. 91, 47.

5."A Couple with Everything but Longevity in Marriage," *The New York Times*, March 25, 2005, Metro section, p. B4.

6.David Kocieniewski, "In New TV Ad, Forrester's Campaign Uses Unflattering Words of Corzine's Ex-Wife," *The New York Times*, November 4, 2005, Metro section, p. B3.

7.Alex Kuczynski, "The 37-Year Itch," *The New York Times*, August 8, 2004, Style section, p. 8.

CHAPTER SIX: ADULT CHILDREN OF LATE-LIFE DIVORCE

1.Judith S. Wallerstein and Sandra Blakeslee, *The Good Marriage: How and Why Love Lasts* (Boston and New York: Houghton Mifflin, 1995). See also Constance

Ahrons, *We're Still Family: What Grown Children Have to Say About Their Parents' Divorce* (New York: HarperCollins, 2005).

2.A. B. Yehoshua, *A Late Divorce* (San Diego: Harcourt Brace, Harvest Books, 1993), pp. 212, 233.

3.Joseph Lelyveld, *Omaha Blues: A Memory Loop* (New York: Farrar, Straus & Giroux, 2005); and "A Memory Loop," *The New York Times Magazine*, March 6, 2005, p. 55.

4.Walter Kirn, "My Parents' Bust-Up, and Mine," in Penny Kaganoff and Susan Spano, eds., *Men on Divorce, The Other Side of the Story* (New York: Harcourt Brace, 1999), p. 153.

CHAPTER SEVEN: SPLITTING OR STICKING

1.Malcolm Gladwell, *Blink: The Power of Thinking Without Thinking* (New York: Little, Brown, 2005), p. 22.

2.Information about Dr. Gottman comes primarily from Gladwell, *Blink;* information about the University of Rochester is from an article posted on Earthlink, "Researchers at University of Rochester Survey 800 Newlyweds," Associated Press, December 26, 2005.

3.Gladwell, *Blink*, pp. 32-33.

4.Amy Goldwasser, "At Home With Paula Scher: Graphics Grande Dame Remakes the World in Type," *The New York Times*, Thursday, January 12, 2006, p. F6; Joan Anderson, *A Year by the Sea: Thoughts of an Unfinished Woman* (New York: Broadway Books, 1999), pp. 154-55.

5.AARP, *The Divorce Experience: A Study of Divorce at Midlife and Beyond*, May 2004, "Table 4: Biggest Fears After Divorce," p. D10.

6.Terry Martin Hekker, "Paradises Lost (Domestic Division)," *The New York Times*, January 1, 2006, Style section, p. 9.

7."America's Model Housewife Turns Feminist as Husband Abandons Her," *Observer* (London), January 7, 2006.

CHAPTER EIGHT: THE TRUE VALUE OF A SPOUSE

1.Pam Belluck, "To Avoid Divorce, Move to Massachusetts," *The New York Times*, November 12, 2004, Week in Review section, p. 12; *The Daily Howler*, November 8, 2004 (www.dailyhowler.com), "Them 'Red State' Blues: Red-Staters Love to Gripe About Blue-State Elites—and to Pocket That Free Blue-State Money."

2.Lenore J. Weitzman, *The Divorce Revolution: The Unexpected Social and Economic Consequences for Women and Children in America* (New York: The Free Press, MacMillan, Inc. 1985).

3.Jennifer Medina, "Divorce Courts: Do They Really Favor the Rich?" *The New York Times*, Westchester section.

4.Geraldine Fabrikant, "Divorce, Corporate American Style," *The New York Times*, August 14, 2005, section 3, p. 8.

5.Weitzman, *Divorce Revolution*, p. 193.

6.*In re Marriage of Brantner*, 67 Cal. App. 3d 416, 419, 136 CAL. Rptr. 635 (1977), cited in ibid.

7.Ibid.

8.Dean E. Murphy and Carolyn Marshall, "Family Feuds Over Soldier's Remains," *The New York Times*, October 12, 2005, p. A14.

9.Information about China is from Jim Yardley, "Women in China Embrace Divorce as Stigma Eases," *The New York Times*, October 4, 2005, p. A9.

10.Ching-Ching Ni, "Entering Splitsville, China," *Los Angeles Times*, May 8, 2006, pp. Al andA12.

11.Leslie Eaton, "A New Push to Loosen New York's Divorce Law," *The New York Times*, November 30, 2004, p. 1, B7.

12.Geoffrey Gray, "Tough Love: What Happens When a Mogul and a Movie Star Get Married," *New York*, March 27, 2006, p. 91.

13.Danny Hakim, "Panel Asks New York to Join the Era of No-Fault Divorce," *The New York Times*, February 7, 2006, pp. 1, B7.

14.For a concise overview of mediation, see Brette McWhorter Sember, J.D., *No-Fight Divorce: Spend Less Money, Save Time, and Avoid Conflict Using Mediation* (New York: McGraw-Hill, 2005).

15.Phyllis Cummings-Texeira, "Finding Ways Toward More Civilized Divorces," *The New York Times*, September 18, 2005, letter to the editor, Connecticut section, p. 7.

16."Preparing the Client for Divorce," Knowles Publishing, Internet advertisement, February 2006.

17.Stephanie Rosenbloom, "Its the Kids. Lock up the China!" *The New York Times*, July 28, 2005, p. G8.

18.From Gayle Rosenwald Smith, "Dollars and Sense," *Divorce*, Fall/Winter 2005, p. 16. See also her book *Divorce and Money: Everything You Need to Know* (New York: Perigee Penguin USA, 2004).

19.The Marriage Project, Rutgers University.

20.Richard Ford, "Occidentals," in *Women with Men* (New York: Alfred A. Knopf, 1997), p. 159.

CHAPTER NINE: THE WAY WE LIVE NOW

1.Title of an article by Alexandria Abramian-Mott, *Los Angeles Times*, February 9, 2006, pp. Fl, F4.

2.Tom Liddy, "Honey, I Blew Up The House," *New York Post*, July 12, 2006, p. 1.

3.Anemona Hartocollis and Cara Buckley, "Divorce, Real Estate and Rubble: When Marriages Go Really Awry," *The New York Times*, July 12, 2006, p. Bl.

4.Stephanie Rosenbloom, "For Men, A Fear of Commitment," *The New York Times*, February 12, 2006, Real Estate section, pp. 1, 14.

5.Liz Seymour, "Inviting Anarchy into My Home," *The New York Times*, March 9, 2006, pp. Fl, F10.

6.Quoted in Abramian-Mott, "When 'Ours' Becomes 'His' and 'Hers,' "p. Fl.

7.CG. Jung, unpublished "Protocols" for *Memories, Dreams, Reflections*. See also Deirdre Bair, Jung: A *Biography* (New York: Little, Brown & Company, 2003), p. 297. Claire Douglas has an interesting discussion of houses in *The Old Woman's*

Daughter: Transformative Wisdom for Men and Women (College Station: Texas A & M University Press, 2006), chapter 4.

8.Quoted in Claudia Wallis, "Women and Relationships," *Time*, October 12, 1987.

9.Jill Brooke, "Home Alone Together," *The New York Times*, May 4, 2006, pp. Fl, F5. Couples whose full names are given are cited in this article; all others are composites from my research.

CHAPTER TEN: THE PASSIONATE LIFE

1.Among these are Diana Holtzberg and Deirdre Fishel, *Still Doing It* (Avery Books/Penguin USA, 2006); Jane Juska, *A Round-Heeled Woman* (New York: Villard Books) and its sequel, *Unaccompanied Women: Late-Life Adventures in Love, Sex, and Real Estate* (New York: Villard Books, 2006); Joan Price, *Better Than I Expected: Straight Talk About Sex After Sixty* (New York: Seal Press, 2006); and Gail Sheehy, *Sex and the Seasoned Woman* (New York: Random House, 2006). Two writers who touch upon the sexuality of older women are Joan Anderson, *A Year by the Sea: Thoughts of an Unfinished Woman* (New York: Broadway Books, 1999), and Karen Baar, *For My Next Act: Women Scripting Life After Fifty* (New York: Rodale Press, 2004).

2.From the jacket copy of Sheehy, *Sex and the Seasoned Woman*.

3.*The New York Times Book Review*, March 5, 2006, letter to the editor.

4.Geoffrey Gray, "With This Ring (and This Contract) I Thee Wed: The Prenup Trickle-down," *New York*, March 27, 2006, p. 51.

5.Erica Jong, *Seducing the Demon: Writing for My Life* (New York: Jeremy P. Tarcher/Penguin, 2006).

6.Teresa Wiltz, ". . . And an Older Erica Jong Learns to Love Zippers," *The Washington Post*, March 26, 2006, p. DO I.

7.Calvin Trillin, "Alice, Off the Page," *The New Yorker*, March 27, 2006, pp. 44ff.

8.Joan Anderson, *A Year by the Sea: Thoughts of an Unfinished Woman* (New York: Broadway Books, 1999).

9.Deborah Tannen, *You Just Don't Understand: Women and Men in Conversation* (New York: William Morrow and Co., 1990).

10.Andrew Hacker, "Divorce a la Mode," *The New York Review of Books*, May 3, 1979, p. 24.

11.Penny Kaganoff and Susan Spano, eds., *Men on Divorce: The Other Side of the Story* (New York: Harcourt Brace, 1999).

12.Tim Parks, "Bedroom Tapestries," in ibid.

13."Equal Rights Initiative in Iowa Attacked," *The Washington Post*, August 23, 1992.

14.Ted Solotaroff, "Getting to the Point," in ibid., p. 26.

15.*AARP the Magazine*, "The Mail," July/August 2006, p. 10.

CHAPTER ELEVEN: THE QUEST FOR HAPPINESS

1.Rachel Donadio, "The Chick-Lit Pandemic," *The New York Times Book Review*, March 19, 2006, p. 31.

2.Mary Wesley, A *Dubious Legacy* (New York: Viking Press, 1992), p. 50.

3.Steve Slon, as quoted in untitled AARP Web article, www.aarp.org/research/press/presscurrentnews/Articles/a2004-05-28-divorce.html, May 27, 2004.

4.Kate Vetrano, chair of the Elder Law Committee of the Family Law Section of the American Bar Association, quoted in Elizabeth Enright, "A House Divided," *AARP the Magazine*, July and August 2004, p. 54.

5.Sue Shellenbarger expresses this view in *The Breaking Point: How Female Midlife Crisis Is Transforming Today's Women* (New York: Henry Holt and Company, 2005).

6.Holly Watson, *The New York Times Magazine*, letter to the editor, November 13, 2005.

7.Deborah Barrow, "My Life as a Tapestry," *New York Home*, December 2005, p. 46.

8.Quoted in Nancy Gibbs, "Midlife Crisis? Bring It On!" *Time*, May 16, 2005, p. 55.

CHAPTER TWELVE: STARTING OVER

1.Charlotte Chandler, "Bette Davis Sighs," *Vanity Fair*, March 2006, p. 256.

2.AARP, *The Divorce Experience: A Study of Divorce at Midlife and Beyond*, May 2004, P. 7.

3."Wounds Linger (Literally) After Marital Strife," *The New York Times*, December 13, 2005, Science Times.

4.Gale Berkowitz, "UCLA Study on Friendship Among Women," based upon S. E. Taylor et al., 2000. See also "Female Responses to Stress: Tend and Befriend, Not Fight or Flight," *Psychological Review* 107, p. 3.

5.Kristen Wyatt, "Graying Set Gets Dating Advice from Young," Associated Press, November 28, 2005.

6.AARP, *The Divorce Experience*, pp. 8, 30.

7.Kristin Kauffman, "Divorced After Decades," Divorce Recovery.net, December 16, 2004.

8.Wyatt, "Graying Set."

9.Claudia Dreifus, "Where Have You Gone, Norman Rockwell? A Fresh Look at the Family," *The New York Times*, June 14, 2005, p. F3.

10.Glenn T. Stanton, "Marriage and Family, Then and Now," *The New York Times*, July 11, 2005, letter to the editor, p. A20.

11.Roslyn Fallick, "Marriage and the Family, Then and Now," ibid., letter to the editor, p. A20.

12.Harvard Law Professor Janet Halley, quoted in Harbour Fraser Hodder, "The Future of Marriage," *Harvard Magazine*, November-December 2004, p. 42.

13.Ibid., p. 39.

14.Judith Wallerstein and Sandra Blakeslee, *Second Chances: Men, Women, and Children a Decade After Divorce* (New York: Ticknor and Fields, 1989), p. 15.

ABOUT THE AUTHOR

DEIRDRE BAIR is the critically acclaimed author of four previous works of nonfiction. She received the National Book Award for *Samuel Beckett: A Biography*, and her biographies of Anaïs Nin and Simone de Beauvoir were also prize finalists. Her biography of C. G. Jung was a finalist for the Los Angeles Times Book Prize and received the Gradiva Award from the National Association for the Advancement of Psychoanalysis. She has been awarded fellowships from (among others) the Guggenheim and Rockefeller foundations and the Bunting Institute of Radcliffe College. She has been a literary journalist and university professor of comparative literature and divides her time between New York and Connecticut.